THE ENGLISH BINOMINAL NOUN PHRASE

The binominal noun phrase, or *of*-binominals, is an important phenomenon in the English language. Defined as a noun phrase that contains two related nouns, linked by the preposition *of*, examples include *a hell of a day* and *a beast of a storm*. This pioneering book provides the first extensive study of the evaluative binominal noun phrases (EBNP) in English, exploring the syntactic rules that govern them, and the (functional) semantic and pragmatic links between the two nouns. Combining quantitative and qualitative methods, corpus data, and two different theoretical approaches (Construction Grammar and Functional Discourse Grammar), it argues that the EBNP now functions as a stage in a grammaticalization path that begins with a prototypical N+PP construction, continues with the head-classifier, and ends with two new *of*-binominal constructions: the evaluative modifier and binominal intensifier. Comprehensive in its scope, it is essential reading for researchers in syntax, semantics, and English corpus linguistics.

Elnora ten Wolde is a postdoctoral researcher at the University of Graz. She has published on *of*-binominals, pre- and postmodification.

STUDIES IN ENGLISH LANGUAGE

General Editor
Merja Kytö (Uppsala University)

Editorial Board
Bas Aarts (University College London),
John Algeo (University of Georgia),
Susan Fitzmaurice (University of Sheffield),
Christian Mair (University of Freiburg),
Charles F. Meyer (University of Massachusetts)

The aim of this series is to provide a framework for original studies of English, both present-day and past. All books are based securely on empirical research, and represent theoretical and descriptive contributions to our knowledge of national and international varieties of English, both written and spoken. The series covers a broad range of topics and approaches, including syntax, phonology, grammar, vocabulary, discourse, pragmatics and sociolinguistics, and is aimed at an international readership.

Already published in this series:
Haruko Momma: *From Philology to English Studies: Language and Culture in the Nineteenth Century*
Raymond Hickey (ed.): *Standards of English: Codified Varieties around the World*
Benedikt Szmrecsanyi: *Grammatical Variation in British English Dialects: A Study in Corpus-Based Dialectometry*
Daniel Schreier and Marianne Hundt (eds.): *English as a Contact Language*
Bas Aarts, Joanne Close, Geoffrey Leech and Sean Wallis (eds.): *The Verb Phrase in English: Investigating Recent Language Change with Corpora*
Martin Hilpert: *Constructional Change in English: Developments in Allomorphy, Word Formation, and Syntax*
Jakob R. E. Leimgruber: *Singapore English: Structure, Variation, and Usage*
Christoph Rühlemann: *Narrative in English Conversation: A Corpus Analysis of Storytelling*
Dagmar Deuber: *English in the Caribbean: Variation, Style and Standards in Jamaica and Trinidad*
Eva Berlage: *Noun Phrase Complexity in English*
Nicole Dehé: *Parentheticals in Spoken English: The Syntax-Prosody Relation*
Jock O. Wong: *The Culture of Singapore English*
Marianne Hundt (ed.): *Late Modern English Syntax*
Irma Taavitsainen, Merja Kytö, Claudia Claridge and Jeremy Smith (eds.): *Developments in English: Expanding Electronic Evidence*

Arne Lohmann: *English Coordinate Constructions: A Processing Perspective on Constituent Order*
Nuria Yáñez-Bouza: *Grammar, Rhetoric and Usage in English: Preposition Placement 1500–1900*
Anita Auer, Daniel Schreier and Richard J. Watts (eds.): *Letter Writing and Language Change*
John Flowerdew and Richard W. Forest: *Signalling Nouns in English: A Corpus-Based Discourse Approach*
Jeffrey P. Williams, Edgar W. Schneider, Peter Trudgill and Daniel Schreier (eds.): *Further Studies in the Lesser-Known Varieties of English*
Jack Grieve: *Regional Variation in Written American English*
Douglas Biber and Bethany Gray: *Grammatical Complexity in Academic English: Linguistics Change in Writing*
Gjertrud Flermoen Stenbrenden: *Long-Vowel Shifts in English, c. 1050–1700: Evidence from Spelling*
Zoya G. Proshina and Anna A. Eddy (eds.): *Russian English: History, Functions, and Features*
Raymond Hickey (ed.): *Listening to the Past: Audio Records of Accents of English*
Phillip Wallage: *Negation in Early English: Grammatical and Functional Change*
Marianne Hundt, Sandra Mollin and Simone E. Pfenninger (eds.): *The Changing English Language: Psycholinguistic Perspectives*
Joanna Kopaczyk and Hans Sauer (eds.): *Binomials in the History of English: Fixed and Flexible*
Alexander Haselow: *Spontaneous Spoken English: An Integrated Approach to the Emergent Grammar of Speech*
Christina Sanchez-Stockhammer: *English Compounds and Their Spelling*
David West Brown: *English and Empire: Language History, Dialect, and the Digital Archive*
Paula Rodríguez-Puente: *The English Phrasal Verb, 1650–present: History, Stylistic Drifts, and Lexicalisation*
Erik. R. Thomas (ed.): *Mexican American English: Substrate Influence and the Birth of an Ethnolect*
Thomas Hoffmann: *English Comparative Correlatives: Diachronic and Synchronic Variation at the Lexicon-Syntax Interface*
Nuria Yáñez-Bouza, Emma Moore, Linda van Bergen and Willem B. Hollmann (eds.): *Categories, Constructions, and Change in English Syntax*
Raymond Hickey (ed.): *English in the German-speaking World*
Axel Bohmann: *Variation in English World-wide: Registers and Global Varieties*
Raymond Hickey (ed.): *English in Multilingual South Africa: The Linguistics of Contact and Change*
Jeremy J. Smith: *Transforming Early English: The Reinvention of Early English and Older Scots*
Tobias Bernaisch: *Gender in World Englishes*
Lorena Pérez-Hernández: *Speech Acts in English: From Research to Instruction and Textbook Development*

Elisabeth Reber: *Quoting in Parliamentary Question Time: Exploring Recent Change*
Marco Condorelli: *Standardising English Spelling: The Role of Printing in Sixteenth and Seventeenth-century Graphemic Developments*
Irma Taavitsainen (ed.): *Genre in English Medical Writing, 1500–1820: Sociocultural Contexts of Production and Use*
Elisa Mattiello: *Transitional Morphology: Combining Forms in Modern English*
Theresa Neumaier: *Conversation in World Englishes: Turn-Taking and Cultural Variation in Southeast Asian and Caribbean English*
Earlier titles not listed are also available

THE ENGLISH BINOMINAL NOUN PHRASE

A Cognitive-Functional Approach

ELNORA TEN WOLDE

University of Graz

Shaftesbury Road, Cambridge CB2 8EA, United Kingdom

One Liberty Plaza, 20th Floor, New York, NY 10006, USA

477 Williamstown Road, Port Melbourne, VIC 3207, Australia

314–321, 3rd Floor, Plot 3, Splendor Forum, Jasola District Centre, New Delhi – 110025, India

103 Penang Road, #05–06/07, Visioncrest Commercial, Singapore 238467

Cambridge University Press is part of Cambridge University Press & Assessment, a department of the University of Cambridge.

We share the University's mission to contribute to society through the pursuit of education, learning and research at the highest international levels of excellence.

www.cambridge.org
Information on this title: www.cambridge.org/9781108926164

DOI: 10.1017/9781108921893

© Elnora ten Wolde 2023

This publication is in copyright. Subject to statutory exception and to the provisions of relevant collective licensing agreements, no reproduction of any part may take place without the written permission of Cambridge University Press & Assessment.

First published 2023
First paperback edition 2026

A catalogue record for this publication is available from the British Library

ISBN 978-1-108-83095-9 Hardback
ISBN 978-1-108-92616-4 Paperback

Cambridge University Press & Assessment has no responsibility for the persistence or accuracy of URLs for external or third-party internet websites referred to in this publication and does not guarantee that any content on such websites is, or will remain, accurate or appropriate.

To Emmerich

Contents

List of Figures	*page* xiii
List of Tables	xv
Acknowledgments	xvii
List of Abbreviations	xviii

1	**Introduction**	1
	PART I CATEGORIZATION	7
2	***Of*-binominal Classification**	9
	2.1 Introduction	9
	2.2 Internal Structure of *Of*-binominals	9
	2.2.1 Head Status	10
	2.2.2 Constituency	14
	2.2.3 Constraints on the Two Nouns	14
	2.2.4 Determiner Selection	20
	2.2.5 Preposition *Of*	20
	2.3 Methodology for Part I	21
	2.4 Conclusion	25
3	**From Prototypical N+PP to Pseudo-partitive**	28
	3.1 Introduction	28
	3.2 N+PP	28
	3.2.1 Head Status	29
	3.2.2 Constituency Tests	30
	3.2.3 Constraints on the Two Nouns	31
	3.2.4 Determiners	32
	3.2.5 Status of *Of*	33
	3.2.6 The Properties of the N+PP	33
	3.3 Head-Classifier	34
	3.3.1 Head Status	35
	3.3.2 Constituency Tests	37
	3.3.3 Constraints on the Two Nouns	38

	3.3.4 Determiners	39
	3.3.5 Status of *Of*	40
	3.3.6 Head-Classifier Types	40
	3.3.7 The Properties of the Head-Classifier	43
3.4	Pseudo-partitive	43
	3.4.1 Head Status	46
	3.4.2 Constituency Tests	50
	3.4.3 Constraints on the Two Nouns	52
	3.4.4 Determiners	56
	3.4.5 Status of *Of*	57
	3.4.6 The Properties of the Pseudo-partitive	59
3.5	Conclusion	60

4 The Evaluative *Of*-binominals — 63

4.1	Introduction	63
4.2	Evaluative Binominal Noun Phrase	63
	4.2.1 Head Status	65
	4.2.2 Constituency Tests	68
	4.2.3 Constraints on the Two Nouns	68
	4.2.4 Determiners	70
	4.2.5 Status of *Of*	72
	4.2.6 The Properties of the EBNP	73
4.3	Evaluative Modifier	74
	4.3.1 Head Status	76
	4.3.2 Constraints on the Two Nouns	77
	4.3.3 Determiners	79
	4.3.4 Status of *Of*	81
	4.3.5 The Properties of the EM	82
4.4	Binominal Intensifier	84
	4.4.1 Head Status	86
	4.4.2 Constituency	87
	4.4.3 Constraints on the Two Nouns	88
	4.4.4 Determiners	90
	4.4.5 Status of *Of*	91
	4.4.6 The Properties of the BI	91
4.5	Conclusion	93

5 Three Case Studies: *Cake*, *Beast*, and *Hell* — 96

5.1	Introduction	96
5.2	Grammaticalization or Lexicalization	97
5.3	Case Study 1: *Cake*	99
5.4	Case Study 2: *Beast*	103
5.5	Case Study 3: *Hell*	106
5.6	Discussion and Conclusions	110

PART II TESTING THE HYPOTHESIS   115

6   Diachronic Evidence   117
    6.1 Introduction   117
    6.2 *Of*-binominal Grammaticalization Pathway   121
    6.3 Methods   124
    6.4 The Pseudo-partitive Strand   124
         6.4.1 *Nub(s)*   125
         6.4.2 *Breeze(s)*   130
         6.4.3 *Husk(s)*   133
         6.4.4 *Snake(s)*   138
         6.4.5 Discussion   143
    6.5 Evaluative Constructions: EBNP, EM, BI   145
         6.5.1 *Whale(s)*   145
         6.5.2 *Bitch(es)*   149
         6.5.3 Discussion   153
    6.6 Conclusion   155

7   Premodification Evidence   157
    7.1 Introduction   157
    7.2 Approaches to Premodification   158
    7.3 Ghesquière's Cognitive-Functional Model   161
         7.3.1 The Classifier Category   164
         7.3.2 Descriptive Modifiers   168
         7.3.3 Classifiers and Descriptive Modifiers   170
         7.3.4 Degree Modifiers   172
         7.3.5 Conclusions   173
    7.4 Methods   173
    7.5 Analysis of Premodification Distribution   177
    7.6 Premodification for the Individual *Of*-binominals   179
         7.6.1 N+PP Constructions   180
         7.6.2 Head-Classifiers   182
         7.6.3 Pseudo-partitive   185
         7.6.4 Evaluative Binominal Noun Phrases   187
         7.6.5 Evaluative Modifiers   189
         7.6.6 Binominal Intensifier   192
    7.7 Discussion and Conclusions   194

PART III THEORETICAL ANALYSIS   201

8   The EBNP Family: A Construction Grammar Analysis   203
    8.1 Introduction to Construction Grammar   203
    8.2 Constructions and Constructional Networks   204
         8.2.1 Constructions   204
         8.2.2 The Construction Grammar Network   209

	8.3 Grammaticalization in Construction Grammar	213
	8.4 Modeling the Evaluative *Of*-binominal Family Network	217
	8.4.1 N+PP	217
	8.4.2 Head-Classifier	220
	8.4.3 Evaluative Binominal Noun Phrase	224
	8.4.4 Evaluative Modifier	227
	8.4.5 Binominal Intensifier	230
	8.5 Conclusion	232
9	The EBNP Family: A Functional Discourse Grammar Analysis	234
	9.1 Introduction to Functional Discourse Grammar	234
	9.1.1 General Overview	234
	9.1.2 Primitives: Units of the FDG Grammatical Component	237
	9.1.3 The Noun Phrase in FDG	240
	9.1.4 FDG Categorization	245
	9.2 A Functional Discourse Grammar Account of the EBNP Family	248
	9.2.1 The EBNP Family	248
	9.2.2 Constructions in FDG	261
	9.2.3 Placement in FDG	264
	9.2.4 Conclusions	267
	9.3 A Diachronic Functional Discourse Grammar Explanation	268
	9.3.1 Grammaticalization in FDG	268
	9.3.2 The FDG Diachronic Analysis	270
	9.4 Conclusion	272

PART IV DISCUSSION — 275

10	Discussion and Conclusions	277
	10.1 Classification Discussion	277
	10.2 Comparing the Two Models	279
	10.3 Future Research	284

References — 286
Index — 306

Figures

5.1	Diachronic development of *cake*, *beast*, and *hell* from N+PP to pseudo-partitive	page 111
5.2	Diachronic development of *cake*, *beast*, and *hell* in the EBNP to BI	111
6.1	Grammaticalization path of the evaluative *of*-binominals	119
6.2	Distribution of *nub(s)* in *of*-binominal constructions from 1910 to 2015	129
6.3	Distribution of *breeze(s)* in the *of*-binominal constructions from 1810 to 2015	134
6.4	Distribution of *husk(s)* in the *of*-binominal constructions from 1820 to 2015	139
6.5	Distribution of *snake(s)* of the *of*-binominal constructions from 1810 to 2015	144
6.6	Distribution of *whale(s)* in the *of*-binominal constructions from 1830 to 2015	150
6.7	Distribution of *bitch(es)* in the *of*-binominal constructions from 1920 to 2015	154
7.1	Ghesquière's cognitive-functional NP model	163
7.2	Premodification in front of Noun 1 and Noun 2	179
7.3	Relative frequency for each zone in the N+PP	182
7.4	Relative frequency percentages for each zone in the head-classifier	184
7.5	Relative frequency percentages for each zone in the pseudo-partitive	187
7.6	Relative frequency percentages for each zone in the EBNP	189
7.7	Relative frequency distribution for each zone in the EM	191
7.8	Relative frequency percentages for each zone in the BI	192
7.9	Overview of the changes of premodifier patterns in the six constructions	195
8.1	The symbolic structure of the construction	205

8.2	Ghesquière's cognitive-functional NP model	208
8.3	Gradient of hierarchic relationships among constructions	210
8.4	The N+PP temporal construction	218
8.5	The N+PP in the construction network	219
8.6	The head-classifier construction	221
8.7	The N+PP and head-classifier in construction network	222
8.8	The EBNP construction	225
8.9	The Head-classifier and EBNP in the construction network	226
8.10	The EM construction	228
8.11	The EBNP and the EM in the construction network	229
8.12	The BI construction	230
8.13	The EM and BI in the construction network	231
9.1	General layout of FDG	236
9.2	Two possible frames triggered by the template at the Representational Level	253

Tables

2.1	First nouns examined in this study	page 23
2.2	Categorization criteria for the internal structure of the NP	26
3.1	Categorization of pseudo-partitives	45
3.2	Overview of the categories N+PP, head-classifier, and pseudo-partitive	61
4.1	The semantic distinctions between first nouns used in EBNPs and EMs	76
4.2	Overview of the evaluative categories: EBNP, EM, and BI	94
5.1	Parallels between lexicalization and grammaticalization	98
6.1	A grammaticalization scenario	123
6.2	Raw figures for first nouns in COCA and COHA	124
6.3	Frequency of *nub(s)* in *of*-binominals in COHA and COCA	126
6.4	Frequency of *breeze(s)* in *of*-binominals in COHA and COCA	132
6.5	Frequency of *husk(s)* in *of*-binominals in COHA and COCA	136
6.6	Frequency of *snake(s)* in *of*-binominals in COHA and COCA	141
6.7	Frequency of *whale(s)* in *of*-binominals in COHA and COCA	147
6.8	Frequency of *bitch(es)* in *of*-binominals in COHA and COCA	152
7.1	Payne and Huddleston's tests to distinguish between compounds and composite nouns	166
7.2	Raw token frequency of modifiers in front of the first and second noun for all constructions	176
7.3	Frequency of modifiers in front of the first and second noun for all constructions	177
7.4	Frequency distribution of premodification between the first and second noun for the four *of*-binominals	178
7.5	Important constellations of variables for premodification in the N+PP	181
7.6	Important constellations of variables for premodification in the head-classifier	183

7.7	Important constellations of variables for premodification in the pseudo-partitive	186
7.8	Important constellations of variables for premodification in the EBNP	188
7.9	Important constellations of variables for premodification in the EM	190
7.10	Important constellations of variables for premodification in the binominal intensifier	193
8.1	Dimensions of constructions	206
9.1	The primitives in the Fund at the different levels	237

Acknowledgments

This work would have never come into life without the unfailing patience and support of Evelien Keizer. I thank her for sharing her knowledge and time – I will always remember our stimulating discussions and feel honored to have worked and still work so closely with her. I would also like to thank Nikolaus Ritt for employing me as a PhD student on his team and introducing me to the philosophy of language sciences. I would like to thank Gunther Kaltenböck for taking me with him to the University of Graz as a postdoc and including me in his research: working with him has expanded my linguistic horizons.

There are a number of people who provided invaluable input for the different chapters, such as Arne Lohmann and Andreas Bauman for the statistics in the premodification study; Nikolaus Ritt for the chapter diachronic studies; Lotte Sommerer, Gunther Kaltenböck, and Ozan Mustafa on Construction Grammar; Lachlan Mackenzie and Evelien Keizer for the chapter on Functional Discourse Grammar. I would also like to thank Freek van de Velde for his suggestions for construction names: the head-classifier came from him. I have had the great privilege to work with so many interesting researchers who have helped me develop as a linguist, in particular I am indebted to Thomas Schwaiger but also Eva Zehenter, Julia Skala, Klaus Puhl, Hella Olbertz, and Henry Widdowson. A special thank you belongs to the editorial team of Studies in English Language: Helen Barton, Isabel Collins, Jacqueline French and Merja Kytö for their input, suggestions, and support.

My other major supporter is of the (non-academic) sort, my partner Emmerich Bezovits. We walked this path together, and when I stumbled, he was always there to keep me on my feet. This book would not have existed but for his unstinting belief.

Abbreviations

Adj	adjective
AI	adjective intensifier
AP	Adjectival Phrase
BI	binominal intensifier
CL	classifier
CxG	Construction Grammar
Cxn	Construction
DEO	descriptive objective modifier
DES	descriptive subjective modifier
Det	determiner
Det_1	first determiner in an *of*-binominal noun phrase
Det_2	second determiner in an *of*-binominal noun phrase
DP	determiner phrase
EBNP	evaluative binominal noun phrase
EM	evaluative modifier *of*-binominal
FDG	Functional Discourse Grammar
FP	functional projection
Int	intensifier
LE	linking element
Mod	modifier
MP	modifier phrase
N	noun
N_1	first noun in an *of*-binominal noun phrase
N_2	second noun in an *of*-binominal noun phrase
NI	noun intensifier
NP	noun phrase
N+PP	prototypical *of*-binominal noun phrase
Obj	object
PDE	Present-Day English
Pseudo-P	pseudo-partitive *of*-binominal noun phrase

PP	prepositional phrase
Subj	subject
V_{tr}	transitive verb

Functional Discourse Grammar

1	singular
2	dual
approx	approximative
Aw	Adjective Word
C	Communicated Content
ComPIF	Combination of Partially Instantiated Frames
f	Property
±id	±identifiable
intens	intensifier
IL	Interpersonal Level
l	location
ML	Morphosyntactic Level
Np	Noun Phrase
Nw	Nominal Word
p^F	phrase-final position
p^{F+N}	position situated N places before the final position
p^I	phrase-initial position
p^{I+N}	position situated N places after the initial position
p^M	phrase-medial position
p^{M+N}	position situated N places after the medial position
PL	Phonological Level
PP	Phonological Phrase
PW	Phonological Word
q	quantity
R	Subact of Reference
Ref	reference function
RL	Representational Level
T	Subact of Ascription
x	Individual
$^m x$	mass Individual
π	operator
φ	function

CHAPTER I

Introduction

In the last forty years, prepositions have shifted from the periphery of linguistic focus, as purely grammatical elements, into the center of multiple lines of research, from being regarded as a surface phenomenon to being appreciated as having an underlying function.[1] Interest in the *of*-binominal (Det$_1$ N$_1$ of Det$_2$ N$_2$), in particular, is inspired by the fact that this phrase's different functions exemplify the semantic indefinability of the preposition *of*. This relatively stable syntactic structure can convey a range of meanings and have diverse functions as the *of*-binominal in example (1.1) demonstrates. This phrase can indicate what the pot is made of, in this case gold (*a golden pot*), or the speaker could be referring to a physical potful of gold (*This is the end of the rainbow. Where are the leprechauns and my pot of gold?*). It could also denote something more abstract like a large quantity (*we are slashing prices, so you won't need a pot of gold to afford this*) or simply success (*our kids are that pot of gold in our life*). The speaker's intended meaning is signaled by the linguistic context.

(1.1)   a pot of gold

Teasing apart and classifying the English *of*-binominals has attracted researchers from a range of theoretical backgrounds, and one central area of research has focused on the genitive variation, more precisely, when and how speakers use the *s*-genitive (1.2a) and *of*-genitive (1.2b) synchronically, diachronically, and in different varieties of English.[2] In comparison, there has been less research on *of*-binominal constructions without a genitive counterpart, some of which are exemplified in (1.3)–(1.5).

---

[1] Since the 1980s, there have been numerous large-scale studies of prepositions in the cognitive-functional paradigm, the most prominent ones being Brugman (1981), Brugman and Lakoff (1988), Dewell (1994), Hoffmann (2004), Kreitzer (1997), Lakoff (1987), and Tayler & Evans (2003).
[2] See Rosenbach (2014) for an overview of this discussion.

(1.2) a. the chair's leg
 b. the leg of the chair

(1.3) a. an idiot of a boy
 b. #a boy's idiot

(1.4) a. a bowl of soup
 b. ?a soup's bowl

(1.5) a. a boat of wood
 b. *a wood's boat

Looking at examples (1.3)–(1.5), the *of*-binominal forms in (1.3a), (1.4a), and (1.5a) are grammatical, but the *s*-genitive alternative either has a different meaning as in (1.3b), is questionable (1.4b), or is completely ungrammatical (1.5b). In (1.3a), the *of*-binominal means that the boy is an idiot or acting idiotically, whereas in (1.3b), the boy possesses an idiot (as did kings in medieval times). *A bowl of soup* in (1.4a) is a quantity of soup that one would order in a restaurant (in theory you could have a bowl of soup in a cup), and the soup is normally not conceived as being able to possess the bowl, hence the questionability of (1.4b). Finally, in (1.5a), the boat is made of wood, but the wood, in (1.5b), cannot own the boat; hence, the phrase's ungrammaticality. The study presented here looks at this latter group of constructions and in particular looks at the development of the evaluative binominal noun phrase, or EBNP, exemplified in (1.3) and how it is related to other English *of*-binominals, such as the pseudo-partitive in (1.4) and the head-classifier in (1.5).

The EBNP construction as a whole has been the interest of linguists since the 1960s. This phrase not only deviates from the "rules"/norms that normally apply to nouns modified by prepositional phrases but also facilitates creative formulations as illustrated by the examples in (1.6). In (1.6a), the first noun ascribes a property onto the second, so *this jewel of a park* refers to a park and not a jewel; the *jewel* expresses the speaker's assessment of the park, i.e. it is magnificent or beautiful. Another non-canonical feature of this phrase is that it also allows proper nouns to function as modifiers as shown in (1.6b). In this example *Dickens* does not refer to Charles Dickens, the author, but a Dickens-like Christmas celebration, most likely referring to *A Christmas Carol*. A further interesting feature of the EBNP is that adjectives that modify the second noun can come in front of the first as in (1.6c), where the book is being qualified as slim and not the gem.

(1.6) a. Rides in *this jewel of a park* south of Half Moon Bay are not technically challenging ... (COCA)[3]
b. You're sure to have *a Dickens of a Christmas* as this South Georgia town transforms itself ... (COCA)
c. I'm halfway through *this relatively slim gem of a book* ... (COCA)

Despite the EBNP's irregular syntax, only touched on here, this construction has existed in English at least since the thirteenth century and has been prolific in many European languages. Variations of this construction have been found in Italian (*un amore di ragazza* 'a love of a girl'), Dutch (*een idioot van een dokter* 'an idiot of a doctor'), French (*un diable d'homme* 'a devil of a man'), German (*ein Engel von einer Frau* 'an angel of a woman'), Spanish (*una bestia di avvocato* 'a beast of a lawyer') among other languages (see Foolen 2004 for further examples). For its irregularities and its productivity, the EBNP has been the focus of much discussion and numerous studies.

This study is the first book-length work dedicated to this construction, and although it addresses questions that have lingered in the EBNP discussion for decades, such as the construction's head, it expands on previous research. Most importantly it does not just focus on the English EBNP, as most previous studies have done, but examines the construction as a member of the English *of*-binominal family, situating it in this network. Family relations, as is often the case in *of*-binominal studies, are assumed when constructions share first nouns, and this study has found evidence for links between the EBNP and the five other *of*-binominals, demonstrated in (1.7) and (1.8b–c) with *hell* as the first noun.

The *of*-binominals in (1.7) are not so obviously related to the EBNP in terms of function, but first nouns used in the EBNP are used in these binominals as well; thus, some sort of family relation is assumed. These constructions include the more prototypical N+PPs, such as the genitive in (1.7a), the head-classifier in (1.7b), and the pseudo-partitive in (1.7c).

(1.7) a. They conjure up hideous visions of howling fiends, with ghastly and wailing spirits, ... they tell us that this is *the hell of the Calvinist*. (COHA)[4]
b. That night, lying in its shallow, hastily dug holes, the remnant of the battalion descended through *further hells of shelling*. (COCA)
c. With a mouse click he could fire *a hell of microwaves* up to the ionosphere. (COCA)

---

[3] The Corpus of Contemporary American English (Davies 2008).
[4] The Corpus of Historical American English (Davies 2010).

Example (1.7a) is a classic *of*-genitive construction as depicted in (1.2b). The first noun denotes the referent, i.e. the speaker is discussing a type of theological hell, and the prepositional phrase denotes the possessors of that hell, i.e. it is a Calvinist's hell. Similar prototypical *of*-binominal phrases are those where the prepositional phrase designates a time (*the hell of the night*) or a source/location (*the hell of Vietnam*). All three types of constructions are grouped together as N+PP constructions (discussed in greater detail in Section 3.2). In example (1.7b), the role of the prepositional phrase is different from the previous example, in that it defines or classifies the first noun, i.e. it is not a biblical hell evoked here, but a hell consisting of shelling. This group of constructions, called head-classifiers, are relatively under-researched in English (see Keizer 2007a and Ten Wolde 2019 where they are called head-qualifiers). Here the prepositional phrase does not ascribe properties onto the first noun but classifies the first noun, functioning similarly to premodifier classifiers, e.g. *head of department* and *department head* (see Section 3.3 for more discussion). Like the N+PP *of*-binominals, the category pseudo-partitive, as demonstrated in (1.7c) and (1.4), includes a number of different *of*-binominals. In (1.7c), the second noun is most likely the head: the speaker is talking about *microwaves* and not a *hell*, and *hell* functions as a non-standard quantifier of the second noun, meaning a large quantity of microwaves were shot into the ionosphere. The construction in example (1.4) and pseudo-partitives with other first nouns (e.g. *a cake of soap*) are very frequent; in contrast, the use of *hell* in this phrase is irregular although attested (see Section 3.3 for more discussion). All three of these *of*-binominals not only share a first noun but seem to share either structural or functional features with the EBNP. This study looks at this group of constructions in more detail, discussing their historical and synchronic relations to each other and the EBNP.

A second central finding presented in this monograph is that some *of*-binominals, which many previous studies have amalgamated under the heading of the EBNP, are in reality three different constructions that are syntactically similar (although not the same) but function differently.

These are exemplified in the examples (1.8a–c): (1.8a) is a classic EBNP, like example (1.3); (1.8b) is a new *of*-binominal that I have called the evaluative modifier (EM), and (1.8c) is a binominal intensifier (BI).[5] In all three constructions, the second nouns are the heads of

---

[5] Trousdale (2012) makes an EBNP and degree modifier/intensifier distinction but only with *hell* as a first noun, arguing that it is an exceptional case. I will show that the intensifier use is more productive and that there is a third category, between the EBNP and the binominal intensifier, the evaluative modifier.

these *of*-binominals: (1.8a) the speaker is talking about a night, in (1.8b) a movie, and in (1.8c) a girl. In the first two examples, *hell* would appear to convey some sort of speaker 'feeling' or evaluation of the thing being referred to; in the final example, it seems to intensify the adjective that follows. Making the distinction between these three constructions not only reshapes the EBNP discussion but provides further evidence in the, as yet, still unresolved discussion on headedness in the EBNP (see Kim & Sells 2015 for an overview).

(1.8)   a. It was *a hell of a night* for a meeting – with the storm going and the river about to blow. (COCA)
b. We are going to show you a scene from this movie, which is by the way *a hell of a movie*, with a tremendous performance by Ms. Stone and everybody involved. (COCA)
c. And if that's flamboyant, well then, yeah, then I'm *a hell of a flamboyant gal*. (COCA)

Looking at the individual examples in more detail, *hell* in example (1.8a) modifies the second noun *night*, ascribing hell-like properties onto the night and can be substituted by the adjective 'hellish' without a change in meaning: *a hellish night for a meeting*. This interpretation of *hell* is supported by the linguistic context where the speaker elaborates on the dangers caused by a storm (see Section 4.2 for more discussion of the EBNP). Whereas the night in (1.8a) is hellish, *hell* has a different function in (1.8b): here, it expresses a positive evaluation of the referent, and the speaker uses *hell* to express his or her appropriation of the movie. This reading is supported by the speaker's elaboration on the *tremendous performance* of the actors.[6] This construction is the EM. In this construction, the first noun ascribes either the speaker's emphatic approbation (e.g. *a honey of a plan*) or disapprobation (e.g. *a dog of a space*) for the referent denoted by the second noun (see Section 4.3 for more discussion). Finally, in (1.8c), *hell* lacks all descriptive properties and emphasizes the property flamboyant, i.e. the gal in question is not just *flamboyant*, but very flamboyant. In these constructions the first noun can intensify a range of gradable adjectives such as *old*, *happy*, or *good*, e.g. *a bitch of a unsatisfactory situation* or *a whale of a good time* (see Section 4.4 for more discussion).

Part I of this monograph presents the classification and description of these six constructions and proposes a hypothesis of how they

---

[6] This distinction can also be found in canonical modifiers such as *great*: *great* still denotes size or quantity, e.g. *a great number of families arrived the evening before* (COCA) or expresses speaker approbation, e.g. *we had a great time* (COCA).

diachronically link together. It begins, in Chapter 2, with an overview of the methods and the classification criteria that have been employed to distinguish between the different *of*-binominal constructions. This includes a comprehensive overview of diagnostic tools used in previous work on *of*-binominals as well as a discussion of the corpus data employed in this part of the study. In Chapters 3 and 4, these diagnostics and criteria are then applied in a qualitative analysis of the corpus data in order to distinguish between the six constructions. This results in the proposal of a grammaticalization path that is then demonstrated in Chapter 5 with three case studies.

This proposed path is then empirically tested in Part II, which addresses the question of whether there is quantitative evidence that would substantiate a link between these six constructions. Chapter 6 presents the first study which is a quantitative and qualitative analysis of the more recent progression of some first nouns through these constructions. The second study, in Chapter 7, examines premodification patterns. As already demonstrated by many of the constructions, either the second noun (in the head-classifiers) or the first nouns (in the pseudo-partitives, EBNPs, EMs, and BIs) fulfill semantic functions prototypically assumed by premodifiers. Therefore, the study answers the question as to whether there is a link between these constructions and premodification.

In Part III the findings from Part I and Part II are examined from the perspective of two linguistic theories: Construction Grammar (CxG) and Functional Discourse Grammar (FDG). These models were chosen for different reasons. CxG was selected because many of the more recent *of*-binominal studies have been conducted using this theory, and because it models language as a network, which shows how the language as a whole affects the changes found in this particular family. CxG theory, the network model, and the analysis of the EBNP data are presented in Chapter 8. For the second theory, FDG was chosen because it is a formal-functional model that provides clearly delineated variables and tools to describe language phenomena and allows for a precise analysis of the data. FDG is a functional model, but unlike CxG, gravitates toward the formal part of the language model spectrum. A brief introduction to the FDG theory and the results of the analysis can be found in Chapter 9. In sum, Part III addresses the following question: when examining the data from Parts I and II from a Construction Grammar and Functional Discourse Grammar perspective, to what extent can each model capture and explain these findings? My answer is presented in Chapter 10, which includes a summary of the key findings and a juxtaposition of these two theories.

PART I

Categorization

CHAPTER 2

Of-*binominal Classification*

2.1 Introduction

This chapter reviews previous studies of *of*-binominals and presents a compendium of the categorization criteria employed in previous work. In particular, it discusses head status diagnostics, constituency tests, criteria for constraints on the two nouns, the status of the preposition, and determiner selection restrictions. It ends with a description of the methods and data used for the classification of the six constructions. In Chapter 3 and Chapter 4, these criteria are then applied to the *of*-binominals discussed in this book not only for the purpose of classifying and distinguishing between each *of*-binominal noun phrase, but also as an argument for these categorical distinctions.

2.2 Internal Structure of *Of*-binominals

The overall aim of the categorization of *of*-binominals is to determine the function of each type of complex noun phrase (NP) and the relation between the different linguistic elements: [Det_1 (Mod) N_1 of Det_2 (Mod) N_2]. For this purpose, a range of semantic and syntactic tests have been applied, and various parameters from the literature have been considered, although different studies, depending on their theoretical foundation, tend toward or require different tests.[1] In this respect, this chapter brings together the

---

[1] For example, Traugott (2008a: 27–8) explicitly states that, in distinguishing between quantifiers and partitives, she looks at determiner–noun agreement patterns, movement, and substitution. Brems (2011: 123–31), in her study of size or measure nouns, predominantly looks at head status (lexicality of N_1 and the co-extensiveness between N_1 and *of*), collocations, semantic prosody, concord between N_1 or N_2, substitution, and premodification. Generative studies such as Selkirk (1977) and Corver (1998), on the other hand, rely on movement tests (pre- and postposition), questions, pronominalization, and coordination.

different parameters used in previous studies, discussing what evidence they provide for the categorization of *of*-binominals. However, it should be emphasized from the start that the grouping of diagnostics here is slightly problematic. One test may offer a range of information, resulting in repeated reference to the same test, e.g. constituency tests provide information about the syntactic constituency of the linguistic elements but also about the status of the preposition, and thus will be discussed in both sections. The analysis begins with one of the most important distinguishing features, headedness, i.e. the question of whether the first noun (N_1) or the second one (N_2) is the head of the complex NP.

2.2.1   Head Status

One of the most critical dimensions along which *of*-binominals are categorized and a feature that impacts various aspects of the internal structure of the NP is the notion of headedness. Headedness "refer[s] to the element in some construction to which all the other parts of that construction are (in some sense) subordinate" (Hudson 1984: 109), and in some cases, which element functions as the head is the only difference between two different binominals. In (2.1), for example, when *pot* is the head, then the noun phrase denotes 'a pot made of steel', and when *steel* is the head, 'a pot full of steel' or 'a pot amount of steel'.

(2.1)   a pot of steel

The notion of a head (in linguistics), as Hudson (1984: 109) points out, has a long history, and different theoretical approaches have developed different diagnostic tests for distinguishing both the syntactic and the semantic head. Much of the work from a generative perspective relies on substitution and syntactic tests (for an overview of generative approaches to pseudo-partitive and EBNP, see Alexiadou, Haegeman & Stavrou 2007). Many of the cognitive-construction-based studies principally adopt semantic evidence (e.g. Brems 2010; Langacker 2010) or semantics in combination with morpho-syntactic diagnostic tests (e.g. Brems 2003, 2004, 2011; Traugott 2008a, 2008b). Keizer (2007a) complies and discusses a range of syntactic, semantic, and pragmatic tests for head status in *of*-binominals.

For determining the semantic head, Keizer (2007a: 10–12) suggests three operational tests: distributional equivalence (McGregor 1997: 64), obligatoriness and omissibility, and the verb's semantic selection (originally discussed for *of*-binominals in Akmajian & Lehrer 1976). Distributional

2.2 Internal Structure of *Of-binominals*

equivalence is used to determine which noun can stand for the construction as a whole without changing the NP's denotation and is very closely linked to the test of obligatoriness/omissibility, a diagnostic showing which of the two nouns is obligatory. This is demonstrated in example (2.2), where the sentence is intelligible only with *hotel* (2.2b), but not with just *hell* (2.2c). Therefore, *hotel* determines the denotation of the construction as a whole and is obligatory, and *hell* does not and can be omitted.

(2.2)   a. He has *one hell of a hotel*.
         b. He has *a hotel*.
         c. *He has *a hell*.

Akmajian and Lehrer (1976) propose verb semantic selection as a diagnostic test: in (2.3a), *spill* requires a liquid, whereas in (2.3b), *broke* requires a solid, which means that in (2.3a) N_2 is the semantic head, and in (2.3b), it is N_1 (Akmajian & Lehrer 1976: 406–7).

(2.3)   a. *A bottle of **wine** **spilled***.
         b. *A **bottle** of wine **broke***.
         (Akmajian & Lehrer 1976: 406–7)

The morpho-syntactic tests determine the morpho-syntactic locus, subject–verb agreement, and determiner–noun concord. Zwicky (1985: 6) defines the morpho-syntactic locus as "the bearer of the morpho-syntactic marks of syntactic relations"; in the case of English, this is the element that carries the inflectional ending, and for *of*-binominals, the syntactic head is the noun that carries the plural marker (Keizer 2007a: 19). This is demonstrated in example (2.4a), where the first noun marks the plurality of the overall referent. This example also illustrates noun–verb concord, since the first noun agrees with the verb in number: plural *were* is selected in (2.4a), whereas a mass noun would select a verb in singular form, as demonstrated in (2.4b) (Keizer 2007a: 12–13).

(2.4)   a. *Two **bottles** of wine **were** standing in a row*.
         b. *The **wine** **is** in the cellar*.
         (Keizer 2007a: 12–13)

Although this is a widely accepted test for establishing headedness in *of*-binominals (see Brems 2011; Quirk et al. 1985: 765–6), Keizer (2007a) and others (e.g. Börjars, Vincent & Walkden 2015: 369; Brems 2011: 129) have cautioned that the results of this test may contradict the semantic findings or could be influenced by other factors, not just the syntactic head status, and therefore, this test can never act as the definitive test of syntactic head.

One example of such factors is the use of collective nouns, which can take single or plural verbs. Other factors are linear proximity to the verb, co-joined subjects, and possibly even animacy (Keizer 2007a: 13–17).

The final morpho-syntactic test is determiner–noun concord. Here the underlying rationale is that the determiner agrees in number with the NP head, and therefore, if the first determiner agrees with the second noun, this could be an indicator that the status of the first noun has changed, as illustrated in example (2.5) (Keizer 2007a: 18; see also Traugott 2008a: 27).[2]

(2.5) **these** kind of pitch **changes** (Keizer 2007a: 18)

The pragmatic-discourse indicators Keizer (2007a, 2011) proposes is pronominalization, in particular personal pronouns and *one*. Proforms have often been used to attest semantic units or syntactic constituency (see Quirk et al. 1985: 863; Stirling & Huddleston 2002: 1461), the underlying assumption being that proforms can replace a constituent, e.g. VP, NP, PP. More specifically, personal pronouns replace a NP and *one* can substitute the nominal head as well as bigger nominal constituents, including whole NPs (see Keizer 2011 for an overview of the literature). Since noun phrases are prototypically referential (in the sense of referring to an entity), they should accept an anaphoric definite pronoun (see Keizer 2007a: 20). In those cases where two nouns do not agree in number, the choice of pronoun can demonstrate which noun functions as head, since it is the head that profiles the referent, hence determining the form of the pronoun chosen (Keizer 2020: 344–5). Thus, in (2.6a), the antecedent of *they* is *reviews*, while in (2.6b) the antecedent of *it* is *a review*. (This test is mentioned again briefly in Section 2.2.3, since the referentiality of the two nouns is also important for their status as nouns.)

(2.6) a. **Some reviews** *of this book* were received. **They** were very laudatory.
b. **A review** *of three books* was received. **It** was very laudatory.
(Keizer 2020: 344)

Keizer (2011) argues that there are many cases where proforms do not actually replace a whole syntactic unit; in the case of the NP, for example, *one* does not have to replace the noun with its complements as demonstrated in (2.7). Instead, *one* prototypically fills the position of the head

---

[2] Zwicky (1985) discusses all three tests (and other indicators of headedness, i.e. subcategorized, governor, and semantic argument), but he claims that the other tests are interrelated, i.e. "subcategorisands are semantic functors … functors agree with their (semantic) arguments and govern them"; ergo the two central "notions" are semantic argument and morpho-syntactic locus (1985: 3).

2.2 Internal Structure of Of-binominals

(2.8) or the head and one or more dependents (i.e. the head plus complement and/or modifier(s)), "[a]s long as the combination of lexical items can be assumed to be accessible to the hearer," as shown in (2.9) (Keizer 2011: 324; for the referential use of *one*, see Stirling & Huddleston 2002: 1513–14). In all these cases, *one* denotes a property that is in turn denoted by its antecedent.

(2.7)   I support *the **ban** on smoking*, but not *the **one** on alcohol*. (Payne & Huddleston 2002: 441)

(2.8)   Well how can (pause) well how can go without *his **keys**?* He's got a spare ***one***. (BNC[3]; Keizer 2011: 308)

(2.9)   First, because *formal **institutionalized procedures*** generally attract more publicity than *informal **ones***. (BNC; Keizer 2011: 309)

Therefore, in the case of the *of*-binominals, *one* can indicate if both nouns still denote a nominal property, i.e. if they function as nouns. Should it not be possible to replace one of the nouns with *one*, as in the case of *hell* in (2.10b), then there is evidence that that noun no longer denotes a property. In the same examples, should the second noun accept *one* as an anaphoric reference, as demonstrated in (2.10a), this would indicate that this noun does denote a property, and as such functions as the head of the whole *of*-binominal. Naturally, there are limitations on the applicability of this test. Should both nouns head their respective noun phrases, then this test merely helps establish the head of each individual NP construction as in (2.11). Moreover, *one* can only be used with countable nouns (Stirling & Huddleston 2002: 1508).

(2.10)   a. That was a funny line, *a **hell** of a **one***, Peter. (COHA)
            b. *That was *a **hell** of a line*. That was *a **one** of a speech*.

(2.11)   a. she hid among *the reeds of the sea* ... (COCA)
            b. she hid among ***the reeds** of the sea* and then moved to hide among the ***ones** of the lake*.
            c. in the morning she hid among *the reeds of the **sea*** and in the evening collected *the reeds of the same **one*** for a bed.

In conclusion, the head status will be determined via a number of semantic, syntactic, and discourse-pragmatic tests.

---

[3] The British National Corpus (BNC)

2.2.2 Constituency

The classic constituency tests – preposing[4] (2.12), postposing (2.13), and coordination of the NPs (2.14) – provide a range of information; logically and primarily, they indicate if the complex NP contains an embedded PP (see McCawley 1988: 47–66; Radford 1988: 69–105).[5]

(2.12)   a. They didn't send us a copy of the exam REGULATIONS, but [the exam PAPER]$_i$ they did send a copy of t$_i$. (N+PP)
b. *[An exam]$_i$, we had to take a bitch of t$_i$. (EBNP)
(Aarts 1998: 135–6)

(2.13)   a. [A copy t$_i$] was received [of the exam regulations]$_i$. (N+PP)
b. *[A monster t$_i$] was delivered [of a machine]$_i$. (EBNP)
(Aarts 1998: 134–5 from Abney 1987: 297)

(2.14)   a. They sent us a copy [of the exam paper] and [of the exam regulations]. (N+PP)
b. *She called him a bastard [of a husband] and [of a father]. (EBNP)
(Aarts 1998: 136)

A negative or ambiguous result to any or all of these tests, as found in examples (2.12b), (2.13b), and (2.14b), then raises the question about the manner in which different linguistic elements stand in relation to each other. This question has been answered in a variety of ways for most of the *of*-binominals discussed here (for a summary of the analysis of the EBNP, see, e.g., Kim & Sells 2015). This, in turn, provides some evidence for the status of the preposition: if NP$_2$ and *of* do not form a prepositional phrase, then clearly *of* cannot be a preposition heading that phrase (Keizer 2007a: 93), and therefore, *of* can only function as some sort of linking element. Finally, this analysis raises other issues such as if the *of*-binominal is not a NP with a PP modifier/complement, then what is the nature and function of the nouns and the role of the determiners?

2.2.3 Constraints on the Two Nouns

Noun phrases are prototypically referential,[6] evoking referents, and therefore they should allow anaphoric reference via a personal pronoun, as

---

[4] Although Aarts (1998: 135) also notes that even with a more canonical *of*-binominal, fronting is a bit awkward unless the right context is created.
[5] Naturally it could also indicate a complement PP. It is difficult to find reliable tests for distinguishing between PP modifiers (adjuncts) and PP complements (see Keizer 2004, 2007a; Payne et al. 2013).
[6] Reference as used here means "if, by using [a linguistic expression] on a given occasion, a speaker intends it to pick out some independently distinguishable entity, or set of entities, in the real world (or in some fictional world)" (Payne & Huddleston 2002: 399).

2.2 Internal Structure of Of-binominals

illustrated in example (2.15a–b): in (2.15a), *Mary* is referential and is co-referential with the pronoun *she*. In (2.15b) *anyone* is not used referentially and therefore does not allow an anaphoric reference (Payne & Huddleston 2002: 399–410).

(2.15) a. Did [Mary]$_i$ telephone while I was out? **She**$_i$ promised to call today.
b. Did [anyone]$_j$ call while I was out? *****She/*He/*They**$_j$ promised to call today.
(Payne & Huddleston 2002: 400)

In the context of this study, this test then shows whether one of the NPs has lost its referentiality. In (2.16), the word *dogs* is the head of the complex NP with the PP indicating location; therefore, the anaphoric referent *they* has the whole complex N+PP as its antecedent. NP$_2$ also has referential value, as shown by the fact that it allows for the use of the anaphoric pronoun *it* (2.16b). This is not the case for NP$_2$ *shells* in (2.17), which cannot be replaced by a pronoun.

(2.16) a. You should know **the vagabond homeless dogs of Lima** inhabit a higher plane of ruthlessness. **They** own the alleys (COCA)
b. You should know *the dogs of **Lima*** inhabit a higher plane of ruthlessness. **It** is not a place for the faint of heart, either dog or man.

(2.17) I bought *a whale of* **shells**. *I wanted to buy you *a mouse of* **them**, but the shop didn't have one.

The *one*-test demonstrates to what extent the noun still represents a lexical element denoting a property (i.e. functions semantically as a noun; see Section 2.2.1). In example (2.18a–b), the noun *nurse* in (2.18a) can be replaced by *one*, whereas the bleached form of *hell* cannot be (2.18b).[7]

(2.18) a. She was *a hell of a* **nurse**. Your sister was a good **one** too.
b. *She was *a* **hell** *of a nurse* and was a **one** of a mother too.

The non-referential nature of the first noun may indicate that we are dealing with incipient stages of grammaticalization (see Chapter 5 for further discussion), and this would then lead to further constraints or changes in the behavior of the nouns. Another prominent indicator is the loss of prototypical noun features, such as plurality; hence some constructions, like (2.19a–c), can accept first nouns only in the singular form (2.19a) and not in the plural (2.19b–c).

---

[7] This use of *hell* will be discussed in greater detail in Section 4.2.

(2.19) a. a hell of day
b. *hells of a day
c. *hells of days

Another potential restriction on nouns in the *of*-binominal is the type of noun selected. For example, the second noun position in the EBNP is habitually filled by singular count nouns, and occasionally by collective nouns, such as *crew* in (2.20a), and plural nouns (2.20b); mass nouns are excluded from this position. If mass nouns are used, the construction would be interpreted as another kind of *of*-binominal construction as demonstrated in example (2.20c), where a likely interpretation of the phrase is a beast made of rice (in which case we are dealing with a head-classifier construction, see Section 3.3).

(2.20) a. those **fools** of a **crew** (Keizer 2005)
b. those Chinese **chopsticks** of **knitting-needles** (Austin 1980: 359)
c. a beast of rice

Other examples show that the function of the construction as a whole may place restrictions on the nouns selected, as in the EBNP in (2.21). In the EBNP, only evaluative nouns or nouns that can be construed as evaluative (such as *idiot* in (2.21a)) can be used in the first noun position; those that cannot be construed as evaluative make the phrase ill-formed, as *teacher* in (2.21b) (Aarts 1998). Therefore, there can be a range of restrictions on noun selection: restrictions on noun form (only singular or plural), restrictions on noun type (e.g. mass, count, collective), and semantic restrictions (e.g. evaluative nouns).

(2.21) a. an **idiot** of a teacher
b. ?that **teacher** of a husband
(Keizer 2007a: 86)

Other defining features are second noun collocates and premodification patterns. Brems (2011: 111–13, 123; for more discussion see Partington 1993) argues, based on her analysis of measure nouns (which she calls size nouns [SNs]), that part of the grammaticalization process of *of*-binominals entails delexicalization, which primarily can be recognized in collocation patterns and semantic prosody (2011: 128–9):

> The degree of lexicality and coextensiveness of course is reflected by the semantic generality of the N_2-collocates; literal and fully lexical SN-uses generally predicate a restricted set of collocates in the *of*-phrase ... Hence, as the collocational range of an SN increases and more collocates are allowed to team up with it, the probability of a quantifier analysis likewise increases.

2.2 Internal Structure of Of-binominals

An example from her study would be *heap-of* in (2.22) and (2.23). For her head use of *heap* (2.22a–c), any second noun can be used as long as it is concrete and 'heapable', i.e. concrete objects like *bricks* (2.22a), animate objects like *bodies* (2.22b), and mass nouns like *rubble* in (2.22c). The quantifier use of *heap* then expands the collocational range to abstract nouns such as *questions* (2.23a) and *humour* (2.23b). Partington's (1993) study of intensifiers demonstrates a similar trend: he argues that the broader the field of collocates, the more delexicalized (i.e. semantically bleached) the intensifier.

(2.22)   a. "My first impression was not that it was an earthquake", said Heinz Hermann, standing by *a heap of **bricks*** that had fallen from his 100 year-old house.
b. While we were attempting to disentangle ourselves from *the heap of crumpled **bodies***, Alain coolly skied off into the distance.
c. Each home belonging to a Croat or Moslem was reduced to *a heap of **rubble***.
(Brems 2011: 134–5)

(2.23)   a. They went through my bags, searched me and asked *a heap of **questions***.
b. Their show has *heaps of **humour***, and you can detect the cheeky influences of Cirus Oz.
(Brems 2011: 140–1)

Further tests that provide evidence of the status of the first nouns and their relationship to other elements within the NP are N–N concord, predicative form, and substitution. Noun concord is whether the construction requires number agreement between the two nouns; prototypically it should not as in *the first beans of the harvest*. However, in the EBNP in (2.24a–b), the first noun ascribes some sort of property onto the second; therefore, the two nouns must agree in number. If not, the construction is ill-formed as in (2.24b) (see Section 4.2 for more details). This provides further evidence that the first noun no longer functions as a prototypical noun.

(2.24)   a. an idiot of a doctor
b. *those **idiots** of a doctor

Another standard diagnostic is whether the first and second nouns are in a predicative relationship as shown in (2.25). One of Den Dikken's (1998, 2006) main contributions to the EBNP discussion is that in some forms of the EBNP, N_1 and N_2 are in a predicative relationship. The final test is substitution, as illustrated in (2.26), where [N₁+of+a] can be substituted by a derived adjective. This test has often been used to deduce the function of certain parts of the phrase and has been explicitly stated as a testing method in many studies (e.g. Brems 2011: 129; Traugott 2008a: 27) and implicitly in others (e.g. Aarts 1998; Keizer 2007a; Trousdale 2012).

(2.25)   a. an idiot of a doctor
          b. The doctor is an idiot

(2.26)   a. An **oaf of a** bus conductor
          b. That **oafish** bus conductor
          (Aarts 1998: 146)

Premodification patterns can provide evidence for two separate features of the binominal: the status of the noun and the function of the construction as a whole. Where the status of the noun is concerned, it is assumed that as *of*-binominals progress along a path of grammaticalization, they tend to lose their 'nouniness' and become more selective with regard to, or resistant toward, premodification. Therefore, the first question is whether the noun can be modified at all. Davidse, Brems, and De Smedt (2008: 149) argue that, in its most grammaticalized form, the element *sort-of* has come to function as a semi-suffix, and has, as such, become integrated into the premodifier zone, where it functions similarly to an 'enclitic' for classifying adjectives or nouns (see also Denison 2002). Hence, the element *sort* can no longer be modified, but modification in front of the first noun modifies the second, as in example (2.27).[8] In the EBNP, where the first noun is less grammaticalized, the ambiguous nominal status of the first noun is reflected in the fact that modifiers in front of the first noun can be selected by the second noun, such as *bitchy* in (2.28a), which is clearly selected by N₂ (*woman*) (Aarts 1998: 133). This interpretation is not available in the regular N+PP construction in (2.28b).

(2.27)   Apparently, her mother was *a* ***keeping-up-with-the-Joneses*** *sort of person*. (Davidse et al. 2008: 149)

(2.28)   a. another **bitchy** iceberg of a **woman** (Aarts 1998: 133)
          b. a **lovely picture** of her father (Alexiadou et al. 2007: 398)

Premodification patterns, furthermore, provide an indication of the function of the first noun and the function of the whole binominal.

---

[8] An alternative analysis would that *keeping-up-with-the-Joneses* does modify *sort*, e.g. *he is the keeping-up-with-the-Joneses sort*. The question here does not so much concern the exact analysis but rather the criteria used to analyze this *of*-binominal.

2.2 Internal Structure of Of-binominals

For example, premodification patterns help distinguish between the attributive use of *sort-of*, as seen in (2.29), and the semi-suffix category, as seen in (2.27): in the attributive use of *sort of* can be modified (2.29), while in the semi-suffix, the premodifiers in front of the first noun modify the second noun, such as *keeping-up-with-the-Jones* in (2.27) (Brems 2011: 289–91).

(2.29) Being *an **accommodating** sort of bloke*, he let me take the car around the paddock at Silverstone. (Brems 2011: 285)

In her analysis of *a lot of*, Traugott (2008a, 2008b) contends that the use of the degree modifier *quite* in front of the first noun is evidence that *a lot* (or, as she argues on the basis of other evidence, *a lot of*) functions as a quantifier (as illustrated in (2.30)). Brems (2011) argues that her head category (similar to my N+PP) accepts all types of premodification in front of the first noun (2.31a), whereas the quantifiers only accept premodifiers that reinforce the quantificational meaning (2.31b) (Brems 2011: 194). Therefore, for the quantifier constructions, adjectives in front of the first noun reinforce the quantifier information, i.e. *whole* in (2.31b), or indicate size, i.e. *hat* in (2.31c) (Brems 2011: 196).

(2.30) the moon had risen and was letting ***quite a lot** of light* into the bank (Traugott 2008b: 232)

(2.31) a. There's always *a **fresh** bunch of **locally grown** dill* at the market. (Brems 2011: 178)
b. The world that awaits me is a bit scary there is going to be *a **whole** bunch of idiot journalists* waiting to ask me stupid questions – then that's life. (Brems 2011: 196)
c. Mccoist made them pay for their failure to convert *a **hat**-load of chances*. (Brems 2011: 196)

In the following chapters, premodification will be briefly discussed in each section, but a more detailed discussion of the general patterns associated with the different categories of N-*of*-N will be reserved for a larger premodification study in Chapter 7. A point that ties into premodification and will not be discussed in the next two chapters is scope, i.e. whether a modifier placed in front of the first noun just modifies the first noun or the whole construction (e.g. Kruisinga 1932: 397). This has been used as a categorization criterion in previous studies (e.g. Kim & Sells 2015: 47–8) and will also be discussed in more detail in the chapter on premodification.

Ultimately, the tests discussed in this section should, first, enable us to determine the extent to which the nouns actually function as prototypical nouns, i.e. their degree of 'nouniness', and second, should help isolate the relationship of the nouns to each other. Third, they should help us to glean as much information as possible about the meaning/function of the complex binominal as a whole.

2.2.4 Determiner Selection

The changing functions of the nouns lead to restrictions on the determiners in the first and second determiner slots. Thus, determiner restrictions provide evidence for, first, the change in noun status: for example, does the first noun function as the head of the NP, as in example (2.32a). Second, it provides evidence for the change of the constituency and function of the construction as a whole, as shown by determiner specification: in (2.32b) the first determiner specifies the second noun, i.e. *those* specifies *creatures* (Denison 2005).

(2.32) a. The mind of the victim of **this kind** *of assault* must be considered equally with the body.
    b. ***Those*** *sort of* ***creatures*** know no bounds when they think they have a purse in view that will answer their impudent demands.
    (Denison 2005)

Furthermore, the preference for or restriction on determiners provides evidence for the function of the construction: in (2.33a), the first determiner slot is open for all types of determination, whereas the second determiner slot is always empty in accordance with the classifying function of the second noun (see Section 3.3). This is different from the EBNP in (2.33b), which allows the definite article in the first determiner zone only in particular contexts, while it is altogether disallowed in the second determiner slot: here, only an indefinite article or a bare article (in the case of a plural N_2) are grammatical.

(2.33) a. a/the/any/this/one book of *a/#the comics
    b. ?the/ that idiot of a/*the/*this/*that/*one/*my doctor
    (variation of Corver 1998: 232)

2.2.5 *Preposition* Of

The change of meaning and function of the preposition *of* is also a defining categorical feature for *of*-binominals, which is not surprising given that *of* is the chameleon under the English prepositions. Langacker (1999: 86) observes that "[s]chematically, *of* profiles an intrinsic relationship between the two participants," and the OED provides no less than sixty entries for *of* (not counting the subentries). Focusing on the binominal use, *of* is said to have semantic content such as 'have'/'with' in (2.34a), 'from' to indicate location or source in (2.34b) or possession such as 'belonging to' in (2.34c) (Kruisinga 1932: 391–5; Quirk et al. 1985: 321–2, 704–5).

(2.34)   a. a man of courage   (Quirk et al. 1985: 704)
           b. the wines of France   (Quirk et al. 1985: 322)
           c. the gravity of the earth   (Quirk et al. 1985: 321)

In more semantically bleached versions, such as (2.35), it has been claimed that *of* functions as some sort of linking device, i.e. a grammatical linker (Löbel 2001: 249), a prepositional copula (Corver 1998; Den Dikken 1998, 2006), or an element of a complex modifier (Aarts 1998; Keizer 2007a). As discussed above, constituent tests also provide information on the status of the preposition, more specifically on whether the preposition functions as head of a PP or not; the conjecture being that, should the PP and NP_2 not be constituents, then the preposition no longer functions as a prototypical preposition, and therefore, no longer has semantic content.

(2.35)   a Kate Moss of a wine (Aarts 1998: 121)

2.3 Methodology for Part I

Use of the EBNP is not restricted to one particular variety of English but is pervasive throughout the English language. For practical reasons, however, this book focuses on American English. The EBNP is not extremely frequent, which means that this study required larger corpora. This project, therefore, predominantly uses the two large modern English language corpora: the Corpus of Contemporary American English (COCA; Davies 2008), which has over 520 million words (the search was conducted in 2014), and its historical English counterpart, the Corpus of Historical American English (COHA; Davies 2008), with over 400 million words and covering the time span from 1810 to 2009 (pre-2021 update). The size of COHA offered the opportunity to examine the development of first nouns in the constructions discussed in Chapter 1 over the last two centuries, while the smaller historical corpora (such as the Penn-Helsinki Corpora, the LAEME Corpus or the Middle English Grammar Corpus) simply offered too few tokens of the relevant constructions to draw any conclusions. The synchronic analysis presented in Chapters 3 and 4 is based on data from COCA; however, examples from COHA, News on the Web Corpus (NOW), and the Internet will also be used to illustrate certain points. A number of different historical corpora are used in the diachronic analysis in Chapter 5.

This project began with a search for the origin and development of the EBNP, and it focused on the first nouns used in this construction. The data was retrieved in a basic type search for nouns that immediately proceeded *of*: [nn* of] in COCA. It was then restricted to the most frequent first nouns which were used in the EBNP in the synchronic data (i.e. selected from the 1,000 most frequent collocates). This resulted in 125 first noun types (see Table 2.1). Looking at the first nouns' functions in the EBNP, they were initially split along two different distinctions, nouns denoting physical objects (first-order entities) and nouns denoting abstract entities (third-order entities),[9] such as beliefs, expectations, or judgments.[10] The former category was then divided into nouns denoting animate entities and nouns denoting inanimate entities;[11] the latter category was simply labeled abstract; hence, the final categories are animate, inanimate, and abstract (see Table 2.1).

Unlike research in the genitive alternation, where animacy is one of the critical variables (for more discussion, see Rosenbach 2002: 42–9), in the EBNP, abstractness is the feature that would appear to most greatly affect the first nouns' potential to grammaticalize into the more evaluative constructions, i.e. whether it is selected to be used in the evaluative modifier and the binominal intensifier. Unsurprisingly, abstract first nouns were found to have the greatest potential, and inanimate first nouns were the least likely to grammaticalize beyond the EBNP. Therefore, the classification was made according to first noun semantics when the noun is used in the EBNP. This distinction was vital in order to balance out the data sample in the premodifier study and when examining

---

[9] This definition of third order adheres more closely to Hengeveld and Mackenzie's (2008: 131–2) definition than Lyon's (1977).

[10] This distinction was based on Lyon's (1977) definitions. First-order entities are physical objects that can occupy a place and time and are observable (Lyons 1977: 442–3). Third-order entities are abstract and cannot be located in space and time; they can be beliefs, expectations, and judgments (Lyons 1977: 443–5).

[11] Unlike Lyons (1977: 443), who makes a tripartite distinction (human, animate, inanimate); a dual distinction has been made here. This is partly because there are so few first nouns referring to humans, and partly because these human first nouns do not seem to develop differently from the other animate first nouns.

2.3 Methodology for Part I

Table 2.1 *First nouns examined in this study*

ABSTRACT	ANIMATE	INANIMATE	
angel	bear	axe	puff
ass	beast	ball	rag
bastard	bird	balloon	reed
bitch	boy	battle	sea
bore	bull	beacon	seal
brat	dinosaur	beak	sigh
brute	dog	bean	slab
bum	eagle	bell	slit
chit	elephant	boat	strip
clunker	horse	bomb	tank
crook	lion	breeze	tomb
demon	mouse	bud	toy
devil	mutt	button	treasure
disappointment	pig	carrot	vault
disaster	snake	cake	whirlwind
dud	swine	castle	whisper
eyesore	whale	cathedral	wisp
fool	workhorse	compass	
freak		doll	
fuck		egg	
giant		fire	
gnome		flower	
hell		gem	
idiot		globe	
jerk		honey	
jewel		husk	
monster		island	
monstrosity		knife	
nightmare		lump	
paragon		mask	
princess		moon	
scorcher		mop	
sham		mountain	
shit		net	
slob		nub	
slut		pearl	
witch		pillar	
waif		plum	

the grammaticalization paths in the diachronic study. It was important that the sample created for these individual studies included first nouns that were less likely to be used as evaluative modifiers and binominal intensifiers as well as those that do grammaticalize further.

The animate group consists primarily of animals (e.g. *horse, whale, snake, beast*); the inanimate group consists of plants (i.e. *carrot, reed*) and lifeless objects (e.g. *jewel, vault, ball, button*). The abstract, third-order entities are slightly more problematic, and there is some overlap with the other two categories. For example, although *boy* is placed with the animate nouns, *princess*, which functions as a title (an abstraction by definition), is part of the abstract category. The abstract category also includes religious and mythical animate beings, like *devil, gnome, angel, giant*, and expletives that often refer to animate things, such as *ass, bitch*, and *bastard. Bitch* and *ass* originally were used to refer to animals, but the abstract use is the predominant one in the EBNP, as demonstrated in (2.36a) for *bitch* and in (2.36b) for *ass*.

(2.36) a. Think of it, Lorry, her lovely Lorry, in bed with *that skinny bitch of a wife*! (COHA)
  b. But that damnable itch always, always returned. *One ass of a doctor* in New York had prescribed a summer at Newport (COHA)

There are some *of*-binominal constructions that appear with a low frequency in the dataset and could not be discussed in detail in this project. First, there were sporadic examples of the partitive; examples can be found in (2.37a) and (2.37b), but they were simply too infrequent to warrant a detailed discussion here. The second construction that would need further discussion in future work is (2.38), where the phrase seems to function similarly to the EBNP, in that the speaker ascribes beast-like properties onto the second noun, but both nouns are referential. Keizer (2007a) categorizes these examples as appositional, but they would have to be examined in more detail, as would their relation to the grammaticalization path argued here. However, in both cases, the frequencies are so low that they do not appear to be central members of the process. Finally, two types of idiomatic phrases periodically appeared in the data: the first is with *it*, in which the pronoun has no clear referent (see example (2.39a)). The second is [the very N of] with *very* modifying the first noun, as shown in (2.39b). In this example *very* seems to indicate 'the core essence of' the first noun. These idiomatic constructions are also excluded from the data.

(2.37) a. He matures into *the most beautiful bird of all*. (COCA)
  b. Atlas was *the alpha dog of the four dogs* she was walking. (COCA)

(2.38) Through the gentle angle of the blinds, I could see midmorning sunlight on green leaves and, across the road, *the great looming beast of the State Hospital*. (COCA)

(2.39) a. The two were rooting for different girls just for *the hell of it*. Neither was invested in the fighters as athletes, women, or even human beings. (COCA)
b. He was over six feet high – a tower of bones, with a complexion absolutely colourless, fair hair, and a light unscrupulous gray eye, twinkling occasionally at *the very devil of mischief.* (COHA)

2.4 Conclusion

This chapter has presented a compilation and review of diagnostic tests that have been applied in previous English *of*-binominal studies and which will be applied to the *of*-binominal constructions introduced in Chapter 1 (see Table 2.2 for summary). Together these tests serve to determine the head and constituency structure of the binominal phrase as well as isolating the meaning and functions of, and restrictions on, the linguistic elements that make up these phrases. In the case of the individual diagnostic tests, there are some that are more cogent than others. Head status, for example, is one of the central tests, but its application is complicated by the fact that there are many different left-headed constructions, e.g. *a bird of prey* (head-classifier) or *the beast of Prague* (locative N+PP), as well as numerous right-headed ones, e.g. *that idiot of a doctor* (EBNP) or *a sort of kitchen* (*sort-of* construction). However, there are constructions like *a pot of steel* (example (2.1)) where headedness is the defining criterion to distinguish between *pot* as a quantifier or as a noun (although both interpretations can be formally distinguished with other tests). The status of the individual nouns and noun phrases also plays an important role, e.g. referentiality, 'nouniness'. However, in *a beast of Prague*, both the construction as a whole and the embedded NP *Prague* can be or are referential.

In Chapters 3 and 4 in Part I, all the diagnostic tests discussed in this chapter will be applied to each of the categories proposed and then, in Chapter 5, three first nouns selected for analysis (*hell* for the abstract nouns, *beast* for the animate nouns, and *cake* for the inanimate nouns) will be discussed in order to exemplify these changes. All three were selected as representatives of their respective categories because they demonstrate the prototypical features of each group and are some of the most frequent first nouns in the data sample. *Hell*, in particular, is not only one of the oldest examples of the EBNP and appears to be one of the first to develop EM and BI interpretations, but also the most frequent form in the corpora used in this study.

Table 2.2 *Categorization criteria for the internal structure of the NP*

1. **Head Status**
    i. *Semantic tests*
        a. Distributional equivalence
        b. Obligatoriness
        c. Verb semantic selection
    ii. *Morpho-syntactic criteria*
        a. Morpho-syntactic locus
        b. Subject–verb agreement
        c. Determinant–noun concord
    iii. *Pragmatic discourse criteria*
        a. Anaphoric reference
            (1) Personal pronouns
            (2) Anaphoric *one*

2. **Constituency (and status of *of*)**
    i. *Preposing*
    ii. *Postposing*
    iii. *Coordination of the PPs*

3. **Constraints on the two nouns**
    i. *Referentiality*
        a. Pronominalization by definite pronouns (anaphoricity)
        b. Pronominalization by *one*
    ii. *Selection restrictions for nouns*
        a. Semantic restrictions
        b. Noun type, e.g. mass, count, collective
        c. Singular/plural form
        d. Collocations
    iii. *Further tests*
        a. N1–N2 number concord
        b. Predicative relationship
        c. Substitution
    iv. *Premodification patterns*
        a. Premodification restrictions
        b. Premodification selection

4. **Determiners**
    i. *Determiner selection*
    ii. *Determiner agreement*

5. **Status of *of***
    i. *Semantic content-function*
    ii. *Constituency tests (see point 2)*

2.4 Conclusion

One major question that remains is to what extent do *of*-binominals have to differ along these parameters to warrant a new categorical distinction. This is not an easy question to answer, and naturally depends on the theoretical background against which the study is conducted. From a functional perspective, there would need to be a change in form to justify a claim of a change in function, the assumption being that a change in meaning leads to a change in form (see Chapter 9 for an FDG analysis). construction grammarians, in particular diachronic construction grammarians, are currently discussing this issue. For some, the change of meaning is enough, while others argue for both a change in meaning and form (see Chapter 8).

CHAPTER 3

From Prototypical N+PP to Pseudo-partitive

3.1 Introduction

This section charts, to a certain extent, the path described in previous research in that it looks at the progression of first nouns from being the head in prototypical N+PP phrases to quantifiers in pseudo-partitive *of*-binominals. However, it differs from other studies in that the majority of the first nouns examined here are not prototypical measure nouns; instead, this study exams first nouns that eventually lend themselves to an evaluative reading in the EBNP. Furthermore, Section 3.3 analyzes the head-classifier category, which most previous studies have either overlooked or grouped with the other left-head constructions. Finally, it is argued that all these syntagms are the beginning stages of the grammaticalization path that leads to the EBNP, and therefore, must be described and classified before progressing to the evaluative constructions (EBNP, EM, and BI) in Chapter 4. This analysis begins, as do many previous studies of the development of the *of*-binominals (e.g. Brems 2011; Denison 2002, 2005, 2011; Trousdale 2012), with the core N+PP construction (Section 3.2), then discusses the head-classifier construction (Section 3.3), and finally the pseudo-partitive construction (Section 3.4), before comparing and contrasting the three constructions and drawing some final conclusions (Section 3.5).

3.2 N+PP

This category represents an amalgamation of *of*-binominals all of which share syntactic features that could be regarded as features of the prototypical or canonical *of*-binominals in English: the first noun is head, and the second noun is part of an NP embedded in a prepositional phrase, functioning as a modifier or complement, with the element *of* denoting a range of relationships between head and second noun phrase (see Quirk et al. 1985: 703). In this particular family of *of*-binominals, the PP tends to function as a modifier specifying possession (3.1a), source/location (3.1b), time (3.1 c), or to simply ascribe a property to the first noun (3.2a–b).

(3.1) a. New American dream: cruisin down the information highway, hand on *the mouse of a new supercharged computer* (COCA)
b. He joined their AHL affiliate, *the Beast of New Haven*, in the fall. (COCA)
c. Kelvin MacKenzie ruled at the Sun – and, among other outrages, alleged that drunkenness among Liverpool football fans led to *the Hillsborough disaster of 1989*. (COCA)

(3.2) a. It was the Cleste, *a small balloon of 900 cubic yards* that had been generously donated by its owner. (COCA)
b. Each one that he considered appeared *a monster of abominable and insolent conceit*. (COCA)

Although this category is not homogeneous, the tests will be applied to a single representative example, and only in those cases when a group of *of*-binominals deviate from the norm will more examples be included.

3.2.1 Head Status

Semantic tests show that the first noun is the head of the whole construction. Examples (3.3) show that the first noun is the obligatory head and is distributionally equivalent to the whole construction, i.e. in (3.3 c), the white citizen being caught would not make sense in the context. This also means that the main verb semantically selects for the first noun, i.e. *caught* for *dog* (3.3).

(3.3) a. When the dogcatchers **caught** *the stray **dog** of a white citizen*, they called the citizen up. (COCA)
b. When the dogcatchers caught *the stray dog*, they called the citizen up.
c. #When the dogcatchers caught *a white citizen*, they called the citizen up.

The first noun is also the syntactic head. As shown in (3.4a), the first noun is the morpho-syntactic locus and agrees in number with the verb. The first and second determiner has concord with their respective noun, e.g. *these* with *beasts* in (3.4b), and *this* with *clime* in (3.4a).

(3.4) a. *The sweet breezes of this happy clime* **came** refreshingly to our nostrils. (COHA)
b. Researchers dubbed some of **these** *exotic beasts of the stellar zoo* "millisecond pulsars" (COCA)

30   3 From Prototypical N+PP to Pseudo-partitive

The pragmatic diagnostic tests are inconclusive when it comes to determining which noun functions as the head. The *one* test in example (3.5 b–c) shows that both nouns act as the head of their individual noun phrases; definite pronouns can take either noun phrase as their antecedents, as shown in (3.6).

(3.5)   a. *The sweet breezes of this happy clime* came refreshingly to our nostrils. (COHA)
        b. *The sweet **breezes** of this happy clime* came refreshingly to our nostrils. Only the **ones** *of the alps* are better.
        c. *The sweet breezes of this happy **clime*** came refreshingly to our nostrils. Only the *sweet views of this **one*** can top it.

(3.6)   a. Phobos and Deimos carry the names of *the chariot horses of the Roman war god Mars* – Fear and Terror. (COCA)
        b. Phobos and Deimos carry the names of **the chariot horses** *of the Roman war god Mars* – Fear and Terror. **They** were known for their prodigious strength.
        c. Phobos and Deimos carry the names of *the chariot horses of **the Roman war god Mars*** – Fear and Terror. **He** was known for his prodigious skill with horses.

In the phrases in this category, each noun ascribes a property and is the head of its respective noun phrase; each noun phrase denotes a separate entity. The semantic and syntactic tests show that the first noun is the head of the binominal as a whole.

3.2.2   Constituency Tests

The constituency tests yield equivocal results. When the PP functions as a complement, with *of* designating intrinsic possession (part–whole relationship), as in (3.7), extraction (preposing/postposing) of the PPs and the embedded NP is possible (examples 3.7a–d).

(3.7)   a. *The globe of the wine glass* dropped to the table. (COCA)
        b. [Of the wine glass]$_i$, it was [the globe t$_i$] that broke.
        c. [The wine glass]$_i$, they broke the globe of t$_i$.
        d. [The globe t$_i$] was broken [of the wine glass]$_i$.
        e. They broke the globes [of his wine glass] and [of his champagne glass].

In the locative (3.8) and temporal (3.9) examples, however, the PP or embedded NP can no longer be extracted; the results are questionable at best, e.g. (3.9d), and absurd at worst, e.g. (3.8d).

(3.8) a. *The stalking beast of his dreams* didn't exist (COCA)
b. *[Of his dreams]$_i$ it was [the stalking beast t$_i$] that he feared most.
c. *[His dreams]$_i$, he met the stalking beast of t$_i$.
d. *[The stalking beast t$_i$] was discovered [of his dreams]$_i$.
e. In one day, he met the stalking beasts [of his dreams] and [of reality].

(3.9) a. He says he considers *the greatest geopolitical disaster of modern times* the dissolution of the Soviet Union. (COCA)
b. $^{??}$[Of modern times]$_i$, it was [the greatest geopolitical disaster t$_i$] that we experience.
c. *[Modern times]$_i$, they discovered the greatest geopolitical disaster of t$_i$.
d. $^{??}$[The greatest geopolitical disaster t$_i$] was discovered [of modern times]$_i$.
e. They discovered the greatest geopolitical disaster [of modern times] and [of this decade].

With the proper context, all three examples allow for coordination as demonstrated in (3.7e), (3.8e), and (3.9e). As already mentioned above, other linguists have noticed that the results of constituency tests with *of*-binominals can be awkward, even with the most prototypical forms (e.g. Aarts 1998: 134–5), and the data here shows that even in these initial constructions, there are restrictions on extraction and coordination of the PP and embedded NP.

3.2.3 Constraints on the Two Nouns

In the N+PP construction, both of the individual nouns head their own individual noun phrase, and both noun phrases are referential and can accept anaphoric reference (as shown in Section 3.2.1). Both nouns can be of any subtype: concrete (e.g. *whale* (3.10) and *glass* (3.7)), abstract (*disaster* (3.9) and *dream* (3.8)), and proper nouns (e.g. *New Haven* 3.1b)). They can appear in singular (e.g. *beast* (3.11) and *citizen* (3.3)) and plural form (e.g. *horses* (3.6) and *times* (3.9)), and as mass nouns (e.g. *honey* (3.11)). Although it is hard to find collective nouns in the sample in this study, intuitively a phrase like *the leader of the group* does not seem to be inappropriate. Both nouns function as prototypical nouns in prototypical, referential noun phrases.

(3.10) a. Among the fossils were *three whales of the same species* huddled together, possibly a family that had died at once. (COCA)
b. Among the fossils were *three whales of the same **species*** huddled together. Nearby were the bodies of *two whales of a different* **one**, also huddled together.
c. Among the fossils were ***three whales*** *of the same species* huddled together. Some distance away were ***ones*** *of a different species*.

(3.11) a. The bees love *the honey of the blue and the white lotuses* the most. (COCA)
b. The bees love *the honey of **the blue and the white lotuses*** the most. **They** only bloom in May.
c. The bees love ***the honey** of the blue and the white lotuses* the most. **It** is sweeter than that of other flowers.

The first and second nouns do not have to agree in number, e.g. (3.11); substitution tests do not apply (since the first noun clearly heads the NPs as a whole), and the two nouns are not in a predicative relation.

As the prototypical N-*of*-N, it is assumed these constructions allow for unrestricted premodification in front of both nouns (with the exception of proper nouns). A cursory review of the corpus data would seem to support this hypothesis, as exemplified by (3.12a–d). Again, the only restrictions are those imposed by the semantics of the nouns themselves.

(3.12) a. the **gentle** breeze of a **forgotten** summer (COCA)
b. one **Arkansas brown** bear of 300 pounds (COCA)
c. the **merest** whisper of Jenkins's own **true** feelings (COCA)
d. a **potential HIV-AIDS** disaster of **unimaginable** proportions (COCA)

In sum, the constructions in this category are made up of two noun phrases both with their own denotation and individual referents. There are no selection restrictions on the nouns except for those specified by the function of the PP modifier/complement, e.g. a temporal modifier/complement requires a referent that can be located in time. Finally, there appear to be no restrictions on premodification in front of the first and second nouns.

3.2.4 *Determiners*

The determiner slots in front of the first and second nouns are unrestricted, as demonstrated by examples (3.13a–d) and (3.14a–b) for N_1 and (3.13a) and (3.14a–e) for N_2. Zero determination is also allowed, e.g. (3.15) for N_1 and (3.13c) for N_2.

(3.13) a. **some** birds of **the** same species (COCA)
b. **that** dreadful nightmare of the Dreyfuseuse (COHA)
c. **any** cat or dog of respectable character (COHA)
d. **its** globe of painted flowers (COHA)

e. **some** monster of the nastier sort (COHA)
f. **one** bomb of 100 pounds (COHA)

(3.14) a. **the** darkest nightmare of **his** iniquitous life (COHA)
b. **a** grotesque gray bird of **some** supernatural region (COHA)
c. some strange monster of **these** buried waters (COHA)
d. the angel of **all my** wretched cadet days (COHA)
e. the devil of **any** other race (COHA)

(3.15) great birds of the air (COCA)

The first determiner indicates the identifiability and number of the referent of the overall NP, the second determiner the identifiability and number of the referent of the embedded NP. The definite and indefinite articles are still the default determiners for both determiner slots.

3.2.5 Status of Of

Despite the ambiguity evidenced in the constituency tests (Section 3.2.2), the element *of* still retains semantic content: 'from', 'with', or 'belonging to'. Examples where *of* most likely means 'from' can be found in examples such as (3.14a–c), where the referent of the NP$_2$ denotes a location, e.g. *some supernatural region* (3.14b). *Of* means 'with' when it ascribes a property or feature to the first noun, as in the case of *respectable character* (3.13 c) or *100 pounds* (3.13 f). Finally, *of* means 'belonging to' when the overall referent is a member of a group designated by the second noun or is possessed by the second NP, e.g. *the nastier sort* (3.16a) and *any other race* (3.16b).

(3.16) a. some monster of the nastier sort (COHA)
b. the devil of any other race (COHA)

Chapter 5 will look at the development of representative members of each of the groups of first nouns, sketching their historical development and their use in the N+PP construction.

3.2.6 The Properties of the N+PP

The category described in this section predominantly consists of core *of*-binominals with the following structure: [$_{NP1}$ [Det$_1$] (Mod) [[N$_1$] [$_{PP1}$ [$_P$ of] [$_{NP2}$ [Det$_2$] (Mod) [N$_2$]]]]]. The first noun is the head of the matrix noun phrase and is modified by a prepositional phrase that ascribes a property, indicates a location, source, or possessor, or provides temporal

34   3 From Prototypical N+PP to Pseudo-partitive

information. Both nouns head their own NP, each denoting a separate referent. The prepositional phrase forms a constituent with the second NP; *of* functions as a preposition with semantic content, denoting either 'from', 'with', or 'belonging to'. The only limitations on the determiner selection are those imposed by the individual nouns themselves.

It should be noted that this category is more a theoretical contingency than an ontological reality in that it consists of a mixture of construction types that share a range of formal properties but are semantically not completely the same and do not perform the same functions. To a large degree the difference between the different functions might be disambiguated by the nouns themselves, but, as shown above, some of the formal features also differ, i.e. the extent to which the PP can be extracted. Nonetheless, these *of*-binominals do set themselves apart from the ones that follow in that they conform more closely to language-internal behavior of core N+PPs than the more grammaticalized forms.

3.3   Head-Classifier

The step from constructions where the prepositional phrase is locative or ascribes a property to the head to constructions where the first noun is categorized by this location or property does not seem to be a big one. Nevertheless, there is a clear difference in interpretation, as demonstrated in example (3.17). In example (3.17a), the *flowers* are ones that appear in a particular spring, although metaphorical; in (3.17b) the temporal relationship designates the type of flowers, i.e. spring flowers as opposed to winter ones.

(3.17)   a. And still the plain truth is that mothers, when their daughters marry, revive their old romance, see again *the flowers of a spring* that was sweet and booming in the long ago ... (COHA; N+PP)
   b. In our meadow where horses graze and *wild flowers of spring* blossom, anise shoots fill the air with aroma. (COCA; head-classifier-type of flowers)

There are a number of examples that would facilitate either reading, as in (3.18). Here the relationship between *silence* and *angel*, even with context, can be interpreted in more than one way: as an angel bringing silence (head-classifier) or as an angel that is ascribed the property of being silent (N+PP), i.e. the silent angel.[1]

---

[1] This would be considered a potential bridging context (for more discussion see Chapter 6).

3.3 Head-Classifier

(3.18) But he stops in midsentence, noticing a hush across the refectory. "Ah, *the angel of silence*," he says, laughing. Without another word, the monks rise and follow the abbot back to the church for the night prayer. (COCA)

In the head-classifier construction, the prepositional phrase does not anchor or identity the first noun but qualifies it (Keizer 2007a: 71; for a general discussion of classifier noun phrases, what they call common names, see also Gunkel & Zifonun 2009: 206–8). The second noun has lost its referential status (i.e. does not refer to a discourse referent) and instead answers the question: *What kind of N?* As such it classifies the overall referent, e.g. in (3.19a), *pleasures* and *pains* classify what type of *beast* is being referred to or assigns ontological status to the first noun (3.19b) (Keizer 2007a: 71–2; cf. Gunkel & Zifonun 2009: 206–8; Ten Wolde & Keizer 2016). The second noun can only be either a bare mass noun or a bare plural count noun. Finally, unlike the previous category, the construction as a whole evokes a referent.

(3.19) a. Like *a beast of lower pleasures*, like *a beast of lower pains*. Mated to a squalid savage, what to me were sun or clime? (COCA)
b. Like *those beasts of burden*, their function is simply to carry (COCA)

The head-classifier category is a relatively unexplored classification, briefly discussed in Keizer (2007a: 71–3), and on the periphery of numerous other functional-cognitive *of*-binominal studies under a range of category names: Jackendoff (1991) calls them constitutive constructions, they form part of Brems' (2011) head-uses category, head-classifiers are included in Traugott's (2008a, 2008b) pre-partitive category, and they belong to Denison's (2002, 2005) binominal category. Furthermore, they are also not exclusive to English; Norde, De Clerck, and Colleman (2014) in their study of the Dutch *massa* (mass) also have a head-classifier-like category (their 'lexical usage'), as shown in example (3.20) (for a more in-depth study of *massa*, see also De Clerck & Colleman 2013).

(3.20) De Zon is *èèn grote massa* van gloeiend waterstof en helium.
'The sun in on big mass of incandescent hydrogen and helium.'
(De Clerk & Colleman 2013: 152)

3.3.1 Head Status

In the head-classifier construction, the first noun is still the head. It designates a referent that the expression as a whole refers to, i.e. in (3.21), the *bitch of kitsch* is a type of bitch. The verb semantically selects for the first noun, as shown in example (3.22a), where *bake* selects *cake* and not the *U.S. foreign policy*, and in example (3.22b), where the *beast* does the 'eating' and not the *burden*.

(3.21) a. I was your mother, goddammit, *the leopard queen bitch of kitsch.* (COHA)
b. I was your mother, goddammit, *the leopard queen* **bitch**.
c. ?I was your mother, goddammit, *the kitsch/?the leopard queen kitsch.

(3.22) a. European decline has been, the phrase you used was **baked** into **the cake** of *U.S. foreign policy*, expectations over the next several years. (COCA)
b. She allowed *the* **beast** *of burden* to **eat** the leaf. (COCA)

Determining the morpho-syntactic locus is problematic, because the second noun must be either a mass noun or a bare plural. However, when the overall referent is plural, the plural marking is on the first noun, as shown in *seas* in (3.23a). The first noun also triggers the plural form in the subsequent verb, as can been seen in (3.23a) when comparing it to the singular form (3.23b).

(3.23) a. Instead, there is horizon like the sea line; there **are seas** *of grass* here, running before an unwearied wind (Knopp 2012: 180)
b. *a vast* **sea** *of grass* **was** still grazed by millions of bison (COCA)

Finally, the second determiner slot is always empty, and the first determiner always agrees in number with the first noun, as can be seen in (3.24), where we find a bare plural *seas* and singular *sea* with the indefinite article, and in (3.25a), where the deictic *this* refers to the dog, *Willis the Pug* (3.25b) and not to *steel* (3.25c). The first noun is therefore the syntactic head.

(3.24) North Korea's Foreign Ministry called the measures an "act of war" and threatened to turn Seoul and Washington into "**seas** *of fire*." Bombastic threats by North Korea about turning Seoul into *a* "**sea** *of fire*" are nothing new ... (COCA)

(3.25) a. Willis the Pug may look as if he's standing on two legs, but *this dog of steel* doesn't really have superpowers. (COCA)
b. Willis the Pug may look as if he's standing on two legs, but *this dog* doesn't really have superpowers.
c. *Willis the Pug may look as if he's standing on two legs, but *this steel* doesn't really have superpowers.

Finally, *one(s)* can only be used to replace the first noun and not the second, even when the second is in plural form, as demonstrated by (3.26a–c): *one* can substitute *snake* in (3.26b), but *ones* cannot substitute *flames* (3.26c). Definite pronouns, as demonstrated in (3.27a–c), can select the whole construction as their antecedent, as shown in (3.27b), but not the second noun as in (3.27c).

(3.26)   a. The picture was from a helicopter and showed the dark mountains and *a glowing orange snake of flames*. (COCA)
b. The picture was from a helicopter and showed the dark mountains and *a glowing orange **snake** of flames* and *a grey **one** of water*.
c. *The picture was from a helicopter and showed the dark mountains and *a glowing orange snake of **flames*** and sporadically *a globe of **ones***.

(3.27)   a. I bought *a whale of **stone***.
b. I bought *a whale of stone*, but **it** broke on the way home.
c. *I bought *a whale of stone*, yesterday. I also wanted to get *a mouse of **it***, but they didn't have one.

Therefore, we may conclude that the second noun does not designate an individual referent and does not head its own noun phrase. This confirms that the first noun must be the pragmatic head. Overall, the semantic, syntactic, and pragmatic evidence points toward the first noun as head.

3.3.2 Constituency Tests

The constituency tests clearly show that the PP is no longer a separate constituent. Neither the PP nor NP$_2$ can be shifted either left or right, nor can the PP be coordinated, as exemplified by *bird of prey* in (3.28) and the less entrenched form of *pig of knowledge* in (3.29).

(3.28)   a. she was *a bird of prey* and my girlfriend was a willing mouse (COCA)
b. *[Of prey]$_i$ she was [a bird t$_i$].
c. *[Prey]$_i$ she was a bird of t$_i$.
d. *[a bird t$_i$] was bought [of prey]$_i$.
e. *She bought him a bird [of prey] and [of paradise].

(3.29)   a. He took some comfort in the three smudged copies of *The Wonderful Pig of Knowledge*. (COCA)
b. *[of knowledge]$_i$ he was [the wonderful pig t$_i$].
c. *[Knowledge]$_i$ he was a pig of t$_i$
d. *[the wonderful pig t$_i$] was found [of knowledge]$_i$.
e. ?He bought a pig [of knowledge] and [of charm].

These syntagms, therefore, no longer consist of a noun with a prepositional phrase as modifier.

3.3.3 Constraints on the Two Nouns

The first noun can appear in both singular and plural form, and there are no restrictions on the type of noun that can be used in this position. The second noun is nonreferential and can only be a bare mass noun, a bare singular abstract noun, or a bare plural count noun.[2] The second noun can be either abstract (e.g. *burden*) or concrete (e.g. *stone*) but is semantically restricted in that it must be able to classify or subcategorize the first noun. Evidence of the nonreferentiality of the second noun phrase can be seen in the fact that it cannot be replaced by a proform, as shown in example (3.27).

The function of the second noun phrase and its subsequent syntactic restrictions means that the first and second nouns do not have to agree in number as demonstrated by example (3.30). Substitution tests do not apply, and the first and second noun are not in a predicative relationship to each other.

(3.30) There are *angels of Silence* and *angels of Anger* and *angels of Intellect*. (COCA)

A variety of premodifiers can be found in front of the first and second nouns, as demonstrated by (3.31a–f). Brems (2011: 194–5) notes that for members of her head-noun category (which includes head-classifiers), modification in front of the first and second noun is unrestricted, and premodification in front of the first noun can modify either the first noun or the whole complex NP (i.e. the referent denoted by the construction). However, premodification in front of the second noun tends toward classifiers such as *international* in (3.31a).[3]

(3.31) a. this **rotten, corrupt, brutal, cynical, bloodthirsty** monster of **international** terrorism (COHA)
b. a lifelong nightmare of **incinerated** birds (COHA)
c. a kind of **political** beast of burden (COHA)
d. a hell of **bitter** self-reproach (COHA)
e. He did it so that you could have a life beyond *this **poor ignorant** ball of dirt!* (COCA)
f. One was *a **snowy-white** ball of fluff*, and the other one could have passed for chocolate bunny. (COCA)

---

[2] There are some exceptions, such as *cancer of the liver or a history of the novel*, where the second noun has a definite article but is nonreferential (see Payne and Huddleston 2002: 408).

[3] Classifiers are in this case defined as words that "subclassify the referent of the head word" (Feist 2012: 10) or "provide further information concerning the subtype of the general type denoted by the head noun they modify. They thus form a functional unit together with the head, which designates the type of which the referent is an instance" (Ghesquière 2009: 319). This category will be discussed in greater detail in Chapter 7.

3.3 Head-Classifier

Premodification in front of the first noun appears to be as unrestricted as Brems claims; examples can be found of classifiers such as *political* in (3.31c), and of descriptive modifiers either ascribing physical properties such as *incinerated* in (3.31b) or providing subjective evaluation, such as *rotten, corrupt, brutal, cynical,* and *bloodthirsty* in (3.31a), and *bitter* in (3.31d). Examples of what Brems describes as premodifiers in front of N_1 with scope over the whole construction, or what I would describe as modifying the exogenous referent, are exemplified in (3.31e–f). In (3.31e), *poor ignorant* cannot modify either the first or the second nouns only the referent designated by the whole construction; the opposite is true for (3.31f), where *snowy-white* can modify either *ball* or *fluff* or the referent designated by the whole construction.

The data discussed in this section shows that the first noun can be filled with a range of nouns and is the head of the whole construction. The second noun is no longer the head of its own noun phrase, and only a plural and mass noun can be selected. However, although the second noun no longer designates a referent, it has retained some attributes of 'nounhood' in that it can still be modified and does not have to agree in number with the head.

3.3.4 Determiners

The first determiner slot is open to a range of determiners; as demonstrated by examples (3.32a–f), there appear to be no restrictions.

(3.32)   a. "And what have you learned from this?" she felt **a** *little demon of defiance* jump into her throat. (COCA)
b. **The** *fire of literacy* is created by the emotional sparks between a child, a book and the person reading. (COCA)
c. He treated this donkey like **any** *beast of burden* and made it carry flour, bricks, and any amount of dried goods (COCA)
d. **My** *boat of compassion* would have sailed to Paradise (COCA)
e. A wild and startling note from **some** *beast of prey*, as it roamed through the trackless and unsubdued forests (COHA)
f. She was not going back into **that** *hell of guns and lights*. (COCA)

In the head-classifier, the second noun, as we have seen, never takes a determiner, and the reason for this restriction is linked to this noun's classifying function. Langacker (1987: 203–4) relates mass and plural nouns, observing that bare plurals can often function and behave like mass nouns. He regards bare plurals as a subtype of mass noun, as designating a higher-order entity (one that construes single entities into unitary ones).[4]

3.3.5 Status of Of

As the constituency tests above show, the PP and NP$_2$ no longer allows movement, and therefore, the element *of* can no longer be considered a prototypical preposition at the head of a prepositional phrase. *Of* in phrases such as *an angel of death* or *a beast of prey* seems to be bleached to the point that it does not specify any semantic relation; instead, it simply functions as a linking element between the two nouns. However, there are other head-classifiers where the second noun designates what material the overall referent is constructed from or consists of, see examples (3.33 a–c). In these cases, one could argue that *of* encodes this 'made of' or 'consists of' meaning. This indicates that there are at least two types of head-classifiers, and the difference will be discussed in the sections below.

(3.33) a. a whale of stone
  b. a bird of wood
  c. a beast of pleasure and pain

3.3.6 Head-Classifier Types

In the head-classifier, the second noun must be a bare plural, a bare singular abstract noun, or a bare mass noun, is no longer referential, and either classifies or qualifies the first noun; however, there seem to be at least two semantic variations of this construction. On the one hand, there is the form where the second noun designates what the overall referent is made of (*a bird of wood* or *a beast of pleasure and pain*) thereby classifying it; what I have called the intrinsic head-classifier. On the other hand, there is a more idiomatic variant, what I have labeled the taxonomic head-classifier, which designates the subtype of the class denoted by the first noun (*a bird of prey*, *a beast of burden*, and *an angel of death*), with the second noun denoting the first noun's ontological category. In this study, the two subcategories of head-classifiers are distinguished based on the function of the second noun in relation to the first noun, i.e. does it denote intrinsic properties of the first noun (the intrinsic head-classifier), or does it designate a taxonomic

---

[4] Bare nouns are NPs that do not have an overt determiner; they usually denote properties or sets (Dobrovie-Sorin & Beyssade 2012: 31). Furthermore, Langacker (1999: 249–54) classifies plural generics as representing (or profiling) a higher-order relationship: plurality "construes component elements as constituting a higher-order thing (albeit one that is mass-like rather than discrete)" (Langacker 1987: 189).

3.3 Head-Classifier

category that the first noun belongs to (the taxonomic head-classifier). Each will be discussed in more detail in the two sections below.

3.3.6.1 Intrinsic Head-Classifiers

In the intrinsic head-classifier construction, the second noun classifies the first by designating what the overall referent, denoted by the first noun, is made of. Thus, in (3.34a) *a boat of wood* is a boat made of wood, and in (3.34b) *a whale of rock* is a whale made of rock (in opposition to flesh and blood). The material in question can be concrete, as seen in the previous examples, or abstract, as illustrated in (3.34c) and (3.34d).

(3.34)   a. The communists try a bold experiment when they substitute *a slow, heavy boat of wood*, owned impersonally by the government. (COHA)
        b. he came the last steep yards of *the great whale of rock* on which he climbed ... (COHA)
        c. President Saddam Hussein's speech should be quite effective. He depicts himself as a submissive servant of God, and President Bush as a tool of *the devil of aggression*. (COCA)
        d. promises of a socialist, Pan-African dream are starting to fade into *a long nightmare of civil wars* (COCA)

In (3.34c), *aggression* classifies the type of *devil* Bush is a tool for, and in (3.34d), the *nightmare* consists of or comprises *civil wars*. Very often, and particularly with the concrete second nouns, this noun can also take the classifier premodifier position: *a rock whale* or *a wooden boat*; however, with abstract second nouns, this is more problematic, e.g. *the aggression devil* or *?the civil war nightmare*. Finally, as example (3.35) demonstrates, modification in front of either noun is acceptable, although in (3.35d) the subjective modifier would most likely trigger a N+PP reading.

(3.35)   a. a **red/dry** boat of wood
        b. a **beautiful** boat of wood
        c. a boat of **red/dry** wood
        d. a boat of **beautiful** wood

3.3.6.2 Taxonomic Head-Classifiers

In the taxonomic use, the second noun does not denote what the first one is made of but the taxonomic category it belongs to, e.g. in example (3.36), the second noun designates *beast* as the type that preys on animals. This taxonomic function also allows the second noun greater semantic flexibility in its categorization system. Therefore, instead of using material as the classification criteria, the second noun can denote a defining activity such as hunting prey (3.36), carrying (3.37a), appearing in spring (3.37b), or bringing death (3.37 c). Example (3.38) illustrates a particularly creative example of this type, namely a globe that appears at noon.

(3.36) I'll be *your "little beast of prey"* ... for fifteen seconds. (COCA)

(3.37) a. therefore I object not unto lending thee *this beast of carriage* (COHA)
b. Isaac knew how much grandmother loved mimosas – *the flowers of spring*. (COCA)
c. She was called *an "angel of death"*, "black widow", all kinds of things. (COCA)

(3.38) From the nearby airport a Concorde, rising to *the blazing globe of noon*, roared by overhead, shaking the ground ... (COCA)

These forms tend to be more idiomatic and thus less productive than the intrinsic head-classifier forms. Formal differences would be that the option of alternating between postmodifier and premodifier positions, which appeared a relatively natural alternative in the intrinsic category, is less so with this form. Interestingly, there are examples, predominantly from the Internet, where the second noun does function as a premodifier of the first as shown in (3.39a–c). All these premodifiers all function as classifiers, designating the noun head's taxonomic category and not ascribing a property, and it has to be said that many speakers would probably find *a carriage beast* (3.39a), *a burden beast* (3.39b), or *the same death angel* (3.39c) rather unnatural.

(3.39) a. If it is desired to raise *a **carriage** beast*, select a mare with a good, animated countenance, sprightly, not too nervous nor too sluggish, but with a general muscular structure. (Kendall et al. 1880: 45)[5]
b. A riding camel is not led on the leash like *a **burden** beast* but it is allowed to run at full trot like a horse. (Cali Abokor 1987: 15)
c. I refuse to have to look over my shoulder, worrying that *the same **death** angel* that took my father is coming for me. (COCA)

Furthermore, the taxonomic forms appear to be more resistant to modification in front of the second noun, as demonstrated in (3.40). In (3.40a), *nocturnal* is natural in front of the first noun but questionable in front of the second (3.40c); the same is true for *beautiful* in (3.40b) and in (3.40d). Finally, for the taxonomic form, premodifiers of the first noun may have scope over the whole construction, as shown in (3.41), where the

---

[5] Intuitively this would seem to be a rather antiquated formulation, probably falling out of use as fast as horses are falling out of use as a mode of transport.

speaker does not dispute David's 'angelicness' but disputes the taxonomic subcategory of angel that is ascribed to him.

(3.40) a. A **nocturnal** beast of prey
        b. A **beautiful** beast of prey
        c. ?A beast of **nocturnal** prey
        d. ?A beast of **beautiful** prey

(3.41) David makes *a good angel of death*, but *an unlikely angel of mercy*.

3.3.7 The Properties of the Head-Classifier

The transition from more prototypical forms of the *of*-binominal to the head-classifier is not difficult to envisage. Logically, every first noun has to be made of something, abstract or concrete, and therefore all first nouns lend themselves to transition into the intrinsic head-classifier. The major change in the head-classifier (in relation to the N+PP) is that the categorizing function of the *of*-phrase requires the second noun to be either a mass noun or a plural, and the second NP no longer refers to a separate entity. Therefore, the first noun retains head status and is ascribed a categorizing/classifying property by the second NP. The underlying form would be $[_{NP1} [Det_1] (Mod) [[N_1] [_{LE}of] [_N (Mod) [N_2]]]]$.

Based on semantic functions and to some extent syntactic restrictions, I have suggested two subcategories of head-classifiers: intrinsic head-classifier and the taxonomic head-classifier. In the former, the PP denotes what the head is made of and in the latter, it links the head to a certain taxonomic category. This second group is more idiomatic and restricts premodification.

Although there often is a premodifier alternative for this construction, e.g. *the boat of wood* and *the wooden boat*, the usefulness of the *of*-binominal lies in the fact that they allow for classification via abstract nouns that may not offer a premodifier alternative, e.g. *the beast of loneliness* is perfectly acceptable, whereas *the loneliness beast* is distinctly awkward. Furthermore, as will be seen again with the EBNP construction, the *of*-binominal allows for progressively more diverse premodification of both the classifying noun and the construction as a whole.

3.4 Pseudo-partitive

The head-classifier and pseudo-partitive are structurally so similar that it is not surprising that there is some historical link between the two. This transition between head-classifier constructions to the pseudo-partitive has also been recorded in measure nouns in Dutch, e.g. *massa* 'mass' as in examples such as: *Allez, ze krijgt er toch massas stress van* ('Well, it does give her loads/?masses of stress) (De Clerck & Colleman 2013, who include head-classifiers in their lexical head category; see also Norde et al. 2014: 212). In English, although no study has looked at head-classifiers in particular, constructions like (3.42a), with the *of*-complement "designating (sub)classes and expressing generic or taxonomic meaning," have been found to develop into constructions where [N_1 of] functions as a quantifier, as can be seen in (3.42b) (Brems 2011: 276).

(3.42) a. Each home belonging to a Croat or Muslim was reduced to *a heap of rubble*. (Brems 2011: 135)
b. A police spokesman said more than a dozen cars have been stolen with "*heaps of cars* broken into." (Brems 2011: 139)

Many researchers have noted the structural similarity between the pseudo-partitive and the head-classifier constructions (e.g. Akmajian & Lehrer 1976; Jackendoff 1977; Ross 1967; Selkirk 1977). As has been pointed out, the prepositional phrase in *a pot of steel* could have a qualifier function, i.e. 'a pot made of steel' (head-classifier), with N_1 as head. However, the first noun could also be interpreted as a container, e.g. 'a pot filled with steel', with some ambivalence as regards headedness. Finally, it could also denote a quantity of iron as a measure noun pseudo-partitive, e.g. 'a pot amount of steel', with N_2 as head (Akmajian & Lehrer 1976; Ross 1967). The primary formal difference between the three readings is a shift of headedness from N_1 as head to an ambivalent head to N_2 as head. In the head-classifier reading, the first noun denotes the referent with the second noun classifying the head, whereas in the pseudo-partitive, the second noun designates the overall referent, and the first noun quantifies it. The shift of head, linguists have argued, then leads to a reanalysis of the internal structure of the construction where [Det (Mod) N_1] is analyzed as a complex quantifier, resulting in the complex NP (N-of-NP) being reduced to a simple NP (Jackendoff 1977; Selkirk 1977).[6]

---

[6] The [Det (Mod) N_1] analysis is from Keizer (2007a) and is only one analysis of the pseudo-partitive. Various alternative syntactic analyses of the pseudo-partitive have been proposed from generative grammarians (examples (1) and (2)), construction grammarians (3), and functional linguists (4). These and other analyses will be discussed in more detail below as they are relevant.

(1) [$_{NP}$ [$_N$ [$_{NP}$ a bunch] of [$_N$ men]]] (Jackendoff 1977: 120; Selkirk 1977: 302–13)
(2) [$_{DP}$D [$_{QP}$ [$_{Q'}$ bottle [$_{NP}$ water]]]] (Löbel 1989: 152)

3.4 Pseudo-partitive

Table 3.1 *Categorization of pseudo-partitives (based on information from Keizer 2020: 349)*

TYPE	EXAMPLES
Quantifier-noun constructions	a number of people, a lot of money
Measure-noun constructions	a pound of meat, a liter of milk
Container-noun constructions	a carton of eggs, a bottle of beer
Part-noun constructions	a piece of pie, a slice of ham
Collection-noun constructions	a gaggle of geese, a group of children

In pseudo-partitives, the first nouns are relational nouns that measure/quantify a portion of the second noun, which is nonreferential and not specified for definiteness (Grestenberger 2013: 94; cf. Abney 1987; Corver 1998; Löbel 1989; Selkirk 1977). The first noun indicates size, shape, or quantity: for example, a tub might have *a bucket of water* in it without the presence of an actual bucket, and there can *be a sea of mud* without a shore. As Langacker (1991: 88–9) explains, "[t]he notion of a discreet physical object has faded, leaving behind the conception of a schematically characterized mass (the mass that, in the original sense, either fills or constitutes the object) whose projection on the scale of magnitude then provides its primary semantic content."

Keizer (2007a: 112–16), based on Vos' (1999) study of pseudo-partitives in Dutch, proposes five types of pseudo-partitives in English, as shown in Table 3.1,[7] where each type is defined by the function of the first noun. From the sample of first nouns analyzed in this study (see Table 2.1), we find examples of part nouns (e.g. *a cake of ice*, *a ball of paper*), measure nouns (e.g. *a mountain of rules*, *a sea of mist*), a few container nouns (e.g. *a boat of lobster*); and one quantifier use (e.g. *a whole hell of people*, as in *a whole hell of people came running*).[8] There are no collection nouns in the dataset.

(3) [$_{NP}$ Det [$_Q$ bunch + of] [$_{N\text{-head}}$ people]] (e.g. Brems 2012: 208–10)
(I have added the first determiner to Brems' representation. The assumption is that the determiner is included, although she does not explicitly state this.)
(4) [$_{NP}$ [$_{Q\text{-compl}}$ [$_{Det}$ a] [$_N$ lot]] [$_{LE}$ of] [$_{N\text{-head}}$ people]] (Keizer 2007a: 149)

It should be noted, however, that this list is not comprehensive. A number of radically different analyses have not been included, e.g. Langacker (2010) who proposes the structure [[$_Q$ a lot] [$_{PP}$ of geese]], and also the various analyses proposed for other languages.

[7] Vos (1999) includes *sort-of, type-of, kind-of* nouns in his categorization; Keizer (2007a) treats these as a separate category.
[8] Although the inanimate first nouns are the ones most prominently used in the pseudo-partitive (since nouns denoting objects can be more readily used for quantification and animate objects, which exhibit behavioral characteristics, used evaluatively), it is not the case that all inanimate first nouns used in the EBNP are used in the pseudo-partitive. Some exceptions would be *doll* or *fire*.

As Table 3.1 indicates, the pseudo-partitives have always been a heterogeneous group, and thus, a problematic category to delineate. This section can only direct the reader to the various arguments proposed by the linguists who have studied this construction[9] and provide a general analysis of the pseudo-partitives found in this study. For, on the one hand, this study automatically must distinguish between the pseudo-partitive and the head-classifier constructions, because both play a role in the development of the EBNP. However, ultimately, the pseudo-partitive plays only a subsidiary role in this analysis; therefore, this section will focus on only those issues, criteria, and distinctions are important for this particular study, and only provide enough background to understand the context of this discussion.

3.4.1 Head Status

The shift from head-classifier to pseudo-partitive involves a rebracketing, i.e. a reversal of the head position from the first noun to the second. The second noun is obligatory, since the first does not have enough semantic content to function independently in the given context, as shown in (3.43 a–c) (Keizer 2007a: 117–18). The second noun agrees with the semantic restrictions of the verb, e.g. *breaking away* in (3.43a), but as previous studies have found, this test is not always decisive, as example (3.44) demonstrates. In (3.44a) *poured out* could select either noun, but in (3.44b) *smashed* clearly selects *bottle* (see Keizer 2007a: 118–20).

(3.43) a. Cold water swirled around my chest. I could feel *the cake of ice* I was lying on **breaking away** from the rest (COCA)
b. #I could feel *the cake* I was laying on **breaking away** from the rest.
c. I could feel *the ice* I was laying on **breaking away** from the rest.

(3.44) a. *The lousy bottle of **wine*** **was poured out**.
b. *The lousy **bottle** of wine* **smashed** to bits when it hit the counter.
(a variation of Akmajian & Lehrer 1976 example)

As Keizer (2007a: 120) demonstrates with examples (3.45a–b), the context might bias the speaker to select one form, but in a relatively neutral context, as in (3.45c), the verb may semantically select and agree with either noun. Overall, however, the evidence points toward the second noun as the semantic head.

---

[9] From generative grammar theories, some of the seminal studies have been Abney (1987), Akmajian & Lehrer (1976), Corver (1998), Jackendoff (1977), Lehrer (1986), Löbel (1989), and Selkirk (1977). From CxG theories, there has been, e.g., Brems (2011, 2012), Denison (2002, 2005), and Traugott (2008a, 2008b). From a functional perspective, this would include primarily Keizer (2007a: 109–51).

(3.45) a. *The **herd** of large African elephants* **was larger** than I thought.
b. *The herd of large **African elephants*** **were stampeding** toward us.
c. *An assortment of responses* to those questions of yours **were/was** considered.
(Keizer 2007a: 120)

The morpho-syntactic diagnostics are even less straightforward, and in particular, subject–verb agreement is rather muddled. We would expect verbal agreement with the second noun, as in (3.46a), but just as often find it with the first (3.46b–d), even in those cases where the second noun fulfills the semantic selection restrictions of the verb, as with *children* and *squirming* in example (3.46d). Even more inconsistent is (3.46b), where the verb in the relative clause agrees with the second noun, but the verb in the matrix clause agrees with the first noun, or (3.46d) where the main clause verb agrees with the first noun, but the pronominal reference in the subordinate clause is plural *they*.

(3.46) a. *A sea of **people*** **were** seen running toward the hills in Phuket (COCA)
b. *The mountain of rape accusations*, which **were given** new attention in a joke from comic Hannibal Buress that went viral, **seems to grow** daily. (COCA)
c. I call for the unity of all Iraqis ... to join together to rebuild Iraq and rescue the country from ***the seas** of blood* that **are spilled** every day. (COCA)
d. ***A sea** of children* in scarlet elf caps **was squirming** around, making a lot of squeaks making a lot of squeaks and thumps as **they took** the odd nose-dive onto the polished wooden floor. (COCA)

Alexiadou, Haegeman, and Stavrou (2007: 422–3) and many others have noticed this confusion and conclude that this indicates that the N_1 has retained some of its transparency/semi-functionality. Löbel (2001: 247–8) explains that because of the co-indexation of the two nouns, this is to be expected. However, Keizer (2007a: 120) argues that the verb-selection behavior of the nouns indicates that they belong to different pseudo-partitive categories: if N_2 has number concord with the verb, then this would indicate a quantificational pseudo-partitive. In cases where the first noun agrees in number with the verb, the agreement might indicate another type of construction, like the head-classifier or a prototypical N+PP (Keizer 2007a: 120–6).

The remaining morpho-syntactic criteria are only slightly less indeterminate. The purely quantificational forms can only take an indefinite article as a first determiner, which would then agree with the first noun, as shown in (3.47a), and in (3.47b), the plural first noun takes a zero determiner. As previous studies have noted (e.g. Brems 2011), the first determiner can sometimes be dropped with a singular first noun, as demonstrated in (3.47c). Therefore, this criterion does not allow us to identify the syntactic head unambiguously.

(3.47)   a. he could fire *a hell of microwaves* up at the ionosphere (COCA)
           b. "We can play pranks on people." I suggested. "Remember last time? We got in *hells of trouble*." She argued. (Jacque_Jackpot 2015)[10]
           c. If force is used, it may cause *hell of problems* in all the Arab world (COCA)

The morpho-syntactic locus is also not easy to distinguish as both the first and the second noun can appear in the plural and in the singular. In constructions with mass second nouns (3.48a–b), it is always the first noun that takes the plural marker, as demonstrated in (3.48b) (Keizer 2007b: 126). However, the question in these cases is if the plural form actually results in a plural referent; if not, the pluralization is just part of the complex quantifier but is not an indicator of headedness, as in the case of (3.48c). Therefore, this test, too, is inconclusive.

(3.48)   a. With every fresh puff of breath from the north, empty air, and dripped into gray pools below *the coiling snakes of snow* grew larger, writhing across the tree-tops and pouring tumultuously into the river-bed. (COCA)
           b. *Cakes of mud* had dried and changed their original white color into something brownish. (COCA)
           c. He took with him *vaults of money*, supplies and equipment, and there was none among his soldiers who did not go out with full equipment and provisions, and thus they spent their day. (COCA)

As to the pragmatic-discourse test, the first noun cannot be the antecedent of anaphoric *one* (even though it is a count noun), as can be seen in (3.49b), and when it substitutes NP_1 (e.g. (3.49c)), the feeling is that it forces a head-classifier reading with N_1 designating the referent and NP_2 qualifying it. Substitution of *ones* for the plural second noun is restricted, since N_2 is often a mass noun. However, as demonstrated in example (3.49d), *ones* can substitute a plural N_2. Therefore, it appears as if anaphoric reference indicates that the first noun no longer heads its own NP and, thus, cannot function as the head of the binominal.

[10] Jacque_Jackpot, One Hell of a Mate [story]. Available at www.wattpad.com/71465531-one-hell-of-a-mate-book-one-chosen-lunas-series (August 19, 2015).

(3.49) a. *A sea of people* were seen running toward the hills in Phuket (COCA)
b. **A **sea** of people* were seen running toward the hills in Phuket and *a **one** of frightened animals* followed.
c. *?A **sea** of people* were seen running toward the hills in Phuket and ***one** of frightened animals* followed.
d. *A sea of **people*** were seen running toward the hills in Phuket and *a sea of braver **ones*** ran the other way.

If a definite pronoun (*it* for mass nouns, *them* for plurals) is used in the position of N_2 (as in *them* in (3.50b)), the construction is no longer a pseudo-partitive but a partitive.[11] This shows that N_2 no longer heads a referential NP. As was the case with many of the constructions already discussed, the first noun cannot be the anaphoric referent of a pronoun, as shown in example (3.50c).

(3.50) a. there are plenty of good no-bake dessert recipes, fields of them, *mountains of them* (COCA)
b. there are plenty of good no-bake dessert recipes, fields of them, *mountains of **them***. In fact, I collect *most of **them*** in a huge box under my sink.
c. *there are plenty of good no-bake dessert recipes, fields of them, ***mountains** of them*. In fact, there are ***them** of Asian stir-fry recipes* as well.

The ambiguous evidence, particularly in the case of the morpho-syntactic tests, has resulted in a variety of interpretations of this form. One well-known example of the N_1 head (or a least partly N_1) head analysis was presented by Corver (1998), who argues that the relationship between the two nouns in the pseudo-partitive is a predicative one, where the predication, through the process of predicate inversion, proceeds the subject, e.g. *a bunch of flowers* and [$_{DP}$ D [$_{Small\ Clause}$ flowers [$_{Pred}$ bunch]]] (Corver 1998: 216).[12] More importantly, Corver (1998) explains the irregular verb concord as

---

[11] Other factors also play a role. For more discussion of the application of pragmatic criteria to pseudo-partitives, see Keizer (2007a: 132–5).

[12] For a full discussion of all four tests, see Corver (1998: 119–22). He bases his arguments on his analysis of the predicative nature of the N_1 (of the surface form), which can, for example, be coordinated with adjective phrases, e.g. *The range of these guns is only **200 meters** but nevertheless **sufficient*** (Corver 1998: 220), and can be used with copular linking verbs other than *be* such as *become*, in examples like *The temperature became **45 degrees** inside the room within minutes* (Corver 1998: 221). He also applies *what . . . like*-questions, where a property is the answer and not an entity, e.g. *What is Sue like? She is nice*, and pronominalization.
   Corver (1998) also links his pseudo-partitive analysis with Den Dikken's (1998) analysis of the EBNP. On the one hand, Corver (1998: 222–30) applies the same tests of predicate inversion that Den Dikken (1998) applied in his analysis of the EBNP (namely, it can be presented as a functional projection (FP) in a DP, the verb agrees with the second noun, inversion of the measure noun requires 'be'). On the other hand, the construction as a whole is very similar to the EBNP (i.e. no *of*-phrase extraction, verb-second noun agreement, modifiers in front of the first noun can modify the second, e.g. *a tasteless cup of coffee*,

shown in (3.51a–b) (example (3.44a–b) repeated here), by making a distinction between quantifier pseudo-partitives, with N_2 as head, and container first noun pseudo-partitives, with N_1 as head. He argues for the distinction between the quantity pseudo-partitives form, what he calls BE predications, in (3.51a), since 'the wine is a bottle amount' and the syntactically similar container pseudo-partitives form HAVE ones (3.51b), i.e. 'the bottle has wine in it'. In the latter construction, the first noun is the head and has semantic concord with the verb (Corver 1998: 234–6; Selkirk 1977).

(3.51) a. *The lousy bottle of wine* was poured out.
        b. *The lousy bottle of wine* smashed to bits when it hit the counter.
        (a variation of Akmajian & Lehrer 1976 example)

In many respects, this is similar to the container and quantifier pseudo-partitive distinction made by Vos (1999), discussed at the start of this section, and similar to the functional explanation presented in Keizer (2007a). Keizer (2007a: 149–51) also concludes that the quantificational pseudo-partitives have a second noun head; the referential constructions (midway position between head-classifier and quantifier) have a first noun head (constructions such as *a half-filled cup of coffee*); and hybrid pseudo-partitive constructions, such as *steaming bowl of food*, have a first syntactic head and second noun semantic head. These distinctions will be discussed in more detail in the following analysis.

In sum, the pseudo-partitive category seems to include a number of different types of *of*-binominals, which function differently. Although most appear to be right-headed, the headedness tests indicate that the analysis is not straightforward. In general, functional and construction grammar research has attributed a right-headed analysis to this category, namely, that N_2 is the head of the construction in which N_1 functions as a quantifier or an element of a complex quantifier. Furthermore, the diagnostic tests for head status seem to point to the second noun as the head of the pseudo-partitive, although the syntactic evidence is inconclusive.

3.4.2 *Constituency Tests*

In a lot of the early work on this construction (e.g. Jackendoff 1977; Selkirk 1977), the pseudo-partitive was placed in juxtaposition with the partitive

---

and no extraction) (Corver 1998: 230–4). As shown in Chapter 3 and Chapter 4, this latter set of criteria is true for many of the *of*-binominal constructions.

3.4 Pseudo-partitive

construction, a left-headed construction (see Traugott 2008a: 27); therefore, we cannot discuss the pseudo-partitive without briefly bringing in the partitive. Selkirk (1977) points out that one of the central distinctions between the partitive (*a piece of that cake*) and the pseudo-partitive (*a piece of cake*) is that the partitive still allows for extraposition of the embedded PP, as illustrated in example (3.52), while the pseudo-partitive does not (see also Jackendoff 1977).[13] This coincides with the findings from examples in this data sample, see examples (3.53); the pseudo-partitives found in this study do not allow for extraposition and the coordination of the embedded PP is questionable.[14]

(3.52)   a. Well over 90 percent of the students who sign up for MOOC do not benefit. (COCA)
        b. [Of the students who sign up for MOOC]$_i$, [well over 90 percent t$_i$] do not benefit.
        c. ?[Well over 90 percent t$_i$] do not benefit [of the students who sign up for MOOC]$_i$.

(3.53)   a. Sets the standard of excellence. Dry and sweet-meated. Not *a whisper of fiber*. (COCA)
        b. *[Of fiber]$_i$ he had not [a whisper t$_i$]
        c. *[Fiber]$_i$ he had a whisper of t$_i$
        d. *[A whisper t$_i$] was had [of fiber]$_i$.
        e. ?It had not a whisper [of fiber] or [of fat].

The fact that extraction is not possible in the pseudo-partitive not only distinguishes it from the partitive but is one of a few observations that led Selkirk (1977) to conclude that the pseudo-partitive has the structure of a simple noun phrase (similar conclusions have been drawn by other studies, e.g. Brems 2012; Jackendoff 1977; Löbel 1989).[15] However, as we

---

[13] There is still some contention on this point. For discussion see Keizer (2007a: 126–31).
[14] The most important difference between partitives and pseudo-partitives is that pseudo-partitives are not constrained by the partitive constraint, neither in its original definition nor in any of its later revisions. Therefore, in the pseudo-partitive, bare mass nouns, bare abstract singular nouns, and bare plural nouns are required in the second noun position, whereas adding a determiner in the Det$_2$ position would result in a partitive (Selkirk 1977: 303–4). Further differences are that complement PPs can be extraposed in pseudo-partitives (e.g. ***A number of stories** soon appeared **about Watergate***) but not in partitives (e.g. ****A number of the stories** soon appeared **about Watergate***) (Akmajian & Lehrer 1976), and pseudo-partitives allow for a different interpretation of modifying relative clauses (Jackendoff 1977: 122).
[15] Other arguments are that in some pseudo-partitives, the preposition *of* is not required, e.g. *a dozen roses*, or is optional as in *a bushel of apples* and *a bushel apples* (Selkirk: 1977: 308). Furthermore, Selkirk observes that there are restrictions on modification. Therefore, she concludes that the PP cannot have an *of*-NP structure (Selkirk 1977: 303–9). On the basis of this evidence, Selkirk argues that [a N$_1$ (of)] functions as a complex modifier in a simple noun phrase.

have already seen in Section 3.4.1, extraction and coordination are also no longer possible for the head-classifier construction, and therefore, constituency tests alone cannot lead to this conclusion.

In sum, the constituency tests demonstrate that pseudo-partitives are formally different from the more prototypical N+PPs. In these pseudo-partitives, *of* no longer functions as a preposition at the head of a prepositional phrase.

3.4.3 Constraints on the Two Nouns

The first noun has been classified in many different ways: as a lexical realization of a functional category (e.g. Abney 1987; Löbel 1989), a semi-lexical head (e.g. Van Riemsdijk 1998; Vos 1999), a noun (e.g. Jackendoff 1977; Selkirk 1977), a predicate (e.g. Corver 1998), and (part of) a complex quantifier (e.g. Brems 2011; Keizer 2007a). As the proform tests show (Section 3.4.1), the first noun in pseudo-partitives does not denote a referent but quantifies or gives a form to the overall referent (designated by the second noun) (e.g. Keizer 2007a: 109–50; Löbel 2001: 247). The first noun designates a quantity, a form, or a conventionalized unit; hence, it must be a noun that can denote a quantity, form, or unit.

The first noun can also be construed to denote a quantity or unit, as in example (3.54a), where the noun *reed* is used to indicate a small quantity, a meaning that is not inherent in the noun itself; the same is true for the metaphorical extension of *ball* into providing *lies* and *fire* a form in (3.54b–c). However, the first noun retains some noun-like features in that it can still take the plural marker (3.54 c) (Löbel 2001: 232). The function of the first noun is that it ensures that the second is countable by providing it with a countable form, aggregating generic masses and sets into countable units (Alexiadou et al. 2007: 403–4).

(3.54)   a. something that, perverse though it seems, offers *a slender reed of hope* (COCA)
         b. From then on, *her ball of lies* began to unravel amid wedding plans. (COCA)
         c. Now, to our "NewsHour" Shares of the day. *Two balls of fire* caught our eye that might be of interest to you, too. (COCA)

The second noun must be a mass noun or a bare plural count noun, i.e. a noun that can be quantified; in Löbel's (2001: 247) terminology, the second noun "contains the feature [+dividable]." Löbel (2001: 251) explains this restriction by adopting Jackendoff's (1991) semantic features

3.4 Pseudo-partitive

analysis of nouns, which categorizes types of nouns based on the variables boundedness and internal structure. He distinguishes between mass nouns: ([- bounded] and [- internal structure]) and count plural nouns: ([- bounded] but with [+ internal structure]).[16] Both count and mass nouns thus share the feature of unboundedness, and the second noun can be either a concrete physical object, as in *apple* and *soap*, or an abstract entity such as *hope* and *lies*.

The pronominalization tests have already been discussed in Section 3.4.1, and the analysis shows that the pronoun *one* cannot replace N_1 even though it is a count noun, and it cannot replace N_2 because it is either a bare plural or a mass noun. Furthermore, the definite pronoun *them* can only replace the NP as a whole (agreeing in number with N_2). The two nouns do not have to agree in number. All these facts present strong evidence against hypothesizing a predicate relationship between the nouns (see Corver 1998 for an alternative analysis).

Pseudo-partitive premodification plays an important role in signaling the type of construction being used, as the different pseudo-partitive types (see Table 3.1) exhibit different premodification patterns.[17] The quantifier pseudo-partitive, as would be expected with the first noun functioning as a quantifier, allows only intensifiers and descriptive modifiers in front of the first noun that reinforce this function of the first noun such as *entire*, functioning as an amplifier in (3.55a) (see Keizer 2007a: 138–43; Kruisinga 1932: 397). Furthermore, quantificational pseudo-partitives collocate with only a limited range of intensifiers, as shown in (3.55b), and do not accept modifiers ascribing descriptive properties to the first noun (Keizer 2007a: 138–9;

---

[16] Note that +/- internal structure and the difference between bare plurals and mass nouns are that "the plurals entail a medium comprising a multiplicity of distinguishable individuals, whereas mass nouns carry no such entailment" (Jackendoff 1991: 21). However, [- internal structure] means "lack of necessary entailment about internal structure" (Jackendoff 1991: 21). This is naturally just one way to represent the nominal categories. Rijkhoff (2002: 53–6) presents a typological model that distinguishes between homogeneity and shape. This allows him to distinguish between six different noun categories.

[17] In a discussion of the differences between pseudo-partitives and partitives, Selkirk demonstrates that in the pseudo-partitive the first noun cannot be postmodified, but the second noun can, which can be extraposed (Selkirk 1977: 305–6). Selkirk (1977: 307–8) notes that relatives clauses modifying pseudo-partitives, as in example (i), "cannot associate with *of daffodils*, only with the full noun phrase, *dozens of daffodils*," whereas in partitives, such as (ii), either noun can be modified by the nonrestrictive relative clause (Selkirk 1977: 307–8). Keizer (2007a: 111, 143–7) gives a more detailed analysis of the different types of pseudo-partitives and their different postmodification patterns.

(i) She bought him *dozens of daffodils*, only two of which were faded.
(ii) She bought him *dozens of those daffodils*, only two of which were faded. (Selkirk 1977: 307)

for a discussion on modification, see also Alexiadou et al. 2007: 417–22; Brems 2011: 191–7; Jackendoff 1977: 128–30).

(3.55) a. If force is used, it may cause *hell of problems* in all the Arab world (COCA)
b. If force is used, it may cause *a **whole**/*complete/*entire/*awful hell of problems* in all the Arab world.

Premodification in front of the first noun for the other pseudo-partitive types is slightly more complex. Descriptive modifiers are problematic in the part, measure, and container pseudo-partitives. If the second noun denotes the overall referent and the first noun only quantifies or shapes the second noun, then the first noun cannot denote an entity for a descriptive modifier to modify. Hence N_1 cannot accept descriptive premodifiers (see Keizer 2007a: 138–42). Therefore, in those cases where descriptive modifiers appear in front of the first noun, the modifier may modify the first noun in its quantitative function, as was the case with the quantifier pseudo-partitive and as demonstrated in (3.56a). In this example *music* can be whispered, but *whisper* seems to indicate 'a small strand' or 'a touch of the country-disco music' is in the song. Therefore, *faint* acts as a downtoner of the quantificational function of *whisper*. An alternative function of the descriptive modifier is that it modifies the overall referent as in *frozen* in (3.56b): both the *ball* and the *ganache* are frozen.

(3.56) a. opening song, "Factory," bolstered with sweeping, mourning strings and brass, comes closest to the group's best work. From there, though, the mood lightens considerably, and disruptively. "Compliments" has *a **faint** whisper of country-disco*, and much of the rest of the album ("Dilly" and' "Older") is redolent of the 1970s soft-rock folkies America. (COCA)
b. we serve it in individual soufflés and put inside *a **frozen** ball of ganache* (soft chocolate cream) that melts as it cooks (COCA)

Jackendoff (1977) observes that descriptive modifiers in front of the first noun can ascribe properties to the second noun, so in (3.57a) the *chocolates* are *delicious*, not the *box*, and in (3.57b) the *coffee* is *tasteless*, not the *cup* (see Alexiadou et al. 2007: 419–22). Therefore, descriptive modifiers in front of the first noun can modify the first noun, the second noun, or the overall referent denoted by the second noun. Alternatively, descriptive modification in front of the first noun could mean a referential reading, in which case the first noun designates the overall referent, as in *broken* in (3.57c), and would indicate a head-classifier reading. With the head-classifier reading, the wine taxonomically classifies the type of bottle that was broken; therefore, sentences such as *I found a broken bottle of wine with oil in it, and the oil ran all over to cupboard,* or *the broken bottle of wine was empty* are acceptable.

(3.57) a. a **delicious** box of Belgian chocolates (Alexiadou et al. 2007: 420)
b. a **tasteless** cup of coffee (Corver 1998: 231)
c. a **broken** bottle of wine

However, as Keizer (2007a: 141–2) notes, not all types of descriptive modifiers can appear in front of the first nouns: evaluative premodifiers can be used appropriately in this position, as demonstrated by *good* in (3.58), but not adjectives such as *red* in (3.59a–b) and *Dutch* in (3.60a–b). For the first point, I would argue that *Dutch* and *red* function as classifiers modifying the second noun: in the case of *Dutch*, it specifies what type of cheese is being referred to and *red* the type of apples (as opposed to yellow or granny smith apples). Classifier premodifiers by definition cannot be separated from the nouns they modify and, therefore, cannot be placed in the first noun premodifier zones. Both these final two points will be discussed in more detail in Chapter 7.

(3.58) a **good** piece of cake

(3.59) a. a pound of **red** apples
b. *a **red** pound of apples
(Keizer 2007a: 141)

(3.60) a. a kilo of **Dutch** cheese
b. *a **Dutch** kilo of cheese
(Keizer 2007a: 141)

Alexiadou et al. (2007: 420 fn. 23) claim that only classifier adjectives are allowed in front of the second noun;[18] however, there are numerous examples of descriptive modifiers in front of N_2 as well: *delicious* in (3.61a), *buttery* in (3.61b), and *pale-green* in (3.61c).

(3.61) a. every 250 ml can contains the juice over *a third of a pound of **delicious** Scottish raspberries* (Keizer 2007a: 141)
b. Mini Pecan Tarts are *a whisper of **buttery** crust* filled with crisp nuts and gooey-rich caramel. (COCA)

---

[18] They argue this based on the evidence that classifier possessives are allowed in front of the second noun, e.g. *a box of women's magazines*, but not possessive genitives, e.g. *?a box of my friend's magazines*. However, I suspect that the unacceptability has more to do with the fact that the second noun has to be non-specific and less with premodification selection.

c. A nearby table of three older guests, who looked as if they would fit right in at the River Oaks Country Club, craned their necks to see parchment-thin disks of green apple flying from *a globe of **pale-green** apple sorbet*. (COCA)

Intensifiers in front of the first noun would be acceptable, as shown in examples (3.62a–b), while intensifiers in front of the second noun, as in (3.63a–b), make the construction ill-formed.

(3.62) a. a **mere** cake of soap.
b. *a cake of **mere** soap

(3.63) a. **whole** cake of soap
b. *a cake of **whole** soap

In sum, in pseudo-partitive constructions, the first noun can usually appear in the singular and plural form and must be able to indicate size, shape, container, or quantity of the referent denoted by the second noun. The second noun is unbounded and can, therefore, only be a plural or mass noun. The pseudo-partitives can only accept restricted premodification in front of the first and second noun, and premodification in front of the first noun can ascribe properties to the referent denoted by the second noun.

3.4.4 Determiners

Alexiadou et al. (2007: 404–5) argue that the inherent measuring character of the pseudo-partitive requires that it take either an indefinite article or a quantificational or cardinal element. Based on evidence from Greek, they also claim that this construction cannot take a definite article: examples with the definite article represent a different type of *of*-binominal. They substantiate this claim with parallels to work on *many* (predominantly Giusti 1991; 1997: 114–19), arguing that *many* and quantifying elements can function either as quantifiers or as adjectives. In an example like *many students liked the show*, *many* functions as a quantifier and therefore cannot accept a definite determiner. In an example like *the many students that were there like the show*, the quantifier functions as an adjective; in that case, use of the definite article is allowed (Alexiadou et al. 2007: 430–1).[19] Brems (2011: 143) offers an alternative explanation in that in the pseudo-partitive, partial decategorialization of the first noun has taken place, which has led

---

[19] As already mentioned above, Brems (2011: 143) does not make this quantifier–adjective distinction and argues that these constructions can take the definite article.

to restrictions on the determination; however, at least some forms of the pseudo-partitive can take the definite determiner, and in this sense it is comparable to *many* (*the many students*).

In the case of English pseudo-partitives, Keizer (2007a: 135–6) argues, it really depends on the type of pseudo-partitive: purely quantificational pseudo-partitive constructions predominantly take an indefinite or the zero article as a first determiner; the zero article can be found both with plural nouns, e.g. *loads* (3.64a), and occasionally with singular nouns, e.g. *hell* in (3.64b). Pseudo-partitives that indicate shape or size can accept definite articles, as in (3.65a), possessive pronouns, as in (3.65b), and demonstratives, as in (3.65c).

(3.64) a. The fact that most of them apparently worked with domestic dogs and made *loads of money* as proclaimed pet therapists did no help to improve this image. (COCA)
 b. If force is used, it may cause *hell of problems* in all the Arab world (COCA)

(3.65) a. I sat with my back to the icebox and could hear **the** *big cake of ice* dripping into the pan beneath. (COCA)
 b. I understood then, for just a moment, what a heady thing it was to be feted by a million or more people waving their Little Red Books and **their** *sea of red flags*. (COCA)
 c. Yes. The judge ruled on June 1st that once this information is released for discovery, there has to be this 30-day period where the defense gets to review **this** *mountain of documentation*, digest it before it's released to the media. (COCA)

The difference may be that in these cases the first determiner indicates identifiability (in the case of the definite article) or ownership (in the case of the possessive pronoun) of the referent. Therefore, the first determiner, as a part of the complex quantifier, agrees in number with the first noun, but at the same time it grounds/identifies the overall referent designated by the second noun (this use of the demonstrative functions similarly to the demonstratives used in the EBNP; see Section 4.2.4). As is the case with the head-classifier, in the pseudo-partitive the second determiner position is empty.

3.4.5 Status of *Of*

In the English pseudo-partitive, the element *of* is obligatory in most cases (Selkirk 1977: 308). However, Selkirk also notes that *of* can be dropped with some first nouns, as in (3.66a–b).

(3.66) a. he feels giddy as she spreads *a **couple of sheets** of paper* on the counter while they sip their coffee (COCA)
b. All you need are *a **couple sheets** of paper*, scissors and tape. (COCA)

Particularly for generative theorists, the persistent presence of the preposition has caused theoretical issues, and *of* in the pseudo-partitive is often analyzed as a dangling preposition (e.g. Jackendoff 1977: 121, 138; Rothstein 2011: 7; Selkirk 1977: 308–9). Alternatively, as proposed by Corver, *of* could be considered "a copula, that is the nominal counterpart of clausal *be*," and both *of* and *be* are surface representations of predication (Corver 1998: 222). More recently linguists have analyzed *of* as being part of the complex determiner (e.g. Löbel 1989; Brems 2011) or argue that it is a linking element (e.g. Keizer 2007a: 109–51).

Evidence for the complex determiner analysis comes from examples such as (3.67a–b) and (3.68a–b), where quantifiers can substitute for the whole [Det noun *of*] unit (see also Keizer 2007a: 148).

(3.67) a. We ran *a **number of** tests*.
b. We ran *some tests*. (Keizer 2007a: 148)

(3.68) a. I know *a **lot of** people*.
b. I know *many people*. (Keizer 2007a: 148)

Keizer (2007a: 149) argues that, as was the case in the head-classifier, the preposition in the pseudo-partitive functions only as a linking device triggered by the two nominal units, a claim strengthened by the fact that there are examples where it is phonetically reduced, as in the more frequent forms *heapsa*, *lota*, *buncha*, and *loadsa* (e.g. Brems 2007).[20] Keizer (2007a: 148–9) points out that in the problematic *dozen* (see fn. 15) or *couple* (3.66) examples, *dozen* and *couple* actually function more like a numeral, like a *hundred* in *a hundred books*, than as a noun and, therefore, does not require a linking element. This is supported by the fact that plural numerals such as *hundreds* in *hundreds of books*, and quantities, *dozens* in *dozens of roses*, do need a preposition. However, this would not explain why both *a bushel corn* and *a bushel of corn* are acceptable (although in COCA, the latter is more frequent). She further points out that the first noun and determiner can function alone as a complex quantifier if the unexpressed noun is retrievable from context, as demonstrated by *a lot* in example (3.69), and this would point to *of* not being a part of the complex quantifier.

---

[20] Interestingly, although there has been orthographic evidence of the phonetic reduction in later constructions (i.e. *hella*, *whaleuva*, in the evaluative modifiers, and binominal intensifiers), this is not the case for pseudo-partitives. This may well be because the pseudo-partitive forms adopted by EBNP first nouns tend to be more the hybrid version and less of the prototypical form.

3.4 *Pseudo-partitive* 59

(3.69) Yeah I don't know how July will is going to hit my classes on Saturday. Some people go away but uhm last year I think I had *quite a lot* you know (Keizer 2007a: 148)

In the end, either analysis would fit this particular study, since *of* is obligatory in the pseudo-partitives discussed, e.g. **a cake soap* or *#a sea people*. One reason why this may not be acceptable is that *cake* and *sea* can be used as a classifier premodifier, where it designates the type of noun, e.g. *cake batter* (as opposed to *cookie batter*) or *sea people* as a type of people who live on or in the sea and not a quantity of people. Ultimately, in pseudo-partitives, *of* neither forms a constituent with the second noun nor has semantic content, and it is only in the general development of first nouns in this family, where the status of the preposition plays a role.

3.4.6 *The Properties of the Pseudo-partitive*

Keizer (2007a: 109–51; cf. Brems 2011: 143) suggests that substitution and the determiner–noun agreement would indicate that [Det_1 (Mod) N_1] forms a complex quantifier (Q-compl). Keizer (2007a: 111, 148–9) argues that the occasional loss of the preposition *of* is evidence that the preposition no longer has semantic content or a function in this particular *of*-binominal; moreover, the fact that [Det N] + *of* can be replaced by a quantifier would show that *of* no longer forms a constituent with the second noun. Keizer's (2007a: 116–51) analysis also addresses the verb–noun agreement issues (see Section 3.4.2), as well as the presence of modifiers in front of the first noun, and ultimately distinguishes between the different pseudo-partitives (or degrees of pseudo-partitiveness): the quantificational pseudo-partitive, with N_2 as head in (3.70a–b), the referential type with N_1 as head in (3.70c), and a hybrid type, illustrated in (3.70d), with the first noun acting as the syntactic head and the second as the semantic head (Keizer 2007a: 139–43, 149–51). It is concluded that the pseudo-partitive consists of a complex quantifier, consisting of the first determiner and the first noun (and possibly an intensifier or a descriptive modifier intensifying the degree function of the first noun. *Of* functions as a linking element between the still noun-like first noun and the second noun: [$_{NP}$ [$_{Q\text{-compl}}$ [$_{Det}$ a] [$_N$ lot]] [$_{LE}$ of] [$_{N\text{-head}}$ people]] (Keizer 2007a: 149). The second noun is the semantic and syntactic head.

(3.70) a. [$_{NP}$ [$_{Q\text{-compl}}$[$_{Det}$ a] [$_N$ lot]] [$_{LE}$ of][$_{N\text{-head}}$ people]] (Keizer 2007a: 149)
        b. [$_{NP}$ [$_{Q\text{-compl}}$[$_{Det}$ a] [$_{A\text{-int}}$ large] [$_N$ quantity]]] [$_{LE}$ of][$_{N\text{-head}}$ water]] (Keizer 2007a: 149)

c. [NP [Det a [ExtN [[A-descr half-filled] [N cup]] [PP [P of] [NP [N coffee]]]]] (Keizer 2007a: 150)
   d. [NP [Q-compl [Det a] [ExtN [A-descr steaming]ᵢ [N bowl]]] [LE of] [N food]ᵢ] (Keizer 2007a: 151)

This general account with the complex determiner including the first determiner would explain first noun and first determiner concord. Furthermore, Keizer (2007a: 135–7) makes the distinction between a pure quantificational pseudo-partitive, which takes only an indefinite or bare article, and the hybrid pseudo-partitive with referential reading that allows for the definite article. Additionally, the hybrid pseudo-partitive construction would account for a descriptive modifier appearing in front of the first noun and modifying the second noun. This analysis also accounts for the ungrammaticality of placing an intensifier in front of the second noun. If, in the pseudo-partitive, [Det (Mod) N] functions as a complex quantifier (like *many*) in a simple noun phrase, then any intensifiers should come before the quantifier (*very many people*) unless they are modifying an adjective (*there are many very ugly dogs*).

Although the pseudo-partitive is formally very similar to the head-classifier, there are some critical semantic and syntactic differences that warrant a distinction between them, such as change in function of the first noun and a shift in headedness. In order to demonstrate the different uses of these constructions, Chapter 5 presents the use of three first nouns (*cake*, *beast*, and *hell*) in these three constructions.

3.5 Conclusion

In the prototypical N+PP and head-classifier binominals, the first noun is head. In the former construction, the preposition *of* often still retains some semantic content and the prepositional phrase denotes possession, location, and time, or it ascribes a property to the first noun. As is expected, the constructions allow for a range of nouns and determiners in the different positions. These positions are more restricted in the head-classifier: the second noun must be a bare plural, bare abstract, or a mass noun and is non-specific and no longer referential. The PP classifies or ascribes a taxonomic category to the head. The pseudo-partitives are a heterogenous group; however, in the examples discussed in the project there seems to be a clear shift of head from the first to the second noun; the first noun indicates the shape or quantity of the second noun. Like the head-classifier, the second noun must be a bare plural or mass noun. Table. 3.2 presents the major features of each of the three constructions.

Table 3.2 Overview of the categories N+PP, head-classifier, and pseudo-partitive

FEATURE	N+PP	HEAD-CLASSIFIER	PSEUDO-PARTITIVE
Of	'Out of', 'with', 'from'	Mandatory, no semantic meaning	Mandatory, no semantic meaning
Determiner 1	Open	Open, canonically definite and indefinite article	Open, canonically indefinite article
Determiner 2	Open	None	None
Head	N_1 is semantic/syntactic/discourse head	N_1 is semantic/syntactic/discourse head	N_2 is semantic/discourse head
Function of construction	Possession, locative, temporal, ascribes a property to N_1	[of N_2] either classifies or ascribes a taxonomic category to N_1	N_1 measures or quantifies N_2
Determiner 1 selection	N_1	N_1	N_1
Modification	Regular	Regular	Irregular in front of N_1
Movement/coordination	Yes	No movement or *of* coordination	No movement or *of* coordination
N_1 lexicality	Yes	Yes	Quantifier/Shape
N_1 & N_2 agreement	No	No	No
N_2	Open	Mass/abstract/plural	Mass/abstract/plural

The proposed grammaticalization path, from more prototypical N+PP *of*-binominals to pseudo-partitive forms, has also been suggested in previous studies focusing primarily on measure first nouns, e.g. *lot-of*, *shred* (Brems 2011, 2012; Traugott 2008b). The present study tracks the progression of first nouns along this path and looks at the developmental stages in more detail, elaborating, in particular, on the head-classifier category, and the link between the head-classifier and the pseudo-partitives – a link neglected in previous accounts. However, not all first nouns found in the EBNP are also used in the pseudo-partitive. Furthermore, this book shows that, contrary to expectations, abstract first nouns have progressed along a similar grammaticalization path (although many never developed a pseudo-partitive function).

Chapter 4 will look at the evaluative constructions in this *of*-binominal family in more detail and, in particular, will argue for a division of what has been called the EBNP, into three separate categories, i.e. EBNPs and what I have named evaluative modifiers (EMs) and binominal intensifiers (BIs). EMs have not been discussed at all in previous research and the BI has only been mentioned peripherally (uses with *hell*).

CHAPTER 4

The Evaluative Of-*binominals*

4.1 Introduction

This chapter addresses the more subjective (evaluative) binominals in this family of *of*-binominals: the evaluative binominal noun phrase (EBNP), the evaluative modifier (EM), and the binominal intensifier (BI). The English EBNP has been discussed extensively in the past, and Section 4.2 provides an overview of this discussion. Section 4.3 introduces the EM, which is a new category that has been overlooked in previous studies. Finally, Section 4.4 discusses the intensifier use of *of*-binominals in this family. A degree modifier stage (BI) has been proposed as the end point of other *of*-binominal grammaticalization paths (e.g. measure nouns, *a lot, sort-of, kind-of, type-of*), but previous studies have never posited it as a possible function of first nouns that have evaluative functions, i.e. first nouns used in the EBNP (although Bolinger [1972] and Trousdale [2012] mention *hell* as an exception). This study shows that evaluative first nouns are more productive as BIs than has been anticipated in previous work and links this progression to the grammaticalization of lexical items such as *great* that develop from a descriptive adjective (*a great distance*) to an affective adjective (*a great man*) and finally an intensifier (*a great big axe*).

4.2 Evaluative Binominal Noun Phrase

Of all the *of*-binominals discussed in this section, the EBNP (e.g. *an idiot of a doctor* or *a beast of a car*) is probably the most idiosyncratic, from a syntactic and discourse-pragmatic point of view. This would then explain its 'allure' to linguists of all theoretical backgrounds (e.g. Aarts 1998; Austin 1980; Den Dikken 1998, 2006; Foolen 2004; Keizer 2007a; Kim & Sells 2015; McCawley 1988; Napoli 1989; Selkirk 1977). This is also a construction found in a surprisingly wide range of languages: German (e.g. Abraham 1998; Leys 1997; Vuillaume, Marillier & Behr 1993), Dutch (e.g. Bennis, Corver & Den Dikken 1998; Everaert 1992; Paardekooper 1956), Italian (e.g. Masini 2016); Spanish (e.g. Villalba & Bartra-Kaufmann 2010), and French (e.g. Bennett 1976; Doetjes & Rooryck 2003; Foolen 2004; Leys 1997). As great as the interest in this phenomenon has been, equally great has been the number of terminological classifications allocated to it: evaluative binominal noun phrase (Trousdale 2012), binominal noun phrase (Aarts 1998; Keizer 2007a; Kim & Sells 2015), expressive binominal noun phrase (Foolen 2004), qualitative binominal noun phrase (Den Dikken 2006: 162), *NoN* (Alexiadou, Haegeman & Stavrou 2007), N of a N (Corver 1998), and adjectival nouns (McCawley 1987). Naturally, with research from various theoretical approaches, there is also disagreement over the description and explanation of the phenomenon itself. Kim and Sells (2015: 52–6),[1] the most recent contribution to the English EBNP discussion, sort previous studies into four basic strands:

(1) Because the PP is obligatory, Napoli (1989) argues that the first noun (N_1) functions as the syntactic and semantic head with a canonical PP complement.[2]
(2) The second noun (N_2) functions as syntactic and semantic head with a grammaticalized [N_1 of a] functioning as modifier phrase (MP) (Aarts 1998; Keizer 2007a).
(3) In EBNPs, N_1 and N_2 have a subject-predicate relationship with N_1 undergoing predicate inversion in a small clause (Kayne 1994). Den Dikken (2006: 162–86) proposes that this construction comes in two types: the first type is the attributive EBNP, where the first noun ascribes a property onto the referent (e.g. *an idiot of a doctor*); the second is the comparative EBNP, where the referent is being compared to the first noun (e.g. *a jewel of a village*).
(4) The construction is a new type of construction called the juxtaposition construction where N_2 is the semantic head and neither noun is the syntactic head (Kim & Sells 2015).

Generally speaking, the EBNP is an *of*-binominal construction in which either the first noun is compared to the second or it ascribes a property (abstract or physical) to the second, as can be seen in examples (4.1a–b). In (4.1a), abstract 'beast-like' properties are ascribed to *thing*, i.e. the thing is

---

[1] See Keizer (2007a: 94–5) for an alternative grouping.
[2] Abney (1987) also proposes that there is an underlying structure with N_1 as head, which is essentially based on syntactic mimicry: the EBNP is structurally similar to more prototypical *of*-binominals and therefore mimics them.

4.2 Evaluative Binominal Noun Phrase

like a beast, and in (4.1b), the *house* (i.e. *thing*) is being compared to/looks like *a wedding cake*, a house that resembles a wedding cake.

(4.1)   a. was thrown out of one slum and only found shelter in another with *a drunken beast of a thing* who would sit tearing at a steak with his bare hands (COCA)
        b. The tallest and most elaborate monument – a multitiered, carved-stone *wedding cake of a thing*. – belongs to the Wiessners, a wealthy family of Baltimore brewers (Jensen & Chalkley 2021: 65)

In the EBNP, the first noun can often be changed into a corresponding adjectival modifier in a simple NP, e.g. *a beastly husband*, without a loss of meaning.[3] Alternatively, some first nouns can take the *-like* suffix and can be used as a premodifier to mean something similar to the EBNP, e.g. compare *this wedding cake of a city* (COCA) to *the cake-like Plaza* (COCA). However, the EBNP not only tends to encode a broader meaning than the simple premodifier use (e.g. the derived adjective *beastly* denotes only manner, where in the EBNP the first noun *beast* can denote both manner and physical size; see Ten Wolde & Keizer 2016) but also sanctions nouns that do not have an adjectival form that would allow them to function as premodifiers, e.g. *a whale of a house* which cannot be **a whaleish/ ?whale-like house*.

The sections below outline the basic features of the EBNP construction according to the criteria laid out in Chapter 2; the different analyses of the EBNP will be tied into the discussion as they relate.

4.2.1 Head Status

When the phrase denotes a referent, it is the second noun that denotes the referent: in example (4.2a), the speaker met a woman and not a mouse. The verb also semantically selects the second noun and not the first: the obligatoriness and omissibility tests would indicate that the second noun usually fulfills the semantic criteria of the verb, as demonstrated in (4.2b) with *park* and *offers*.

(4.2)   a. I **met** *a colourless little mouse of a **woman*** yesterday, and we drove to the beach together. (Aarts 1998: 118)
        b. *This jewel of **a** park* near downtown Oakland **offers** numerous pleasures for little ones. (COCA)

---

[3] This is naturally controversial: see Den Dikken (2006) and Kim and Sells (2015).

However, some examples yield ambiguous results, as shown in examples (4.3a–b). As shown in (4.3a–b), there are cases when either noun could represent the construction as a whole without a change in meaning (for a discussion of relevant data, see Keizer 2007a: 95–6). Aarts (1998: 118) points out that there are contexts in which a certain metaphorical interpretation is triggered by the first noun, making it the more appropriate recipient of the verb semantics in certain contexts, as shown in (4.4): *described* selects the metaphorical description *a colourless mouse*, not the element *a woman* (Keizer 2007a: 96). However, in general it would seem that the second noun is the semantic head.

(4.3) a. We should have fired *that plonker of a plumber*.
b. We should have fired *that plonker/that plumber*.
(Keizer 2007a: 95)

(4.4) She is usually **described** as *a colourless mouse/*$^{??}$*a woman*.
(Aarts 1998: 118)

A possible explanation for the variable results in the semantic tests might be the nondefault function of the first noun. The fact that the first noun functions as a modifier might well explain the equivocality of verb selection test, i.e. in the regular NP, *a pretty woman* in (4.5a–b), *describe* also selects *pretty* and not *woman*. Furthermore, the first and second nouns can be used interchangeably in those constructions where the denotation of both the first and the second noun can represent or be construed to metaphorically represent, the referent (Keizer 2007a: 95–6). Since in many cases the two nouns are in a predicative relation, either noun can be left out without changing the underlying message. This is demonstrated in example (4.6a–d), where *fired* can select either *beast* or *man*, but it would not work for *scrapped* with *whale of a car* (4.6c–d). Therefore, although N_2 clearly determines the referent, in figurative usages of the EBNP, the first noun can also be used to represent the referent.

(4.5) a. She is usually **described** as *a pretty woman*.
b. She is usually **described** as pretty/$^{??}$*a woman*.

(4.6) a. We should have **fired** *that beast of a man*.
b. We should have **fired** *that beast/that man*.
c. We should have **scrapped** *that whale of a car*.
d. We should have **scrapped** **that whale/that car*.

Morpho-syntactic evidence is in general inconclusive, since most of the tests do not apply. The first and second nouns must agree in number;

4.2 Evaluative Binominal Noun Phrase

therefore, the morpho-syntactic locus and subject–verb agreement tests do not apply here. The only exceptions are those few cases where collective nouns are used, as in example (4.7a–c) (Bennis et al. 1998: 96–9). In (4.7a), the noun–verb concord would appear to be with the first noun. Although *jury* can also trigger either a singular or a plural verb as shown in (4.7b), this is never true with a demonstrative pronoun (4.7c) (Keizer 2007a: 97).

(4.7)   a. *Those prejudiced **fools** of a jury* **were**/***was** totally unreliable.
        b. *The jury* **were/was** *a bunch of prejudiced fools*.
        c. ***That*** *jury* ***were/was** totally unreliable.
        (Keizer 2007a: 97)

Pronominalization, as seen in example (4.8) and (4.9), shows that *one* can only take the second noun as an anaphoric referent and indicates that N₂ is the head. As demonstrated by (4.10), the form of the personal pronouns is determined by the second noun, as in (4.10a), but not the first, as demonstrated in (4.10b). The first noun no longer has referential status; thus, it seems justified to conclude that the second noun functions as the pragmatic-discourse head (see Keizer 2007a: 93–101).

(4.8)   We had *an absolute beast of a **party***; the next one won't be so good, I'm sure. (Keizer 2007a: 100)

(4.9)   A: He had *a **hell** of a time* getting from one part of the country to the other.
        B: *I had (a) *one of a row* because I refused to even try.
        (Keizer 2007a: 100)

(4.10)   a. An old rascal had managed to capture *that flower of **a girl***, and made **her** believe that to save **her** dead father's good name **she** must marry him. (COHA)
        b. *An old rascal had managed to capture *that **flower** of a girl*, and made **it** believe that to save **its** dead father's good name **it** must marry him.

As explained in Section 4.2 above, there has been some discussion on the headedness of EBNPs. McCawley (1987: 459) and Napoli (1989) argue for either an N₁ as head or a two-headed solution, N₁ as syntactic head and N₂ as semantic head. The first noun as head would simply place the syntactic evidence above the semantic-pragmatic facts; a conclusion that would not coincide with a functional approach selected here. A two-head analysis begs the question of the explanatory benefit of such conclusion. Keizer (2007a: 106) argues that the semantic and pragmatic tests clearly point to N₂ as head; the syntactic evidence is inconclusive. Headedness is essentially a semantic and pragmatic phenomenon, and therefore, it would have the greatest explanatory power to make the second noun head (for further discussion see Aarts 1998: 126–30). It is concluded here that the second noun is the head. This conclusion is strengthened by the constituency tests as well as the other criteria laid out in Section 4.2.2.

4.2.2 Constituency Tests

Neither the PP nor the NP$_2$ can be extracted or coordinated, as demonstrated in (4.11a–e).[4] Therefore, the *of*-phrase is clearly neither a complement nor a modifier of the first noun,[5] and *of* is not a prototypical preposition. However, the EBNP can be clefted as in (4.11f) (Kim & Sells 2015: 48–9). This shows that the individual noun phrases and the prepositional phrase are no longer individual constituents, but the EBNP, as a whole, is a constituent.

(4.11) a. David sits and begins to rotate *his shiny egg of a head* while kneading the base of his neck. (COCA)
b. *[of a head]$_i$ he had [a shiny egg t$_i$]
c. *[a head]$_i$ he had a shiny egg of t$_i$
d. *[a shiny egg t$_i$] was painted [of a head]$_i$
e. *He had a shiny egg [of a head] and [of a belly].
f. It is [his shiny egg of a head] that he begins to rotate.

This is also true for the following two constructions (EM and BI) and, therefore, will not be repeated in the sections below.

4.2.3 Constraints on the Two Nouns

The second noun in the EBNP can denote an entity, but the first one does not. Instead, it denotes a semantic value that is ascribed to the second noun, as shown by the paraphrase of (4.12a) given in (4.12b) (Den Dikken 1998: 177–8; Napoli 1989: 222). This value must be construable as some sort of evaluative judgment, hence the awkwardness of *teacher* in (4.13a) (Aarts 1998: 121). As we have seen, N$_1$ can also be metaphorical, such as *mouse* in

---

[4] Kim and Sells (2015: 50) argue that the NPs also cannot be coordinated; however, the nouns can. Therefore, this is why it is possible to find examples such as *some little mouse of a boy and girl* and *a self-appointed bastard of a judge, jury, and God* (both from COHA), but not examples like *some little mouse of a boy and a girl*.

[5] Abney (1987), however, argues that the PP is a constituent, and that the thematic role is not stipulated by the first NP (for further discussion of the problematic aspects of this analysis, see Aarts 1998: 136–7).

4.2 Evaluative Binominal Noun Phrase

(4.13b), but it is not a requirement: the *fool* in *a fool of a doctor* is not metaphorical.

(4.12) a. her nitwit of a husband
         b. her husband is a nitwit
         (Keizer 2007a: 88)

(4.13) a. *a teacher of a husband (Keizer 2007a: 86)
         b. a mouse of a child

This relationship between the first and second noun is further supported by the evidence that although N_1 can still appear in singular (4.12) and plural form (as shown in (4.14)), it must agree in syntactic number (4.14a) or semantic number (4.14b) with N_2 (Keizer 2005; 2007a: 96–7, 99).

(4.14) a. if that wasteful old hussy isn't getting up a feast for *those beasts of Indians*! (COHA)
         b. those fools of a crew (Keizer 2005: 303)

N_2 can be a count noun (as demonstrated by most of the examples in this section), a collective noun (4.15a), or a proper noun (4.15b). It cannot be a mass noun, as a mass noun would trigger a head-classifier reading, as in the case of *glass* in (4.15c) (Keizer 2007a: 91–2; see Section 3.3).

(4.15) a. those fools of a **crew** (Keizer 2005: 303)
         b. that clever little wench of a **Rebecca** (Austin 1980: 361)
         c. a jewel of **glass** (Keizer 2007a: 92)

Den Dikken (1998) notes that the first and second nouns in the EBNP form a predicative relationship, as shown in (4.16a–b). He therefore proposes two underlying constructions, the comparative binominal noun phrase (e.g. *the wine is like Kate Moss*) and the attributive one (e.g. *the doctor is a fool*). However, this is not true for all EBNPs, as examples (4.17a–b) demonstrate.

(4.16) a. a fool of a doctor
         b. the doctor is a fool
         (Keizer 2007a: 107)

(4.17) a. You're sure to have *a Dickens of a Christmas* as this South Georgia town transforms itself into a scene straight from "A Christmas Carol" for Victorian Christmas . . . (COCA)
         b. *A Christmas is a Dickens.

This distinction between the EBNPs has been discussed but not generally adopted in later studies, and although it is indisputable that the distinction exists, the question is whether it justifies two underlying representations.

Keizer (2007a: 87, 107) contends that in English the distinction does not affect the syntactic structure and, thus, does not warrant a new construction.

Although the first noun needs to agree in number with the second, it can still take individual modification. There are numerous examples of premodification of N$_1$ in the corpora, and an idiosyncratic feature of premodification in the EBNP is that modifiers placed in front of the first noun can be selected by N$_1$ or N$_2$ (Aarts 1998: 132). This means that they can have scope over the first noun or the whole construction. Kim and Sells (2015: 47), among others, claim that these premodifiers can also have scope over N2; however, it is difficult to define the scope of a modifier. Examples in (4.18) to (4.20) demonstrate some premodification patterns and restrictions in the EBNP.

(4.18) a. a **ravening** beast of a cartridge (COCA)
        b. a magnificent **anecdotal** monster of a **novel** (COCA)
        c. a **hungry-looking** mere wisp of a **fellow** (COCA)

(4.19) a. ?the ten fools of a crew
        b. ?many beasts of Indians

(4.20) that **very** wonder of a city (Aarts 1998: 147)

In (4.18a), *ravening* is clearly selected by N$_1$ and may, arguably, have scope over either N$_1$ or the whole construction. In (4.18b), *anecdotal* is clearly selected by N$_2$ and has scope over the whole construction. In (4.18c), *hungry-looking* is clearly selected by *fellow* and *mere* by *wisp*. Keizer (2007a: 92) first pointed out that an intensifying modifier, such as *mere* in (4.18c), can only modify the first noun; it is the descriptive modifiers that can have scope over the whole construction as is the case with *hungry-looking*. It seems that the use of both numerals (example (4.19a)) and quantifiers (example (4.19b)) are inappropriate in front of the first noun. Aarts (1998: 147–8) finds that the fact that intensifiers such as *very* can sometimes modify the first noun is further evidence for its modifying function, as in (4.20) (see Chapter 7 for a study of premodification patterns).

In sum, in the EBNP, the first noun ascribes a property to the second noun, and this property must be evaluative. The second noun denotes the referent of the whole construction. The first noun has lost some properties of nounhood in that it must agree in number with the second noun and cannot be quantified.

4.2.4 Determiners

The first determiner slot is open for all types of determination (see Keizer 2007a: 88–90), but the prototypical determiner is the indefinite article

4.2 Evaluative Binominal Noun Phrase

(e.g. Keizer 2007a: 88; Kim & Sells 2015: 44). There is some discussion about the use of the definite article, but as Payne in a personal communication with Aarts (1998: 120) argues, it is only used when referring to a referent already introduced into the discourse (as seen in (4.21)) (see also Keizer 2007a: 89).

(4.21) I want to see my bank manager, but *the sly fox of a man* has just left. (Aarts 1998: 121)

As noted in Quirk et al. (1985: 1285) and others (Aarts 1998: 131; Austin 1980: 361; Napoli 1989: 212), when a possessive pronoun appears in the first determiner position, it specifies the second noun (4.22a–c). As shown in example (4.22c), the second noun cannot take its own (postnominal) possessive because a noun cannot be marked twice for possession. This analysis would also explain why an indefinite article is not allowed in the first determiner position when a proper noun fills the second noun position, exemplified in (4.23) (Aarts 1998: 132). Furthermore, if the EBNP is a referential expression, the first determiner designates the type of reference: *your jerk of a brother* has definite reference and *a Dickens of a Christmas* in (4.17) has indefinite reference.

(4.22) a. your jerk of a brother
b. your brother is a jerk.
c. *your jerk of a brother of yours
(Aarts 1998: 131)

(4.23) *a creep of a James (Aarts 1998: 121 taken from Van Caspel 1970)

However, there are some exceptions, as demonstrated in (4.24). In (4.24a–b), the first determiner shows number concord with the first noun, as shown by the use of the plural demonstrative determiner in (4.24a). The plural determiner *those* cannot, however, be used with *jury*, e.g. **those jury*, even though *jury*, as seen above, can be interpreted as having a plural referent (*The jury* **were/was** *a bunch of prejudiced fools*).

(4.24) a. *Those prejudiced fools of a jury* were totally unreliable. (Keizer 2007a: 97)
b. ***That*** *jury* **was** totally unreliable.

For these examples, Keizer (2005; 2007a: 101–2) argues that the demonstrative does not function like a prototypical demonstrative in these cases; instead, it functions as an intensifier of the evaluative judgment expressed by the first noun (and as such agrees in number with the first noun), and at the same time, as an indicator of definiteness for the expression as a whole (something similar can be found with *one* and *some* in the EM and BI constructions).

The second determiner is canonically the indefinite article,[6] even when a proper noun fills the second noun position, as demonstrated in (4.25a–b) (Austin 1980: 361). It still marks number, meaning that there is no article in those rare cases where the first and second nouns are both plural (see (4.26); Keizer 2005). Quantifiers such as *some* or *many* are not allowed.

(4.25)   a. this colourless little mouse of **a** woman/*the woman (Aarts 1998: 118)
          b. that creep of **a** James (Aarts 1998: 121)

(4.26)   if that wasteful old hussy isn't getting up a feast for *those beasts of Indians*! (COHA)

Summing up, in the EBNP, the Det₁ position is open although it only allows the definite article in particular discourse contexts. Det₂ position allows only the indefinite article and in the plural N₂, no article.

4.2.5   Status of Of

The element *of* is mandatory; however, its status depends greatly on the general analysis of the construction (see the four suggestions in Section 4.2). Abney (1987), Napoli (1989: 215 for Italian), and Quirk et al. (1985: 1285) interpret *of* as a preposition; others, however, argue that it no longer functions like a prototypical preposition (Aarts 1998: 134–7; Alexiadou et al. 2007: 445; Keizer 2007a: 97–9). To the first analysis, the constituency tests clearly show that the PP and NP₂ are not constituents; therefore, there is no evidence that *of* functions like a prototypical preposition. Instead, Den Dikken (2006: 164) and others (Alexiadou et al. 2007: 445) analyze *of* as a functional element, a "nominal copula" that acts as an alternative for the copula *be* with N₂ as subject and N₁ as object. This means that examples (4.27a,c) can be paraphrased as (4.27b,d) (Aarts 1998: 118). However, as already discussed above, *of* cannot be used as a nominal copula in all EBNPs. This means that although it might have a grammatical (or linking) function, it no longer appears to have semantic value.

(4.27)   a. the plonker of a plumber
          b. The plumber is a plonker.
          c. that idiot of a prime minister
          d. That prime minister is an idiot.

---

[6] Generative theories see the restriction of the determiners in front of the second noun in the EBNP as evidence of a loss of the DP-layer for the second noun (see Alexiadou et al. 2007: 398–9).

4.2.6 The Properties of the EBNP

Most studies tend to agree on the syntactic features that characterize the EBNP; the debate, instead, focuses on the headedness question. The decision whether the first, second, or both nouns are selected as head greatly influences the underlying analysis of the construction. Based on the evidence presented above, it is unclear how a left-headed analysis can be supported unless the semantic evidence is ignored. Furthermore, there appears to be no value in deciding that neither noun is head and that the first noun and second noun are in apposition; here, too, we would be ignoring a large amount of evidence that supports the idea that the second noun is, at the very least, the semantic head. Aarts (1998) and Keizer (2007a) suggest that we should view the [N_1 of a] unit as a complex modifier phrase.

A number of features of the EBNP would support this account, namely the fact that the EBNP is unable to accept extraction or coordination; that the first noun does not appear to have referential value and has lost most of its features of nounhood; that personal pronouns and modifiers in front of the first noun are semantically selected by the second noun and can modify the whole construction; that the second determiner marks for number but not (in)definiteness; and that both nouns have to agree in number. The combined evidence points to a reanalysis of the syntactic structure of the *of*-binominal. Aarts' and Keizer's complex modifier account explains the change of properties in the first determiner as well as the irregular premodifier selection in front of the first noun. They argue that in the attributive form it modifies the property of the noun, [Det (Mod) [$_{MP}$ N_1 of a] (Mod) N_2], and in the comparative version the extended noun phrase consists of two properties each ascribing a property to the referent: [$_{NP}$ [$_{Det}$ a] [$_{ExtN}$ [[$_{MP}$ fool of a] [$_{N\text{-head}}$ doctor]]]] (Keizer 2007a: 107).

Kim and Sells (2015: 54) have two central arguments against this analysis. First, this analysis does not explain the loss of the second determiner in plural forms, and second, there is no synchronic or diachronic evidence that [N of a] forms a constituent. The following section addresses the first argument in that I propose that the EBNP represents a transition stage and only in the EM is the reanalysis complete. To the second, as they themselves point out, this analysis accounts for the scope of the pre-N_1 adjectives and determiner, and conforms with the findings from the constituency tests, and in the context of the further grammaticalization stages, this analysis would appear to be the most plausible.

4.3 Evaluative Modifier

The EBNP and the pseudo-partitive, respectively, mark the beginning of the process that results in the further loss of internal structure as new uses develop. One such new *of*-binominal is the EM; it consists of constructions that have, in previous studies, been aggregated to EBNPs. I argue here that they are a separate construction: with a separate function and form. In the EM, the first noun's ascription of physical properties found in EBNPs is lost, and the underlying subjective-evaluation semantics is foregrounded. The construction construes the first noun as expressing a bounded, either a negative or positive, extreme on a profiled scale.[7] What scale is implied and what feature of N_2 the speaker wishes to enforce, very often depends on the second noun and requires context and/or social/cultural knowledge to interpret (see examples (4.28a–b)).

(4.28) a. It was *a hell of a night* for a meeting – with the storm going and the river about to blow. (COCA)
b. "Y'ever hear what Kennedy said three hours before he was shot?" he asked, putting on his best Massachusetts accent. "You know, last night would've been *a hell of a night* to kill a President." (COCA)

Example (4.28a) is a potential example of a bridging construction between the two categories: it clearly marks the speaker's emphasis on the negative features of the night (i.e. stormy, dangerous) and could be analyzed either as a negative evaluative modifier, *a very bad night*, or as an EBNP, in which case 'hellish' features are ascribed to that particular night (*a hellish night*). The premodifier alternative allows us to distinguish between some EBNPs and EMs, particularly in those cases where the first nouns are, in the EBNP construction, already abstract, as in the case of *hell*. In the case of *hell*, once the construction loses the premodifier alternative, then it has clearly transitioned to the EM. This transition can

---

[7] Boundedness has been discussed in relation to nouns (e.g. Jackendoff 1991: 20–1). However, boundedness is also used by Paradis (2001) as a criterion to classify adjectives. Paradis (2001: 48) argues that boundedness in adjectives, similarly to boundedness in nouns and verbs, is a basic property of adjectives and in the case of adjectives associated with gradeability. She explains that boundedness has to do with the presupposed mental scale encoded by adjectives. For example, *long* and *short*, both unbounded adjectives, imply a range of values on a scale. However, extreme adjectives such as *brilliant* or *terrible*, i.e. bounded adjectives, represent the end values on a scale (Paradis 2001: 51–2).

be seen in example (4.28b), where the semantic prosody has unmistakably changed: the irony hinges on the fact that Kennedy is claiming that it would have been a very propitious night to kill a president. Therefore, *hell* denotes a positive subjective evaluation of the second noun.

The [N of a]$_{MP}$ unit in the EM functions similarly to extreme adjectives such as *gigantic, gorgeous,* and *fantastic* (see Morzycki 2016; Paradis 1997, 2001). As Paradis (1997: 54–7) explains in her categorization of extreme adjectives: "[they] can be described as implicit superlatives in that they express a superlative degree of a certain feature." In a similar way, the semantics of the EM can be broken down into two elements: on the one hand, there is the subjective, affective semantics that expresses speaker evaluation of the overall referent, and on the other hand, there is an implied scalar extreme, either negative or positive; for example, *a hell of a day* is not just *a good day* but *the best of days*. Evidence for this analysis can be found in more creative uses where *hell* is given a superlative morphological ending when used in the EM, as illustrated in (4.29).

(4.29)   there's heaven in *the **hellest** of holes* (NOW)

In this example, the superlative does not indicate degree in relation to other entities such as *hole* but emphasizes the properties of *hell*. It functions very similarly to examples such as *the most excellent day*, where *most* emphasizes *excellent*, although *excellent* is an extreme modifier.[8] This example also indicates that speakers conceptualize *hell* in the EM as functioning like an adjectival modifier.

Unfortunately, most of the syntactic tests Paradis (1997: 54–7) proposes for determining extreme modifiers do not apply to the *of*-binominal;[9] however, the one test that does apply is that of premodification. Paradis's (1997: 56–7) test proposes that extreme modifiers cannot be modified by degree modifiers, except for *most* and maximizers, and there are examples of *hell* and *beast* being modified by *most* in (4.30a) and by *absolute* in (4.30b). The emphatic value of a phrase can most clearly be seen when *what* acts as an intensifier (though this emphatic value can also be found in the EBNP), as seen in (4.30c) (Brems 2011: 145–6; Davidse 2009: 287–8).

---

[8] This is also similar to phrases such as *totally untrue* or *completely dead*.
[9] The tests that Paradis (1997: 56) suggests are (i) being comparable (although this in general is a problematic test), (ii) asking for scale: *How x is it?* (extreme adjectives should be awkward in these formulations), (iii) functioning in exclamatory expressions: *How x!*, (iv) having a scalar antonym, e.g. *excellent – terrible*, and (v) resisting scalar degree modifiers, e.g. *slightly, fairly*, but accepting *most* and most maximizing modifiers.

(4.30) a. You're *the **most** hell of a officer* I ever seen in my life. (Cave 2007: 331)
b. Headline: It's *an **absolute** beast of a laptop* (NOW)
c. "I love you," I said. And I do. I really do. And I remember thinking **what** *a hell of a man* a man could become. (COHA)

There are not many first nouns which have transitioned from the EBNP to the EM, and those that have are from either the abstract or the animate groups of first nouns. Table 4.1 shows those first nouns that were found in this study. The following sections discuss the different features of the EM in more detail.

4.3.1 Head Status

If the EM is referential, the second noun defines the overall referent of the construction as shown in (4.31a–c) and is also semantically compatible with other elements in the linguistic context (e.g. *turn* in (4.32a) and *where* and *play* in (4.32b)); this suggests that N_2 is the semantic head.

(4.31) a. making the point that Washington is *a hell of a party town* (COHA)
b. making the point that Washington is *a party town*
c. #making the point that Washington is *a hell*

(4.32) a. They're tumblers of sorts, people who know how to **turn** *one hell of a spiritual somersault.* (COHA)
b. It was two years ago at Bethpage Black, *a beast of a **golf course*** anyone **could play** for $31, **where** raucous New Yorkers cheered (COCA)

Table 4.1 *The semantic distinctions between first nouns used in EBNPs and EMs*

FIRST NOUN	EBNP	EM
hell	hellish	something or someone very good or very bad
beast	large-size, beastly manner, beast-like appearance	something is difficult, someone or something is wonderful, great, challenging
whale	large	something or someone very good
bitch	malicious or treacherous animate object	something difficult, very bad or very good
dog	ugly	someone or something bad
devil	devilish	someone or something difficult or very good
honey	sweet animate object	something or someone very good
bastard	vicious, despicable person; something difficult or bad	something or someone very good

4.3 Evaluative Modifier

As to the syntactic head, both N_1 and N_2 are predominantly used in singular form, and therefore, the verb agreement diagnostic does not apply. As with the EBNP, a possessive pronoun in the Det1 position specifies the second noun, as in example (4.33) (two exceptions are the emphatic *some* and *one*). In almost all the tokens found, the first and second nouns agree in number and are always singular; thus, the first determiner agrees in number with both nouns. This suggests that N_2 is the syntactic head.

(4.33) China, with **its** 1.3 billion people and *beast of **an** economy*, is shopping the world for oil. (COCA)

Either the whole construction or only the second noun can function as a pronominal antecedent, as in (4.34), indicating that N_1 no longer has referential status and indicating that the second noun is the head of the construction. Moreover, only the second noun can be the antecedent of the personal pronoun, as shown in (4.35).

(4.34) A: We had *an absolute beast of a **party***; the next **one** won't be so good, I'm sure. (Keizer 2007a: 100)
B: *We had **one** *of a sleepover.*

(4.35) *A hell of **a warrior**.* Too bad **she** is paying such a cost. (COCA)

The headedness tests show that, unlike in the case of the EBNP, in the EM the second noun is the unambiguous head of the *of*-binominal.

4.3.2 Constraints on the Two Nouns

N_1 has decategorialized: it no longer exhibits the form or function of a prototypical noun. It no longer codes concreteness or animateness, which are the semantic criteria of nounhood (Givón 1993: 55–7); structurally, the determiner in the Det1 position specifies the referent denoted in N_2; N_1 cannot take the plural form or take a possessor (in example (4.36) *his* specifies *presence*). N_1 does not function as the head of its NP or the *of*-binominal.

(4.36) a. Perseverance and encouragement were its virtues, and *his hell of a harrowing presence* in the line leading into the New Womb were well-deserved. (Baker 2014: 300)
b. *This harrowing presence of his* in the line leading into the New Womb . . .
c. #*This hell of his* in the line leading into the New Womb . . .

There is very little modification that appears in front of the first noun, but the modifiers that do appear in this position are usually selected by N_2 and have scope over the whole construction (see Ten Wolde 2019). In example (4.37a), *hard-charging* could have been selected by either N_1 or N_2, as opposed to example (4.37b), where *red-carpeted* is clearly selected by *time*, not *whale*. In other cases, the premodifier in front of the first noun can function as two different types of modifiers depending on which noun it modifies: in example (4.37c), *poor* is a value judgment if modifying *contrivance* (speaker judgment of the *contrivance*'s relation to a prototypical contrivance of this sort); if, however, *poor* modifies *devil* it conveys speaker empathy, but in that case *devil* would evoke a referent (i.e. not be an EM).[10] As demonstrated in example (4.38), maximizers can also appear in front of N_1.

(4.37) a. The Social Network is *a,* **hard-charging beast** *of a* **movie** with a full tank of creative gas (COCA)
       b. the national Committeemen and women are having *a* **red-carpeted whale** *of a* **time** (COHA)
       c. here it stood, **poor** *devil of a contrivance* that it was! with only the thinnest vesture of human similitude about it ... (COHA)

(4.38) Director Tomas Alfredson ... hits and sustains just the right tone throughout, aided by *one* **absolute** *hell of a cast.* (COCA)

The second noun is predominantly realized by singular count nouns and, therefore, usually denotes a specific referent. The use of proper nouns in the N_2 slot, in the case of EBNPs, is lost in this form. Canonically the N_2 is countable (4.37a) or a collective noun (4.39a). However, there are also some examples with mass nouns (4.39b); although in examples like (4.39b), where a mass noun takes an indefinite determiner, *rain* is most likely being construed as a countable object, i.e. a rain storm. Plural or mass nouns used in the second noun position usually indicate another *of*-binominal construction, e.g. a quantifying construction (4.39c), and in this case, the *hell* most likely means 'a large amount' (see section 3.4).

(4.39) a. "We know Syracuse is *a hell of a team,*" said Dean Smith. (Maiorana & Pitoniak 2005: 45)
       b. Wow! I can see that we had *one hell of a rain* last night. It's the heaviest rain we've had in a couple of years. (COCA)
       c. With the click of a mouse he could fire *a hell of microwaves* up at the ionosphere. (COCA)

---

[10] This use of *poor* expresses a speaker's subjective attitude to the designated referent (see, e.g., Butler 2008).

4.3 Evaluative Modifier

Premodification in front of the second noun tends to take the form of classifiers (4.40a). There are, as can be expected, ambiguous occurrences such as (4.40b), where [*hell of a*] could be intensifying *strong* (i.e. [*a* [*very strong*] *grip*]; see Section 4.4 below) or modifying the Adj+N combination: [*a* [[*hell of a*] [*strong grip*]]]. The EM exhibits increased syntactic scope in that it can also modify an EBNP (4.41a) and increased syntactic freedom in that [N of (a)] can be used in the semi-fixed constructions (4.41b) and may violate the word boundary (4.41c).

(4.40) a. George Bush has cultivated his Texas roots and grown himself *one whale of a **political** career.* (COHA)
b. "One of those kids," he said sadly, "has *a hell of a **strong** grip.* (COHA)

(4.41) a. A hell of a poor slob of a bastard (COHA)
b. Bottom line you need much training, experience and be *in hell of shape* just to complete "Selection" (COCA)
c. "Hey, yourself," Ryan replied, smiling back. "*Triple bitch of a jump*, eh?" (COCA)

Both nouns in the EM are usually found in the singular form and, therefore, agree in number. However, there are a few examples with plural second nouns as in (4.42), and in these examples the first noun remains singular, but the indefinite article might be triggered by *couple*.

(4.42) You know, nobody's going to talk about the Hastert revolution like they talk about the Gingrich revolution. But he gets things done. He got the nuclear waste bill done, the budget, he got the supplemental bill, the Catholic chaplain – he's had *a **hell** of a couple **weeks*** in his quiet understated way. (COCA)

To conclude, in the EM, the first and second nouns agree in number, and both almost always occur in the singular form. Premodification in front of both nouns is restricted, and premodifiers in front of the first noun can be selected by the second. Unlike the EBNP, the EM is no longer a fixed construction but demonstrates increased syntactic scope and the syntactic flexibility of modifiers or expletives, i.e. expletive infixing.

4.3.3 Determiners

The first determiner slot can be filled with all types of determination but, like the EBNP, is canonically filled by the indefinite determiner, as in (4.43a), or by emphatic *one/some*, as in (4.43b) and (4.44b). There is a difference between the regular use and the intensifier use of *one* and *some*. This can be seen in examples (4.44a–b), where the *some* in the EBNP in (4.44a) refers to the referent's unidentifiability, whereas the *some* in the EM in (4.44b) intensifies the approbation features of *hell* in this construction.

(4.43) a. that Beasley is ***a beast of a scorer*** on the low block (COCA)
b. he stood up, stretched and smiled down at her. "You're ***one hell of a chess player***, Harmon," he said. (COHA)

(4.44) a. ***Some dragon of a receptionist*** refused to let him see her boss without an appointment. (Kim & Sells 2015: 44)
b. Fantastic! What a picture! Unbelievable! Fantastic! What a picture! ***Some hell of a team***, eh, boys! (COHA)

There are corpus examples in which the initial determiner has been dropped, particularly when the EM is in clause-initial position (4.45), a phenomenon seen in the grammaticalization of other *of*-binominals (Traugott 2008a: 229). As discussed in Section 4.3.1, the first determiner has scope over the whole construction, and if the EM is referential, the first determiner specifies the definiteness of the referent denoted by the second noun.

(4.45) Late the first day. *Hell of a way* to make an impression on his new boss. (COCA)

As is also the case with the EBNP, the second determiner slot is predominantly filled with an indefinite article; there are a few cases, however, where it is left empty. However, whereas in the EBNP the second determiner still encodes number (one of Kim & Sells [2015: 54] central arguments against analyzing [N1 of a] as a MP constituent), in the EM this function has been lost. This is supported by the fact that corpus and internet examples can be found where the second determiner has been dropped (see examples (4.46a–c)). Although these forms still sound awkward, this variation was only found in EM, not the EBNP, and occurs in published works such as books as in (4.46a).[11]

(4.46) a. Together we all learned to ride and had *a hell of time* doing it. Over the years, nothing's really changed. Snowboarding remains something that I really enjoy because of the friends I get to ride with. (Gallagher 2009: 17)

---

[11] In COCA 2020, there are 248 tokens for the search string: *hell of* Noun(s). In this sample 34 tokens are EMs without a second determiner; there is only one potential EBNP. It seems that this phenomenon, despite its awkwardness, is not just a typo.

b. A little wild blood would breed a good horse. And *a hell of man* too, it might be. (COCA)
c. Just want to call to congratulate you, and tell you you're doing *a hell of job*. (COCA)

4.3.4 Status of Of

As in the EBNP, the element *of* is mandatory, although it does not carry semantic meaning. In the EM, *of* no longer functions as a linking element and usually cannot be replaced with a copular verb as in (4.47).

(4.47) a. What we forget in all this piling-on is that Beasley is *a beast of a scorer* on the low block (COCA)
b. #the scorer is a beast

The preposition's lack of semantic content and the second determiner that appears to no longer mark number or definiteness in the second noun makes it very plausible that [N of a] is reanalyzed as a single unit. There is also orthographic evidence to support this in that, as demonstrated in examples (4.48a–b), [*hell of a*] has been reduced to *helluva* and finally to *hella* (this reduction is also discussed in Austin 1980: 360; Bucholtz et al. 2007; Trousdale 2012).[12] *Helluva* is the most frequent form, but there are also examples with *whaleuva* (see example (4.49a)).[13] The reanalysis of the internal structure of the *of*-binominals is not unique to this construction but has also been observed in the grammaticalization of other *of*-binominal constructions, e.g. *kinda, sorta, lota* (e.g. Traugott 2008b: 227).

(4.48) a. "And *a **helluva** recommendation* we would get from him, too, I bet yer!" (COHA)
b. you'd better be *one **hella** witch* to keep me from strangling you (COHA)

(4.49) Tom Hirst, who has done *a **whaleuva** job of organizing everything*, hopes those of you within a couple hours drive will plan to join us for the day. (Creesy 1986)

---

[12] Austin (1980: 360) attributes this reduced form to the EBNP (although her examples are of the EM). Trousdale (2012) links *hell*'s phonological reduction to the intensifier usage, i.e. the next stage, and Bucholtz et al. (2007) studies this reduction in California English.
[13] This is also not conclusive evidence, since phonological reduction has also been found to be a frequency effect (Brems 2011: 375).

4.3.5 The Properties of the EM

As discussed in Section 4.2, the main argument that Kim and Sells (2015) present against analyzing the EBNP as a construction where [N_1 of a] has become a single modifying phrase (MP) is that there is no external evidence for this change, whereas the fact that the second determiner still reflects number would argue against such an analysis. However, making a distinction between the EBNP and the EM shows that the EBNP is, in fact, the first stage in this reanalysis. In the EBNP, Det_2 still denotes number; this has been shown to be no longer the case in the EM. Furthermore, the orthographic reduction found in the most frequent forms of the EM, where [N of (a)] is reduced to a single orthographic unit that functions as a modifier, provides external evidence for this reanalysis in the EBNP. In the EM, [N_1 of a] has functions as an evaluative modifier that "signal[s] the subjective preference of the speaker toward an entity" (Givón 1993: 63). The formal structure of this construction is [[Det_1] [$_{MP}$ N_1 **of (a)**] (Mod) [N_2]].

The EM differentiates itself from the EBNP both semantically and morpho-syntactically. Semantically, the first noun expresses an evaluative, scalar extreme judgment of the overall referent, the exact interpretation of which depends on the context. Structurally, *of* and the second determiner no longer have a clear syntactic function and, in some very frequent examples, have been reduced. In some examples the second determiner has even been omitted. The first determiner slot allows for a range of determiners, including emphatic *one* and *some*. The first noun has lost its nounhood: it no longer evokes a referent and no longer takes the plural form, and it demonstrates very restricted premodification patterns. Therefore, it would be safe to conclude that, in the EM, [N_1 of a] is a single constituent.

Distinguishing between the EBNP and the EM constructions solves some of the issues that have arisen in the analysis of the EBNP. First, it might explain why some forms, such as [*hell of a*] and [*whale of a*], have been reduced and other first nouns that are generally frequent in the EBNP, but infrequent or not used as all in the EM, such as *jewel*, *jerk*, and *fool*, are not. Furthermore, this construction strengthens Aarts' (1998) and Keizer's (2007a) analysis of the EBNP and presents a scenario in which the EBNP is the initial stage of a reanalysis of the internal structure of the *of*-binominal, a reanalysis which is complete in the EM. This would make the final stage, the binominal intensifier's integration into the MP (see Section 4.4), more plausible.

4.3 Evaluative Modifier

The EM's semantic function has already been discussed in the context of adjectives. For example, needing world/encyclopedic knowledge to interpret a lexical item is not unknown in an adjective-noun symbiosis. There are Giegerich's (2004: 577) associative adjectives, where the modifiers can only be understood with world knowledge: *papal murder* (pope is the object), *papal visit* (pope is the subject), and *papal emissary* (the emissary is associated with the pope). Pustejovsky (1995) and Jackendoff (1997) note that *good* can only be understood in relation to the noun; *a good knife* is one that cuts well, and this *good* is different from the *good* in *a good nap* (Vendler 1967). Bouchard (2002: 57–146) goes so far as to argue that *good* cannot be interpreted in a vacuum but only in connection with a noun.

An extreme case is Dixon's (1982, 2010) VALUE modifier. A VALUE modifier "qualifies not the head noun, but some other adjective" (Dixon 1982: 25), and this "other adjective" can be either expressed or unexpressed. Therefore, he claims that *a good fast car* is a *good car* because it is *fast* (not a *good* and *fast car*), and in *a good box*, *good* does not qualify the head *box* but some unexpressed value in the mind of the speaker, e.g. *sturdy, big* (Adamson 2000: 44). Essentially, if a VALUE adjective appears alone "then it has manner function with respect to an implicit non-value adjective" (Dixon 1982: 30).[14] Therefore, even in the case of prototypical, single lexical modifiers, there can be an interplay between modifier semantics and context, either linguistic (e.g. collocations) or situational (e.g. discourse). This is, therefore, not a function unique to the EM construction.

This development from a descriptive modifier to a subjective-evaluative modifier has also already been discussed in relation to individual lexical items. In her seminal paper on the grammaticalization of *lovely*, Adamson (2000) argues (primarily on the evidence of context and collocations) that it developed from having a descriptive adjective meaning 'loving' or 'amiable' (4.50a) via a description of physical beauty (4.50b) to subjective-evaluating modifier (4.50 c) via what she calls an affective modifier. This shift is accompanied by a change in *lovely*'s place in premodifier word order, as the premodifier moves from the more objective right to the more subjective left of the premodifier zone (for more discussion see premodifier Chapter 7).

---

[14] Matthews (2014: 119) points out that *good* as a value adjective may function as Dixon outlines in examples, e.g. *a good hot bath*, where the bath is good because it was hot, but this is less likely in cases like a *good long film*, where the film is less likely to be good because it is long (see also the discussion in Adamson 2000: 44; Alexiadou et al. 2007: 300–2; Ghesquière 2014: 36).

(4.50) a. with *much hearty and **lovely** recommendations* (Adamson 2000: 47)
b. *the tears ... like envious floods ore-run her **lovely** face* (Adamson 2000: 48)
c. *Mr Lewes had 'a **lovely** time'* at Wybridge (Adamson 2000: 48)

The change from noun to (part of a) modifier phrase has also been described in other groups of *of*-binominals: both SKT, i.e. *sort of, kind of, type of* nouns,[15] and size noun binominals, such as *a lot of, load of,* have developed modifier functions. SKT binominals have developed attributive modifier functions (originally Denison 2002, but for a detailed analysis, see Brems 2011: 284–92). The first modifier usage is that of the semi-suffix construction (Denison 2002; see also Brems 2011). The semi-suffix is used after attributive and classifying words or phrases: *a Spielberg Kinda Christmas* (Brems 2011: 290–1). The second is the attributive modifier *of*-binominal such as *an accommodating sort of bloke* or *a lingering kind of swim*; they denote "the qualities named by the adjective premodifying the TN-expression apply to an instance of N₂, not to type" (Brems 2011: 286). As in the case of the EM, there is general bleaching of the first noun involved, as well as a narrowing of the semantic scope. Furthermore, certain pseudo-partitives[16] have grammaticalized into what Brems (2010, 2011) calls valuing (quantifier) uses, e.g. *a bunch of hamfisted dimwits* (Brems 2010: 84). In this example, "*a bunch of* mainly serves to emphasize the negative value of *hamfisted dimwits*, rather than quantifying the referents" (Brems 2010: 84), and in general, Brems (2010: 97–8) defines value quantifiers as "thriv[ing] on the sharing of affective or emotively colored values between the nodal SN and its collocates." Again, there are parallels to the EM in that, like the EM, the valuing construction relies on collocates and context for its semantic values. Therefore, in the context of the whole *of*-binominal family, this transition of full nouns into modifiers is not unique; what is important here is that in the context of EBNP research, this distinction has not been made.

4.4 Binominal Intensifier

The final stage of the EBNP's grammaticalization path is a change into an intensifier. In this final construction, the gradability inherent in the EM shifts to the foreground, and the meaning of the first noun bleaches, from having propositional and degree content to indicating pure degree.

---

[15] Brems (2011: 270) calls them type noun constructions (TN).
[16] Brems (2011: 84) calls them size noun constructions (SN).

4.4 Binominal Intensifier

Intensification is defined by Partington (1993: 178) as "a direct indication of a speaker's desire to use and exploit the expression of hyperbole." Intensifiers can be used "for impressing, praising, persuading, insulting, and generally influencing the listener's reception of the message" (Partington 1993: 178). Intensification differs from quantification (as in the pseudo-partitive) in the degree of precision, in that the intensifiers are indefinite and answer the question: *To what extent?* rather than *how much?* (Athanasiadou 2007: 556; Paradis 1997: 12).

In the BI, [N₁ of a] functions as an intensifier or booster, emphasizing or praising the quality denoted by the adjective (and in some cases the adverb) that follows, e.g. *better* in (4.51a), *powerful* in (4.51b), and *fine* in (4.51c). This means that the *job* is not just *better* but *a lot better*, the *MS PowerPoint* is not just a *powerful tool* but *a really powerful one*; and the *fellow* is not just *a great guy* but *a really great guy*. The first noun has completely delexicalized[17] in that the noun no longer has any individual lexical content and simply intensifies a quality in the following adjective: there seems to be little difference between *what a hell of a good day, what a whale of a good day,* and *what a beast of a good day*.

(4.51)   a. he supported the injunction but added that the city can do *a "hell of a better job"* giving young people alternatives to gang life (COCA)
         b. MS Powerpoint is *a beast of a powerful tool* (COCA)
         c. He's had a chance all evening to tell you what *a whale of a fine fellow* he is. Now it's my turn. (COHA)

The adjectives modified are usually unbounded, gradable adjectives denoting evaluation, physical properties or dimensions, and human propensity, although there are also some tokens with age as well (see Bolinger 1972: 17; for similar analysis with *really*, see also Lorenz 2002).[18] There are also tokens with extreme adjectives, such as *one hell of a gorgeous grandson* (COCA), but these cases are rare, and these adjectives would appear to be construed as unbounded adjectives in these instances (for more discussion see Paradis 2008: 323).

First nouns used in the BI are not only from the abstract category of first nouns, e.g. *bitch* in (4.52a) and *hell* in (4.51a); some members from the

---

[17] Delexicalization as used here is "the reduction of the independent lexical content of a word, or group of words, so that it comes to fulfil a particular function but has no meaning apart from this to contribute to the phrase in which it occurs" (Partington 1993: 183).
[18] Interestingly there are no corpus examples with color, and in examples from the Internet (*a hell of a blue color, a hell of a black eye,* or *one hell of a white knuckle ride*), the color functions as a classifier or is part of a compound; this means that the construction is an EM, not a BI.

animate category have shown initial signs of progressing to this stage, e.g. *whale* in (4.52b) and *beast* in (4.52c).

(4.52) a. You know, friend, this is *a goddamn bitch of a unsatisfactory situation*. (COCA)
  b. It's gonna have *one whale of a hard time* making it in Nashville. (COCA)
  c. Aussie cricketer and *beast of a fast bowler* Mitchell Johnson (NOW)

The sections below will present the semantic and syntactic features of this construction before comparing it with similar developments in the *of*-binominal network.

4.4.1 Head Status

The second noun determines the NP's overall denotation, as demonstrated in examples (4.53a–c). Thus, in example (4.53a), the subject *he* is *having a good time singing* (as shown in (4.53b)). The alternative *having a whale*, given in (4.53c), might mean (if one accepts the metaphorical extension of *whale*) that the subject is birthing or possibly eating a whale; however, the context eliminates these alternative meanings. The verb thus clearly selects the second noun, as can also be seen in examples (4.54a–c). As in the case with the EM and EBNP, the second noun is the semantic head.

(4.53) a. It's Crazy 88 MIKI's turn at the mike and he's having *a whale of a good time* singing Dionne Warwick's "Walk On By" (COCA)
  b. he's having *a good time* singing
  c. #he's having *a whale*

(4.54) a. He'd **do** *a hell of a better job* than anyone else in the United States. (COCA)
  b. He'd **do** *a better job* than anyone else.
  c. *He'd **do** *a hell* than anyone else.

In the few cases where the two nouns do not agree in number, the second noun takes the plural marker (as in the case of *times* in (4.55a)). Subject–verb agreement is not so easy to determine because either the examples with a plural N_2 found in the dataset did not have the BI in subject position, or if it was, the sentence is not in the present tense. Based on constructed examples in (4.55b–c), verb agreement with the second noun sounds intuitively more appropriate. There is clearly confusion over the function and requirements for articles in the second determiner position, as demonstrated in (4.56), with a singular countable second noun without any determiner in the Det₂ position (for further discussion, see the section on determiners).

(4.55) a. We all had good times, *hell of good times*. (Iannuzzi 2008: n.p.)
 b. *hell of good times* **have** come and gone.
 c. ?*hell of good times* **has** come and gone.

(4.56) I had *a hell of good life* after I retired. (NOW)

A possessive pronoun in Det₁ position has scope of the second noun, as in (4.57). The first determiner has scope over N₂ as can be seen in (4.58a–c). All in all, we may conclude that the second noun is also the syntactic head.

(4.57) **His** "*hell of a good run*" ended in 2002. (Star Tribune 2008)[19]

(4.58) a. It's *one helluva big varmint* I got to shoot. (COCA)
 b. It's *one big varmint*.
 c. #It's *one helluva*.

Finally, as with all the previous constructions (except the N+PPs and the head-classifiers), anaphoric reference shows that *one* can substitute the second noun, but not the first, as demonstrated by *hell* in (4.59a–b), and the second noun determines the form of the prenominal referent; *they*, in (4.60b), refers to nude paintings. Therefore, the second noun denotes the nominal reference and is clearly the head of the whole binominal; the second noun is the undisputable head.

(4.59) a. This is *some hell of a big* **tree** "The biggest **one** I could find" (COCA)
 b. *This is *some **hell** of a big tree* and this, *some **one** of a small tree*.

(4.60) a. Chase could paint *a hell of a good nude* when sufficiently moved (COCA)
 b. Chase could paint ***a hell of a good nude*** when sufficiently moved – **they** are the best examples of his work.

4.4.2 Constituency

As is the case with most of the evaluative *of*-binominals, neither the *of*-phrase nor the second NP can be extracted or coordinated. However, a difference is that it can be used in the predicative position, as shown in (4.61a–b). Therefore, [N₁ of (Det) Adj] would appear to be a single constituent.

---

[19] Michelle M. O'Connor [obituary], *Star Tribune*, Minnesota, August 27, 2008 (www.startribune.com).

(4.61) a. The vanilla eclairs *are hell of good* (min_jimn blog 2007)[20]
b. They would have been *hell of fun* to play with (NOW)

Further evidence for [N of (Det) Adj] being a separate constituent is the fact that this unit exhibits greater syntactic freedom than in any of the previous constructions; thus, in some contexts, [N_1 of (Det) Adj] no longer needs the first determiner, as seen in example (4.62a), and can modify a quantifier in (4.62b) (see Trousdale 2012).[21]

(4.62) a. These riders ride *hell of fast* in ziz zaz. (NOW)
b. But what *a devil of a lot of knives* we use in everyday life, he thought. (COCA)

4.4.3 Constraints on the Two Nouns

The first noun in the BI functions as a bleached intensifier, but it retains traces of semantic content, as opposed to a fully grammatical intensifier like *very* which does not (Adamson 2000: 53–4). The first noun is always in singular form, and the whole syntagm can be substituted with a single intensifier without an obvious change in meaning as demonstrated by *very* in (4.63a–b). Although the two nouns usually agree in number, both taking singular form, examples such as *hell of good times* in (4.55) show that first and second noun agreement is not obligatory in this construction.

(4.63) a. *a whale of a good time* singing (COCA)
b. a very good time singing

As was the case in the EM, the first noun is not referential, and it cannot take an antecedent. Therefore, the first noun in the BI no longer denotes a property. The second noun is prototypically a count noun (see examples above) or a collective noun, as in (4.64a). Sporadic examples of mass nouns can be found on the Internet (4.64b), and there seems to be no plausible reason why these constructions should not accept mass nouns. As mentioned above, there are a few examples with plural nouns.

(4.64) a. They have to believe what *a hell of a good football team* we've got now (NOW)

---

[20] min-jimn, A festival of furry things [blog], March 31, 2007 (http://minneapolis.metblogs.com/20 07/03/31/)
[21] Other studies have created a separate category for this form: the adverbial (Denison 2002, 2005), free adjunct (Trousdale 2012), or free adverbs (Traugott 2008a, 2008b).

b. 2 c. skim milk (for a richer and somewhat softer ice cream, use whole milk; if whole milk makes you panic but skim milk makes you sad, use 1% or 2% . . . one way or another, this is *a hell of a good ice cream*) (caribourgrrl blog 2016)²²

Adamson's (2000) analysis of the grammaticalization of lexical items from descriptive modifiers to intensifiers uses premodifier placement as evidence of change in meaning through grammaticalization, i.e. the fact that premodifiers tend to move from descriptive modifier positions at the right of the noun phrase, i.e. closer to the noun head as in *jolly* in (4.65a), leftward to the intensifier positions, further from the head as shown in example (4.65b) (Adamson 2000: 54). This is supported by a range of premodification studies (see Chapter 7 for a more detailed discussion). Therefore, when [N₁ of a] functions as an intensifier, premodification should only be restricted in front of N₁, as demonstrated by example (4.66a). Descriptive modifiers should not be able to appear in front of the first noun, as exemplified by (4.66b) (see Section 7.3.2 for a more detailed analysis).

(4.65) a. A small **jolly** woman
b. A **jolly** small woman (Adamson 2000: 54)

(4.66) a. A **whole**/?**very**/***mere** hell of a long time
b. a ***beautiful**/***red**/***bright** hell of a good day

The BI modifies unbounded descriptive modifiers. In (4.67a) *hell of* is not intensifying *daily* (not gradable) but instead is an EM modifying the combination *daily driver*, meaning *an excellent daily vehicle*. In (4.67b), *dead* is usually a bounded adjective (something is customarily either dead or alive); consequently, the most likely interpretation of this example is that the metaphorical dead rat is very unsatisfactory (i.e. an EM), but not a very dead rat (BI). Finally, the modifiers following the [N of (a)] are usually descriptive modifiers; however, in addition to the descriptive modifier, the second noun can also accept classifiers such as *football* in (4.67c) (see Chapter 7 for more discussion of premodification).

(4.67) a. . . . a body-colored jerry can and a bottle opener on the front bumper (a nice little Easter egg) come together to make *one hell of a **daily driver**. (Campbell 2017)²³

---

²² Recipe for lavender icecream, *The Moose Curry Experience: Eat Real Food* [blog], January 27, 2016 (moosecurrry.blogspot.com).
²³ Bryan Campbell, This hot rod vintage land cruiser is what dreams are made of, April 18, 2017 (www.gearpatrol.com/cars/a349617/fj-company-vintage-land-cruiser/).

b. Given Labour's grand vision is to sweep the boards on September 23 and conquer all of the Maori seats, holding a referendum in a bid to ace them would be *a hell of a dead rat* for Labour to swallow (NOW)
  c. one hell of great **football** player (COCA)

The first noun has lost all lexical content, no longer takes the plural form, and in general, cannot be modified. Therefore, the first noun has lost its 'nounhood'.

4.4.4 Determiners

The first determiner tends to be either emphatic *one/some* in (4.68a–b) or the indefinite article in (4.68c) but can also be left out as in (4.68d). The definite article can also be found, as demonstrated in (4.68e) (Trousdale 2012: 182), but less frequently.[24] Personal pronouns tend not to be found in this position. In sum, determiners in the Det₁ position are predominantly either the *some/one* or an indefinite article.

(4.68) a. it's gonna be **one** *hell of a cold night* to fool around looking for a ride (COHA)
  b. But I'm going to have to have **some** *hell of a good years* to catch Connie Mack. (COCA)
  c. You know, Joey, you're going to make some faithful woman *a hell of a fine fugitive.* (COHA)
  d. *Hell of a sweet kid,* to come from such cruddy parents. (COHA)
  e. And **the** *hell of a fine story* you gave them; you must have enjoyed hearing yourself talk. (Trousdale 2012: 182)

As in both the EBNP and the EM, the second determiner is typically indefinite, and as is seen in the EM, examples can be found where it has been omitted, e.g. in (4.69a), and the second determiner also does not mark number, as seen in (4.69b). A determiner in the Det₂ position is usually an indefinite article; it no longer marks number and does not agree with the second noun.

(4.69) a. once a nervous PROBIE, now a seasoned vet. And *one hell of proud father* (COCA)
  b. We set ourselves *hell of a high standards.* I make no apologies for that (NOW)

---

[24] It can also be found in the EBNP but only in the very infrequent contexts where it is used to refer to an identifiable entity (Keizer 2007a: 89).

4.4.5 Status of Of

As in the EM, the preposition *of* is often present but no longer appears to have semantic content or a function. Reduced forms can be found, as shown in (4.70a–c). Although the majority of the BIs include the preposition, there are some examples with *hell* in use as an intensifier without a preposition as in (4.71a–b). However, in general, the preposition cannot simply be omitted, as demonstrated in (4.71c).

(4.70)   a. the New Deal meant *a whaleuva lot* to the followers of the rod and reel game (Motorland 1933: 13)[25]
         b. we'll have a great fire and cook wienies and coffee and dance and have *a helluva good time* (COHA)
         c. The people who work here are *hella cool*. (COHA)

(4.71)   a. We have *hell good leadership* in both party's [*sic*]. (COCA)
         b. there are *some hell tough ladies* in those books (COCA)
         c. *he had *a whale good yard*

4.4.6 The Properties of the BI

The BI form is the final stage of the grammaticalization process, where the first nouns used in this construction have lost all features of nounhood and their original semantic content. They function as intensifiers of other adjectives and less frequently quantifiers. Partington (1993: 179) provides three central attributes for the behavior of intensifiers: (1) they modify verbs and/or adjectives and adverbs, and some exclusively modify one group or the other (e.g. *very* modifies adjectives and adverbs, and *dearly* exclusively modifies verbs); (2) there are restrictions on the collocates that intensifiers modify; and (3) they are an open word class that recruits heavily.[26] The analysis above demonstrates that all three points apply to the BI. To point (1), [N₁ of a] clearly modifies the adjectives and in rarer cases even adverbs. There are some restrictions, point (2), in that the modified adjectives tend to be unbounded gradable adjectives. To point (3), intensifiers are often recruited from descriptive and evaluative modifiers (e.g. Adamson 2000; Lorenz 2002; Paradis 2000; Partington 1993) and

---

[25] *Motorland* (1933), vols. 32–37: 13. Available online at Google Books (www.google.at/books/edition/Motorland/MloPAAAAIAAJ?hl=en&gbpv=0&bsq=%22whaleuva%20lot%22).
[26] It should be added that some linguists make a closed and open class distinction with the closed class consisting of strongly grammaticalized and therefore bleached elements, e.g. *much, rather, quite,* and *very*, and the open class with lexical items that retain some remnant of their original semantics, e.g. *highly, terribly, horrifically, absolutely* (e.g. Ghesquière 2014: 35–6; Lorenz 2002: 144).

are often recruited from *of*-binominals (e.g. Brems 2003; Davidse 2009; Denison 2002, 2005; Traugott 2008a, 2008b; Trousdale 2012).

Syntactically, [N of (a)] has gone from being the head of an adjectival phrase (AP) in the EM to being a part of the AP in the BI, i.e. an adjectival intensifier. Therefore, the underlying structure of the BI is [_NP_ [Det] [[_AP_ [_INT_ N_I of a] [Adj]] [N_2]]]. It is at this stage that there is unequivocal evidence of the reanalysis posited by Aarts (1998) for the EBNP, namely, the combination [[N of (a)] [Adj]] can stand alone as a constituent.

Adamson (2000: 44, 54) claims that the affective adverb *lovely* has developed an intensifier form; see example (4.72) where *lovely* means [*very* + approval] and intensifies *warm*. On the basis of this analysis, she argues that there is a link between affective adjectives and intensifiers, i.e. it suggests a semantic relation between affective adjectives and adverbs. This shared function might explain why affective adjectives often develop intensifier functions (Adamson 2000: 53–5).

(4.72)   a lovely warm room

Matthews (2014: 87–104) also argues that adjectives such as *great*, *little*, and *dirty* can also function as intensifiers and demonstrates this with lexical items with opposing semantics, e.g. a *pretty face*, *an ugly face*, and *a pretty ugly face* (Matthews 2014: 101). Matthews (2014: 103) explains that

> [i]f either adjective were subordinate, it would be the adjective of value that 'qualifies', as Dixon puts it, the one that follows, not the opposite. In such a use it can easily be thought of as intensifying: *a lovely large garden*, for example, would be said of a garden pleasingly and thus especially large.

Of-binominals transitioning to intensifiers have also been found in other *of*-binominal families: Denison (2002, 2005) and Traugott (2007, 2008a, 2008b), for instance, both find a similar final stage for the English partitive constructions (*a lot of NP*, *a kind of NP*) grammaticalization path in constructions such as *lots of fun*. Furthermore, numerous researchers in both synchronic (Aijmer 2002: 175–209; Keizer 2007a: 153–84) and diachronic studies (Brems 2010, 2011; Denison 2002, 2005; Margerie 2011; Traugott 2008a, 2008b) have found that both *kind-of* and *sort-of*, as well as *bit-of*, *bunch-of*, *a lot-of*, become approximators: *kind of lousy*, *kinda wicked*.

Traugott (2007) argues that EBNPs do not generally develop into degree modifier or intensifier constructions because there is no inference of quantity. However, Trousdale (2012: 181) points out that *hell* in [*hell of a*] does indeed develop an intensifier function and specifically functions as a booster similar to *a lot*. Nonetheless, Trousdale (2012), in his analysis, does not claim that this evidence refutes Traugott's claim, merely that *hell of* would be the exception. This study agrees with Trousdale that *hell* is used as an intensifier in BI constructions, but *hell* is not unique in this respect; other first nouns found in this dataset are used productively in this construction.

Why the constant push along this cline or movement toward intensity? Lorenz (2002) suggests that there is a link between novelty and expressivity, and that the most unusual formulations are the most expressive. This means that nouns progressing along this path bleach to the extent that they can be used in both the EM and the BI. If they become frequent in these forms, they lose their novelty and, thereby, their expressivity value, which is the central function of intensifiers (Lorenz 2002: 143). As Bolinger (1972: 18) explains, with the intensifier category "all means of emphasis quickly grow stale and need to be replaced," meaning this construction is maintained by the constant need for creative expression.

4.5 Conclusion

This chapter has sketched out a process in which the first noun in the EBNP designates properties, whether subjective evaluative or physical evaluative, and ascribes these to the referent. In the EM, it is the abstract 'evaluativeness' of the EBNP that remains, while the *of*-binominal becomes a subjective-evaluative modifier, profiling a scalar extreme of a property defined by context. The implied degree implicit in the EM is then profiled in the BI, while the subjective content is backgrounded or lost. This historical development is therefore a schematic shift from a noun functioning as a modifier to an extreme modifier, and subsequently to a scalar intensifier (see (1)–(3) below).

(1) **EBNP** [N_1] or [N_1 of a] ascribes physical or abstract evaluative properties to N_2.
(2) **EM** [N_1 of a] ascribes abstract, evaluative properties to N_2: functions as an extreme modifier, and predominantly occupies the leftward position of the NP.
(3) **BI** [N_1 of a] functions as a scalar degree modifier: co-occurs with another descriptive or value adjective and has a fixed leftward position in the AP.

Through this development, the [N_1 of a] completes a grammaticalization path similar to lexical items described by Paradis (2000) and Adamson (2000), moving from descriptive uses in the EBNP and subjective ones in the EM to intensifying uses in the final stage, the BI. This analysis is not only

Table 4.2 *Overview of the evaluative categories: EBNP, EM, and BI*

FEATURE	EBNP	EM	BI
Of	Mandatory, no semantic meaning	Mandatory no semantic meaning	Usually required, no semantic meaning
Determiner 1	Open, canonically indefinite article, limited definite article	Open, can be absent, canonically indefinite article or *some/one*	Open, can be absent canonically indefinite article *some/one*
Determiner 2	Indefinite or zero article/marks number	Indefinite or absent/no longer marks number	Indefinite or absent/no longer marks number
Head	N_2 is semantic/discourse head, syntactic evidence inconclusive	N_2 is semantic/syntactic/discourse head	N_2 is semantic/syntactic/discourse head
Function of construction	N_1 ascribes property to N_2	[N_1 of a] functions as an extreme modifier	[N, of a] functions as an intensifier of following adj
Determiner 1 scope	Prototypically whole construction	Whole construction	Whole construction
Modification	Irregular in front of N_1/open in front of N_2	Limited in front of N_1/open in front of N_2	Almost exclusively before N_2
Constituency	No movement or *of*-coordination	No movement or *of*-coordination	No movement or *of*-coordination
N, lexicality	Yes plural, yes modification	No plural, limited modification	No plural, no modification
N_1 & N_2 agreement	Agree in number	Usually agree in number	Do not have to agree in number
N_2	Count/collective	Count/collective	Count/collective/mass

4.5 Conclusion

supported by Adamson's (2000) study of *lovely* but also reciprocally supports her hypothesis that there is indeed a link between evaluative modifiers and degree modifiers. However, the grammaticalization of *of*-binominals to degree modifiers has also been documented in studies of measure *of*-constructions, and therefore, it is not clear if it is the internal semantics of these phrases that have led to this development or its analogy between similar syntactic forms in the family.

The general analysis shows that there are pragmatic, semantic, morpho-syntactic, and phonological criteria to support a categorical differentiation between EBNPs, EMs, and BIs. Pragmatic-semantic differences are seen in the different functions that these *of*-binominals fulfill (i.e. modifying, intensifying), and in differences in semantic prosody between the EBNP and EM. These changes are then evinced in the variation in determiner and second noun selection, changes in the syntactic structure and premodification patterns. They eventually allow for conflation of [N of (a)] to a single lexical item.

Finally, previous work on the grammaticalization of the *of*-binominals has almost exclusively focused on the quantity/size forms of these constructions and not the evaluative forms such as the EBNP. Moreover, work on the evaluative forms of the *of*-binominal has predominantly focused on the EBNP category in isolation. Therefore, this book contributes not only to the discussion of the EBNP but also to the discussion on premodification by demonstrating that the *of*-binominals, like single lexemes (e.g. *very*, *lovely*), have progressed along this grammaticalization path from descriptive functions to intensifier ones (see Chapter 7 for more details).

CHAPTER 5

Three Case Studies: Cake, Beast, *and* Hell

5.1 Introduction

So far, this book has primarily discussed the present state of this family of constructions as found in corpus data. However, as Lehmann (2002: 210) points out, a synchronic variation is the result of diachronic processes. This chapter will discuss some of these processes. Concretely, I apply the classification criteria discussed in Chapters 3 and 4 in order to examine the path of the first nouns *cake, beast,* and *hell* through these constructions. This chapter examines the realizations of these three first nouns in the six *of*-binominal constructions: the prototypical N+PP, the head-classifier, the pseudo-partitive, the EBNP, the EM, and the BI. The first nouns were chosen because *cake* is a frequent, conventionalized pseudo-partitive, *beast* as a very frequent, animate first noun that is used in the EBNP and EM, and *hell* as it has grammaticalized furthest and is the most frequent first noun in the EM and BI in Present-Day English (PDE). Each noun illustrates a slightly different function in the constructions.

Another question that a study of these first nouns addresses is whether progression along this path leads to the grammaticalization or lexicalization of the first nouns (the difference between the two will be discussed in more detail in the following section). The reason that this path may be considered lexicalization is that there is evidence of univerbation in the most frequent forms, such as *helluva, hella, whaleuva,* and possibly *beasta*; the most frequent of these new lexical forms then join the adjectival and intensifier paradigms. Furthermore, intensifiers that function similarly to the BI are still lexical, meaning that they are not fully grammatical items that would be the result of a more prototypical grammatical cline.

Looking at first attestations in the Penn-Helsinki Parsed Corpus of Middle English (PPCME; 1150–1500) the *Oxford English Dictionary* (OED), the corpus of *Early English Books Online* (EEBO; 1471–1690), the Archer Corpus (Archer; 1600–1999), and the Corpus of Historical American English (COHA; 1810–2015),[1] this study tries to piece together the diachronic development of these three nouns before discussing in more detail the question of whether this process could be considered grammaticalization or lexicalization.

5.2 Grammaticalization or Lexicalization

Lexicalization, in the most general sense of the term, is "the process by which new items that are considered 'lexical' ... come into being" (Brinton & Traugott 2005: 32). It is, therefore, the process

> whereby in certain linguistic contexts speakers use a syntactic construction or word as a new *contentful* form with formal and semantic properties that are not completely derivable or predictable from the constituents of the construction or the word formation pattern. Over time there may be further loss of internal constituency, and the item may become more lexical. (Brinton & Traugott 2005: 96; my emphasis)

This definition of lexicalization conceptualizes the process as gradual, and entails fusion, increasing degrees of lexicality, a decrease in type or token productivity, and univerbation (Lightfoot 2011: 445).

In general terms, grammaticalization is a gradual process in which a linguistic element becomes grammatical or more grammatical (Lehmann 2002: 11), meaning that it is "[t]he process whereby lexical material in highly constrained pragmatic and morpho-syntactic contexts is assigned grammatical function, and once grammatical, is assigned increasingly grammatical, operator-like function" (Traugott 2003: 645). A number of different processes have been proposed for grammaticalization (see Hopper 1991: 22–33; Lehmann 2002); however, the processes that are important for this study are those that distinguish grammaticalization from lexicalization.

The distinction between grammaticalization and lexicalization is still being debated (see further Anttila [1972] 1989; Giacalone Ramat 1998; Himmelmann 2004; Van der Auwera 2002). Part of the issue is that a clear distinction between lexical and grammatical categories is problematic, which muddies the distinction between the grammaticalization and lexicalization processes. This means, as Brinton and Traugott (2005: 89–110) argue, both processes share similar features and changes and,

---

[1] Data extracted before the 2021 update.

Table 5.1 *Parallels between lexicalization and grammaticalization*
(Brinton & Traugott 2005: 110)

FEATURES	LEXICALIZATION	GRAMMATICALIZATION
Gradualness	+	+
Unidirectionality	+	+
Fusion	+	+
Coalescence	+	+
Demotivation	+	+
Metaphorization/metonymization	+	+
Decategorialization	–	+
Bleaching	–	+
Subjectification	–	+
Productivity	–	+
Frequency	–	+
Typological generality	–	+

therefore, are easily conflated (see Table 5.1; see also Fischer 2008; Haas 2007; Heine & Narrog 2010).

Brinton and Traugott (2005: 110) argue that although there is overlap between lexicalization and grammaticalization, there are several processes that are unique to grammaticalization, such as decategorialization, bleaching, subjectification, greater productivity, an increase of frequency, and typological generality. The first three processes include the loss of semantic content and morpho-syntactic features and an increase of speaker orientation; the final three predict greater type and token use. This first three processes relate to this study.

Decategorialization deals with morpho-syntactic class markers, bleaching involves loss of meaning, and subjectification entails a shift from external to internal speaker meaning. In detail, decategorialization involves the loss of word-class features, e.g. *face* in *in the face of* can no longer take a demonstrative **in that/this face of* (Hopper 1991: 30–1). In this context *face* is losing the features of nounhood. Semantic bleaching is a process in which the semantic meaning of a word changes or fades to the point where it eventually signals only a grammatical function: for example, the auxiliary verb *will* initially was a full lexical verb meaning 'want' and, now, has become an auxiliary verb indicating intention, predictions, or future (Hopper & Traugott 2003: 97–8). Finally, Traugott (1995: 32) defines subjectification as:

broadly speaking, the development of a grammatically identifiable expression of speaker belief or speaker attitude to what is said. It is a gradient phenomenon, whereby forms and constructions that at first express primarily concrete, lexical, and objective meanings come through repeated use in local syntactic contexts to serve increasingly abstract, pragmatic, interpersonal, and speaker-based functions.

Traugott (1982: 253) proposes that the change of meaning in the propositional content tends to shift from "less personal to more personal" with the more personal meaning being "more anchored in the context of the speech act, particularly the speaker's orientation to situation, text, and interpersonal relations." Langacker (1990: 16) similarly claims that "meanings tend to become increasingly situated in the speaker's subjective belief/attitude toward the situation" and "at least some instances of grammaticalization involve subjectification." An example would be the development of epistemic modals such as *must*, which first meant 'I ought to' in *I must be home by 10* to 'I conclude that' in *it must be raining* (Hopper & Traugott 2003: 92)

The assumption is that if we find evidence of these three changes in the data, that we are indeed looking at grammaticalization. Section 5.6 will discuss this in more detail.

5.3 Case Study 1: *Cake*

According to the OED, the noun *cake* entered English in the thirteenth century (see Example (5.1a)) and was initially used, similarly to *loaf* (as can be seen in (5.1b)), as a measure term for a bread-like substance. The sweetened version, which is the one that eventually developed evaluative semantics, began to appear in the fourteenth century, as shown by example (5.1c). There appear to be examples of *cake* in the N+PP as early as the fourteenth century (5.1d).

(5.1)   a. *Hire cake* bearneð o þe stan. (*ca* 1230 OED)
'Her cake is burning on the stone.' (my gloss)
b. That … he offre a silueren peny, and *a round kaak of breed*. (1382 OED)
'… he offers a silver penny and a round cake of bread.' (my gloss)
c. Wymmen sprenge togidere talwȝ þat þei make *swete cakis* to þe qween of heuene (ante 1382 OED)
'Women mixed together flour that they make sweet cakes for the queen of heaven' (my gloss)
d. *Gloss. W. de Bibbesworth* (Cambr.) (1929) 462   Kakenole [*glossed*] *a cake of spices* [*a*1325 *Arun.* a spiced kake, *a*1325 *Trin. Cambr.* a kake wyth spices] (ante 1325 OED)

In N+PP *of*-binominals, the PP can provide a range of information, such as indicating possession (5.2a) or ascribing a feature to a cake (5.2b): for example, either highlighting an important ingredient in (5.2c) or describing an attribute of a cake in (5.2d). *Cake* in this construction can take the plural form (5.3).

(5.2) a. in respect of his body, as being fed by raues [ravens] and by *the little cake of a poore widow*, dwelling in zarepta, 1: Kings 17 (1631 EEBO)
b. ye shall geue *a cake of the first* of youre dowe vnto an heue offerynge ... (1530 EEBO)
c. let it be *a swete cake of fyne floure* myngled with oyle (1540 EEBO)
d. twentie persons attending came aboord, brough a Bullocke, bread, quinces, and other Fruites, and *a cake of great roundness and thickness* ... (1625 EEBO)

(5.3) they baked *swete cakes of the dowe* (1530 EEBO)

The first clear historical examples of *cake* in the head-classifier construction appear at the end of the sixteenth century (5.4). When *cake* is used in the N+PP, the PP modifier often describes a feature of the *cake* (5.2 c–d); in the head-classifier the *cake* is classified by the material it is made of, such as *rye* in (5.4). Through metaphorical extension, *cake* in the head-classifiers becomes abstract or collocates with abstract second nouns, such as *sluttery* in (5.5), and, more clearly, *sincerity* and *truth* in (5.6). *Cake* appears predominantly in the intrinsic head-classifier, where we find both metaphorical cakes in (5.5) and (5.6) and physical cakes in (5.4). Example (5.6) also illustrates that *cake* takes the plural form in this construction.

(5.4) for he accustomed, to feade him selfe with *a cake of rye*, the whiche he grounde, and baked vppon the coles ... (1556 EEBO)

(5.5) than remove *the incrustated Cake of Sluttery*, the constant Nursery of Flies and Beet (1672–81; PPCEME)

(5.6) let us keepe the feast, not with old leven, neither with the leven of malice and wickednesse; but with *the unlovened cakes of sincerity and truth* (1627 EEBO)

It would appear that the pseudo-partitive construction with *cake* as the first noun appears before the head-classifier use (see Chapter 6 for a discussion of the implications of this). In the OED, examples of *cake* in the pseudo-partitive can be found as early as the fourteenth century as in (5.7a), and in the fifteenth century there are examples of *cake* used as a measurement or form meaning outside of the pseudo-partitive as in

5.3 Case Study 1: Cake

(5.7b) (OED). *Cake* is primarily used in a part noun pseudo-partitive; the first noun indicates a certain form, and the second noun is the head (the alternative, with *cake* as head, would make *cake* referential and the construction a head-classifier): [NP[Q-compl[Det *a*] [N *cake*]] [LE *of*] [N-head *soap*]]. The first noun most frequently co-occurs with solid second nouns such as *bread* (5.7a), *ice* (5.8), and later *soap* (5.8b). However, in general, *cake* denotes an indistinct form and can therefore be used with a range of other first nouns such as *tallow* in (5.9a) and *rosin* in (5.9b). *Cake* takes the plural marker as demonstrated in (5.9a–b).

(5.7) a. That ... he offre a silueren peny, and *a round kaak of breed*. (1382 OED)
'... he offers a silver penny and a round cake of bread' (my gloss)
b. Take fayre Flowre & raw 30llkys of Eyroun, & Sugre, & Salt, & pouder of Gyngere, & Safroun, & make *fayre cakes* & þan take marow ... (ante 1450 cookbook OED)

(5.8) a. when it thawed, *the great cakes of yce* brake down many great bridges ... (1565 EEBO)
b. Then again I find a stone imitation of *a cake of soap* in the water to wash with ... (1887 COHA)

(5.9) a. Hole cakes of rendred Tallow (1541 OED)
b. Wee have taken here in a Vessel, *14 cakes of Rosin*. (1652 OED)

Cake usually refers to a physical object in the N+PP and the head-classifier and refers to a quantity or shape in the pseudo-partitive. The EBNP use is different. The first attestations of *cake* in the EBNP, as exemplified by (5.10a), appear in the late twentieth century. *Cake* appears predominantly in Den Dikken's (2006: 162) comparative EBNP (or what he calls a comparative qualitative binominal noun phrase [QBNP]), drawing a comparison between the shape or optical features of *a cake* and the exteriors of physical things such as *a building* in (5.10a). In later examples, *cake* is used with abstract second nouns such as *career* in (5.10b), entailing more a sense of approval than ascribing physical characteristics, and thereby developing an EM function. No plural examples in the EBNP were found in the corpora.

(5.10) a. as much as the industrial exhibit now housed in the former palace of Soviet-Chinese Friendship in Shanghai differs from what was originally intended when *that towering wedding cake of a building* was gratefully received as a present from the Soviet Union (1973 COHA)
b. Emmy would just be extra icing on *her already-rich she-devil's food cake of a career*. (1991 COCA)

The animate and abstract first nouns tend to represent the more prototypical first nouns in the EM. In the case of *cake*, the corpus data shows a metaphorical extension from ascribing cake-like 'properties' to physical second nouns to approbation of abstract nouns such as *careers* in (5.10b). Nevertheless, the premodification such as *already-rich* and *devil food* would indicate that this is still the EBNP use. There are no clear examples of *cake* used in the EM in the corpora, but a few can be found on the Internet, as demonstrated in (5.11), where it modifies the very abstract concept of 'a time'. In (5.11), it is unclear if *cake* is a positive evaluation (*wonderful time*) or negative (*difficult time*), but it no longer refers to physical features of cakes, as was the case in the EBNP but purely speaker evaluation. There are no examples with *cake* used in the plural form in either the EBNP or the EM. Furthermore, there were no examples found with *cake* being used in the BI.

(5.11) The JLA would have *a cake of a time* getting this done (Comic clint post 2016)[2]

In sum, the fact that the pseudo-partitive constructions appeared first would indicate that this construction is not directly involved in the primary grammaticalization path (see Chapter 6 for more discussion). The development of this first noun shows that *cake* was used in the first three constructions much earlier than the evaluative ones: even in the larger corpora, the EBNP examples appear toward the end of the twentieth century, and the EM examples can only be found on the Internet. This transition to the evaluative function may have been facilitated through the semantic extension in the head-classifier from reference to a physical cake to an abstract one in the nineteenth century. This transition may also have been supported by changes in the meaning of *cake* itself, where it becomes more subjective and comes to refer to someone foolish or silly in the eighteenth century, or used to refer to a prostitute or an attractive woman in the twentieth century (OED). This section shows then the semantic meaning of *cake*, in these *of*-binominals, changes from a typical noun evoking a referent in the N+PP and head-classifier and a quantity or shape in the pseudo-partitive, to a speaker's evaluation of a physical form in the EBNP, and finally just subjective evaluation in the EM. This demonstrates a typical subjectification path and will be discussed in more detail in Section 5.6.

---

[2] Comic clint, Stealing from the collector: The water cooler [Forum post], Comic Collector Live, Feburary 7, 2016 (www.comiccollectorlive.com/forum/default.aspx?g=posts&t=44913).

5.4 Case Study 2: *Beast*

The noun *beast* enters the English language in the Middle English period (OED), with the earliest attested uses in the *of*-binominal found in the PPCME appearing at around the thirteenth century in constructions indicating a locative relation. In this form, the prepositional phrase identifies or specifies the first noun by denoting the overall referent's source or location, such as hell, as seen in example (5.12).

(5.12) þet te *beast of helle*, hwen he snakereð toward ow forte biten on ow ... (ca 1200 PPCME)
'So that the beast of hell, when he sneaks towards you in order to bite you ...' (Lundskær-Nielsen 1993: 139)

In the EEBO, *beast* in N+PP is used not just in locative (5.13a) and source constructions (both physical in (5.13a) and abstract in (5.12)), but also with prepositional phrases denoting possession (5.13b) and ascribing attributive properties (5.13c). As demonstrated in examples (5.13d), *beast* can be used in plural form.

(5.13) a. they after this manner sealed with the marke of *the grett beast of the erth*. (1528 EEBO)
b. here foloweth the iudgement and sentence of god against all them whiche worship *this beast of antichrist* (1549 EEBO)
c. there is also founde *a foure foted beast of monstrous shape* (1553 EEBO)
d. surely the mountaines bring him forthe grasse, where *all the beasts of the field* playe (1561 EEBO)

The first examples of *beast* in the head-classifier in the corpora can be found in the mid-sixteenth century, as shown in (5.14a–b). With this first noun, there are examples of both types of head-classifiers: the intrinsic uses in (5.14a) and taxonomic forms as in (5.14b). The transition from *beast*'s use in *of*-binominals where the prepositional phrase specifies the first noun's location (*beasts of the field* as opposed to *beasts of the sky*) to ones where it categorizes the head in terms of its material or its taxonomic status (e.g. *a beast of burden* and *a beast of prey*) is not so easy to identify. The loss of the definite article in *beasts of the field* to *beasts of field*, is a strong indication of this change.[3] However, one feels that even in examples like *beasts of the field*, *the field* is non-specific, so this transition might have taken place in several stages. Example (5.15) is another instance where both readings, N+PP and head-classifier, are potentially possible: *sinners* may be the possessor of the

---
[3] *Beast of field* sounds a bit antiquated, but there are some modern examples, e.g. "We comprehend our position as a 'higher' organism superior to *the beast of field and water* ..." (Pins 2018: n.p.).

beast (N+PP) but might also define the type of *beast* (head-classifier). As shown in examples such as (5.16), *beast* can appear in head-classifiers in both singular and plural form.

(5.14)   a. vpon the seyd *beast of destruccyon* (1545 EEBO)
          b. and in that pastyme hauyng to *euery beast of venery* but two dogges at the moste (1541 EEBO)

(5.15)   would he haue *the beasts of sinners* die & their vices lieu? (1593 EEBO)

(5.16)   to sell all *the beasts of burthen*, except a fewe nedefull (1578 EEBO)

As mentioned above, predominantly inanimate first nouns tend to develop pseudo-partitive meanings, and unsurprisingly, *beast* does not appear to be used in this form. However, there are some animate first noun exceptions to this general trend, such as *snake* (for further discussion of *snake* as a pseudo-partitive, see Chapter 6). Historically, *beast* extended from referring to or evoking a physical animal or a group of animals (as seen in the N+PP and the head-classifier) to signifying abstract properties such as 'animal-like manner or nature', as demonstrated in (5.17a). The first examples of *beast* in the EBNP are in the sixteenth century with *beast* describing the referent's manner as in (5.17b–c). Only in later examples, when collocating with inanimate objects does the first noun start to signal physical dimension, i.e. largeness (5.17d). This first EBNP use of *beast*, indicating manner, entails a strong sense of opprobrium, missing in the later physical dimension examples. There are also examples of plural EBNPs in the EEBO, as demonstrated in example (5.18)

(5.17)   a. O powerfull Love, that in some respects makes *a Beast a Man*: in some other, *a Man* a beast. (1616 OED)
          b. he shal so abace him selfe, that he shal become seruante vnto synne now receaued, &; beyng geuen there vnto, how great *a beast of a man* (a cruell thyng to be spoken) shal he be made then? (1555 EEBO)
          c. Enter Mrs. Guzzle, drunk Guzzle: Where's *my drunken beast of a husband*? (1770 ARCHER)
          d. we got friendly at once – couldn't help it, scrambling into *that beast of a boat* while the rest laughed at us. (1886 COHA)

(5.18)   see (said summer) how some of *these beasts of advocates* use their clients, like tennis-balls, sending'em from post to pillar, and tossing them backward and forward ... (1692 EEBO)

A bleached form of *beast* is used in the EM: the ascription of physical properties prominent in *beast*'s use in the EBNP has disappeared, and the opprobrium aspect shifts to the forefront. The first examples of potential

5.4 Case Study 2: Beast

EMs, such as (5.19a–b), begin to appear in the seventeenth century: in (5.19a), the context would allow for a large reading (EBNP), but also the speaker's subjective evaluation of the *horse* (EM). The use of the definite article in front of the first noun would also indicate an EM reading. In example (5.19b), the properties of manner and size that *beast* ascribes in the EBNP are no longer a potential reading: the speaker is clearly expressing their evaluation of the argument, and the premodifier *horned* intensifies *beast* instead of ascribing a descriptive property to it (the fact that it is horned makes the argument even more difficult). In this example, no beast-like properties, either manner or physical size, are being ascribed to the second noun, but the speaker gives an evaluation of the second noun. Only the singular form was found in the corpora.

(5.19) a. aye, I lost *the finest beast of a mare* in all Devonshire (1678 EEBO)
        b. now this ... is *a horned beast of an argument*: it is a curst dilemma, which hath long horns (1687 EEBO)

Although *beast* began to be used in the EM very early, tokens of the BI can only be found in the last decade in COCA, as in (5.20). In these examples, *beast* intensifies the following modifier. Examples of the BI are only found in singular form.

(5.20) a. what Americans face – or rather refuse to face – on their doorstep is *a beast of a frightening new order*: A Clockwork Orange set to ranchera music. (2010 COCA)
        b. MS Powerpoint is *a beast of a powerful tool*, and immensely popular for giving people the ability to make presentations without making them think much. (2012 COCA)

Beast in both the EM and BI constructions appears to have a shortened form, *beasta*. Although the urban dictionary (urbandictionary) defines it as denoting someone who has a low hanging chain or sporting diamonds and other fancy jewelry, that would not explain its uses in examples (5.21a–b). In the first example *beasta* appears to be an EM and in the second a BI.

(5.21) a. They better thake [sic] things to another level, fast, because this is *an absolute beasta benchmark* (iWeb [Davies 2018])
        b. Barthelemys [sic] *a beasta big guy* who is very strong (iWeb [Davies 2018])

As was the case with *cake*, in these constructions *beast* demonstrates semantic bleaching, changing from a noun evoking a referent in the N+PP and head-classifier to, in the EBNP, indicating a large size or beast-like manner to, in the EM, ascribing difficulty or approbation, and then merely functioning as a booster in the BI. It has clearly moved from denoting an external referent to ascribing an internal speaker evaluation. Finally, before looking at the final case study, it should be noted that instances of the oblique construction (e.g. *every beast of theirs* [1683 EEBO]) and the partitive (e.g. *the most subtle beast of all* [1661 EEBO]) appear in the corpus data, although infrequently. Whether they play a role in this grammaticalization path and what that role might be is still unclear. Further research is needed.

5.5 Case Study 3: *Hell*

Both synchronically and diachronically, *hell* is the most frequent first noun found in the dataset. Of Germanic origin, it begins to appear in Old English denoting a dwelling place of the dead and the grave, before being metaphorically extended to denote a terrestrial place of misery and suffering: example (5.22a) is listed as its first use for the dwelling place of the dead, and (5.22b) is its first use as a metaphorical extension to describe a person (OED).

(5.22)   a. (Mercian) cyme deað ofer hie & astigen hie in *helle* lifgende. (early Old English OED)
'Death came over them and they descended into hell alive.' (my gloss)
b. Hee was called *the Hell of the worlde* (1586 OED)
'He was called the hell of the world' (my gloss)

In the N+PP, we find examples in the sixteenth century of *hell* used as both a place in the afterlife (5.23a) and a metaphorical extension into the secular world (5.23b). The *of*-binominal can be used to specify possession (5.23c) or to ascribe a feature to *hell* (5.23d). It can appear in plural form (5.24).

(5.23)   a. our sauiour Jesus christ, did in his owne person, go downe into *the hell of the damned* (1571 EEBO)
b. king: *the hell of life* that hangs vpon the Crowne, the daily cares, the nightly dreames ... (1594 EEBO)
c. Thair was also infernus partum, *the hell of the fatheris* (1552 EEBO)
d. it should also cause the vtter losse and dampnacion in *hell of many thousand souls* (1530 EEBO)

(5.24)   give us new heavens and *new hells of his own invention* (1645 EEBO)

For all three first nouns discussed in this chapter, *hell, beast,* and *cake,* there are ambiguous contexts in which an N+PP or a head-classifier reading

5.5 Case Study 3: Hell

is possible. Examples for *hell* can be found in (5.25a), where the speaker may wish to ascribe the attribute of having *fire* to *hell* (N+PP), or he/she may be defining what type of *hell*, *a hell of fire* as opposed to *a hell of ice* (head-classifier). The first clear uses of *hell* in this construction can be found at the end of the sixteenth century (5.25b) (although with so few tokens it is hard to say definitely). *Hell* is primarily found in the intrinsic head-classifier in the data. *Hell* can be used in the head-classifier in singular (5.25) and plural forms (5.26).

(5.25) a. than hauying two fete to be cast in *the hell of unquencheable fyre* (1538 EEBO)
b. She made no reckoning of his importunate and diligent seruice, which drewe *a Hell of tormentinge thoughts* vppon Tarisius. (1588 OED)

(5.26) Heauen of hopes I haue midst *hells of Feares* (1616 EEBO)

Although primarily inanimate first nouns tend to develop pseudo-partitive meanings, *hell* is an exception to this trend. There are examples that indicate that *hell* has developed quantifier uses, as demonstrated by (5.27a–b); however, the examples are extremely rare in the dataset. In (5.27a), the most likely semantic interpretation of *hell of* is 'a large number of problems', and in (5.27b), many or a lot of microwaves were fired. The clearest examples are in the more contemporary corpora, but there are some potential pseudo-partitive readings in some tokens from the EEBO, as in (5.28): the intensifier *very* strengthens the quantifier reading (*very many woes*) and the verb *heaped* selects the second noun as head.

(5.27) a. If force is used, it may cause *hell of problems* in all the Arab world, especially the friends of the United States. (2002 COCA)
b. With the click of a mouse he could fire *a hell of microwaves* up at the ionosphere (2006 COCA)

(5.28) heere woe and there woe, and *a very hell of woes* is heaped vppon mee (1601 EEBO)

Although rare, these examples are interesting for two reasons: one, *hell* is the only abstract noun from the data sample used in the pseudo-partitive, and two, it is the only first noun to develop a quantitative pseudo-partitive function. Unlike the head-classifiers, the second noun is clearly the head in these constructions; *hell* functions as a more emotive version of 'a lot of':
[$_{NP}$ [$_{Q\text{-compl}}$[$_{Det}$ *a*] [$_N$ *hell*]] [$_{LE}$ *of*] [$_{N\text{-head}}$ *microwaves*]].

In general, *hell* in the EBNP is used in an abstract sense in that it no longer refers to the abode of the dead but transposes hell-like properties onto some entity and has primarily an affective meaning. The *hell* used in the EBNP expresses a strong speaker subjective evaluation comparable to its adjectival form *hellish* (Aarts 1998: 136). Trousdale's (2012: 182) diachronic study of *hell* found that the first examples of *hell* in the EBNP, although ambiguous, began to appear in the seventeenth century, as shown in (5.29a) and (5.29b). Example (5.29a) comes from Shakespeare's Sonnet 120, and while the characteristic indefinite article in the second determiner position is missing, *hell* would appear to function as a modifier of *time*, i.e. *a hellish time*. The context excludes a quantifier or head-classifier reading. In (5.29b), we find a more prototypical EBNP with the indefinite article in the second determiner position.

(5.29) a. For if you were by my unkindness shaken, As I by yours, y' haue past *a hell of time* (1609 OED)
b. Old Nick, I am sure, would not be a Whore, It's grown such *a Hell of a calling* (ca 1680 OED).

Because *hell* and most of the first nouns from the abstract group, such as *bitch, devil, bastard*, and *honey*, are already used metaphorically in the EBNP, it is difficult to pinpoint the exact transition between the EBNP and the EM use. This is particularly true in the case of *hell*. The transition between *hell* ascribing 'hellish' properties and *hell* operating as an evaluative modifier, meaning 'very bad', is indistinct, as demonstrated in example (5.30). Instead, EMs with the noun *hell* (or any of the other nouns in this group) are characterized by the loss of the adjectival alternative (if they have one), e.g. *hellish*, and even more clearly with a change in semantic prosody.

(5.30) This is *a hell of a council of war*. (1776 OED)

Historically, unambiguous examples of *hell* in the EM begin to appear in the nineteenth century with the change from negative to positive prosody, as demonstrated in examples (5.31a–b): in (5.31a) *hell* seems to function like *great* and in (5.31b) as *great/wonderful*. In the more contemporary forms, there is also a change in the collocation patterns, in that *hell* in the EM starts to modify animate second nouns in (5.31c), and in these linguistic contexts, *hellish* is no longer an alternative. The first reduced EMs appear in COHA at the beginning of the twentieth century with *helluva* (5.32a) and *hella* at the start of the twenty-first century (5.32b).

(5.31) a. an' tell de boys he in *a hell of a hurry*, sah! (1867 COHA)
b. He walked over to Maggie and whispered in her ear. "Ah, what deh hell, Mag? Come ahn and we'll have *a hell of a time*." (1893 COHA)

5.5 Case Study 3: Hell

c. When I ask about John Wayne, his eyes light up. "He's my favorite," he says with a shyness that manifests itself in conversation as great enthusiasm for whatever question is asked. "He was a great actor and *a hell of a man*." (1999 COCA)

(5.32) a. "And *a helluva recommendation* we would get from him, too, I bet yer!" (1912 COHA)
b. You mess with them even once, believe me, you'd better be *one hella witch* to keep me from strangling you. (2006 COHA)

The fact that *hell* might have an intensifying function in the *of*-binominal is first noted peripherally by Bolinger (1972: 59) and is later discussed in more detail in Trousdale (2012). *Hell* is the most frequent first noun in the BI (in both COCA and COHA) and might, therefore, well be the forerunner of this construction. *Hell* in the BI functions as a booster, meaning 'to a high degree', and is similar to but more emotive than *very*; expletive semantics most likely allows it greater expressiveness. The first tokens of the intensifier use of *hell* in COHA appear in the nineteenth century (see examples (5.33a–b)). The binominal intensifier collocates with gradable unbounded adjectives, such as *long, good, fine, nice*, and *bad*.

(5.33) a. Thomas Burchard, testified that several nights since he had been fleeced at *the same hell of a large sum* (1839 COHA)
b. If any of them old stogies tries to pump hot air into you, I've got *a hell of a good bull dog*. (1885 COHA)

The distinction between the EM and BI reading can most clearly be seen in examples (5.34a–c): example (5.34a) could have either an EM or a BI reading. Example (5.34b) is an EM construction, expressing a strong, positive evaluation of the criminal defense lawyer, while (5.34c) is a BI construction, where the speaker emphasizes the degree of 'criminalness' of the defense lawyer. It is possible that the BI stemmed from similar bridging contexts, in which only the stress patterns could disambiguate the two meanings.

(5.34) a. One hell of a criminal defense lawyer. (1992 COCA)
b. [$_{NPi}$ [$_{DETi}$ one] [[$_{MP}$ hell of a] [$_{Ni}$ criminal defense lawyer]]]
c. [$_{NPi}$ [$_{DETi}$ one] [$_{AP}$ [$_{INT}$ hell of a] [$_{ADJ}$ criminal]] [$_{Ni}$ defense lawyer]]

In the corpus data *hell* is the only one of the three nouns (*hell, beast*, and *cake*) that is widely productive in the BI. This form is so productive that the reduced form of 'hell', *helluva*, also has an OED entry as an intensifier starting around the early twentieth century (see online OED). The COHA examples below confirm this with *helluva* starting around the 1930s (5.35a);

hella appears later in the twenty-first century and is even used predicatively (5.35b).

(5.35) a. we'll have a great fire and cook wienies and coffee and dance and have *a helluva good time*. (1931 COHA)
b. even if you find it, it's *hella expensive* ... (2007 COHA)

There are examples from the Internet of *beast* functioning as an intensifier, and *bitch*, *whale*, and *devil* are also shown to be productive in this construction (the development of *bitch* and *whale* will be discussed in more detail in Chapter 6).[4] Similarly to *cake* and *beast*, *hell* in this family of constructions changes from evoking the already emotive referent of a biblical hell to denoting negative properties in the EBNP to denoting a positive evaluation in the EM and intensification in the BI. Unlike other abstract first nouns, it also develops a pseudo-partitive use. Although tokens of *hell* used in the *of*-binominals begin to appear later in this dataset than the other two first nouns, it begins to be used in the EBNP long before *cake* and only slightly after *beast* and is the most productive first noun in the evaluative constructions in PDE.

5.6 Discussion and Conclusions

The representatives of the three semantic groups of first nouns (*hell* for abstract, *beast* for animate, and *cake* for inanimate) demonstrate different developments in this group of constructions (see Figures 5.1 and 5.2). Although *cake* is productive in the earlier binominals and the EBNP, there are only sporadic examples of its use in the EM and none as a BI. Interestingly, its use in both the EBNPs and the EMs begin hundreds of years after the three initial constructions. However, inanimate first nouns are the staple for the pseudo-partitive, and *cake* appears to be used very productively in the construction long before the first head-classifiers appear. *Beast*, used in both the EBNP and the EM, has grammaticalized a stage further although it shows only initial signs of transitioning to the BI. Finally, *hell* has progressed the furthest and might actually be the forerunner in the development of the EM *of*-binominals and BIs. However, examples of *hell* in the first three constructions appear long after *cake* and *beast* have established themselves in the *of*-binominals (see Figure 5.1).

---

[4] Some inanimate first nouns have also developed intensifier functions, but this is probably via the pseudo-partitive: this is a grammatical path already greatly discussed in *of*-binominal literature (see Chapter 8 for a more in-depth discussion).

5.6 Discussion and Conclusions

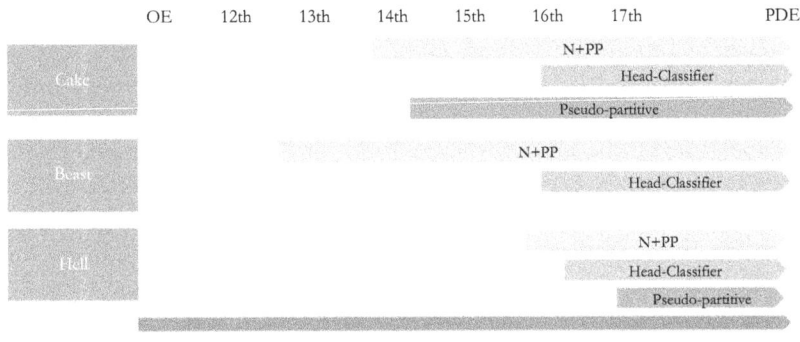

Figure 5.1 Diachronic development of *cake*, *beast*, and *hell* from N+PP to pseudo-partitive

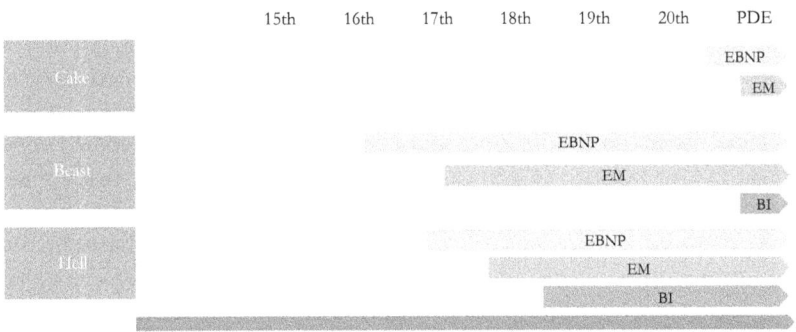

Figure 5.2 Diachronic development of *cake*, *beast*, and *hell* in the EBNP to BI

The first question to be addressed is whether the path illustrated in the three examples above is a case of lexicalization or grammaticalization. The case studies above and the analysis in Chapters 3 and 4 show that first nouns that progress along this grammaticalization path undergo decategorialization. From the head-classifier construction, there have been major structural changes in the construction, i.e. a shift in the construction's head from first to second noun and internal reorganization of the phrase, during which [N of a] develops into an MP preceding a noun and, finally, an intensifier modifying an adjective or quantifier. A first noun used in these constructions also undergoes changes.

The reanalysis of [N of a] triggers a gradual debonding process, in this case where a noun becomes an adjective (see Van Goethem & De Smet 2014: 252). For the N+PP and the head-classifier, the first noun is the head. The status of the first noun in the EBNP is still ambiguous: it still marks number and can be found in plural form, but it agrees in number with the second noun; N_1 is no longer the head of a NP, and first determiner has scope over the whole construction. In the EM, N_1 has clearly become part of a modifying phrase [N_1 of a] in [[Det$_1$] [$_{MP}$ N_1 of (a)] [N_2]]: the preposition and second determiner appear to have lost their semantic values and grammatical functions and are, in the most frequent cases, conflated to form a single lexical item together with N_1. The first noun only appears in singular form. Finally, in the BI, this [N_1 of a] phrase is integrated into the MP and functions as an intensifier of the adjective that follows. Decategorialization of the first noun but also of the preposition and second determiner has clearly taken place.

All three case studies show that there was a semantic shift from a lexical first noun evoking a referent to a lexical first noun ascribing descriptive properties to the second noun, and finally, to the first noun functioning as a more grammatical intensifier. All three first nouns denote referents in the initial constructions: both *beast* and *cake* denote physical referents, while *hell* is more abstract. In the EBNP, *beast* and *cake* have a descriptive, referent-oriented meaning as well as a subjective, speaker-oriented evaluation required by this construction. In both first nouns, the semantic transition from EBNP to EM is distinct; in this process the descriptive properties of the first noun are backgrounded and the abstract subjective evaluation shifts to the forefront. With *beast*, the size or the beast-like characteristics in the EBNP are lost and the speaker's approval, disapproval, or simple evaluation (i.e. difficulty) is foregrounded. With *cake*, the physical comparison to *cake* and the ascription of cake-like features onto the referent in the EBNP is lost. This represents a clear shift to a more subjective, speaker-oriented meaning. With *hell* this transition is not so clear. Owing to the abstract quality of *hell*, the noun has already shifted semantically to principally ascribing a subjective evaluation to the referent. Unlike the other two examples, for *hell*, which is already used in the abstract sense in the EBNP, the transition can be most clearly seen in the change of semantic prosody from negative to positive, after which it then becomes an intensifier. Degree modifiers are considered intrinsically subjective since they, by definition, evoke a scale on which the speaker/writer assesses a property (Ghesquière 2014: 72). This shift from modifier to intensifier also mirrors subjectification paths documented in diachronic

5.6 Discussion and Conclusions

studies of single lexical premodifiers which change from objective to subjective modifiers and finally to intensifiers (Adamson 2000: 44, 55–9).

Thus, although the ultimate end of the historical process has resulted in new lexical items, e.g. *helluva*, *whaleuva*, *hella*, and *beasta*, the overall changes are attributable to grammaticalization. This is most likely not a case of lexicalization. The creation of these lexical items is an example of univerbation, a process that can be involved in both lexicalization and grammaticalization (see Table 5.1). Univerbation is a process in which syntactic constructions are converted into lexical items such as the French *pomme-de-terre* (apple-of-earth) for 'potato' (Lehmann 2020: 209). Brinton and Traugott (2005: 105), but also other studies (e.g. Heine & Narrog 2010: 405), have pointed out that both grammaticalization and lexicalization can have a reductive component. Therefore, univerbation, in this case the grouping of [N of a] into a chunk, can be found in both lexicalization and grammaticalization (see Lehmann 2020: 213), and if fusion (i.e. the transition from [hell of a] to *helluva*) is the central argument for this process to be considered lexicalization, then this evidence is not decisive. What is interesting is that in phrasal univerbation, the new lexical item assumes the category membership of its head (Lehmann 2020: 214); this is interesting in this case because *hella*, *helluva*, and *whaleuva* are all adjectives or adverbs, not nouns. This would indicate that the change in the first noun's function did indeed occur in the EBNP. This observation would conform with the findings of other *of*-binominal studies such as Brems and Davidse (2010).

Finally, although the role of the pseudo-partitive in this grammaticalization path is unclear, the main path from the N+PP to head-classifier and then the EBNP, EM, and BI (Figure 5.1) would be supported by this study. The role of the pseudo-partitive in this cline will be discussed in more detail in Chapter 6.

PART II

Testing the Hypothesis

CHAPTER 6

Diachronic Evidence

6.1 Introduction

The synchronic analysis presented in Chapters 3 and 4 and the diachronic analysis presented in Chapter 5 suggest a scenario for the development of the evaluative constructions: the EBNP, EM, and BI. This scenario began with the N+PP and the reconceptualization of the relationship between the two nouns in this *of*-binominal: the noun in the PP no longer ascribed a property to the head (locative, temporal, etc.) nor indicated a possessor. Instead, the ascribed property denoted by the PP was interpreted as the defining or taxonomic feature of the first noun: the prepositional phrase categorizes the first noun either by denoting the substance the nominal referent consists of or by ascribing it a taxonomic category. This semantic change was either triggered by or resulted in the preposition *of* losing semantic content and gave rise to the head-classifier construction. This change in function resulted in formal changes: the loss of semantic content in the preposition resulted in *of*-NP no longer functioning as a separate constituent, and N_2 became nonreferential. The preposition's loss of content might have facilitated a reinterpretation of the role of the first noun as a quantifier, measure, part, or container noun that imposes a shape, measurement, or quantity on the second noun in the pseudo-partitive construction. Particularly inanimate first nouns, such as *cake*, *nub*, or *breeze*, are amenable for this reinterpretation. This new function of the first noun may have triggered an internal reorganization of the whole construction: the second noun became the head, the two nouns became co-ascriptive, i.e. the whole NP involves reference to only one entity (as opposed to the N+PP with an embedded NP with its own referent), and both nouns ascribe a property to that referent. This step meant that the semantics of the first noun has had to, to some extent, bleach, and the first noun now functions in a [Det N] complex quantifier. In essence, the original N-*of*-N construction has become a simple NP.

There are two possible scenarios for the role of the pseudo-partitive construction and the transition to the EBNP. The first is a direct link between the pseudo-partitive and the EBNP.[1] In this scenario, the change of head and subsequent loss of semantic content in the first noun, and the reconceptualization of the internal structure in the pseudo-partitive, may have directly facilitated the grouping and chunking of linguistic elements into [N of a], resulting in the EBNP. This process began with inanimate first nouns, and later, animate first nouns developed a direct link between the head-classifier and the EBNP.

The second potential link is an indirect one: the use of certain first nouns in the pseudo-partitive facilitates a reinterpretation of the role of the first noun in the EBNP, but the two constructions are not consecutive stages in the grammaticalization path. In this scenario, the role of the pseudo-partitive might be more peripheral. There might have been a split at the head-classifier stage that resulted in the first nouns used in the pseudo-partitive and then later the EBNP. If the split does indeed take place at this stage, this would mean that the existence of the pseudo-partitive with inanimate first nouns may have facilitated a change of head reanalysis reading with inanimate first nouns in the EBNP.[2] This scenario would mean that the pseudo-partitive and the EBNP would constitute two different grammaticalization paths, and some first nouns progress along both (see Figure 6.1). We can assume that there is a link between the head-classifier and the EBNP, since animate and abstract first nouns are not usually used in the pseudo-partitive construction. Therefore, the question is what path do the inanimate nouns take?

After the EBNP, the path becomes clearer. In the EBNP, the change in head and change in function results in the further loss of semantic content in the first noun (which now only ascribes physical or subjective evaluative

---

[1] The EBNP may have already existed in English before the development of this path – this grammaticalization path might be the result of what Torrent (2015) calls the Construction Network Reconfiguration Hypothesis, namely that links between constructions can change so that new links can be formed with already existing constructions. In this case, the EBNP supposedly stems from constructions such as *monstrum mulieris* (monster woman.GEN 'a monster of a woman'; Curme 1914: 56; 1931: 85), and Aarts (1998: 120) found EBNP examples from as early as the thirteenth century. It is believed that the EBNP stems from Latin and entered English via French (Aarts [1998: 120], who quotes Austin [1980], and Curme [1914]). As far as I am aware, no one has presented strong evidence to substantiate this hypothesis. However, even if the EBNP in English stemmed from a similar French or Latin construction, it could still be requisitioned by this grammaticalization path.

[2] There is actually a third scenario which will be explored in future work and would entail an *of*-apposition construction, such as *the snarling superannuated beast of a watchdog*, as a transition between the head-classifier and EBNP. This will only briefly be discussed in this chapter. This alternative would not fundamentally change the path proposed here but simply add an intervening step between the head-classifier and the EBNP.

6.1 Introduction

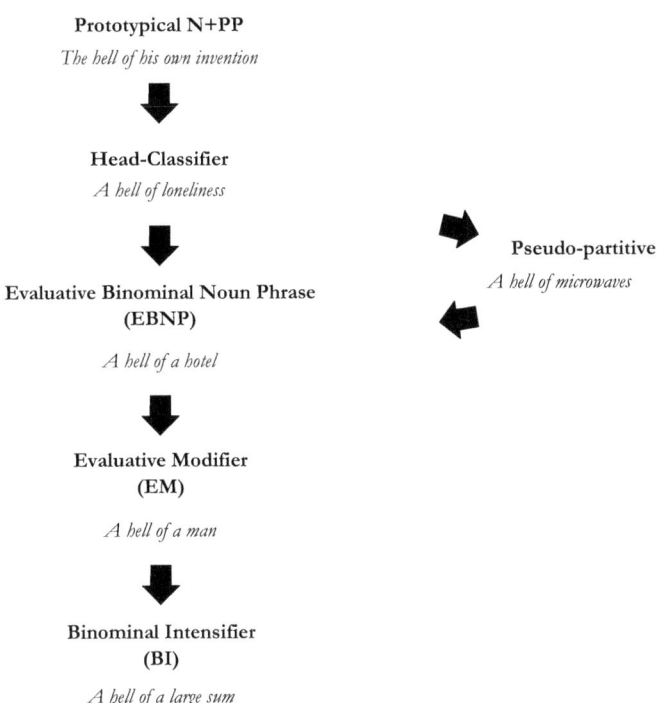

Figure 6.1 Grammaticalization path of the evaluative *of*-binominals

properties to the second noun), the reorganization of internal components (hence, the irregular premodification patterns and second determiner restrictions), and the internal restructuring into a [N of a] chunk. In the EM, this new form solidifies into the [Det [N of (a)] N] reanalysis. The first noun can no longer denote physical properties; the second determiner no longer marks number or identifiability. Finally, in the BI, the first noun has bleached to the point that it retains only its emphasizing meaning and functions as an intensifier of the following modifier. In the most frequent cases, [N of (Det) Adj] becomes a seperate constituent.

In these last three constructions (EBNP, EM, and BI), the features of nounhood in the first noun slowly disappear, and the first noun becomes more subjective. The EBNP requires a noun that denotes evaluative properties, and the first noun agrees in number with the second. The first noun in the EM denotes only a subjective evaluation, appears only in singular form, and takes restricted premodifiers. Finally, in the BI, the first noun is an intensifier, can appear only in singular form, and does not take modification.

In essence we are discussing two different processes here: the first is the creation of the different N-of-N templates, what Noël (2007: 192) calls schematization, and the second is the grammaticalization of first nouns in these constructions. Schematization leads to partially or fully schematic syntactic elements (Noël 2007: 183; see further Gisborne & Patten 2011: 100–2). A diachronic study looking at this creation of templates is always hampered by two difficulties. One is that the EBNP is a relatively rare construction, and unlike *sort-of, kind-of,* and *a lot-of,* it is not easy to find tokens of this form, particularly if one follows the development of specific first nouns, as *of*-binominal studies have done in the past. The solution to this problem would be that one does not look at just specific first nouns but all *of*-binominals. However, this leads to the second problem, namely the quantity of the date. Three of the first four constructions (the N+PP, the pseudo-partitive, and the EBNP) have existed since the Old English or Middle English periods (Aarts 1998: 85; Brems 2011; Mustanoja 2016: 396, 79–80). No one has looked at the head-classifier in more detail, but the OED has examples of *bird of prey* from the fourteenth century (OED), and Mustanoja (2016: 387) explains that in Middle English head-classifier-like constructions were used to denote material and color (e.g. *John hadde clothe of the heeris of cameylis and girdil of skyn*). This means that such a project would have to sift through all the *of*-binominals in all the historical periods from Old English (OE) onwards. Therefore, this project has focused on first nouns that may have progressed along this path more recently and has used the larger modern corpora (the Corpus of American English [COCA] and the Corpus of Historical American English [COHA]).

This chapter thus looks at what evidence the more modern corpus data can provide us about the relationship between the constructions discussed in Chapters 3–5. In particular, it will look for evidence of the grammaticalization path proposed above, discuss the possible roles of the pseudo-partitive in this development, and examine the evidence for the tripartite distinction between the EBNP, EM, and BI. In order to do this, a corpus analysis of the first nouns *nub, breeze, husk, snake, whale,* and *bitch* has been conducted.

This chapter is broken down into six sections. Section 6.2 introduces importance concepts in grammaticalization theory that play a role in this analysis. Section 6.3 presents the methods, the reasoning behind the choice of first nouns, and the results of the study. Section 6.4 presents the study of inanimate first nouns, and Section 6.5 discusses the study of the evaluative *of*-binominals. Finally, Section 6.6 presents the conclusions drawn from these results.

6.2 *Of*-binominal Grammaticalization Pathway

Chapter 5 presented arguments for considering this path as an example of grammaticalization. Recent work shows that grammaticalization can be not only loss or reduction but also a process of expansion (Himmelmann 2004), or the process may stop midway (e.g. Fischer 2000; for more discussion and reconciliation of these two approaches see Traugott 2015).[3] Himmelmann (2004: 31–3) focuses on expansion in grammaticalization and delineates three types of expansion: host-class, syntactic, and semantic-pragmatic. In host-class expansion, a grammaticalizing form will increase its range of collocations with members of the relevant part of speech (noun, adjective, verb, or adverb) or in our case, the types of nouns (concrete, abstract, proper, or common, etc.). For example, in the case of demonstratives, in the process of their grammaticalizing to articles, they begin to be used with nouns that they previously had not co-occurred with, such as proper nouns or nouns denoting unique entities (e.g. *sun* or *queen*) (Himmelmann 2004: 32). This results in an increase in productivity. Syntactic expansion involves extension to larger contexts, such as from core argument positions (e.g. subject and object) to adpositions (e.g. directional and temporal phrases). In semantic-pragmatic expansion, as a grammaticalizing form develops new meanings, it expands the pragmatic and/or semantic contexts in which it can be used; for example, the grammaticalization of a demonstrative to articles requires context expansion from dietic reference to broader usage, evoking a referent and associative anaphoric functions (e.g. *a wedding – the bride*; Himmelmann 2004: 32). According to Himmelmann (2004: 33), in grammaticalization all three contexts expand (but not necessarily together); the first and last processes play a role here.

Brems (2011: 103–5; see also Brems 2003) in her work on pseudo-partitive *of*-binominals argues that semantic change in these constructions is indicated by the broadening of the collocation range of second nouns. She argues that "[t]his redistribution of meaning also entails overall semantic generalization in the [measure *of*-binominal], which allows for the collocational extension of N_2," (Brems 2011: 104). In other words, as the semantic content of the first noun generalizes, it

---

[3] A similar distinction is made in lexicalization (see Diewald 2011).

allows for a wider collocation range of the second noun, i.e. host-class expansion. For Brems this means an expansion from concrete (see (6.1a)) to abstract (see (6.1b)) second nouns.[4] Barðdal and Gildea (2015: 15) point out that changes in collocational restrictions also demonstrates a change in form: changes in collocational patterns often coincide with a change in the categorical status of certain words in a construction. Therefore, a change in collocation patterns is also one of the criteria examined in the analysis below.

(6.1)   a. *Six plane loads of food* are also being flow today to the city of Mogadishu. (Brems 2011: 130)
   b. Both children and adults have been seriously attacked and I think there's *loads of evidence* that something fairly drastic should be done. (Brems 2011: 130)

Change is usually thought, at least from a functional perspective, to begin in the semantics and pragmatics and in situations where the context of an utterance allows for an alternative interpretation of an expression (Heine 2003; Heine & Narrog 2010). Should these situations occur often, frequency leads to conventionalization and both patterns coexist. These contexts of change have been called bridging contexts (Evans & Wilkins 1998: 5), critical contexts (Diewald 1999; see also Auwera, van Olmen & Du Mon 2015: 639), and pivot contexts (Traugott & Trousdale 2013: 193).

Bridging contexts, critical contexts, and pivot contexts are similar concepts (Heine 2002: 84; Traugott 2011: 26 fn 3) with all three of them being defined as contexts exhibiting structural and/or semantic ambiguity and, thereby, inviting alternative interpretations. However, it is important to keep in mind that the bridging context is only the beginning of the change and does not necessarily need to lead to a change. What is also required is a switch context (Diewald's isolating contexts), where the new meaning is then separated from the original meaning: the context has a property that does not allow for the original interpretation, thus ruling it out, but the new interpretation is not yet conventionalized and is still very context dependent. Conventionalization is, then, the final stage of the process (Heine 2002: 85; see Table 6.1). For the present study, finding bridging contexts between two constructions would thus strengthen the claim that the progress of first nouns through the six

---

[4] This is abstract or concrete as defined by Quirk et al. (1985: 247). The referents of concrete nouns are perceivable by our senses; those of abstract nouns are unobservable (see also Lyons' [1977: 442–3] first-order and third-order entities discussed in Chapter 2).

6.2 Of-binominal Grammaticalization Pathway

Table 6.1 *A grammaticalization scenario* (Heine 2002: 86)

STAGE	CONTEXT	RESULTING MEANING
Initial stage	Unconstrained	Source meaning
Bridging context	There is a specific context giving rise to an inference in favor of a new meaning.	Target meaning foregrounded
Switch context	There is a new context which is incompatible with the source meaning.	Source meaning backgrounded
Conventionalization	The target meaning no longer needs to be supported by the context that gives rise to it; it may be used in new contexts.	Target meaning only

constructions takes place in a certain order (Figure 6.1). Naturally, an inability to find these contexts in the data would have the opposite effect.

In her study of measure pseudo-partitive constructions, Brems (2011: 130) argues that "[s]ynchronically ambiguous SN-constructions are interesting in that they may represent transitional contexts of grammaticalization and delexicalization and may point up [*sic*] factors that diachronically allowed the lexical SN-meaning to be pragmatically enriched with quantifier meaning." As she points out, vague and ambiguous examples exemplify the tensions between lexical items and the grammar, and I would even add the tension between lexical items and the whole *of*-binominal network.

The empirical study below examines the changes in the first nouns to support my hypothesis of the grammaticalization of the N-of-N frame. Furthermore, the theoretical discussion above provides us with several features to look for in the data. If the proposed pathway is correct, then not only should the analysis show first occurrences to appear in a particular order, but in addition, there should be evidence of bridging contexts between the different categories in the data. Since a corpus provides only the linguistic context of an expression, the analysis below will look for contexts where there are alternative readings. In this case linguistic context includes second noun collocates shifting from concrete second nouns to abstract second nouns.

6.3 Methods

The analysis uses data from the Corpus of Historical American English (COHA, 1810–1989) and the Corpus of Contemporary American English (COCA, 1990–2015) and is broken down into two different strands examining two different parts of this grammaticalization path. The first study examines the role of the pseudo-partitive and the second the development of the EM and BI. The dataset consists of all tokens of the first noun types selected: *nub(s)*, *breeze(s)*, *husk(s)*, *snake(s)*, *bitch(es)*, and *whale(s)* (see Table 6.2 for the raw frequencies). Using information from the OED, these nouns were chosen for a variety of reasons, and these will be discussed at the start of each section. Once the data was extracted, each token was then coded for the construction type and second noun type, i.e. abstract or concrete. The sample was divided into ten-year time periods with the last time period in COCA being a five-year period.

Section 6.4 will examine the development at the start of the cline (N+PP, head-classifier, pseudo-partitive, and EBNP) and look at first nouns that appear to develop along this path, in particular, those with a pseudo-partitive form: *nub(s)*, *breeze(s)*, *husk(s)*, and *snake(s)*. Section 6.5 will look at the later stages of this development (EBNP, EM, and BI), discussing the first nouns *bitch(es)* and *whale(s)*.

6.4 The Pseudo-partitive Strand

The predominant criterion for the selection of the four nouns examined in this section was that they enter the English language late enough that it might be possible to catch their development along the proposed path in data from the eighteenth to the twenty-first-century. *Nub(s)*, *breeze(s)*, and

Table 6.2 *Raw figures for first nouns in COCA and COHA*

	N_1	COHA	COCA
Pseudo-partitive	nub(s)	93	146
	breeze(s)	356	126
	husk(s)	116	144
	snake(s)	112	100
Evaluative	whale(s)	154	113
	bitch(es)	35	69

6.4 The Pseudo-partitive Strand

husk(s) were chosen because they represent the more conventional pseudo-partitive first nouns. *Snake(s)* is interesting as one of the only animate nouns in the dataset that is used in the pseudo-partitive construction.

6.4.1 Nub(s)

Nub, meaning 'lump', enters the English language at around the end of the seventeenth century (as seen in (6.2a)), and it is etymologically related to the cognate *knub*, meaning 'a small lump, a protuberance' (as illustrated in (6.2b)) (OED). In the OED at the start of the nineteenth century, there is an example that would suggest a pseudo-partitive reading (6.2c), and at the same time the meaning of *nub* also extends to mean, on the one hand, 'something cut off short or imperfectly grown' (as demonstrated in (6.2d)) and 'the heart of the matter' or 'the crux', as shown in (6.2e) (OED). Since it was unclear if this last meaning is a case of homonymy or polysemy, the tokens with *nub* meaning 'the heart of' or 'crux' were excluded from the dataset.

(6.2) a. Another little brass pessell & morter with *two nubbs*. (1696 OED)
       b. If a hawkes feete be but swolne, & haue not *any knubs* in the ball of the foote. (1575 OED)
       c. It will not hurt oxen nor milch cows to give them once in a while *a nub of corn or some potatoes*. (1806 OED)
       d. And soft in her lap her Baby she lay'd *With his pretty Nubs of Horns* a-sprouting, And his pretty little Tail all curly-twirly. (1834 OED)
       e. That's pretty much *the nub of the business*. (1834 OED)

Table 6.3 below shows the frequency of all the constructions in each of the time periods. The first part represents the data from COHA, and the figures in the last three columns are from COCA. The first tokens from the corpora all exemplify the 'crux' meaning of *nub* in examples such as *the nub of the business* (like the OED example in (6.2e)), and tokens of *nub* denoting a form begin to appear only at the start of the twentieth century. The first two examples are ambiguous and will be discussed below (see examples (6.8) and (6.9)). The first N+PP instance is (6.3), and in general the prepositional phrase in the first examples denotes innate possession. The few head-classifier tokens found show both concrete collocates, such as in *flesh* in (6.4a), and abstract ones, as in *life* in (6.4b). Head-classifiers become more frequent only after 1990; all the corpus examples are intrinsic head-classifiers denoting what the nub is made of.

(6.3) Boone lay on his belly, screened by the quaking asp that grew on *the nub of a hill*. (1946 COHA)

Table 6.3 *Frequency of* nub(s) *in* of*-binominals in COHA and COCA*

			COHA															COCA			
		1810s	1820s	1830s	1840s	1850s	1860s	1870s	1880s	1890s	1900s	1910s	1920s	1930s	1940s	1950s	1960s	1970s	1980s	1990s	2000s	2010-2015
N+PP	raw	0	0	2	0	0	2	0	1	1	0	2	9	7	15	14	10	13	9	49	36	17
	pmw	0.00	0.00	0.15	0.00	0.00	0.12	0.00	0.05	0.05	0.00	0.09	0.35	0.28	0.61	0.57	0.41	0.55	0.36	0.24	0.17	0.14
	%	0.00	0.00	100.00	0.00	0.00	100.00	0.00	100.00	100.00	0.00	100.00	90.00	100.00	100.00	87.50	100.00	92.86	81.82	71.01	69.23	68.00
Head-Cl	raw	0	0	0	0	0	0	0	0	0	0	0	1	0	0	2	0	1	0	13	9	6
	pmw	0.00	0.00	0.00	0.00	0.00	0.00	0.00	0.00	0.00	0.00	0.00	0.04	0.00	0.00	0.08	0.00	0.04	0.00	0.06	0.04	0.05
	%	0.00	0.00	0.00	0.00	0.00	0.00	0.00	0.00	0.00	0.00	0.00	10.00	0.00	0.00	12.50	0.00	7.14	0.00	18.84	17.31	24.00
Pseudo-P	raw	0	0	0	0	0	0	0	0	0	0	0	0	0	0	0	0	0	0	2	3	0
	pmw	0.00	0.00	0.00	0.00	0.00	0.00	0.00	0.00	0.00	0.00	0.00	0.00	0.000	0.00	0.00	0.00	0.00	0.00	0.01	0.01	0.00
	%	0.00	0.00	0.00	0.00	0.00	0.00	0.00	0.00	0.00	0.00	0.00	0.00	0.00	0.00	0.00	0.00	0.00	0.00	2.90	5.77	0.00
EBNP	raw	0	0	0	0	0	0	0	0	0	0	0	0	0	0	0	0	0	2	5	4	2
	pmw	0.00	0.00	0.00	0.00	0.00	0.00	0.00	0.00	0.00	0.00	0.00	0.00	0.00	0.00	0.00	0.00	0.00	0.08	0.02	0.02	0.02
	%	0.00	0.00	0.00	0.00	0.00	0.00	0.00	0.00	0.00	0.00	0.00	0.00	0.00	0.00	0.00	0.00	0.00	18.18	7.25	7.69	8.00

Note: For each construction the raw figures are given at the top, normalized figures in the middle (normalized per hundred million words), and the percentage of all examples in that period at the bottom.

(6.4) a. she tucked *the nub of flesh* from sight and, disdainfully closing the robe, crossed her knees, signaling, apparently, an end of the exhibition. (1971 COHA)

b. She bent to release her skirt from the reaching twig and felt *the hard little nubs of bursting life* against the dry wood. (1955 COHA)

The pseudo-partitive and EBNP tokens appear at about the same time. The first potential pseudo-partitive examples can be found in the 1990s. Example (6.5) could represent a possible bridging context between the head-classifier and pseudo-partitive; even with a context, it is unclear if the speaker means 'a nub made of hazelnut' (head-classifier) or 'hazelnut in the form or quantity of a nub' (pseudo-partitive). The use of a demonstrative would point toward the former analysis; the context (the other imprecise amounts, e.g. *bit* and *blob*) would indicate the latter.

(6.5) ... insecure because you wonder, after all, if it is worth it – the many-blocks walk on such a cold dull day, the loss of loose change, a perhaps too hopefully expectant state of mind – just for this bit of butterscotch, *this nub of hazelnut*, this soft blob of perhaps unmerited reward, this precious though transient gift of pleasure – ruinous to the teeth, the figure, the complexion ... (1992 COCA).

Unambiguous pseudo-partitive tokens with clear measure functions appear at the start of the twenty-first century (as seen in example (6.6a)). The first tokens take concrete second nouns like *hazelnut* in (6.5) and *butter* in (6.6a); pseudo-partitives with abstract second nouns appear a decade later, as demonstrated with *shame* and *regret* in (6.6b).

(6.6) a. I melt *a nub of butter* in the blackness, crack an egg on its hard, capable side (2003 COCA)

b. He could feel his face getting hot, and *a little nub of shame and regret* formed in his chest. (2004 COCA)

The first clear EBNP examples appear only slightly earlier in the mid-1980s, and with the first noun ascribing a certain shape to the second, as demonstrated in (6.7a), where *nub* ascribes a smallish, roundish shape to *nose*, and in (6.7b), where *nub* ascribes a similar shape onto a man's body. There are no examples of the EM and the BI.

(6.7) a. The Abbot was a tall, emaciated man with an elegant monkey like face, all tiny bones, *a nub of a nose*, and querying little brown buttons for eyes. (1984 COHA)

b. Narcissa's Negro overseer, *a black-skinned nub of a man* named Joseph, explained the custom to Oliphant. (1985 COHA)

The evidence presented here offers only speculative support to the grammaticalization path proposed. However, some of the ambiguous examples, such as (6.8) and (6.9), demonstrate how these constructions may have been reconceptualized. Examples (6.8) and (6.9) both appear very early in the dataset but do not fit into a single category:

(6.8)   So the march went on and on: big, Southern-bred steer grappling the problem of his first Northern winter; thin-flanked cow with shivering, rough-coated calf trailing at her heels; humpbacked yearling with *little nubs of horns* telling that he was lately in his calfhood . . . (1907 COHA)

(6.9)   It is a well-known fact that the dwellers in the most ancient ranges, such as the Jura in Switzerland, which Time has worn down to *mere nubs of mountains*, find that the hills make a place for themselves in the heart which grand peaks of the Alps cannot fill. (1909 COHA)

In both (6.8) and (6.9), the two nouns are co-ascriptive (i.e. the whole NP denotes a single referent, and both nouns ascribe properties to that referent), which would point to either a pseudo-partitive or an EBNP reading. In (6.8), *little* might be conceptualized as a descriptive modifier denoting the size of the referent designated by N_1 (which would indicate a head-classifier construction) or function as an intensifier of the property denoted by N_1 (which would indicate a pseudo-partitive construction). Therefore, this construction appears to represent a bridging context between the head-classifier and the pseudo-partitive form.

The verb *worn down* in (6.9) could have been semantically selected by either noun, but would point to the first noun *nub*, a head-classifier or N+PP reading. However, in (6.9), *mere* would seem to indicate an evaluative reading of the first noun, and therefore, this reading points in the direction of an EBNP interpretation. The EBNP reading for (6.9) is further supported by the evaluative word choice: it is rather unennobling to call a mountain a nub. What would argue against the EBNP reading is the fact that the next EBNP token appears over seventy-five years later. However, this example would appear to demonstrate a potential bridging context between the head-classifier and EBNP.

As shown in Figure 6.2, the first clear uses of *nub* are in the N+PP, baring the two ambiguous examples. Although we would have expected head-classifier tokens to appear much earlier in the data sample, they do appear before clear examples of the pseudo-partitive and EBNP. Based on this

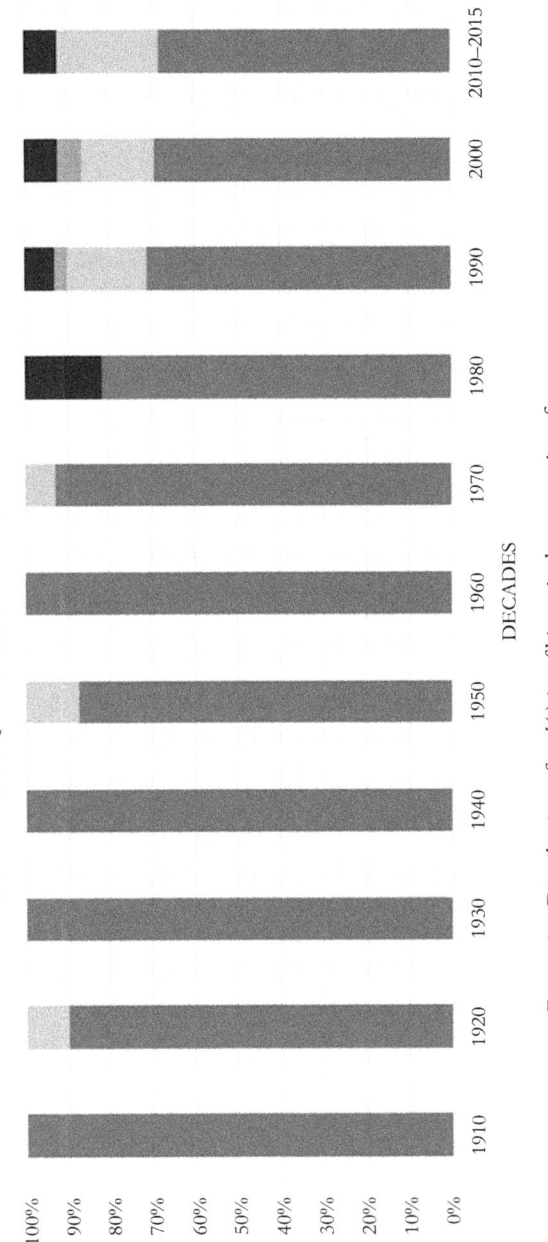

Figure 6.2 Distribution of *nub(s)* in *of*-binominal constructions from 1910 to 2015
Note: Before 1910 only N+PP constructions (see Table 6.3)

evidence the transition from *nub* as a noun denoting the overall referent of the head-classifier to a measure or form meaning in the pseudo-partitive and the shift to a descriptive, evaluative semantics in the EBNP might not have happened sequentially (the pseudo-partitive then the EBNP); instead, both pseudo-partitive and EBNP may have developed from the head-classifier, and these two changes may have occurred at about the same time.

The two initial examples are the most controversial and demonstrate a potential bridging context between head-classifier and pseudo-partitive and, at the same time, between the head-classifier and EBNP. However, they, as well as information from the OED, also lead to the suspicion that, at least in the case of *nub*, the corpus data does not represent what is happening in the language. The OED provides examples much earlier than the corpora.

6.4.2 Breeze(s)

Breeze also entered the English language rather late, toward the end of the sixteenth century, and first denoted 'a north or north-easterly wind' (6.10a) (OED). It developed its more modern use of 'a gentle wind' in the seventeenth century (as shown in (6.10b)); in the nineteenth century, *breeze* underwent a metaphoric extension to mean 'a rumor' or 'a breath of news', as shown in (6.10c), and 'a quarrel', as shown in (6.10d) (OED).

(6.10)   a. Against *the breze* and easterwind. (1596 OED)
         b. A calme, *a brese*, a fresh gaile. (1626 OED)
         c. There came *a breeze* that Spirit Séguier was near at hand. (1879 OED)
         d. The cession would create *a breeze* in the Konkan. (1803 OED)

Not unexpectedly, *breeze* is more frequent than *nub* (see Table 6.4), and at the start of the nineteenth century, both N+PPs and head-classifiers are frequent. In the N+PP examples, the prepositional phrase ascribes location (6.11a) or temporal properties (6.11b) to the matrix noun, and it is particularly this second form that is amenable to the head-classifier construal, i.e. *a breeze of the night* becomes *a breeze of night* as in (6.11c) or *a night breeze*. The noun *breeze* is used in both the taxonomic head-classifier in (6.11c) and the intrinsic head-classifier in (6.11d).

(6.11)   a. One day, while walking on the water's edge, to breathe *the wholesome breezes of the sea*; I left my friends and climb'd the fearful rocks ... (COHA 1815)
         b. Or like those strange unearthly lyres, Whose hearts are strung with unseen wires, That wake but to the winds of heaven – *The breezes of the morn and even* ... (1819 COHA)

c. Of soldier-hymning when it comes Upon *the shifting breeze of night*, In farewells to the dying light (1819 COHA)
   d. Had I been forced to tread these low brow'd caves. Where *gentle breeze of vital air* ne'er play'd … (1812 COHA)

Initial examples provide ambiguous contexts where both a head-classifier and a pseudo-partitive reading are possible. Abstract second nouns in the head-classifier, i.e. *passion* in (6.12a) and *thoughts* in (6.12b), force a metaphorical reading of *breeze*. This ambiguates the meaning of the first nouns: in (6.12a) and in (6.12b), the speaker may be referring to a metaphorical breeze consisting of *passion* and *sad and gentle thoughts* (head-classifier), or 'a brief passion' and 'brief passing thoughts' (pseudo-partitive). In (6.12a), *complaisance* selects *passion* (you comply with every passion and not every breeze) and the pseudo-partitive reading (something small and short-lived). In (6.12b) *visit* could select either *breeze* or *thoughts*.

(6.12) a. it does not require an unqualified complaisance to *every sudden breeze of passion* or to every transient impulse which the people may receive from the arts of men, who flatter their prejudices to betray their interests (1817 COHA)
   b. Perhaps, indeed, *a summer breeze of sad and gentle thoughts* would sometimes visit him; but, in these brief memories of his love, he did not wish that it should be revived, or mourn over its event. (1828 COHA)

By the 1860s, there are clear examples of *breeze* in the pseudo-partitive construction, as demonstrated in (6.13a). *Breeze* would normally semantically entail 'slow moving air', and therefore, in (6.13a), for the speaker to select *wind* as the second noun would appear to be a tautology since *breeze* already entails 'wind'. Therefore, *breeze* can be assumed to function as a measurement of a small amount. In the pseudo-partitive, the second noun tends to be abstract such as *commonsense* in (6.13b). Later there are pseudo-partitives that select proper nouns, as seen in (6.13c); here *breeze* appears to mean a 'small taste of something'.

(6.13) a. "How are you, Captain John?" shouted the young pilot. "Why, Lawry! How are you?" replied the skipper of the sloop. "What are you doing here?" continued Lawry. "Waitin' for *a breeze of wind*. I had a good freight promised to me if I got to Burlington by tomorrow morn-in'" (1866 COHA)
   b. The blast was *a welcome breeze of commonsense atmosphere* sicklied o'er with false humanitarianism. (1937 COHA)
   c. Plus My Best Friend's Wedding, *the first summer breeze of Julia Roberts*, to be followed by Julia and Mel Gibson in Conspiracy Theory. (1997 COCA)

Table 6.4 Frequency of breeze(s) in of-binominals in COHA and COCA

										COHA												COCA		
		1810s	1820s	1830s	1840s	1850s	1860s	1870s	1880s	1890s	1900s	1910s	1920s	1930s	1940s	1950s	1960s	1970s	1980s	1990s	2000s	2010-2015
N+PP	raw	2	6	17	33	23	13	12	17	16	8	12	5	8	4	4	6	3	4	30	31	13
	pmw	0.85	0.86	1.23	2.09	1.39	0.77	0.64	0.85	0.78	0.36	0.52	0.19	0.32	0.16	0.16	0.25	0.13	0.16	0.14	0.15	0.11
	%	25.00	42.86	48.57	75.00	51.11	56.52	46.15	53.13	64.00	50.00	54.55	55.56	61.54	57.14	80.00	35.29	60.00	40.00	53.57	60.78	68.42
Head-Cl	raw	4	8	17	10	22	9	14	13	9	7	10	3	4	3	1	9	2	3	22	12	4
	pmw	1.69	1.15	1.23	0.63	1.33	0.53	0.75	0.65	0.44	0.32	0.43	0.12	0.16	0.12	0.04	0.37	0.08	0.12	0.11	0.058	0.034
	%	50.00	57.14	48.57	22.73	48.89	39.13	53.85	40.63	36.00	43.75	45.45	33.33	30.77	42.86	20.00	52.94	40.00	30.00	39.29	23.53	21.05
Pseudo-P	raw	1	0	0	1	0	1	0	2	0	1	0	1	1	0	0	2	0	2	4	5	1
	pmw	0.42	0.00	0.00	0.06	0.00	0.06	0.00	0.10	0.00	0.05	0.00	0.04	0.04	0.00	0.00	0.08	0.00	0.08	0.02	0.02	0.01
	%	12.50	0.00	0.00	2.27	0.00	4.35	0.00	6.25	0.00	6.25	0.00	11.11	7.69	0.00	0.00	11.76	0.00	20.00	7.14	9.80	5.26
EBNP	raw	0	0	0	0	0	0	0	0	0	0	0	0	0	0	0	0	0	0	0	2	0
	pmw	0.00	0.00	0.00	0.00	0.00	0.00	0.00	0.00	0.00	0.00	0.00	0.00	0.00	0.00	0.00	0.00	0.00	0.00	0.00	0.01	0.00
	%	0.00	0.00	0.00	0.00	0.00	0.00	0.00	0.00	0.00	0.00	0.00	0.00	0.00	0.00	0.00	0.00	0.00	0.00	0.00	3.92	0.00
unclear	raw	1	0	1	0	0	0	0	0	0	0	0	0	0	0	0	0	0	0	0	1	1
	pmw	0.42	0.00	0.07	0.00	0.00	0.00	0.00	0.00	0.00	0.00	0.00	0.00	0.00	0.00	0.00	0.00	0.00	0.00	0.00	0.01	0.01
	%	12.50	0.00	2.86	0.00	0.00	0.00	0.00	0.00	0.00	0.00	0.00	0.00	0.00	0.00	0.00	0.00	0.00	0.00	0.00	1.96	5.26
Total	raw	8	14	35	44	45	23	26	32	25	16	22	9	13	7	5	17	5	9	56	51	19

Note: For each construction the raw figures are given at the top, normalized figures in the middle (normalized per hundred million words), and the percentage of all examples in that period at the bottom.

6.4 The Pseudo-partitive Strand

The first EBNP examples appear in the twenty-first century, much later than the pseudo-partitive ones. Initially, *breeze* is used with inanimate second nouns, as shown in (6.14a) where it means 'easy', and then also with animates second nouns, as seen in (6.14b), where it indicates physical appearance or manner. There are no examples with potential bridging contexts between the pseudo-partitive and the EBNP or the head-classifier and the EBNP. There are no examples of EMs or BIs.

(6.14)   a. But in the seventh inning, Schilling's last in *this breeze of an outing*, the Yankees' Jorge Posada walks with one out. That's hardly a crisis in a 9-1 game. (2001 COCA)
         b. A photographic portrait made at the time shows a girl as slender and graceful as a tulip stem, with long, ringletted [*sic*] masses of black hair, deepest dark eyes, high Slavic cheekbones and skin as pale as January snow. ... *A perfect breeze of a girl* is how the Salonblatt, Vienna's snob-society newspaper, described the young Anna. A perfect breeze who turns into an exquisite storm when seated before the 88 black and white keys. (2003 COCA)

With *breeze* the diachronic development appears to be more straightforward than with *nub* (see Figure 6.3). Both N+PP and head-classifier uses appear to be relatively conventionalized at the start of the nineteenth century. Already there are ambiguous contexts with possible pseudo-partitive readings. Over the 200-year time period, examples of the pseudo-partitive become more frequent even though it is never as frequent as the first two constructions (see Table 6.4). The first tokens of the EBNP appear long after the pseudo-partitive; however, there are too few instances and no real bridging contexts to indicate which construction it developed from.

6.4.3 Husk(s)

According to the OED, *husk* appears in Late Middle English (*ca* 1400) and is of unknown origin. It originally referred to 'the outer covering of seeds or fruit' in (6.15a) or later, in American English, to 'the outer covering of an ear of corn' in (6.15b). In the seventeenth century, it extended to include animal coverings (as demonstrated in (6.16a)), and not long after its meaning expanded to comprise the outside of anything, including people (i.e. the human husk), as shown in example (6.16b). It was often applied in a depreciatory sense, as we will see below (OED).

(6.15)   a. Þe macez er þe huskes of þe nutemuge. (*ca* 1400 OED)
           'The outer covering or the husks of the nutmeg'

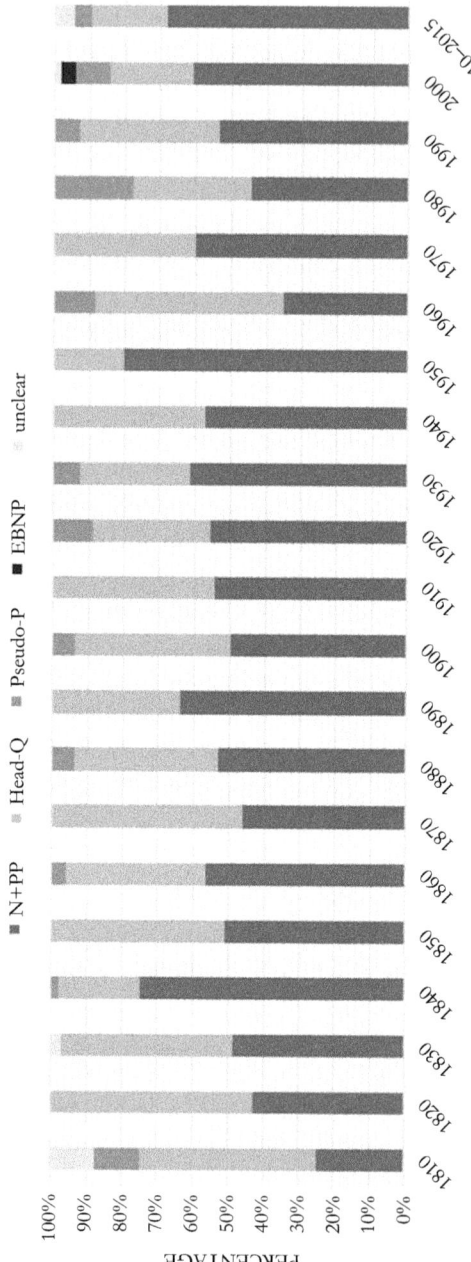

Figure 6.3 Distribution of *breeze(s)* in the *of*-binominal constructions from 1810 to 2015

b. the furniture of those huts, consisting of mats braided from *the husks of the Indian corn*, and baskets woven from splinters of the ash and hickory, together with a few utensils of the most primitive sort for the preparation of food (1849 COHA)

(6.16) a. Euerie one [silkworm] shutting vp himselfe in his scale or *husk*, which they make and build vp in two daies. (1600 OED)
'Every silkworm, shutting himself up in his shell or husk, which they make and build in two days.'
b. May not our Soul … challenge a good share of our time … or shall *this mortal husk* engross it all? (1677 OED)

Already in the seventeenth century, possible bridging contexts between the head-classifier and the pseudo-partitive appear, as demonstrated in example (6.17). In this example, *husk* might be a metaphorical extension of real husks (i.e. 'we just know the outer layer of reason'), or a pseudo-partitive, where *husk* means a small amount.

(6.17) But because he boasts so much of setling mens Consciences on warrant from Scripture … and thus would perswade men, as if he had all Scripture for him; we nothing but *a few huskes of reason for us*: Let him not thinke to carry it thus away with vaunts and big words … (1644 OED: P. Hunton, *Vindic. Treat. Monarchy*)

As the OED entry would lead us to expect, the tokens of *husk* from the nineteenth century already show frequent use in the N+PP, as demonstrated in (6.18a), and the head-classifier, as in (6.18b) (see also Table 6.5). There are also early examples with abstract second nouns in both constructions, as demonstrated in (6.19a) for the N+PP, and (6.19b) for the intrinsic head-classifier.

(6.18) a. The white floor was carefully sanded, and at each door a broad mat, made of *the husks of the Indian corn*. (1824 COHA)
b. Of knowledge e'er he gain his fill, he Must diet long on *husks of Lily* (1820 COHA)

(6.19) a. Great truths would bring him to God; the soul of science would do the same; he must shut himself up to little truths, and feed on *the husks of external knowledge*, phenomenal, experimental, fragmentary, partial, unconnected. (1835 COHA)
b. But it is doing violence to the soul, to its innate love of truth, and of growth by the nutriment of truth, to feed it thus with *the mere "husks of knowledge*, rather than knowledge itself." (1855 COHA)

In (6.19a), the verb *feed*, although used metaphorically, would still seem to indicate that *husk* is the head of the construction; in (6.19b), *feed* could

Table 6.5 Frequency of husk(s) in of-binominals in COHA and COCA

		COHA																			COCA		
		1810s	1820s	1830s	1840s	1850s	1860s	1870s	1880s	1890s	1900s	1910s	1920s	1930s	1940s	1950s	1960s	1970s	1980s	1990s	2000s	2010-2015s
N+PP	raw	0	1	0	5	6	2	2	1	3	3	6	4	3	1	0	2	3	6	8	20	21
	pmw	0.00	0.14	0.00	0.32	0.36	0.12	0.11	0.05	0.15	0.14	0.26	0.16	0.12	0.04	0.00	0.08	0.13	0.24	0.04	0.10	0.18
	%	0.00	50.00	0.00	71.43	54.55	40.00	20.00	14.29	37.50	33.33	54.55	44.44	42.86	20.00	0.00	40.00	37.50	85.71	17.02	38.46	46.67
Head-Cl	raw	0	1	1	2	5	3	6	6	5	6	5	4	4	4	2	1	4		34	23	18
	pmw	0.00	0.14	0.07	0.13	0.30	0.18	0.32	0.30	0.24	0.27	0.22	0.16	0.16	0.16	0.08	0.04	0.17	0.00	0.16	0.11	0.15
	%	0.00	50.00	100.00	28.57	45.45	60.00	60.00	85.71	62.50	66.67	45.45	44.44	57.14	80.00	50.00	20.00	50.00	0.00	72.34	44.23	40.00
Pseudo-P	raw	0	0	0	0	0	0	2	0	0	0	0	0	0	0	0	0	0	0	0	0	0
	pmw	0.00	0.00	0.00	0.00	0.00	0.00	0.11	0.00	0.00	0.00	0.00	0.00	0.00	0.00	0.00	0.00	0.00	0.00	0.00	0.00	0.00
	%	0.00	0.00	0.00	0.00	0.00	0.00	20.00	0.00	0.00	0.00	0.00	0.00	0.00	0.00	0.00	0.00	0.00	0.00	0.00	0.00	0.00
EBNP	raw	0	0	0	0	0	0	0	0	0	0	0	1	0	0	2	1	1	1	5	9	5
	pmw	0.00	0.00	0.00	0.00	0.00	0.00	0.00	0.00	0.00	0.00	0.00	0.04	0.00	0.00	0.08	0.04	0.04	0.04	0.02	0.04	0.04
	%	0.00	0.00	0.00	0.00	0.00	0.00	0.00	0.00	0.00	0.00	0.00	11.11	0.00	0.00	50.00	20.00	12.50	14.29	10.64	17.31	11.11
unclear	raw	0	0	0	0	0	0	0	0	0	0	0	0	0	0	0	1	0	0	0	0	1
	pmw	0.00	0.00	0.00	0.00	0.00	0.00	0.00	0.00	0.00	0.00	0.00	0.00	0.00	0.00	0.00	0.04	0.00	0.00	0.00	0.00	0.01
	%	0.00	0.00	0.00	0.00	0.00	0.00	0.00	0.00	0.00	0.00	0.00	0.00	0.00	0.00	0.00	20.00	0.00	0.00	0.00	0.00	2.22
Total	raw	0	2	1	7	11	5	10	7	8	9	11	9	7	5	4	5	8	7	47	52	45

Note: For each construction the raw figures are given at the top, normalized figures in the middle (normalized per hundred million words), and the percentage of all examples in that period at the bottom.

6.4 The Pseudo-partitive Strand

select either noun but the context, i.e. the comparison with *knowledge itself*, indicates that the first noun *husk* is the head of the *of*-binominal. As particularly seen in (6.19b), *husk* can portray a certain implied opprobrium, where speaker's disproval is also reflected in the choice of *mere*, and the fact that *husk of knowledge* is placed in opposition to *knowledge itself*.

Example (6.20) would appear to be a bridging context between the head-classifier and the pseudo-partitive. Based on the semantics gleaned from the narrow context provided, and the use of the premodifier *dry*, *husks of logic* would appear to be a head-classifier. However, in this example the verbs *hammer* and *slash* semantically select the second noun. Furthermore, the following *scraps of creed*, part of the same example, is clearly a pseudo-partitive. Thus, it appears to be a hybrid pseudo-partitive (see Section 3.4). *Dry* does not have an intensifier function and therefore either modifies the second noun or the overall referent.

(6.20) They hammered and slashed about, – *Dry husks of logic* – old scraps of creed, – And the cold gray dreams of doubt, – And whether Just or Justified Was the Church's mystic Head . . . (1871 COHA)

Distinct pseudo-partitive examples can be found toward the end of the eighteenth century, as in (6.21). Like the *breeze of wind* example above, *chaff* here means the husks of grains, so if *husk* denotes 'the outer covering of a grain' then this would be a tautology; therefore, it is more likely a pseudo-partitive with *husk* meaning a small amount or piece. This reading is further supported by context: *scarcely* and *so much as* would support a quantity reading.

(6.21) Then think of the vast numbers of editor-people and orator-people whom he has set to beating straw throughout the country, old straw, musty straw, straw that has scarcely so much as *a husk of chaff* in it – at which they thresh away day after day, week after week, with all the zeal of men garnering a harvest! (1872 COHA).

Finally, this depreciatory sense expressed in (6.19a–b) is accentuated in the EBNP. Most of the EBNP examples with *husk* (72 percent) refer to humans, indicating some flaw in a person's personality, as in (6.22a), or the person's body, as in (6.22b). In addition, examples can be found of *husk* being used to refer to inanimate entities, such as buildings as in (6.23).

(6.22) a. Then, finally, I realized I was just going to be *a burned-out husk of a person*, full of bitterness and nothing else . . . (1992 COCA)
b. If it is nothing, then for nothingness I offer thanks; if another mode of existence, with *this worn-out husk of a body* left behind, like a butterfly extricating itself from a chrysalis . . . (1979 COHA)

(6.23) He was born into *a ramshackle husk of a house* that had no indoor plumbing except for cold running water that froze in the pipes come winter – and the occasional hot running rat. (2008 COCA)

The EBNP appears to draw on the opprobrium found in many of the head-classifier examples; thus, it would seem more likely that the EBNP would stem from the head-classifier and not the pseudo-partitive (although this is hardly conclusive). Example (6.24) is the first EBNP example, and despite the noncanonical use of the definite determiner in the first determiner position, the context (i.e. *burned-out*, and *full of bitterness and nothing else*) makes it clear that by using *husk*, the narrator is negatively evaluating his stature or personality and not referring to an actual husk. There are no EM or BI tokens.

(6.24) The NORTH had done that for him; the north with its wonderful forests, its vast skies, its rivers, and its lakes, and its deep snows – the north that makes a man out of *the husk of a man* if given half a chance. (1921 COHA)

An analysis of *husk* would seem to support the divergence scenario for the pseudo-partitive appearing first and the EBNP much later (see Figure 6.4). The data does provide potential bridging contexts between the head-classifier and the pseudo-partitive; although this is not the case with the EBNP, semantically it seems likely that there is a head-classifier and EBNP link.

6.4.4 Snake(s)

Snake was already used in Old English to denote a "limbless vertebrate constituting the reptilian order Ophidia (characterized by a greatly elongated body, tapering tail, and smooth scaly integument)," as exemplified in (6.25a) (OED). In the sixteenth century, snake-like properties were also applied to people as a designation of contempt or pity, as in (6.25b); at the start of the seventeenth century, figurative uses of *snake* appeared, as seen in (6.25c) (OED). Although belonging to the animate group of first nouns, the noun *snake* is included in this section because it is one of the few animate first nouns used in the pseudo-partitive construction.

(6.25) a. Ic sealde eow anweald to tredenne ofer næddran & *snacan*. (*ca* 1000 OED)
'Behold, I gave you the power to tread upon adders and snakes.' (my gloss)
b. Thou Cupid worke, that I (*poore Snake in loue*). (1597 OED)
c. I feare me, you but warme *the starued Snake*, Who cherisht in your breasts, will sting your hearts. (1623 OED)

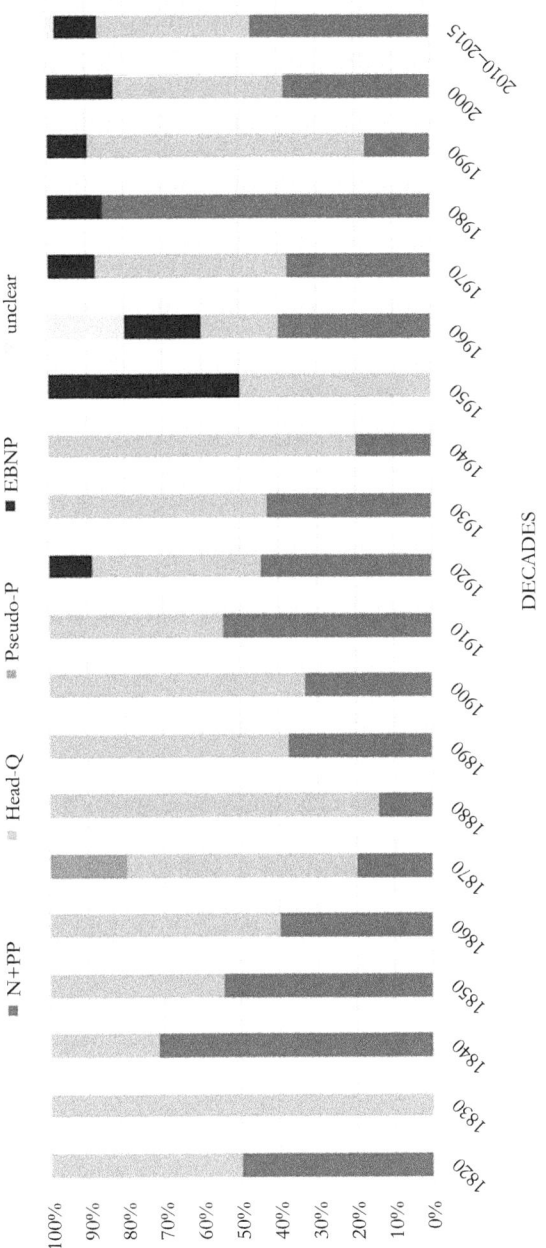

Figure 6.4 Distribution of *husk(s)* in the *of*-binominal constructions from 1820 to 2015 in COHA (see Table 6.5).
Note: No instances found in 1810.

As seen in Table 6.6, the first tokens in the COHA are N+PPs and head-classifiers, illustrated in (6.26a–b) and in (6.27a–b) respectively. In the first N+PP examples, the prepositional phrase indicates possession (6.26a) or location (6.26b). In (6.27a), *hell* in *snake of hell* may no longer designate a location, but the taxonomic category that the snake (Bonaparte) belongs to, thus indicating a particular type of snake. First examples of the head-classifier usually have abstract second nouns, as demonstrated in (6.27a–b), and they either designate a taxonomic category, as in (6.27a), or qualify the first noun, as in (6.27b).

(6.26) a. Or like *the brazen snake of Moses*, Cure your crackt skulls and batter'd noses? (1820 COHA)
b. Go thy ways, *snake of the sea*, spawn of a water devil! (1838 COHA)

(6.27) a. Officer O: soul wretch! *Thou snake of hell*!
Bonaparte: Stabs him again. (1815 COHA)
b. No more Permit its heat to warm to life *the snakes Of vice*, &; belch them from the envenom'd womb O'er all the earth, bearing within their mouths The sting of death. (1815 COHA)

Ambiguous examples, where the speaker could be using either the head-classifier or the pseudo-partitive, can be found in the 1880s, as seen in example (6.28).

(6.28) From one low threatening cloud, that rose to meet us, leaped out suddenly *A crinkled snake of fire*, then darted in; And thunder trampled with tumultuous roar (1886 COHA)

Example (6.28) is a case of personification and, thus, would appear to be a head-classifier; however, *snake* or *fire* could be semantically selected by the verbs *leap* and *dart*, and *crinkled* could modify *fire* as well as *snake*, which would indicate a hybrid pseudo-partitive.[5] Furthermore, *snake* and *fire* are co-ascriptive, and *snake* provides the fire only with a form, very similarly to *cake* in the pseudo-partitive (see Section 5.3). In these examples, we can see the possible confusion between the different readings, and how these contexts might invite a pseudo-partitive reading. Clearer pseudo-partitives appear later, as demonstrated by example (6.29), where *snake* indicates the shape the hair forms.

---

[5] There are also examples where the opposite is true, i.e. examples where semantically the construction appears to be a pseudo-partitive, whereas the premodifier in front of the first noun would point to a referential reading of the first noun, e.g. *the coiling snakes of snow* (COHA).

Table 6.6 Frequency of snake(s) in of-binominals in COHA and COCA

		COHA																			COCA			
		1810s	1820s	1830s	1840s	1850s	1860s	1870s	1880s	1890s	1900s	1910s	1920s	1930s	1940s	1950s	1960s	1970s	1980s	1990s	2000s	2010-2015
N+PP	raw	0	2	2	8	1	2	1	2	11	3	4	6	2	8	4	5	1	2	17	14	10
	pmw	0.00	0.29	0.15	0.51	0.06	0.12	0.05	0.10	0.54	0.14	0.17	0.23	0.08	0.33	0.16	0.21	0.04	0.08	0.08	0.07	0.08
	%	0.00	100.00	66.67	88.89	100.00	66.67	25.00	33.33	91.67	60.00	57.14	75.00	28.57	66.67	40.00	45.45	33.33	28.57	40.48	41.18	41.67
Head-Q	raw	2	0	0	1	0	1	3	3	1	0	0	0	1	0	4	4	1	2	7	3	3
	pmw	0.85	0.00	0.00	0.06	0.00	0.06	0.16	0.15	0.05	0.00	0.00	0.00	0.04	0.00	0.16	0.17	0.04	0.08	0.03	0.02	0.03
	%	100.00	0.00	0.00	11.11	0.00	33.33	75.00	50.00	8.33	0.00	0.00	0.00	14.29	0.00	40.00	36.36	33.33	28.57	16.67	8.82	12.50
Pseudo-P	raw	0	0	1	0	0	0	0	1	0	1	2	1	2	2	1	0	1	1	14	11	7
	pmw	0.00	0.00	0.07	0.00	0.00	0.00	0.00	0.05	0.00	0.05	0.09	0.04	0.08	0.08	0.04	0.00	0.04	0.04	0.07	0.05	0.06
	%	0.00	0.00	33.33	0.00	0.00	0.00	0.00	16.67	0.00	20.00	28.57	12.50	28.57	16.67	10.00	0.00	33.33	14.29	33.33	32.35	29.17
EBNP	raw	0	0	0	0	0	0	0	0	0	1	1	1	2	2	1	2	0	2	2	5	3
	pmw	0.00	0.00	0.00	0.00	0.00	0.00	0.00	0.00	0.00	0.05	0.04	0.04	0.08	0.08	0.04	0.08	0.00	0.08	0.01	0.02	0.03
	%	0.00	0.00	0.00	0.00	0.00	0.00	0.00	0.00	0.00	20.00	14.29	12.50	28.57	16.67	10.00	18.18	0.00	28.57	4.76	14.71	12.50
unclear	raw	0	0	0	0	0	0	0	0	0	0	0	0	0	0	0	0	0	0	2	1	1
	pmw	0.00	0.00	0.00	0.00	0.00	0.00	0.00	0.00	0.00	0.00	0.00	0.00	0.00	0.00	0.00	0.00	0.00	0.00	0.01	0.00	0.01
	%	0.00	0.00	0.00	0.00	0.00	0.00	0.00	0.00	0.00	0.00	0.00	0.00	0.00	0.00	0.00	0.00	0.00	0.00	4.76	2.94	4.17
Total	raw	2	2	3	9	1	3	4	6	12	5	7	8	7	12	10	11	3	7	42	34	24

Note: For each construction the raw figures are given at the top, normalized figures in the middle (normalized per hundred million words), and the percentage of all examples in that period at the bottom.

(6.29)   Nearer by a woman's figure bent over a kettle black on a bed of embers, then a girl's fire-touched form, with raised arms, shaking down *a snake of hair*, which broke and grew cloudy under her disturbing hands. (1910 COHA)

The first EBNP token appears at the start of the twentieth century, not long after the first pseudo-partitive token. *Snake* in the EBNP is used both with humans, as in (6.30a), and with inanimate objects, as in (6.30b). In both examples *snake* conveys a sense of opprobrium reinforced through the pre-modifiers, *mud-eating* and *horse-thieving* in (6.30a) and *confounded* in (6.30b).

(6.30)   a. Murders him like *the mud-eating, horse-thieving snake of a Greaser* that he is; but being within the law, the kid drawing on him first, he don't stretch hemp the way he should. (1903 COHA)
b. He may be over later when he gets *that confounded snake of an instrument* figured out. (1910 COHA)

Snake also denotes shape in (6.31a) and (6.31b), which appear to be neither pseudo-partitives nor EBNPs. Shape is not evaluative, and therefore, semantically they do not appear to be EBNPs. Although the definite article can be used in the first determiner slot in the EBNPs when referring to an entity that has or can be identifiable from context, the context indicates that this is not the case here. Moreover, the second nouns, *train* in (6.31a) and *measuring tape* in (6.31b), denote the referent of the whole construction (which means it cannot be an N+PP), and semantically *snake* would be ascribing a snake-like shape to both second nouns (very similar to the pseudo-partitive). However, the second nouns are not plurals or mass nouns (excluding a pseudo-partitive reading). As we have seen in previous examples, this shows a transitionary construction that is neither a pseudo-partitive nor an EBNP but functions as a bridge to the EBNP.[6]

(6.31)   a. There slope the hills beyond, Besprinkled with white houses and dark groves, Along whose base *the white snake of the train* Steals vanishing and nearer at my feet … (1886 COHA)
b. Over in the corner was the tall "dress form" which his mother used in her work. It had a quilted bosom and quilted hips, with wire mesh in the back and below. Saucers of pins and *the flat snake of a measuring tape* lay before it like votive offerings. (1934 COHA)

---

[6] These examples could be an example of another *of*-binominal construction (an appositional *of*-binominal) that functions as a transition between the pseudo-partitive or head-classifier (or N+PP, which would explain the definite article in the second determiner position) and the EBNP (see Keizer 2007a: 73–83). They were not included in this project because they are relatively infrequent.

6.4 The Pseudo-partitive Strand

A final point, although these constructions were not found to be frequent enough to be discussed in this project, partitive uses with *snake* were found in the earliest COHA examples, as in (6.32). There were no examples of EMs and BIs.

(6.32) As to the black snake, and viper and common water snake, you may amuse yourself with taking them in your hand. Or take St. Patrick's plan, Mr. Swansdown; cut a hazel rod, and if you use it properly you may conjure *every snake of them*, out of striking distance. (1832 COHA)

Interestingly, the first examples are head-classifiers, but since N+PPs appear soon afterwards there is no evidence that the head-classifier was first (see Figure 6.5). Uses in the pseudo-partitive appear the decade following. The EBNP appears much later. For *snake*, evidence for the transition between head-classifier and the pseudo-partitive can be found in the data, but none between head-classifier and EBNP. On the other hand, there is a potential link between the pseudo-partitive and the EBNP.

6.4.5 Discussion

This analysis cannot tell us anything about the historical link between the N+PP and the head-classifiers. All the nouns analyzed here entered English before the nineteenth century and were, therefore, most likely already used productively in the more prototypical and productive *of*-binominals before 1810. The corpus data appears to support this supposition in that most of these nouns are frequent in both constructions early in the nineteenth century. However, for constructions with the more prototypical pseudo-partitive first nouns (i.e. *nub*, *breeze*, and *husk*), the analysis indicates that the grammaticalization path diverges after the head-classifier, one direction leading to the pseudo-partitive and the other to the EBNP. In the case of *nub*, the pseudo-partitive and the EBNP appear at around the same time, whereas with *breeze* and *husk*, the EBNP appears much later. The data contains ambiguous constructions that would allow for both a head-classifier and an EBNP reading, potential bridging contexts. There are also, as would be expected from the shared formal features, cases where both a head-classifier and a pseudo-partitive reading is possible. Only with *snake* are there examples that might indicate a potential link between the pseudo-partitive and the EBNP, and therefore, the EBNP use might have developed from the pseudo-partitive. However, the *snake* examples are at best peripheral, hybrid pseudo-partitives denoting a shape and not a quantity. Furthermore, the case study with *cake* would also seem to

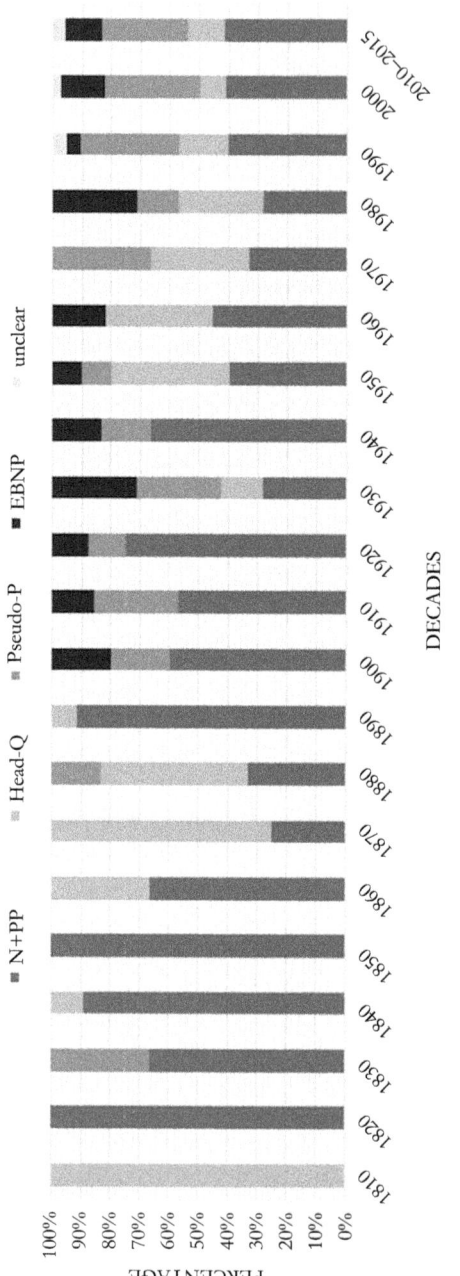

Figure 6.5 Distribution of *snake(s)* of the *of*-binominal constructions from 1810 to 2015

indicate that the pseudo-partitive plays a subsidiary role in this grammaticalization path, not part of the central path, since the pseudo-partitive with *cake* is frequent long before the first head-classifier constructions appear and even longer than the first EBNP (see Section 5.3).

The bridging or ambiguous contexts indicate how these constructions might have been reconceptualized and provide clues as to how the grammaticalization path is constructed. The progression of these first nouns would support the path proposed. However, many of the first nouns used in these constructions, as the first nouns discussed in this chapter demonstrate, appear infrequently in the corpora; thus, first examples probably do not represent when these constructions were first used in the language. This point is illustrated most clearly in *husk*: where the OED indicates that *husk* was used in the pseudo-partitive in the seventeenth century, the first examples in the corpus appear at the end of the nineteenth century. Therefore, the dates should be considered conservative estimates.

6.5 Evaluative Constructions: EBNP, EM, BI

This section focuses on the later stages of the proposed grammaticalization cline, in particular the transitions from the EBNP to the EM and from the EM to the BI. Both first nouns examined in this second study, *whale* and *bitch*, have been in the English language since the OE period; however, this is generally true for all the first nouns that progress to the BI. These two nouns have been chosen because *whale* represents the concrete nouns and *bitch* the abstract ones (at least in its use as an EBNP). *Whale* as an EM and BI is most likely an American phenomenon (OED), and therefore, the hope is that it has developed later than other first nouns. *Bitch* also most likely progressed into the EM and BI more recently, since its abstract use (i.e. not referring to a female dog) has only gained greater acceptability in modern American English (see Schneider 2011: 44–6). In the following analysis, first *whale* will be discussed (in Section 6.5.1) and then *bitch* (in Section 6.5.2).

6.5.1 Whale(s)

As mentioned in the introduction, *whale* already existed in OE (*hwæl*) as a lexical item denoting a large marine mammal, as demonstrated (6.33) (OED). The OED marks *whale*'s metaphorical extension from a physical creature to figurative uses such as "having a great capacity or appetite for," "very good at or keen on," or "no end of" at the end of the nineteenth century (OED; as demonstrated in (6.33b)); the OED also groups BIs under this definition (see example (6.33c)). However, "no end of" might work as a paraphrase for the example they provide (i.e. example 6.33c)), but not for the majority of the other BI examples as in (6.34). Still, this does indicate that although *whale* has been in English since Old English, the figurative uses and hence its use in the evaluative constructions (EBNP, EM, and BI) began to occur after 1810.

(6.33) a. Se hwæl bið micle læssa þonne oðre hwalas. (ca 893 OED)
'This whale is much smaller than other whales.' (my gloss)
b. He was not, as he put it himself graphically, *a whale* on geography. (1893 OED)
c. [They] had what the Americans call "*a whale of a good time*" (1913 OED)

(6.34) For instance, *a whale of a big sofa*, not only wide and cushiony but stretching from here to there, calls for more than two spindly chairs flanking it. (1965 COHA)

Table 6.7 shows only a few examples of *whale* in the N+PP and head-classifier constructions, which would be expected, since *whales* are not often discussed in normal day-to-day language use.[7] However, *whale* can occur in head-classifiers, usually as an intrinsic head-classifier designating the material the *whale* is made of, e.g. *a whale of stone*. The EBNPs begin to appear in the twentieth century, in which *whale* ascribes properties of large size to the second noun as in example (6.35a), and in this construction the second nouns are predominantly physical objects: in (6.35a) *fellow* refers to a cinder, and a person as in (6.35b), where *jumbo* in the previous sentence indicates that the man in question is indeed large (the fact that both *the whale of a man* and *Jumbo* refer to the same person would also explain the use of the definite article in the EBNP). There are also some tokens with abstract second nouns, such as *difference* in (6.35c).

(6.35) a. Hold still – just a – Hold still – There you are. No wonder you squirmed. That was *a whale of a fellow*. (Showing the cinder to Jim.) How's that for size, to get in a lady's eye? (1918 COHA)
b. "You could get that sarsaparilla across the bar at the Bird Cage, couldn't you, Jumbo?" the boy grinned. *The whale of a man* looked at him reproachfully. (1921 COHA)
c. Economic laws are immutable, and the first of these is that it makes *a whale of a difference* whose ox is gored. (1923 COHA)

---

[7] The eighteen tokens from the 1850s are from a single source, i.e. *Moby Dick*.

Table 6.7 *Frequency of whale(s) in of-binominals in COHA and COCA*

											COHA											COCA	
		1810s	1820s	1830s	1840s	1850s	1860s	1870s	1880s	1890s	1900s	1910s	1920s	1930s	1940s	1950s	1960s	1970s	1980s	1990s	2000s	2010-2015
N+PP	raw	0	0	1	0	18	3	0	1	0	1	2	4	0	3	0	0	4	2	6	18	9
	pmw	0.00	0.00	0.07	0.00	1.09	0.18	0.00	0.05	0.00	0.05	0.09	0.16	0.00	0.12	0.00	0.00	0.17	0.08	0.03	0.09	0.08
	%	0.00	0.00	100.00	0.00	100.00	100.00	0.00	100.00	0.00	100.00	25.00	9.76	0.00	21.43	0.00	0.00	40.00	40.00	13.64	39.13	39.13
Head-Q	raw	0	0	0	0	0	0	1	0	0	0	0	0	0	0	1	0	0	0	1	1	0
	pmw	0.00	0.00	0.00	0.00	0.00	0.00	0.05	0.00	0.00	0.00	0.00	0.00	0.00	0.00	0.04	0.00	0.00	0.00	0.00	0.00	0.00
	%	0.00	0.00	0.00	0.00	0.00	0.00	100.00	0.00	0.00	0.00	0.00	0.00	0.00	0.00	5.26	0.00	0.00	0.00	2.27	2.17	0.00
EBNP	raw	0	0	0	0	0	0	0	0	0	0	3	11	10	5	2	5	3	0	9	3	4
	pmw	0.00	0.00	0.00	0.00	0.00	0.00	0.00	0.00	0.00	0.00	0.13	0.43	0.40	0.20	0.08	0.21	0.13	0.00	0.04	0.01	0.03
	%	0.00	0.00	0.00	0.00	0.00	0.00	0.00	0.00	0.00	0.00	37.50	26.83	55.56	35.71	10.53	35.71	30.00	0.00	20.45	6.52	17.39
EM	raw	0	0	0	0	0	0	0	0	0	0	3	21	6	2	8	5	2	1	19	17	10
	pmw	0.00	0.00	0.00	0.00	0.00	0.00	0.00	0.00	0.00	0.00	0.13	0.82	0.24	0.08	0.32	0.21	0.08	0.04	0.09	0.08	0.08
	%	0.00	0.00	0.00	0.00	0.00	0.00	0.00	0.00	0.00	0.00	37.50	51.22	33.33	14.29	42.11	35.71	20.00	20.00	43.18	36.96	43.48
BI	raw	0	0	0	0	0	0	0	0	0	0	0	5	2	4	8	4	1	2	4	5	0
	pmw	0.00	0.00	0.00	0.00	0.00	0.00	0.00	0.00	0.00	0.00	0.00	0.19	0.08	0.16	0.32	0.17	0.04	0.08	0.02	0.024	0
	%	0.00	0.00	0.00	0.00	0.00	0.00	0.00	0.00	0.00	0.00	0.00	12.20	11.11	28.57	42.11	28.57	10.00	40.00	9.09	10.87	0.00
unclear	raw	0	0	0	0	0	0	0	0	0	0	0	0	0	0	0	0	0	0	5	2	0
	pmw	0.00	0.00	0.00	0.00	0.00	0.00	0.00	0.00	0.00	0.00	0.00	0.00	0.00	0.00	0.00	0.00	0.00	0.00	0.02	0.01	0.00
	%	0.00	0.00	0.00	0.00	0.00	0.00	0.00	0.00	0.00	0.00	0.00	0.00	0.00	0.00	0.00	0.00	0.00	0.00	11.36	4.35	0.00
Total	raw	0	0	1	0	18	3	1	1	0	1	8	41	18	14	19	14	10	5	44	46	23

Note: For each construction the raw figures are given at the top, normalized figures in the middle (normalized per hundred million words), and the percentage of all examples in that period at the bottom.

The transition between the EBNP and EM might have been facilitated by a link to the conventional metaphor IMPORTANCE IS SIZE, e.g. *Gates is a big man in the large community* (COCA) (Grady, Oakley & Coulson 1999: 112). There is only a single example of a potential EBNP to EM bridge context, example (6.36), before the EMs and even the EBNPs begin to appear in the dataset at the start of the twentieth century. The premodifier makes this example ambiguous.

(6.36)   And, as luck would have it, as I swept the glass round, what should I see but a long rakish corvette in company with *a huge whale of a line-of-battle ship*, with her double tier of ports glimmering away in the slanting rays of the sun, both on the wind … (1864 COHA)

Example (6.36) has two possible readings. The first is that *whale* is being used in an EBNP construction to denote 'largeness', and *huge* functions as an intensifier of that property. The second is that *huge* ascribes size onto the second noun, and *whale* simply signals speaker approbation (an irregular EM). The fact that there are bridging constructions between the EBNP and the EM in the data, despite the paucity of EBNP examples before the twentieth century, would lead one to suspect that *whale* was used in the EBNP before this time period. Example (6.36) also appears almost fifty years before the next EM token.

As already mentioned above, the first examples of the EM appear at the start of the twentieth century, and in these constructions, *whale* no longer denotes size (as in the EBNP) and just indicates approval or greatness, as seen in example (6.37a). The EM also takes human second nouns but only indicates importance, not size (6.37b). Even with the earliest examples of *whale* in the EM, the second nouns are concrete animate objects (6.37b), inanimate objects (6.37c), and abstract concepts (6.37a).

(6.37) a. "Then you get Dad into a game of billiards, play as well as you can and – lose." "*A whale of an idea!*" exclaimed Trask. (1913 COHA)
    b. And the railroad people he'd been with before had been shifted around so much that they'd forgotten all about him. He wasn't the kind to tell' em what *a whale of a guy* he was, and nobody else did it for him. (1920 COHA)
    c. I've seed many a gold camp in me day, boy, and plenty as good as the Klondyke before I ever struck that Canadian bird; but I never got into ground so rich as this. I tell you, boy, it not only makes me eyes bug out, but it makes me hair stand on end, fur it's *a whale of a gold creek!* (1910 COHA)

6.5 Evaluative Constructions: EBNP, EM, BI

The BIs begin to appear slightly after the EBNPs and EMs in the 1920s, although not with the same frequency (see Table 6.7). The bridge between the EM and BI might lie in the ambiguity between classifier and descriptive modification in front of the second noun. If the premodifier *gold* in (6.37c) is conceptualized as a classifier, the most likely reading is that [*whale of a*] modifies the head, and the construction is an EM. Should the context allow a descriptive modifier reading of *gold*, i.e. *a very golden creek*, then [*whale of a*] could be reconceptualized as an intensifier, and the construction is a BI. In the BI examples, [*whale of a*] intensifies both gradable modifiers (see example (6.38a)) and quantifiers such as *a lot* (see example (6.38b)).

(6.38)   a. He's had a chance all evening to tell you what *a whale of a fine fellow* he is. (1920 COHA)
          b. "Oh, do let us! I think it would be lovely to present 'Romeo and Juliet'!" yearned Ella Stowbody. "Be *a whale of a lot of fun*," Dr. Terry Gould granted. (1920 COHA)

Figure 6.6 shows that, unlike in the other first nouns, *whale* in the N+PP was used only sporadically at the start. Table 6.7 shows an increase in frequency with the transition of *whale* into the evaluative constructions (EBNP, EM, and BI), and Figure 6.6 shows that the evaluative uses dominate the dataset. As already mentioned at the start of this section, this result is not unexpected; one does not often talk about the animal but with a change in function in the evaluative constructions, where *whale* comes to denote only something big or wonderful, or just intensifies a modifier, the first noun becomes more serviceable for non-maritime conversations. This increase in frequency would be predicted by grammaticalization theory (see Section 5.2).

6.5.2 Bitch(es)

According to the OED, *bitch* denoting a female dog already existed in Old English (see example (6.39a)), and in the sixteenth century, it metaphorically extended to a censorious reference ascribed to a female human (as demonstrated in (6.39b)). In the eighteenth century this form then extended to include men, as shown in (6.39c), though less negatively (OED).

(6.39)   a. Canicula, bicge. (*ca* 1000 OED)
          b. Come out thou *hungry nedy bytche*. (1575 OED)
          c. Landlord is *a vast comical Bitch*. (1749 OED)

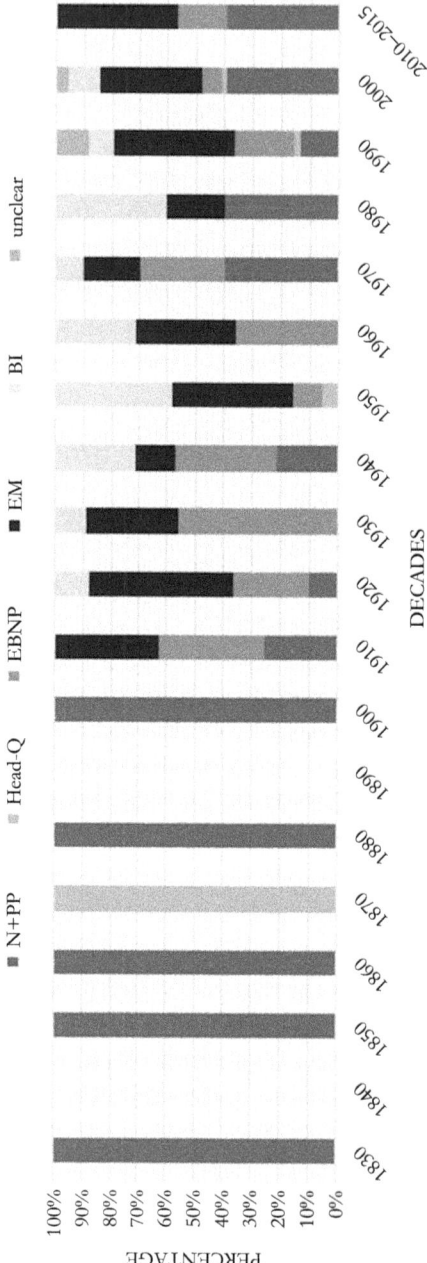

Figure 6.6 Distribution of *whale(s)* in the *of*-binominal constructions from 1830 to 2015
Note: First tokens in COHA found in 1830 (see Table 6.7).

6.5 Evaluative Constructions: EBNP, EM, BI

There are very few tokens with *bitch* in the *of*-binominal in the corpora, and most of the examples appear in the twentieth century (see Table 6.8). However, the data does propose an interesting scenario for the transition between the EBNP and the EM. In the EBNP, *bitch* usually collocates with human second nouns, as demonstrated in (6.40a). In this example, *bitch* is used to express the speaker's negative evaluation of the referent's behavior and is interchangeable with the adjective *bitchy*. This function is extended to second nouns denoting objects that are often referred to, conceptualized, or personified as human, i.e. *the tub* (boat) in (6.40b), and England (often referred to as Mother England) in (6.40c). This results in vagueness about the exact semantic properties that *bitch* ascribes to the referent, which is shown by the unnaturalness of the adjectival alternative (e.g. ?*England, they all said, was a bitchy nation*). This change then facilitates the general acceptance of inanimate second nouns, as demonstrated by examples (6.41a) and (6.41b), both of which are EMs, but results in the loss of semantic value in *bitch*. In (6.41a–b), *bitch* no longer ascribes 'bitchiness' to the referent; instead, both cases have strong negative connotations (Heine's switch context).

(6.40) a. Think of it, Lorry, her lovely Lorry, in bed with *that skinny bitch of a wife*! Think of it! Oh, God! (1936 COHA)
b. God damned *old crummy bitch of a tub*. (1930 COHA)
c. England, they all said, was *an old bitch of a nation* who was everlastingly sticking her imperial nose into the affairs of others ... (1941 COHA)

(6.41) a. "We'll have *a bitch of a job* getting through the plasmasphere, though," said the chief. "That fraction of a second will--" "It'll jolt us," Mike agreed, interrupting. "But it won't wreck us. Let's get going." (1962 COHA)
b. It's those foul Paris drawing rooms did me in, sweetheart, that foul middle-class disease passed on by women, to rise, to rise. *You bitch of a city*, you finally did me in. (1976 COHA)

In the EM, *bitch* first means 'difficult', similarly to *beast* in the EM, as demonstrated by (6.41a), and 'very bad' as in (6.41b). At some point there is a change in prosody, and *bitch* in the EM develops a positive connotation, as demonstrated in (6.42). In this example, *bitch* clearly denotes a positive evaluation of the car that has *four barrel, headers*, and *mags*. There is only a single example of a BI, as demonstrated in (6.43).

Table 6.8 Frequency of bitch(es) in of-binominals in COHA and COCA

		COHA									COCA		
		1920s	1930s	1940s	1950s	1960s	1970s	1980s	1990s	2000s	2010-2015
N+PP	raw	1	0	1	4	0	3	0	6	2	6
	pmw	0.04	0.00	0.04	0.16	0.00	0.13	0.00	0.03	0.01	0.05
	%	100.00	0.00	33.33	57.14	0.00	37.50	0.00	30.00	8.00	25.00
Head-Q	raw	0	0	0	0	0	0	0	2	0	1
	pmw	0.00	0.00	0.00	0.00	0.00	0.00	0.00	0.01	0.00	0.01
	%	0.00	0.00	0.00	0.00	0.00	0.00	0.00	10.00	0.00	4.17
EBNP	raw	0	2	2	2	1	2	4	9	9	9
	pmw	0.00	0.08	0.08	0.08	0.04	0.08	0.16	0.04	0.04	0.08
	%	0.00	40.00	66.67	28.57	33.33	25.00	50.00	45.00	36.00	37.50
EM	raw	0	0	0	1	2	3	4	3	12	6
	pmw	0.00	0.00	0.00	0.04	0.08	0.13	0.16	0.01	0.06	0.05
	%	0.00	0.00	0.00	14.29	66.67	37.50	50.00	15.00	48.00	25.00
BI	raw	0	0	0	0	0	0	0	0	1	0
	pmw	0.00	0.00	0.00	0.00	0.00	0.00	0.00	0.00	0.01	0.00
	%	0.00	0.00	0.00	0.00	0.00	0.00	0.00	0.00	4.00	0.00
unclear	raw	0	3	0	0	0	0	0	0	1	2
	pmw	0.00	0.12	0.00	0.00	0.00	0.00	0.00	0.00	0.00	0.02
	%	0.00	60.00	0.00	0.00	0.00	0.00	0.00	0.00	4.00	8.33
Total	raw	1	5	3	7	3	8	8	20	25	24

Note: For each construction the raw figures are given at the top, normalized figures in the middle (normalized per hundred million words), and the percentage of all examples in that period at the bottom.

6.5 Evaluative Constructions: EBNP, EM, BI

(6.42) I'm saving for this guy's Camaro. Man, it is *one bitch of a car*. Four barrel, headers, mags. Give me your fifty bucks and I'll drive you around anytime you want. (1996 COCA)

(6.43) You know, friend, this is *a goddamn bitch of a unsatisfactory situation*. (2000 COCA)

The extension of N_2 in the EBNP from nouns denoting humans to those denoting personified objects, and then, finally, to those denoting all types of objects could plausibly explain the transition between EBNP and EM. Furthermore, this scenario would conform to Heine's three stage grammaticalization process discussed in Section 6.2; clearly, lexical context (i.e. second noun collocates) plays an important role in facilitating an alternative analysis of *bitch* in the EBNP and aided the transition to the EM. As was the case with *whale*, this noun is not very frequent in the N+PP and head-classifier, but as soon as it is used in the EBNP the frequency increased, particularly in the EBNP and the EM (see Figure 6.7).

6.5.3 Discussion

An analysis of *whale* and *bitch* provides evidence of a transition between the EBNP and the EM. With *whale* this transition is more subtle. First the general context would allow for a size (EBNP) or approbation (EM) reading, as seen in the ship example (6.36). Then the construction begins to recruit second nouns that can take only the approbation reading and not the size one. With *bitch*, the second noun collocates play a more central role in facilitating this reanalysis, moving from female entities to inanimate entities personified as female and then inanimate entities. Unfortunately, one can only speculate on the development of the BI; *whale* appears to transition into BI at about the same time it is used in the EBNP and EM. In the case of *bitch*, it appears to be a consecutive change, i.e. first the EM, and only recently the BI with only a single BI token of a *bitch*, which appears almost forty years after the first EM token.

Semantically, there is a clear shift of meaning from the first noun denoting some concrete entity in the N+PP, e.g. *a whale of England* or *the little yapping terrier bitch of Edward of Wales*, to ascribing a descriptive feature such as in 'large size' in the EBNP, e.g. *a whale of a man*, or personality traits in *his bitch of a wife* to speaker evaluation in the EM, e.g. *a whale of a job or a bitch of a headache*. This clearly demonstrates a path from denoting external situations to internal situations or states.

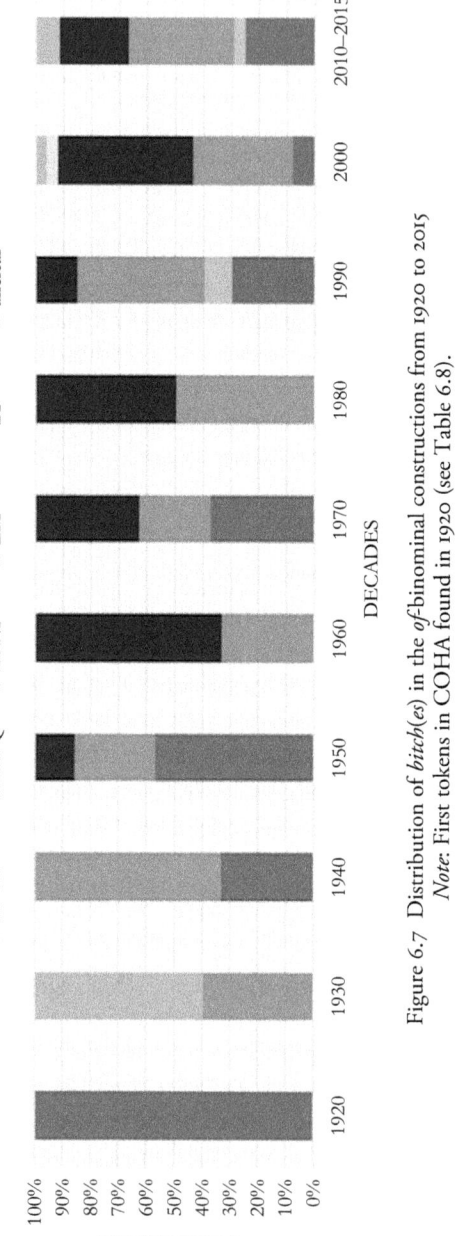

Figure 6.7 Distribution of *bitch(es)* in the *of*-binominal constructions from 1920 to 2015
Note: First tokens in COHA found in 1920 (see Table 6.8).

Furthermore, the transition from the head-classifier to the EBNP, from the EBNP to the EM and then the BI is characterized by a shift from the first noun denoting an objective property to the first noun, *a whale of a man*(EBNP) to expressing the speaker's attitude, belief, or evaluation of the object or event denoted by the second noun, *a whale of a time* (EM) to an intensifier of a gradable property, *a whale of a good time* (BI): this is a clear case of subjectification (for discussion see Section 5.2).

6.6 Conclusion

The data from this analysis provides evidence of bridging contexts between the head-classifier and pseudo-partitive, head-classifier and EBNP, the EBNP and EM, and the EM and the BI. Therefore, this empirical analysis provides evidence supporting the grammaticalization path in Figure 6.1. Furthermore, it would indicate that in most cases, there is divergence after the head-classifier. At this stage, first nouns develop, in the case of inanimate first nouns, the pseudo-partitive function and then (usually) subsequently, the EBNP uses from the head-classifier. This means that the pseudo-partitive might have a more auxiliary role. Animate and abstract first nouns transition into the EBNP from the head-classifier. However, there are naturally exceptions, *snake* being the one examined in this chapter. The data gives some indication that the EBNP with *snake* might have developed from the pseudo-partitive. Particularly with *snake*, this is plausible, since it is only used in the hybrid-pseudo-partitive form and never develops into a prototypical quantificational pseudo-partitive. Therefore, ambiguity between a head-classifier, pseudo-partitive, and EBNP reading is understandable.

The transition between the EBNP and the EM in both *whale* and *bitch* results in expansion of the range of N_2 collocates and subsequent increase in frequency. Particularly in the case of *bitch*, the change from selecting animate second nouns to inanimate ones most likely facilitated the reanalysis from an EBNP construction to that of the EM. Finally, in the BI, [N of (a)] shifts into the adjectival phrase and intensifies either gradable adjectives or quantifiers.

The findings also show that there is a clear semantic and pragmatic expansion which has resulted in diversification and layering.[8] First the

---

[8] Layering (a term taken from Givón 1984: 32–5) means that more than one form can adopt a certain function. However, the term can also refer to the retention of older forms in semantic change, in that older meanings are still retained alongside younger ones (Traugott & Dasher 2002: 12).

study shows that diachronically the first nouns indeed change, thus allowing expansion into other constructions and collocations with more diverse second nouns. Second, the study shows that the older constructions continue to exist despite the development of the new forms, and the different meanings of the first noun also tend to coexist: the intensifier use of *whale* in the BI, *a whale of a beautiful day*, did not oust the original *whale* that denotes the oceanic mammal, and in frequent cases this may result in polysemy. However, particularly in the case of *whale*, this resulted in an increased frequency and expansion into more diverse contexts. The first nouns discussed in this chapter show different degrees of attrition, e.g. *breeze* changes from referring to a type of movement of air to simply denoting a small amount; *whale* transitions from referring to a large mammal that swims in the sea to expressing speaker approbation. The first nouns used in the pseudo-partitive constructions shift from referring to a referent to denoting a quantity to expressing an evaluative property; those used in the evaluative *of*-binominals semantically shift from denoting physical properties to abstract properties to a subjective evaluation of a referent to an intensifier.

The study shows that the 'younger' constructions, such as the BI and EM, are more selective. Therefore, all six nouns are used in the older N+PP, head-classifier, and the EBNP. Four of the six nouns are used in the pseudo-partitive, even the animate *snake* although it would not prototypically belong to this group (which tends to prefer inanimate first nouns). However, only *bitch* and *whale* are used in the EM and BI, and the former only tentatively. Returning to the discussion in Chapter 4, altogether only a few first nouns in the dataset are used in the EM and even fewer can be found in the BI. This would provide evidence that these are newer forms.

In sum, this chapter examined the development of the first nouns to infer the development of the syntactic forms. The evidence of this analysis would then support the grammaticalization path proposed in Chapter 5. It would also appear to indicate that the pseudo-partitive has a more subsidiary role in this grammaticalization process, and the reanalysis of the left-headed construction to that of a right-headed one in the pseudo-partitive facilitated the use of these first nouns in the EBNP. However, it does not appear to be directly linked to the EBNP, and the more plausible historical link is between the head-classifier and the EBNP. The EM does appear to have developed out of the EBNP and the BI from the EM.

CHAPTER 7

Premodification Evidence

7.1 Introduction

The link between premodification patterns and the different binominal constructions discussed in Part I of this study is threefold. First, previous studies (e.g. Aarts 1998; Keizer 2007a; Kim & Sells 2015) have noted that the EBNP exhibits irregular premodification patterns in that modifiers clearly selected by the second noun can appear before the first noun, in examples such as *a bitchy iceberg of a woman* (example from Aarts 1998: 133); this chapter looks for a systematic explanation for this development.

Second, premodification restrictions have been used in previous research on *of*-binominals as support for distinctions between binominal categories. For example, Keizer (2007a: 142) uses premodification patterns, particularly in her analysis of pseudo-partitives, as support for her distinction between five subtypes of pseudo-partitives, as well as for the distinction between pseudo-partitive constructions, on the one hand, and referential (head-classifier) constructions, on the other. Similarly, Brems (2011), in her extensive study on size and type *of*-binominals, takes changes or restrictions in premodification patterns to substantiate her arguments for recognizing a new *of*-binominal category, and emphasizes "the importance of systematically studying premodification patterns in arguing for the grammaticalization status of changes in binominal constructions" (Brems 2011: 191).[1] Alexiadou, Haegeman, and Stavrou (2007: 418) note in their study of the pseudo-partitive that premodification patterns offer clues as to the function of the two nouns in the *of*-binominal, since "[i]f N_1 is functional it rejects adjectival modification."

Finally, in Part I, I propose that in the evaluative constructions (the EBNP, EM, and BI), the [N of a] chunk has developed into a modifier in

---

[1] Partington (1993) also uses collocates as evidence for delexicalization of intensifiers and also modifier collocates to help decipher intensifier meaning.

the EBNP and EM, and an intensifier in the BI. This would lead to the assumption that the [N of a] chunk functions like a more prototypical premodifier, making it logical to assume that this chunk would integrate into the already existing premodification patterns. Therefore, evidence either supporting or refuting this finding should appear in the distribution of the premodifiers in EBNPs, EMs, and BIs.

The central aim of this chapter is to see if a study of the premodification patterns found in the various *of*-binominals discussed in Part I does indeed provide evidence for the grammaticalization path hypothesized in this book. The empirical project described in this chapter thus addresses the following questions:

(1) Do the six constructions show unique, individual premodification patterns? If so, what are the premodifier patterns of these constructions?
(2) Are there distinctions between the EM and BI and the EBNP that would substantiate my claim to distinguish between the three? If so, then what features distinguish each *of*-binominal?
(3) Is the selector of modification, the first or the second noun (the feature so characteristic of the EBNP), a significant feature found in other premodification patterns?

This chapter will first introduce the different approaches to categorizing premodification and explain the premodifier classification used for the data coding in this project. Second, the corpus study which was conducted to determine the significant features and trends in the premodification patterns of all six related *of*-binominals will be presented to see if these can provide evidence for the changes hypothesized in Part I.

7.2 Approaches to Premodification

It is generally agreed upon that prototypical adjectives "make a statement that something has a certain property" (Dixon 2010: 70) or function "as a specification that helps identify the referent of the head noun" (Dixon 2010: 71; see also pp. 62–108; Ferris 1993). English adjectives are prototypically placed in either the attributive or the predicative positions, are typically gradable, and can themselves be modified (Quirk et al. 1985: 402–3).

This is a very straightforward definition of a category with many exceptions due to the ambiguity inherent in the semantics of many premodifiers, and it is both the exceptions and the polysemous forms that raise so many questions about premodifier classification and word order. For example, is *massive*, in (7.1a), a descriptive modifier, as in *the injections are massive*, or a quantifier, as in *a massive amount of injections?* The following horse comment would support the former and the *one at a time* comment the latter interpretation. In (7.1b), two premodifiers are of interest: *Ebola* and *highest*.[2] As for the former, *Ebola* cannot be used predicatively in a copular construction: we cannot say **the patients are Ebola* (only *the patients have Ebola*). Therefore, *Ebola* does not assign a property to the patient but indicates what sort of patient it is. As to *highest*, whether *highest* classifies the type of level or functions as a subjective descriptive modifier (like *best*) can only be answered by Trump. Furthermore, not only does an adjective's semantic variability play a role in the discussion, but, in addition, the choice of noun may effect a change in its interpretation: the *small* in *a small elephant* is not the same *small* as the one in *a small microbe*.

(7.1)   a. No more **massive** injections. Tiny children are not horses – one vaccine at a time, over time. (Trump Tweet 2014)[3]
       b. Stop *the* **EBOLA** *patients* from entering the U.S. Treat them, at *the* **highest** *level*, over there. (Trump Tweet 2014)[4]

To some extent, syntactic placement helps to disambiguate the different readings of one and the same adjective, as there seems little dispute over the fact that there is a link between the adjectival meaning or function and syntactic placement (e.g. Alexiadou et al. 2007: 288–394; Bolinger 1967; Dixon 1982). English has essentially three different syntactic slots for nominal modification: prenominal (7.2a), predicative (7.2b), and (infrequently) postnominal (7.2c).

(7.2)   a. the **visible** star
       b. the star is **visible**
       c. the star **visible**

Bolinger (1967) was the first to point out that should a modifier be allowed in both prenominal and postnominal positions, these different positions encode a different meaning. Thus, in (7.3a) the property *observable* would be interpreted as a property that is generally permanent or true, while in (7.3b), it would be interpreted as a temporary property. This can be seen in the possible strangeness of (7.3c), but the acceptability of (7.3b).

---

[2] *Ebola patients* might also be analyzed as a compound (see Section 7.3.1.1 for more discussion).
[3] Donald J. Trump. Twitter post. September 3, 2014. 3:29 p.m. (http://twitter.com/realDonaldTrump)
[4] Donald J. Trump. Twitter post. August 1, 2014. 2:22 p.m. (http://twitter.com/realDonaldTrump).

However, this distinction in English is not as clearly defined as it is in Romance languages such as French and Spanish (for further discussion see Bouchard 2002; Cinque 2010).

(7.3)   a. The North Star is one of *the **observable** stars*.
        b. The North Star is one of *the stars **observable*** at the moment.
        c. ?The North Star is one of *the **observable** stars* at the moment.

Similarly, in the premodifier position, syntactic placement plays a role. Larson (1999) noted that premodifiers close to the head tend to designate permanent properties, and those further away from the head temporary properties, as demonstrated in examples (7.4a–b). Example (7.4a) thus communicates that stars that are usually visible are now invisible, which is a plausible event. The opposite would be true for (7.4b), which would explain the unnaturalness of this sentence. Therefore, there is a difference not only in the meaning and function of modifiers placed in the predicative, prenominal, and postnominal positions, but also in the order of the premodifiers.

(7.4)   a. *the **invisible visible** stars* include Capella
        b. ?*the **visible invisible** stars* include Capella
        (Larson 1999)

Based on these observations, linguists have postulated a set premodifier ordering or premodifier zones; therefore, a change in syntactic position potentially relates to a change in meaning. Numerous premodification linear orderings or taxonomies have been presented. On the one hand, there are the various premodification distinctions and hierarchies proposed by generative grammarians (e.g. Cinque 1994, 2010, 2014; Laenzlinger 2005; Scott 1998, 2002; Sproat & Shih 1988, 1991). On the other hand, there are various zone-based approaches to premodification, implicitly suggested in Dixon's (1982) taxonomy of descriptive modifiers and more explicitly in Quirk et al.'s (1985: 437, 1338–40) zones. The Quirk et al. zone-based approach to categorizing premodification divides the space between the determinative and the head into four premodifier zones: the precentral, central, postcentral, and head, and this model has then been adopted and elaborated on by contemporary cognitive-functional linguists such as Breban (2010), Davidse and Breban (2019); Feist (2012), and Ghesquière (2014, 2017).

From the range of premodification approaches and categories proposed for the English NP (e.g. Cinque 1994, 2010; Dixon 1982; Feist 2012; Ghesquière 2009, 2014, 2017; Quirk et al. 1985; Scott 1998, 2002),

I choose a linear, zone-based classification in the present study. One important consideration was that the model chosen had to be amenable to a functional-cognitive view of language, since the two theories in Part III are functional-cognitive theories. Second, a grammatical class-based approach to premodification (e.g. Dixon 1982; Quirk et al. 1985) would be inadequate because the hypothesis proposed at the start of the chapter maintains that in the EM, the [N of (a)] chunk functions as an evaluative modifier: it would be difficult to classify this chunk as belonging to a particular grammatical class. Furthermore, a functional-based categorization offers a more flexible set of parameters for the categorization of premodifiers, one not found in the Dixon or Quirk et al. models, which focus on minute semantic distinctions such as speed, size, etc. (see Cinque 1994, 2010; Dixon 1982; Scott 1998, 2002).[5] The relevant issue here is not the semantic content of the premodifiers, which will predominantly be restricted by the nouns chosen, but the functional categories of premodification found.

Ghesquière's (2014) cognitive-functional model was chosen, first because of its theoretical foundation in Construction Grammar (discussed in greater detail in Chapter 8), and second, because the categorical distinctions the model makes are (with only a few exceptions) similar to the modification categories in the second theory discussed here, Functional Discourse Grammar (see Chapter 9), making the two models comparable. Furthermore, it offers broad categories that facilitated data coding. Section 7.3 will introduce the Ghesquière model and issues related to this model; Section 7.4 introduces the methods and results of the empirical project. Section 7.5 concludes the chapter with an explanation and discussion of these results.

7.3 Ghesquière's Cognitive-Functional Model

To denote Ghesquière's (2014) model as purely linear is a bit of a misnomer because, unlike other models (e.g. Feist 2012; Quirk et al. 1985: 1340), it does attempt to take into account scope relationships between the different functional categories. Ghesquière (2014: 13) theoretically orients herself to a constructional approach, defining constructions (as per Croft 2001; Fried 2010) as "functional structures in which grammar and lexis are integrated with each other, i.e. as distinct form-meaning pairings" (Ghesquière 2014: 14), and her model builds on Halliday's Systemic Functional Grammar NP model

---

[5] For example, Scott (1998: 71) proposes the following taxonomy: Ordinal > Cardinal > Subjective Comment > Evidential > Size > Length > Height > Speed > Depth > Width > Temperature > Wetness > Age > Shape > Color > Nationality/Origin > Material.

(Halliday 1985, 1994, Halliday & Matthiessen 2014), Bach's (2000) functional zone model of the English NP, and Langacker's (1991, 2002) work in cognitive grammar. Essentially this model assumes a function-based rather than a grammatical category or semantic-based approach to premodification (see also Breban 2010), i.e. there is no one-to-one correlation between a word's grammatical category and a word's premodifier function. This model breaks up the prototypical NP template into three primary zones according to their function: categorization, modification, and determination (see Figure 7.1).

The categorization zone potentially consists of two elements: the head, designating the type of referent, and classifiers "which indicate a subtype of the type denoted by the head" (Ghesquière 2014: 25). The modification zone consists of two types of modifiers, descriptive and degree modifiers. The former attributes subjective and objective properties and qualities to the head, to some extent comparable to Feist's (2012) epithet and descriptive modifier zones. However, unlike Feist, Ghesquière distinguishes between two different degree modifiers. She defines degree modifiers as lexical items that "measure the degree of gradable properties referred to by the descriptive modifiers (adjective-intensifiers) and/or the head of the NP (noun-intensifiers)" (Ghesquière 2014: 25; see also Adamson 2000). In the outer-left zone, we find the determiners, and the linguistic elements in this zone ascribe identifying and quantifying information (Ghesquière 2014: 25). The present chapter focuses on the modification and the categorization zones, which will be discussed in more detail below.

The principle behind a zone-based approach to premodification is that the existence of zones would explain why *smart* can classify or define the type of bomb in (7.5a), ascribe a descriptive, observable property to the boy in (7.5b), and ascribe a subjective speaker evaluation of the bonnet in (7.5c). Hence position in the premodifier zone (naturally disambiguated by the semantics of the head and context) helps the hearer/reader disambiguate the meaning of *smart* that the speaker intended. This can be seen more clearly when noncanonical lexical items or complex structures serve a particular premodifying function, as demonstrated in example (7.6); in this case a whole clause functions as a classifier of the head *day*. Another important feature of the zone-based approach is that as a premodifier grammaticalizes, it tends to move from right to left along the premodifier zones, from more objective to subjective (e.g. Adamson 2000; Ghesquière 2014).[6]

---

[6] There are also studies where elements from the determiner zones become intensifiers, left to right, e.g. Davidse 2009.

Instantiation of a type of entity							
determination			modification			categorization	
secondary	primary	secondary	degree modification		descriptive modification		
			noun-intensifier	adjective-intensifier	subjective	objective	classifier	head
				bleached				
				non-bleached				
all	those		utter	really	pretty	little	garden	flowers
	those			lovely		long		madness legs

Figure 7.1 Ghesquière's cognitive-functional NP model (Ghesquière 2014: 24)

(7.5)   a. an American **smart** bomb
        b. a **smart** Viking boy
        c. a **smart** blue bonnet
        (Feist 2009: 309)

(7.6)   It's a **I-wish-I-never-got-outta-bed** day.

Although there is a lot of agreement between the Ghesquière zones and other zone-based categorizations, some of Ghesquière's zone distinctions are controversial and proved to be problematic in the data analysis. Therefore, Sections 7.3.1–7.3.3 will describe the zones in more detail and discuss some issues before presenting the final coding based on this discussion.

7.3.1   The Classifier Category

In the categorization zone, Ghesquière (2014: 26) explains, the head can be realized by a noun or a compound noun. The main evidence for compounding is that the component part of compounds cannot be separated by coordination and modification, e.g. *ice-cream* by **ice-Italian cream* and **ice-and custard-creams*. Ghesquière (2014: 27) defines English classifiers as premodifiers that provide information specifying the head's type or class and are very often organized into groups or sets, e.g. *electric trains/steam trains*. Classifiers usually cannot be used in the predicative position[7] and normally do not allow degree modification (except those that modify class membership, e.g. *almost, exclusively*) (Ghesquière 2014: 27; Quirk et al. 1985: 1324). Furthermore, Davidse and Breban (2019: 336) point out that they also cannot be separated from the head noun, e.g. **an electric brand-new train*. Nouns used in this zone denote a permanent feature even if they do not implicitly encode permanency: *the corner table* (i.e. 'the table in the corner') but not **the corner man* (i.e. 'the man in the corner'; Quirk et al. 1985: 1331; see also Halliday & Matthiessen 2014: 377–8).

Jespersen (1924: 97) has been accredited with first describing the classifier function in English with examples such as *a nice young lady*. He analyzed *young lady* as being one idea, therefore, one constituent: [nice [young lady]]; however, today, almost a century later, the classifier category

---

[7] This is very similar to the Quirk et al. (1985: 432) classifier-like category called denominal adjectives or adjectives related to noun; denominal adjectives are usually non-gradable and attributive, i.e. cannot take intensifiers (see Halliday & Matthiessen 2014: 377 for discussion on the difference between classifiers and what he calls epithets (Ghesquière's subjective descriptive modifiers)).

7.3 Ghesquière's Cognitive-Functional Model

is still a difficult one to delineate (Matthews 2014: 90). The first issue is distinguishing between compounds and classifiers (see Section 7.3.1.1), and the second issue is delineating between classifiers and descriptive modifiers (see Section 7.3.3). The latter will be discussed after a brief introduction of the descriptive modifiers.

7.3.1.1 Classifiers versus Compounds
One major issue that arises with this classification is the question of distinguishing between classifiers and compounds; an issue particularly relevant in English because of the lack of adjectival endings and the orthographic variation found in the spelling of compounds, with certain compounds being spelled as one word or with a hyphen, others as two, and some with all three spellings as viable forms. This issue is particularly problematic for this study because the classifier plays a critical role in indicating (loss of) nounhood, i.e. if a noun does not take classifiers, this would be one indication that it is no longer being used as a noun.

The Ghesquière (2014: 27) model, based primarily on work from Halliday (1994), distinguishes between classifier noun phrases and compounds primarily along semantic criteria. She argues that the difference is that classifiers specify the taxonomy that the head belongs in, e.g. *electric trains/steam trains*, whereas compounds do not (Ghesquière 2014: 27). Furthermore, she claims that for a classifier-noun sequence to become a compound, "it has to undergo a process of semantic specialization," which would also mean the loss of compositionality (Ghesquière 2014: 27; see also Matthews 2014: 114–15). She includes two syntactic tests: coordination and stacking (see Table 7.1 below). This distinction is controversial in many respects because stress and orthography, not semantics, have been common indicators of compound or phrase status.

Payne and Huddleston (2002: 448–51) propose multiple syntactic, semantic, morphological, orthographic, and phonological tests to distinguish between compounds (*ice-cream*) and composite nouns both A+N (*some new cars*) and N+N (*two London colleges*). Table 7.1 below lists the tests they propose to distinguish between the composite nouns and compounds.

As can be seen in Table 7.1, a phrase or composite noun should allow for coordination of the modifier and of the head where compounding does not (see also Ralli & Stavrou 1998: 244–5). Composite nouns also allow modification and stacking, resulting in a change of scope (illustrated by examples such as *the urban athletic center*), while a compound does not (Ralli & Stavrou 1998: 245–6). In an example like [*urban* [*athletic center*]], both *urban* and *athletic* are classifiers, and *urban* has scope over both *athletic* and *center*, i.e. indicates

Table 7.1 *Payne and Huddleston's tests to distinguish between compounds and composite nouns*

TESTS	COMPOSITE NOUNS	COMPOUNDS
Modifier coordination	[new and used] cars various [London and Oxford] colleges	*[ice- and custard-] creams
Head coordination	new [buses and cars] various London [schools and colleges]	*ice-[lollies and creams]
Delayed right constituent coordination	[four new and two used] cars [two London and four Oxford] colleges	*[two ice- and ten custard] creams
Submodification	two [reasonably new] cars two [south London] colleges	*[crushed ice-] cream
Stacking	two new [diesel-driven cars] two London [theological colleges]	*ice-[Italian cream]
Compositional transparency	new cars: newly made cars (compositional) London colleges: colleges in London	ice-cream: not a cream made of ice (less transparent)[8]
Productive	new cars, electric cars, diesel cars London colleges, US colleges	ice-cream is not the same as chocolate-cream
Orthography	two words	one word
Stress	second element stress	first element stress[9]

a particular type of athletic center. If the order is reversed, there is a change in meaning with *athletic* indicating the type of urban center. Like Ghesquière, Payne and Huddleston argue that compounding requires a loss of compositionality, e.g. *cold war* has nothing to do with the temperature (cf. Ralli & Stavrou 1998: 248), and both Payne and Huddleston and Ghesquière point out that composite nouns, but not compounds, form taxonomies and are productive. In general, orthography seems to be a rather unreliable criterion to distinguish compounds: *blackberry*, *blue fish*, and *greyhound* are compounds, but *black bean*, *blue cheese*, *gray squirrel* are phrases; therefore, orthography can be nothing more than supporting evidence (Bauer 2004: 11–12; examples from Bauer 2004: 20).

---

[8] Historically the phrase was originally *iced cream*. Only with the loss of the past particle ending did it become irregular (OED).

[9] *Ice cream*, however, has second element stress; this is possibly a remnant of its composite use as *iced cream* (OED)

7.3 Ghesquière's Cognitive-Functional Model

Another test that could be applied is *one*-substitution (see also discussion in Section 2.2.1). As Keizer (2011) shows, anaphoric *one* substitutes the head of an NP; therefore, in the case of classifier premodification, *one* should be able to substitute the left-element (i.e. noun), as in (7.7a), which would not be possible in a compound as shown in (7.7b). In (7.7b), *ice* would have to be included in the substitution.

(7.7)   a. I want to ride on *the little steam train* and Bob likes *the huge electric one*.
        b. *I bought *a small ice cream* and she bought *a huge one/*huge ice one*.

Payne and Huddleston (2002: 451) admit that none of the tests provides, by itself, a clear distinction between the two categories: orthography is variable, productivity gradient, and compounds such as *raindrop* or *backache* are transparent. There can even be conflicting evidence: *cutlery boxes* and *matchboxes* seem very similar, despite the orthographic differences; however, *cutlery box* would seem to pass the coordination test, e.g. *I need cutlery and wine-glass boxes*, but *matchbox* would not, e.g. ^{??}*I need match and cigarette boxes*.

Stress has been applied as a commonly accepted primary diagnostic for compounding: first-element stress (on the adjective in an adjective–noun composite or the left noun in a noun–noun composite) signals compounds, e.g. *blackbird*, and second-element stress (on the noun in adjective–noun composite or the right noun on a noun–noun composite) signals a phrase, e.g. *black bird* (Bauer 2004: 7–8; e.g. Bloomfield 1933: 180; Lieberman & Sproat 1992). However, recent work on N+N compounds (e.g. Bauer 1998; Bell & Plag 2013; Giegerich 2004, 2009; Olsen 2000; Plag 2006, 2010; Schlücker & Plag 2011; see Giegerich 2009 for a more detailed discussion) suggest that stress on N+N pairs is motivated by numerous factors beyond the simple morpho-syntactic relationship of the two nouns. Thus, stress can be assigned to indicate analogy to or to distinguish between similar forms (e.g. Plag 2010; Bauer 2004 talks about saliency), can stem from semantics (e.g. Giegerich 2009; Olsen 2000; Plag et al. 2007; Plag et al. 2008), can add informativity (e.g. Bell & Plag 2013), and can be assigned for structural reasons (e.g. Bell & Plag 2012; Giegerich 2004).

For example, Giegerich (2004) observes that in N+N constructions, although phrasal constructions have right-stress, compounds can have left or right stress. This can be illustrated by examples such as *London Road* (stress on *Road*) but *London Street* (stress on *London*). Plag's (2006: 158–61) empirical testing of Giegerich's (2004) hypothesis found robust evidence to support Giegerich's claim that the modifier-head compounds can take stress on either element. Therefore, one must conclude that stress in N+N constructions is an unreliable indicator of compound or syntactic status.

Giegerich (2005) demonstrates that similar problems can be found with classifer+noun phrases (what he calls associative AdjNs). These phrases "have an irreconcilably hybrid status in English: their structural characteristics identify them as objects of the lexicon [i.e. compounds], while at the same time they may behave as though they are syntactic constructions [i.e. phrases]" (Giegerich 2005: 572). Giegerich (2005: 589) and Bauer (2004) argue that although some Adj+N phrases would be categorized as phrases based on the semantic and syntactic criteria, stress would categorize them as compounds, as in the examples in (7.8a–b). In (7.8a), *dental building* would take first-element stress but is still relatively compositional, and *one*-substitution is acceptable, as demonstrated by (7.8b). Essentially, like the N+N constructions, the stress patterns in classifier+noun constructions are only relatively predictable; these phrases demonstrate both left and right stress patterns (Giegerich 2005: 587; Portero Muñoz 2013: 125).

(7.8)   a. dental building
      b. Is this *the medical building* or *the dental one*? (Giegerich 2005: 588)

The compound-phrase distinction is not a central issue here; nonetheless, the distinction is important for the empirical study described below, as elements needed to be classified either as classifiers or as parts of compounds. For the purposes of this study, I adopted Ghesquière's original semantic compositionality test and adopted Payne and Huddleston's tests in Table 7.1. In ambiguous cases, the decision was made based on the results from *one* substitution (which classifiers should allow) and stress patterns.

7.3.2 Descriptive Modifiers

Ferris (1993: 4) explains that the difference between classifiers (what he calls associative modifiers) and descriptive modifiers is that the former classify the head and the latter qualify the head, i.e. descriptive modifiers ascribe a property to the head (see also Davidse & Breban 2019: 341). Thus, descriptive modifiers are the prototypical premodifiers and "attribute a certain quality or property to the instances referred to by the NP" (Ghesquière 2014: 29). They can occur in the attributive and predicative positions, tend to be gradable, and allow for degree modification. Ghesquière, furthermore, makes the distinction between objective and subjective descriptive modifiers: where objective modifiers "indicate objectively recognizable, purely descriptive and potentially defining qualities," subjective ones "express the speaker's attitude towards the instance referred to by the NP" (2014: 30; like the affective adjective in Adamson 2000, the Epithet in Feist 2012, or the subjective comment Scott 2002). The two categories are not discrete but represent two ends on a continuum (Ghesquière 2014: 29). This distinction between more objective and more subjective descriptive modifiers, as well as the observation that they are ordered (starting from the noun head) from objective to subjective and that those closest to the head are those modifiers denoting the most inherent properties, transcend theoretical boundaries (Quirk et al. 1985: 1341; for a more detailed discussion of this distinction from a cognitive-functional perspective, see Breban 2010: 40–56; for a discussion of the subjective–objective distinction, see also Adamson 2000; Cinque 1994; Hetzron 1978; Scontras et al. 2017; Scott 1998; Seiler 1978; Trueswell 2009). Therefore, although it is not always easy to draw the exact line between the two categories (i.e. is *intelligent* in *an intelligent person* subjective or objective), this is a distinction that is generally agreed upon.

Although many studies support the supposition that there is an objective to subjective ordering of descriptive modifiers, making them two separate categories is problematic (see Davidse & Breban 2019: 344–8). For example, there is no clear objective and subjective line between calling something *red*, *big*, *ugly*, and *excellent*, as these lexical items clearly exhibit different degrees of subjectivity. *Red* is a relatively strong objective property, whose attribution can be refuted via visual evidence. *Big* might be considered more subjective because it presupposes some kind of norm, and this norm may vary for each speaker, i.e. a tall person for someone small might be different for a speaker who is also tall. *Ugly* can be considered even more subjective, as it expresses the speaker's evaluation of something or someone; however, it is still based on physical properties. Finally, a modifier like *excellent*, expressing the speaker's evaluation of the referent, has an even higher degree of subjectivity. These distinctions are difficult to capture in Ghesquière's subjective and objective descriptive modifier categories.[10] Davidse and Breban (2019: 346) attempt to formalize this cline defining more subjective as "(individually) evaluative, momentaneous, and not potentially defining" and more objective as "collectively accessible, permanent, inherent, potentially defining." The cline between

---

[10] Halliday and Matthiessen (2014: 376) talk about an experiential epithet and the interpersonal epithet; however, the problem still remains: where is the line between experiential and interpersonal?

these two extremes is affective category > dimension > epithet > age > physical quality > color.

Generative approaches try to distinguish between the different degrees of subjectivity by applying such distinctions as referent and reference modification, absolute and relative modification, and restrictive and non-restrictive modification, because these distinctions influence the word order. However, this degree of detail greatly exceeds the goals of this particular project. Ghesquière's main criterion is to model the relative word order and more importantly to model the functions of premodifiers, and for this reason the Ghesquière categories have been retained for this study, and *red* and *big* are categorized as objective modifiers and *ugly* and *excellent* as subjective modifiers. This issue and its repercussions on this study will be discussed in more detail in Chapter 10.

7.3.3 *Classifiers and Descriptive Modifiers*

It is a problem to distinguish not only between subjective and descriptive modifiers but also between classifiers and descriptive modifiers. Ghesquière (2014: 27–34) distinguishes between the two in terms of their function, placement, and modification: classifiers denote the type of class that the head noun belongs to, cannot take the predicate position, and does not take degree modification. Descriptive modifiers, however, ascribe a property to the head, can be used in a variety of syntactic positions, and prototypically have no restrictions on modification.

This distinction between the two classes becomes problematic because many modifiers can function as both classifiers and descriptive modifiers. Halliday (1985: 164) describes prototypical classifiers as words that denote "material, scale and scope, purpose and function, status and rank, origin, mode of function."[11] In particular, many modifiers from these word classes can take both functions, as exemplified by *wooden* in (7.9). In this example, *wooden* not only ascribes the property 'made of wood' to the *table* (descriptive modifier) but also situates it in the category of 'tables made of wood' (classifier) (Alexiadou et al. 2007: 318–19). Therefore, depending on the context, *wooden* might be analyzed as a descriptive modifier or a classifier.

(7.9)   John just picked up *the wooden table*.

---

[11] Alexiadou et al. (2007: 319–20) point out that neither evaluative adjectives nor size adjectives tend to develop this function. Feist (2009: 305) gives the example of *smart*, which is evaluative in examples such as *a smart outfit* but can also be a classifier in examples such as *a smart bomb* (see example (7.5)).

7.3 Ghesquière's Cognitive-Functional Model

Matthews (2014: 113–15) explains the difference between the two categories in terms of compositionality, as demonstrated by example (7.10). *Green* in (7.10a) can be either a classifier indicating the bird's species *Picus viridi* (7.10b)[12] or a descriptive modifier describing the bird's color (7.10 c) (Matthews 2014: 114). If, in example (7.11), *green* and *beautiful* are compositional (the meaning of the noun phrase is composed of the semantic meanings of all three lexical items: *the bird is green and is beautiful*), then the use of *green* would be descriptive; if, on the other hand, *green* describes the species of bird, it is no longer transparent or compositional, and therefore *green* functions as a classifier.

(7.10) a. juvenile green woodpecker
        b. [juvenile [green woodpecker]]
        c. [juvenile [green [woodpecker]]]

(7.11) a **beautiful green** bird (Matthews 2014: 114)

In other words, both classifiers and descriptive premodifiers restrict the head, but each exhibits a different type of restrictiveness: classifiers predominantly function as type restrictors, as shown in example (7.12a), and descriptive modifiers function as referent restrictors, as demonstrated in (7.13) (FDG makes a similar distinction see Chapter 9). However, as already mentioned above, in certain contexts classifiers can be used to identify a certain referent, e.g. example (7.12b) (for further discussion see Davidse & Breban 2019: 334–6).

(7.12) a. stream train/electric train (type restrictor)
        b. My train is electric. (referent restrictor)

(7.13) a black horse/ a white horse (referent restrictor)

Alexiadou et al. (2007: 323) distinguish between classifying and descriptive modifiers through flexibility of word order. Classifying adjectives combine in a hierarchical pattern (have different scopes), and a change in word order results in a change in scope relations and meaning, e.g. *urban athletic center* vs. *athletic urban center*. However, if two descriptive modifiers are used together, they can be reversed without changing the meaning of the phrase, e.g. *a big colorful shirt* and *a colorful big shirt*. Finally, when descriptive modifiers and classifiers are used together, the order cannot be reversed, as the descriptive modifier must precede the classifier, e.g. *a new*

---

[12] Matthews (2014: 114; my emphasis) hedges saying "*[i]f it is not a larger compound*, it would instead be a syntactic unit modified as a whole within a larger syntactic unit."

Gucci shirt and not ?*a Gucci new shirt* (unless the speaker's intention is to highlight *Gucci* in some way).

In conclusion, English classifiers are defined in this study as premodifiers that often denote a subset in a larger set, i.e. function as type restrictors, cannot take the predicative position, and cannot take modification except for very limited degree modification. They cannot be coordinated with other premodifiers, and a change of premodification order would result in a change of meaning. English descriptive modifiers function as referent restrictors, and when sharing the same zone, can be coordinated and have more flexible word order.[13] They can be modified by degree modifiers.

7.3.4 Degree Modifiers

As with the descriptive modifiers, Ghesquière (2014: 34–44) distinguishes between two different degree modifiers. The first, adjective-intensifiers, "modify or indicate the extent of a quality or property denoted by a descriptive modifier they precede" (Ghesquière 2014: 35), e.g. *a **very** nice book* or *a **really** fast car*. For this category, she then makes the distinction between more or less bleached adjective-intensifiers; the more bleached category includes adverbs such as *very* or *fairly*, and the less bleached are those such as *lovely* in *lovely long legs* (Ghesquière 2014: 35–6). The second kind of degree modifiers, noun-intensifiers, "have scope over and modify the degree of all gradable qualities in the whole NP," e.g. *a **complete** idiot*, ***utter** darkness* (Ghesquière 2014: 36–7; like emphasizers [Quirk et al. 1985] or reinforcers [Paradis 2001; Feist 2012]).

Whereas the adjective-intensifiers have been much discussed (e.g. Kennedy & McNally 2005; Lorenz 2002; Quirk et al 1985), Ghesquière's (2014: 36–7) noun-intensifier category is a conglomerate of a variety of categories, including what Quirk et al. (1985: 429–30) call emphasizers and what Paradis (2000) and Feist (2009, 2012) call "reinforcers" (Ghesquière 2014: 36). She includes in this category modifiers such as *true*, *real*, and *utter*; grammatical lexical items such as *such* or *too*, although they initially had identifying functions; and adverbs as in *quite* or *rather* (Ghesquière 2014: 37). Ghesquière (2014: 37) explicitly includes *true* in her noun-intensifier category, explaining that, based on work from Kennedy and McNally (2005), there are two types of scalarity in degree modification:

---

[13] It would be acceptable to say *an urban and athletic center*, but the speaker is most likely referring to two different centers, *an urban center* and *an athletic center*. However, with descriptive modifiers it would be fine to say *a beautiful and large complex*, when describing one complex.

open scales and closed scales (Kennedy & McNally 2005: 349, 352–3). Modification along open scales "involves measuring the actual degree of a quality on a scale with some form of assumed measure units"; in the case of noun-intensifiers this type of modification would be exemplified by *mere*, in *a mere question* (Ghesquière 2014: 39). Closed scales would "involve comparing the degree of a quality to a boundary as either approximating or reaching it," as in *complete* in *a complete failure* (Ghesquière 2014: 39). Some issues in these distinctions will be discussed in more detail in the conclusion.

7.3.5 Conclusions

Essentially there are five different premodifier classes or zones that play a role in this study: classifier, objective descriptive modifier, subjective descriptive modifier, adjective degree modifier, and noun degree modifier. The classifier specifies the noun head, and in the empirical study classifier–noun pairs and compounds were distinguished primarily through the syntactic criterion (potential predicative use and/or restrictions on modification), and the semantic distinctions suggested by Ghesquière (2014). In cases of doubt, I used both stress patterns and the *one*-substitution test to decide. The objective and subjective descriptive modifier distinction is, as Ghesquière (2014: 30) herself explicitly states, scalar. Those modifiers that exhibited some physical property, like *orange* or *limp*, were categorized as objective, and modifiers that ascribe some subjective evaluation of character, such as *kind* or *innocent*, were classified as subjective. Finally, adjective intensifiers modified adjectives; however, the noun-intensifier category included not only modifiers of degree, but also modifiers with pragmatic information. In cases where two readings are possible, even taking into consideration the contextual information, I tagged the example for both options (see Methods in Section 7.4).

7.4 Methods

This study uses data from the Corpus of Contemporary American English (COCA) to capture the premodification patterns of the two nouns in the *of*-binominal constructions introduced in Part I.[14] The dataset was derived by a basic type search for nouns that co-occur with *of a*, i.e. [N of a] (the

---

[14] The search was conducted in 2014, and since then COCA has undergone a number of changes in that the data was substantially expanded and the blog, movie, and web data were added.

indefinite article was used since this is a defining feature of the EBNP) and the results were restricted to the 1,000 most frequent collocates. The first nouns which are used in the EBNP in the synchronic data were then selected and this resulted in 119 types. Of these 119 types, all the tokens in COCA were compiled into a dataset. This large dataset of over 30,000 tokens was then reduced according to a number of criteria. First, because the EBNP, EM, and BI are predominantly used with singular nouns, the premodification study includes only examples where the first nouns are in singular form. Second, those first noun lexical items that have developed to EM usages were automatically included in the dataset, i.e. *bastard, beast, bitch, devil, dog, hell, honey,* and *whale*. The other types that were included were chosen from the three semantic first noun groups: animate (e.g. *warhorse, lion, bear*), inanimate (e.g. *ball, egg, cake, whisper*), and evaluative (e.g. *demon, disaster*). Therefore, the dataset consists of two parts: one, those nouns that are used in the evaluative modifier, and two, tokens from the three first noun categories: abstract, inanimate, and animate. In this second part, types from each group made up about one-third of the tokens (the frequency distributions were based on raw figures, i.e. both modified and unmodified tokens), meaning one-third animate, one-third inanimate, and one-third abstract.

The individual first nouns from these three semantic groups were chosen on the basis of the following criteria. Each of the three groups had at least one first noun type that has a larger token sample, i.e. between 400 and 500 tokens, and each category contains no more than two high-frequency items (so that no one first noun would dominate the sample). The remaining first nouns selected had a token frequency between 50 and 250 tokens; this token amount is large enough to be sure that the first noun is an established member of this family but not so big as to disproportionately dominate the data sample. Because the animate group is a relatively small group with only twenty first-noun types, almost all animate first nouns were included.[15] For the other two groups, the selection was based on representativeness. In this case, representativeness means to what extent they represent the variation in the category; for example, *globe, moon,* and *ball* are used very similarly, particularly in the pseudo-partitive form. Therefore, only *globe* was included. For each first noun chosen, all instances with premodifiers were extracted and included in the dataset. From this smaller dataset, tokens were excluded based on the following criteria. Those that form semantic collocates with the verb, as in example

---

[15] *Boy* was not included because of its relatively large frequency, which would skew the animate data.

7.4 Methods

(7.14a) and (7.14b), were excluded. Idiomatic uses were also deleted, as in (7.14c), where the *of*-phrase no longer ascribes the property of color to the horse, but now means 'a different matter altogether' (naturally the token was retained if it did refer to a horse's color). Polysemous forms of first nouns (that do not develop an EBNP usage), such as *bull* for *papal bulls*, were also excluded from the sample.

(7.14)   a. She'd made *a complete fool of herself*. (COCA)
         b. The U.S. military is a machine that's basically going to kick *the ass of every other country around the world*. (COCA)
         c. Walt was *a horse of a different color*. (COCA)

Each instance was then tagged for a range of variables: the type of construction (using the criteria discussed in Chapters 3 and 4) and the premodifier's syntactic place (in front of the first noun [N_1] or the second noun [N_2]). Since one goal of this investigation is to look at the frequency of premodifiers in front of the first noun being selected by the second, in order to test if the premodifiers placed in front of the first noun semantically selected by the second noun is a significant pattern for the EBNP, the premodifiers in front of the first noun were also tagged for their selector. Premodifiers in front of the first noun that could be interpreted as modifying either noun (as in (7.15a)) were grouped with those selected by the first noun (as in (7.15b)); both were tagged as group 0 (it was assumed that if a modifier could have been selected by either noun, it was selected by the first noun or both). Those clearly selected by the second noun (either placed in front of N_1 or N_2), as in example (7.15c), were placed in group 1. This resulted in two selector categories, 0 and 1. Finally, each premodifier was tagged for the zone that it filled. In some cases the premodifier function was ambiguous even with the context, and for these examples both zones were tagged, e.g. in (7.16), *immense* could be either an objective or a subjective descriptive modifier, and it was tagged as both.

(7.15)   a. an **eternal** nightmare of pain (COCA)
         b. the **mean** monster of the playground (COCA)
         c. the **F5-category** monster of a funnel cloud (COCA)

(7.16)   an **immense** globe of water (COCA)

The statistical method used is the Hierarchical Configural Frequency Analysis (HCFA; cf. Von Eye 2002; Gries 2009; Hilpert 2013). This is a multifactorial analysis that essentially functions as a chi-square test for multiple vectors. It is an exploratory method that tests the significance of all variable combinations against the frequencies expected by chance (Gries 2009:

248–52; Hilpert 2013: 56). If a two- or three-way configuration has a significantly higher frequency than expected, then it is defined as a type for that construction; if a combination of variables is significant in its low frequency, it is an anti-type (Gries 2009: 248–52; Hilpert 2013: 55–6). Therefore, the questions being addressed here are (i) whether it is possible to identify types and anti-types in the premodification patterns of these *of*-binominals constructions, and if so (ii) which features characterize the patterns for each of these constructions. The results are calculated using Gries's (2009) HCFA 3.2 package for R, using the Holm's test.[16]

Two analyses were conducted. The first was for the premodification distribution between the first and second noun in each construction, based on the raw frequency premodification figures shown in Table 7.2. The second analysis included all the variables: construction, premodifier placement (N_1 or N_2), selector, and zone. In order to not skew the results to more premodification-heavy constructions (such as the N+PP and the EBNP), and because the ultimate question addressed in this chapter is the use of which premodifier zones/type are characteristic for each construction, the second analysis counted the filled zones (see Table 7.3) and not the number of premodifiers. This means that in an example such as *a tall bearded bear of a man*, the two objective descriptive modifiers would count only once, since together they fill a single slot.

In Section 7.5, the results for both analyses are presented and, in each case, followed by a brief discussion.

Table 7.2 *Raw token frequency of modifiers in front of the first and second noun for all constructions*

of-binominals	Noun$_1$	Noun$_2$	Total
N+PP	1019	752	1771
Head-classifier	486	247	733
Pseudo-partitive	59	45	104
EBNP	428	87	515
EM	16	87	103
BI	2	205	207

---

[16] The HCFA program provides the choice of one of two options to adjust the p-values for post hoc tests: the Bonferroni correction and Holm adjustment. The more conservative Holm's test was chosen for this analysis (see Gries 2009: 249).

Table 7.3 *Frequency of modifiers in front of the first and second noun for all constructions*

of-binominals	Noun$_1$	Noun$_2$	Total
N+PP	946	679	1625
Head-classifier	457	231	687
Pseudo-partitive	54	43	96
EBNP	369	80	449
EM	15	84	99
BI	2	205	207

7.5 Analysis of Premodification Distribution

The results of the first analysis, concerning the concentration of premodification in front of the first and second noun, are listed in Table 7.4. Although most variations of the combinations of variables (construction and placement) were found to be significant, some patterns turned out to be more significant than others. For the N+PP, in comparison with the other *of*-binominals, the observed frequency in front of the first noun was higher than that in front of the second noun; however, neither figure was significant in relation to the rest of the group. Thus, for the N+PP constructions, there are no defining types or anti-types for premodification placement in front of the first or second noun. For the head-classifier, the premodification placement is only marginally significant in comparison to the other constructions, with placement in front of the first noun being more characteristic than that in front of the second noun. This means that premodification in front of the first noun is a head-classifier type and modification in front of the second a head-classifier anti-type. For the pseudo-partitive, the premodification is relatively equally distributed between the first and second noun, and therefore, in comparison with the other constructions, neither are a defining feature (neither a type nor anti-type).

The patterns become more distinctive for the evaluative constructions (e.g. the EBNP, EM, and BI). The EBNP demonstrates a significant preference for premodifiers in front of the first noun, and a significant dispreference to those in front of the second. Therefore, premodification in front of the first noun is a significant type and premodification in front of the second noun a significant anti-type. The opposite is true for the EM, where premodification in front of the second noun is a type, and in front of the first noun is an anti-type. This pattern is even stronger in the BI, where

Table 7.4 *Frequency distribution of premodification between the first and second noun for the four of-binominals*

Construction	Placement	Observed frequency	Expected frequency	X^2 contribution	p value	Effect size
N+PP	$Noun_1$	1019	1036.91	0.31	ns	0.007
N+PP	$Noun_2$	752	734.09	0.44	ns	0.007
Head-classifier	$Noun_1$	486	429.17	7.53	0.01	0.02
Head-classifier	$Noun_2$	247	303.83	10.63	0.002	0.02
Pseudo-partitives	$Noun_1$	59	60.89	0.06	ns	0.001
Pseudo-partitives	$Noun_2$	45	43.11	0.08	ns	0.001
EBNP	$Noun_1$	428	301.53	53.05	$2.8e^{-12}$	0.04
EBNP	$Noun_2$	87	213.47	74.93	$5.94e^{-23}$	0.04
EM	$Noun_1$	16	60.31	32.55	$7.61e^{-11}$	0.01
EM	$Noun_2$	87	42.69	45.98	$9.55e^{-09}$	0.01
BI	$Noun_1$	2	121.2	117.23	$2.49e^{-49}$	0.04
BI	$Noun_2$	205	85.8	165.59	$1.03e^{-27}$	0.04

Note: The types (i.e. those where the observed frequency is higher than the expected frequency) are highlighted in light gray, and the anti-types (i.e. the observed frequency is lower than the expected frequency) are in dark gray. The white rows are not significant. (X^2 = 509.37, df = 5, $p < 0.05$, N = 3433).

premodification in front of the first noun is a significant anti-type, and premodification in front of the second, a significant type. For an overview of the distribution, see Figure 7.2, which shows the raw frequency of premodification in front of the first and second nouns.

In sum, in the first three constructions there tends to be a relatively even distribution between premodification in front of the first noun and the second noun. Only in the head-classifier is the preference for premodification in front of the first noun significant, as is a lack of premodification in front of the second noun. In comparison, premodification in front of all three evaluative constructions demonstrate clear patterns. The EBNP favors premodification in front of the first noun and exhibits less premodification in front of the second. The opposite is true for the EM and the BI; both constructions predominantly accept premodifiers in front of the second noun and demonstrate a general paucity of premodification before the first noun.

7.6 Premodification for the Individual *Of*-binominals

In this section information from the analysis in Section 7.5 will be integrated into the more detailed results from the second analysis, looking at the usage of the individual zones in front of each noun in each of the *of*-binominal constructions, in order to create an overall profile for each construction.

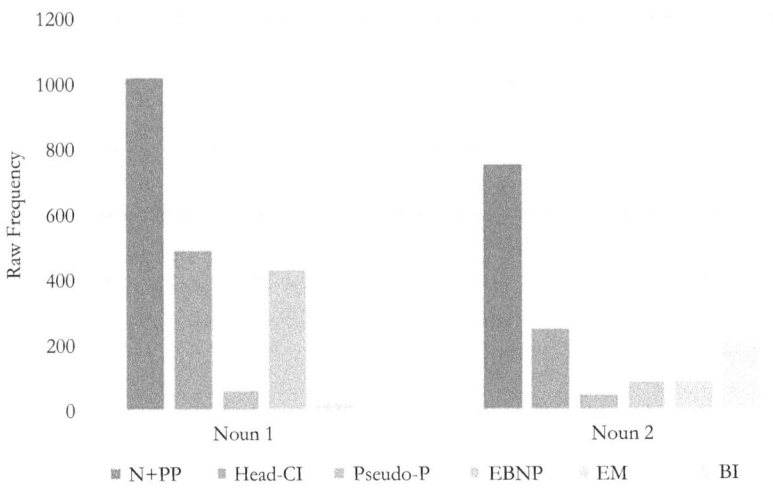

Figure 7.2 Premodification in front of Noun 1 and Noun 2

7.6.1 N+PP Constructions

As stated in Section 7.5, despite the higher raw frequency numbers in the N+PP constructions for first noun premodification (1,019 tokens) compared to second noun premodification (752 tokens), the use of neither set of premodification zones is significant (see Table 7.4).[17] This result is not unexpected. Given the fact that the head-classifier and the EBNP prefer premodification in front of the first noun, and the EM and BI for premodification in front of the second, it makes sense that in relation to the other *of*-binominals, the use of N_1 and N_2 zones in the N+PP construction would not be significant, despite the high frequency of premodifiers in front of both nouns.

When looking at the individual zones (Table 7.5), a clearer picture appears. The premodification patterns of the N+PP construction are characterized by its use of both of the classifier zones with their respective nouns as selectors, i.e. 0 for N_1 and 1 for N_2 as the selector of the classifying modifier. The same applies for both the objective descriptor zones and both subjective descriptor zones in front of N_1 and N_2, the use of all these zones is significant in relation to the other *of*-binominal constructions in the sample. What is most interesting is that the adjective-intensifier zone and the noun-intensifier zone in front of second noun are a type, albeit a marginally significant one. These zones are still in use, and although they are not frequently used, they are used more frequently than in all the other constructions. The graph in Figure 7.3 provides a visual overview of the distribution between zones.

The N+PPs are characterized by the use of all the zones except for the intensifier zones in front of the first noun. On the basis of observed frequency, this indicates that all zones in front of the nouns are open, and therefore, as expected, there are no premodifier restrictions on either of the nouns in this construction (except for those stemming from the lexical item itself, e.g. proper nouns do not tend to take premodification). One interesting feature is that this is the only construction where the use of the noun-intensifier slot in front of second noun is a defining feature. The observed frequency for

---

[17] In a smaller scale version of this project (Ten Wolde 2019), without the pseudo-partitive and the BI, this construction and the EM are the only ones which are characterized by frequent use of the zones in front of the second noun. In relation to the high frequency of premodification in front of the second noun in the BI, this is no longer significant in the N+PP.

Table 7.5 Important constellations of variables for premodification in the N+PP

Selector	Zone	Placement	Observed frequency	Expected frequency	X^2 contribution	p-value	Effect size
0	classifier	$Noun_1$	453	189.87	364.64	$3.8e^{-62}$	0.09
0	obj descriptive	$Noun_1$	279	204.68	26.98	$1.53e^{-05}$	0.03
0	subj descriptive	$Noun_1$	183	129.56	23.06	0.0001	0.02
0	adj-intensifier	$Noun_1$	15	13.03	0.3	ns	0.001
0	noun-intensifier	$Noun_1$	16	9.78	3.96	ns	0.002
1	classifier	$Noun_2$	334	139.58	275.56	$1.26e^{-45}$	0.07
1	obj descriptive	$Noun_2$	216	79.5	234.37	$7.25e^{-36}$	0.04
1	subj descriptive	$Noun_2$	113	65.16	35.12	$2.94e^{-06}$	0.02
1	adj-intensifier	$Noun_2$	8	1.95	19.69	ms	0.002
1	noun-intensifier	$Noun_2$	8	1.95	19.69	ms	0.002

Note: The types (i.e. those where the observed frequency is higher than the expected frequency) are highlighted in light gray, and anti-types in darker gray. In white are the nonsignificant features important for the discussion. (X2 = 6606.59, df = 104, p < 0.05, N = 3165).

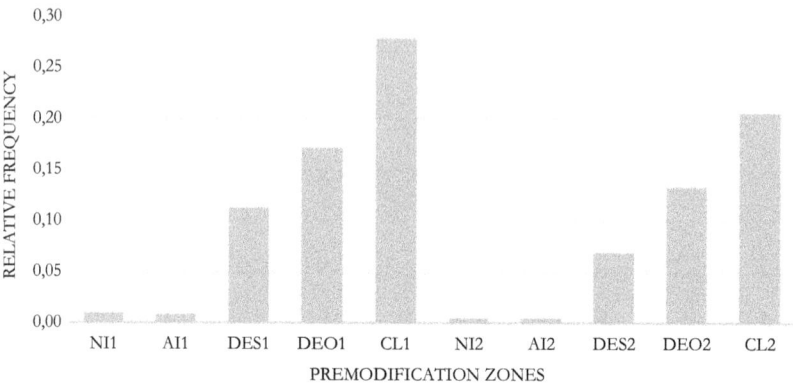

Figure 7.3 Relative frequency for each zone in the N+PP

CL = classifier, DEO = objective descriptive modifier, DES = subjective descriptive modifier, AI = adjective-intensifier, NI = noun-intensifier. 1 as in CL1 is a classifier in front of the first noun; CL2 is a classifier in front of the second noun etc. (Percentages are based on the total number of N+PP premodifiers.)

modification in the intensifier zones is low even in the large N+PP sample, but N_2 degree modifiers almost completely disappear after this construction.

7.6.2 Head-Classifiers

In the head-classifier, the difference between the frequencies of N_1 modification and N_2 modification is only slightly significant, with first noun premodification as a weak type and second noun premodification a weak anti-type (Table 7.4). When looking at the individual zones, the defining zones are the classifier, subjective and objective descriptor zones in front of the first noun, and the classifier and objective descriptive modifiers in front of second noun. The use of all these zones is significant, making them types. There are examples with subjective descriptive modifiers in front of the second noun, but this zone does not have the observed frequency of other members of this family, meaning it is not significant. The same holds true for the intensifiers in front of the first noun. Table 7.6 provides the exact results, and Figure 7.4 shows the distribution of premodifiers in all ten zones.

None of the intensifier zones are significant for the head-classifier. However, what deserves comment is the fact that there is only one example with a noun-intensifier in the noun-intensifier zone in front of the second noun. This lack of use of this zone is not an anti-type, since this zone is not frequently used by any of the other constructions, and

Table 7.6 Important constellations of variables for premodification in the head-classifier

Selector	Zone	Placement	Observed frequency	Expected frequency	X^2 contribution	p value	Effect size
0	classifier	$Noun_2$	125	80.39	24.76	0.0001	0.01
1	classifier	$Noun_1$	2	59.95	55.02	$2.78e^{-21}$	0.02
0	obj descriptive	$Noun_1$	188	86.66	119.51	$6.17e^{-20}$	0.03
0	subj descriptive	$Noun_1$	123	54.43	86.39	$5.01e^{-14}$	0.02
1	subj descriptive	$Noun_1$	2	39.91	36.01	$2.99e^{-13}$	0.01
0	adj-intensifier	$Noun_1$	9	5.52	2.2	ns	0.001
0	noun-intensifier	$Noun_1$	8	4.14	3.60	ns	0.001
1	classifier	$Noun_2$	138	59.67	107.25	$3.33e^{-17}$	0.03
1	obj descriptive	$Noun_2$	68	33.66	35.04	$9.09e^{-06}$	0.01
1	subj descriptive	$Noun_2$	23	27.59	0.76	ns	0.001
1	adj-intensifier	$Noun_2$	0	0.24	0.04	ns	0
1	noun-intensifier	$Noun_2$	1	0.83	0.36	ns	0

Note: The types (i.e. those zones where the observed frequency is higher than the expected frequency) are highlighted in light gray, and anti-types (i.e. where the observed frequency is lower than the expected frequency) in darker gray. The rows in white are the nonsignificant features important for the discussion. ($X^2 = 6606.59$, df = 104, p < 0.05, N = 3165).

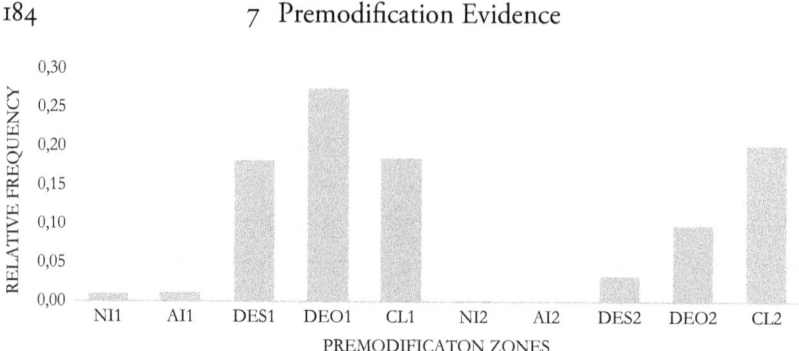

Figure 7.4 Relative frequency percentages for each zone in the head-classifier

even with the N+PP, where the zone is a type, the noun-intensifier use is very infrequent. The single noun-intensifier token in front of the second noun is *freaking*, a substitute for the expletive *fucking* (see example (7.17)), and expletives are well-documented for not respecting phrase or word boundaries, i.e. *that is un-fucking-believable*, and for defying word order rules. Therefore, this example does not provide robust proof that this zone is still in use. However, it would appear that there is a clear restriction on the use of this zone as demonstrated by examples (7.18) and (7.19). In example (7.18), *proper* can modify the referent when in front of the first noun in (7.18a), can modify *burden* when on its own in (7.18b), but not *burden* in the head-classifier as in (7.18c). The same is true for *very uncompromising* in (7.19). The MP can modify the referent in (7.19a), but not in the head-classifier prepositional phrase in (7.19c), or the more likely reading of (7.19c) would be a pseudo-partitive one, and *boat* functioning as a quantity, rather than a head-classifier.

(7.17)   the angel of **freaking** death (COCA)

(7.18)   a. a **proper** beast of burden
           b. a **proper** burden
           c. * a beast of **proper** burden

(7.19)   a. a **very uncompromising** boat of love
           b. a **very uncompromising** love
           c. ?a boat of **very uncompromising** love

Noncanonical selection, i.e. the second noun selecting premodification in front of the first noun, was not found in the dataset. However, some interesting premodification anomalies were encountered, as demonstrated in (7.20). In these examples of endocentric premodification, a premodifier in front of the first noun, although ascribing a property to the overall referent of the phrase, is not selected by either the first or the second noun. In example (7.20), *poor ignorant* is most likely selected by (modifies) the overall referent, the earth, not *ball* and not *dirt* (7.20).

(7.20) He did it so that you could have a life beyond *this **poor ignorant** ball of dirt*! (COCA)

7.6.3 Pseudo-partitive

Pseudo-partitives demonstrated a relatively equal distribution between the first and second nouns, neither of which is significant (see Table 7.4). Furthermore, when examining the individual zones, these are either not significant or only minimally significant. In front of the first noun, the use of the objective descriptive and the adjective-intensifier zones form two important types (see Table 7.7). The other important features are the use of the classifier and objective descriptive modifier zone in front of the second noun. The subjective descriptive zones in front of either noun are rarely used. Otherwise, as seen in the head-classifier, there are no instances of intensification in front of the second noun (see Figure 7.5). Thus, the general pattern that evolves is that of a preference for objective descriptive modifiers in front of the first noun, and classifiers and objective descriptive modifiers in front of the second noun. Although intensifier use in front of the first noun was anticipated by previous research, it was found to be only minimally significant.

There are two points to be considered when looking at the figures for the objective modifiers in front of the first noun. First, this dataset was not coded for scope and the selector was often very ambiguous. Therefore, in examples like (7.21a), *dark* and *red* could very easily have been selected by *blood*, but since they could also have been selected by *pearl*, it was coded 0. The same is true for (7.21b), where *new* could be selected by either *cake* or *soap*. Furthermore, they could modify the referent of the construction as a whole, but again this was not accounted for in the study. These sorts of examples made up the majority of the pseudo-partitive sample. Second, as proposed by Keizer (2007a: 138), descriptive modifiers in front of the first noun could function as an intensifier, as, for example, *faint* in (7.22a), and *thin* in (7.22b), but these readings cannot always be disambiguated (not even in context). This might have inadvertently resulted in the low number of intensifiers and the inconclusive result for this configuration in this dataset.

Table 7.7 *Important constellations of variables for premodification in the pseudo-partitive*

Selector	Zone	Placement	Observed frequency	Expected frequency	X^2 contribution	p value	Effect size
0	classifier	Noun$_1$	5	11.33	3.54	ns	0.002
0	obj descriptive	Noun$_1$	39	12.22	59.71	$6.83e^{-08}$	0.008
0	subj descriptive	Noun$_1$	3	7.67	2.85	ns	0.001
1	subj descriptive	Noun$_1$	1	9.96	7.07	ns	0.003
0	adj-intensifier	Noun$_1$	5	0.78	22.91	ns	0.001
0	noun-intensifier	Noun$_1$	0	0.58	0.58	ns	0
1	classifier	Noun$_2$	23	9.27	26.22	0.001	0.01
1	obj descriptive	Noun$_2$	14	4.75	19.05	0.03	0.003
1	subj descriptive	Noun$_2$	6	3.89	1.14	ns	0.001
1	adj-intensifier	Noun$_2$	0	0.12	0.12	ns	0
1	noun-intensifier	Noun$_2$	0	0.12	0.12	ns	0

Note: The types (i.e. the observed frequency is higher than the expected frequency) are highlighted in light gray, and in white are nonsignificant features important for the discussion. (X2 = 6606.59, df = 104 p < 0.05, N = 3165).

7.6 Premodification for the Individual Of-binominals

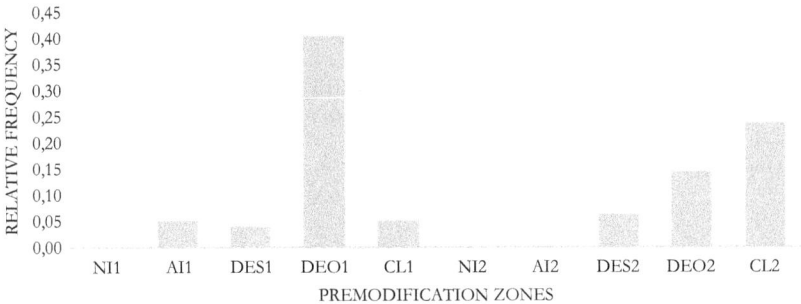

Figure 7.5 Relative frequency percentages for each zone in the pseudo-partitive

(7.21) a. a **dark red** pearl of blood (COCA)
        b. a **new** cake of soap (COCA)

(7.22) a. a **faint** whisper of yuzu-kosho (COCA)
        b. its **thin** whisper of cobalt pinstripes (COCA)

7.6.4 Evaluative Binominal Noun Phrases

In the EBNP, there is a significant shift of premodification from the zones in front of the second noun to those in front of the first one; premodification before N₁ is a characterizing feature for this construction, as is the lack of premodification before N₂ (Table 7.4). The figures in Table 7.8 show that both descriptive zones in front of the first noun are distinctive features. It is also in these two zones that examples of premodifiers selected by the second noun can be found; however, both of these constellations (i.e. objective descriptive modifiers with N₂ as selector and placed in front of N₁, and subjective descriptive modifiers with N₂ as selector and placed in front of N₁) are anti-types. Most of the N₂ premodifier zones are not significant.

Previous work on the EBNP claims that the second noun can function as a selector for modification in front of the first noun; this was not found to be significant in this dataset. However, this finding does not contradict previous work but simply shows how ambiguous noun selection is as a criterion. Since this dataset contained a large number of animate first nouns taking animate second nouns, many premodifiers, such as *big* and *lovable* in example (7.23a), could be selected by either noun. It is only in cases when a more specific property is ascribed, such as *bearded* in (7.23b) which requires a human referent, that the selector is clear. Even when the

Table 7.8 *Important constellations of variables for premodification in the EBNP*

Selector	Zone	Placement	Observed frequency	Expected frequency	X^2 contribution	p value	Effect size
0	classifier	$Noun_1$	53	52.46	0.01	Ns	0
1	classifier	$Noun_1$	1	39.47	36.5	$6.06e^{-14}$	0.01
0	obj descriptive	$Noun_1$	180	56.56	269.44	$5.18e^{-38}$	0.04
1	obj descriptive	$Noun_1$	3	41.47	35.69	$9.45e^{-13}$	0.01
0	subj descriptive	$Noun_1$	110	35.52	156.16	$5.41e^{-22}$	0.02
1	subj descriptive	$Noun_1$	6	26.05	15.42	0.0002	0.01
0	adj-intensifier	$Noun_1$	9	3.60	9.1	Ns	0
0	noun-intensifier	$Noun_1$	7	2.7	6.84	Ns	0
1	classifier	$Noun_2$	52	39.29	4.91	Ns	0.004
1	obj descriptive	$Noun_2$	22	21.97	0.0001	Ns	0
1	subj descriptive	$Noun_2$	6	19.01	9.004	Ms	0.004
1	adj-intensifier	$Noun_2$	0	0.54	0.54	Ns	0
1	noun-intensifier	$Noun_2$	0	0.54	0.54	Ns	0

Note: The types (i.e. the observed frequency is higher than the expected frequency) are highlighted in light gray, the anti-types (i.e. the observed frequency is lower than the expected frequency) are in dark gray, and in white are nonsignificant features important for the discussion. ($X^2 = 6606.59$, df = 104, $p < 0.05$, N = 3165).

7.6 Premodification for the Individual Of-binominals

two nouns are not from the same category, such as *workhorse* and *standard* in (7.23c), *amazingly successful* could be selected by either noun, although one feels intrinsically that it applies to *standard* as the noun that denotes the referent. Often what is found is mixtures of modifiers, as exemplified in (7.23d): *big* and *hairy* is selected by *bitch*, but *favor-laden* by *law*. There are no classifiers selected by the second noun found in front of the first noun.

(7.23)   a. her **big lovable** bear of a husband (COCA)
           b. a huge, **black-bearded** bull of a man (COCA)
           c. an **amazingly successful** workhorse of a standard (COCA)
           d. a **big, hairy, favor-laden** bitch of a law (COCA)

Although the classifier and objective descriptive zones in NP_2 are used, their numbers are not significant, and the subjective descriptive modifier is a minimally significant anti-type. Other nonsignificant features are all the intensifier zones, and particularly those in front of the second noun, which are empty. Figure 7.6 shows the distribution of EBNP premodifiers for each zone.

7.6.5 Evaluative Modifiers

The difference between the frequencies of N_1 modification and N_2 modification in the EM is the inverse of that of the EBNP: a significant feature of this construction is premodification in front of N_2, and an anti-type is the lack of premodification in front of N_1 (Table 7.4). Distinguishing features of the EM premodification profile in Table 7.9 are the use of the classifier zone in front of the second noun (with modifiers selected by the second noun) and the lack of classifiers in front of the first noun (with N_1 selectors). Another anti-type is the lack of objective descriptive modifiers in front of the first noun, which was so characteristic for the head-classifier (Table 7.6)

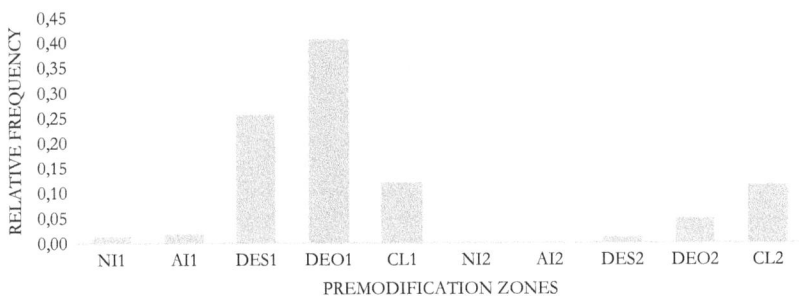

Figure 7.6 Relative frequency percentages for each zone in the EBNP

Table 7.9 *Important constellations of variables for premodification in the EM*

Selector	Zone	Placement	Observed frequency	Expected frequency	X^2 contribution	p value	Effect size
0	classifier	Noun₁	1	11.57	9.65	0.008	0.003
0	obj descriptive	Noun₁	0	12.47	12.47	0.0002	0.004
1	obj descriptive	Noun₁	1	9.14	7.25	ns	0.003
0	subj descriptive	Noun₁	7	7.83	0.09	ns	0
0	adj-intensifier	Noun₁	4	0.79	12.95	ns	0.001
0	noun-intensifier	Noun₁	2	0.6	3.31	ns	0
1	classifier	Noun₂	76	9.44	540.58	1.83e-43	0.02
1	obj descriptive	Noun₂	5	4.84	0.01	ns	0
1	subj descriptive	Noun₂	3	3.97	0.24	ns	0
1	adj-intensifier	Noun₂	0	0.12	0.12	ns	0
1	noun-intensifier	Noun₂	0	0.12	0.12	ns	0

Note: The types (i.e. the observed frequency is higher than the expected frequency) are highlighted in light gray, the anti-types (i.e. the observed frequency is lower than the expected frequency) are in dark gray, and in white are nonsignificant features important for the discussion. ($X^2 = 6606.59$, df = 104, $p < 0.05$, N = 3165).

7.6 Premodification for the Individual Of-binominals

and the EBNP (Table 7.8). The lack of subjective and objective descriptive modifiers selected by and in front of the second noun is not significant. The lack of use of the intensifier zones is also not significant. Again, there are no examples of intensifiers in front of the second noun.

The few descriptive modifiers in front of the first noun are either selected by the second noun, such as *little* in (7.24a), or potentially selected by either noun, such as *beautiful* or *intelligent* in (7.24b). With the subjective descriptive modifiers, in many examples it was problematic to distinguish between descriptive modifier use and classifier use. For example, *sexy* in example (7.24 c) could be either a subjective evaluation of the speaker or classifying her. The difference would mean that this is either [*a* [[*hell of a*] [*sexy lady*]]] (an EM) or she is 'a very sexy lady' (a BI); the token was tagged for both. In (7.24d), *killer* would normally function as a classifier or an element of a compound, but in this construction, it functions as an intensifier for *whale*: it is not only *a whale of a tale*, but *a killer whale of one*, with *killer whale* denoting greater intensification than *whale*.

(7.24) a. his **little** honey of a mule (COCA)
b. a **beautiful, intelligent** bitch of a life (COCA)
c. "And you," he says, kissing my nose, "are *one hell of a **sexy** lady*." (COCA)
d. The fisherman does have *a **killer** whale of a tale* to tell. (COCA)

This analysis shows that there is a clear difference between the EBNP and EM premodification patterns (compare Figure 7.6 and Figure 7.7). In the EM, the first noun predominantly no longer accepts premodification, and principally, only the classifier zone in front of the second noun is used. When subjective and objective descriptive modifiers are used in front of

Figure 7.7 Relative frequency distribution for each zone in the EM

the second noun, then it is ambiguous as to whether the speaker intended an EM construction or a BI construction.

7.6.6 Binominal Intensifier

Like the EM, the BI shows a preference for premodification in front of the second noun, and a significant absence of premodification in front of the first (see Table 7.4). The premodification pattern is strongly marked by the use of the second noun's descriptive zones, both subjective and objective (both significant types), as well as by the lack of modifiers in the first noun's classifier and descriptive zones. In general, none of the intensifier zones are used, except for the two instances with noun-intensifier modification. With these two examples, the situation is similar to that of the head-classifier: one token is an expletive *goddamn* in (7.25), and the second is *whole* in (7.26a), where it would appear to be modifying *bunch-of* and not *hell-of*. This intuition is substantiated by the fact that (7.26b) with *whole* modifying *bunch-of* is felicitous, whereas (7.26c) is not grammatically incorrect but would be an example of another construction, most likely the pseudo-partitive or N+PP. Table 7.10 and Figure 7.8 provide an overview of the premodifier distribution.

(7.25) a **goddamn** bitch of a unsatisfactory situation (COCA)

(7.26) a. a **whole** hell of a bunch of German prisoners (COCA)
        b. a **whole** bunch of German prisoners
        c. #a whole hell of German prisoners

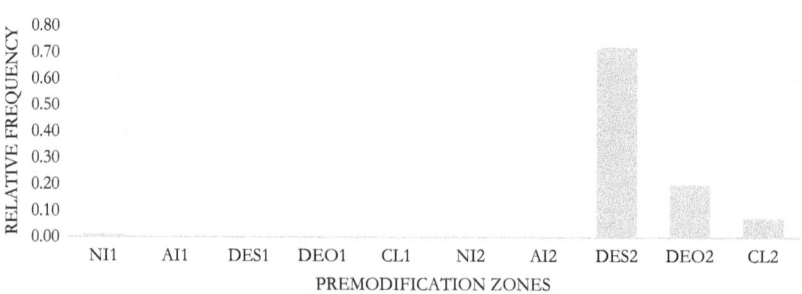

Figure 7.8 Relative frequency percentages for each zone in the BI

Table 7.10 *Important constellations of variables for premodification in the binominal intensifier*

Selector	Zone	Placement	Observed frequency	Expected frequency	X^2 contribution	p value	Effect size
0	classifier	Noun$_1$	0	24.19	24.19	$2.6e^{-09}$	0.008
0	obj descriptive	Noun$_1$	0	26.07	26.07	$3.96e^{-10}$	0.008
0	subj descriptive	Noun$_1$	0	16.38	16.38	$6.29e^{-06}$	0.005
0	adj-intensifier	Noun$_1$	0	1.25	1.25	ns	0
0	noun-intensifier	Noun$_1$	2	1.66	0.07	ns	0
1	classifier	Noun$_2$	15	17.65	0.4	ns	0.001
1	obj descriptive	Noun$_2$	41	10.13	94.12	$2.14e^{-11}$	0.01
1	subj descriptive	Noun$_2$	149	9.3	2384.83	$3.12e^{-127}$	0.05
1	adj-intensifier	Noun$_2$	0	0.25	0.25	ns	0
1	noun-intensifier	Noun$_2$	0	0.25	0.25	ns	0

Note: The types (i.e. the observed frequency is higher than the expected frequency) are highlighted in light gray, the anti-types (i.e. the observed frequency is lower than the expected frequency) are in dark gray, and in white are nonsignificant features important for the discussion. (X^2 = 6606.59, df =104, p < 0.05, N = 3165).

7.7 Discussion and Conclusions

The empirical evidence presented in this analysis allows for the following conclusions concerning each construction's premodification patterns. The N+PP exhibits predominantly prototypical premodification in front of N_1 and N_2; nonetheless, despite the high raw frequency, the difference between first and second noun modification in terms of relative frequency is not significant. Otherwise, the use of almost all the zones is significant except the intensifier zones in front of the first noun (which is not significant in any of the constructions) and the adjective-intensifier zone in front of the second noun. Of note is the frequent use of the second noun-intensifier zone. In the head-classifier, none of the intensifier zones have been found to be significant, and the construction is characterized by its use of most of the remaining zones. There is an absence of noun-intensifiers in front of the second noun. With the pseudo-partitive, the use of premodification in front of both nouns is non-significant. However, both the use of adjective intensifiers and objective descriptive modifiers in front of the first noun, and classifiers and objective descriptive modifiers in front of the second noun are significant features of the modification patterns for this construction. In the EBNP, the premodification is predominantly found in front of the first noun and characteristically in the descriptive zones (unsurprisingly since the function of the construction is evaluative), and the descriptive modification in the second noun zones are not significant. In the EM, premodification is found in front of the second noun, predominantly taking the form of classifiers. Finally, in the BI, the lack of premodification in front of the first noun is important, as is the use of the descriptive zones in front of the second noun. Figure 7.9 models these changes.

The findings show that the EBNP, the EM, and the BI demonstrate different premodification patterns, and thus these findings would support making a distinction between these three constructions. Furthermore, the evidence would substantiate the hypothesis that in the EM and the BI, at least, the two separate NPs (NP_1 of NP_2), with their two separate premodifier zones, were conflated into one set of zones in a simple NP. This would mean that potentially the radical shift of premodification to the front of the first noun seen in the EBNP is simply the beginning of this process. In the EBNP, the first

7.7 Discussion and Conclusions

N+PP

Det1	NI1	AI1	DES1	DESO1	CL1	N1	of	Det2	NI2	AI2	DES2	DEO2	CL2	N2
A		very	pretty	black	lap	dog		the	true		ugly	small	mutt	breed

Head-classifier

Det1	NI1	AI1	DES1	DESO1	CL1	N1	of	Det2	NI2	AI2	DES2	DEO2	CL2	N2
A		very	proud	little	divine	angel		-			sweet			mercy

Pseudo-partitive

Det1	NI1	AI1	DES1	DESO1	CL1	N1	of	Det2	NI2	AI2	DES2	DEO2	CL2	N2
A		very		thin		whisper		-			cobalt			pinstripes

EBNP

Det1	NI1	AI1	DES1	DESO1	CL1	N1		NI2	AI2	DES2	DEO2	CL2	N2
A		very	bitchy			iceberg of a		nasty			white		women

EM

Det	NI	AI	Des	CL	N
One		very	helluva	catering	job

BI

Det	NI	AI	Des	CL	N
One	helluva		wonderful	catering	job

Figure 7.9 Overview of the changes of premodifier patterns in the six constructions

Note: CL = classifier, DEO = objective descriptive modifier, DES = subjective descriptive modifier, AI = adjective-intensifier, NI = noun-intensifier. 1 as in CL1 is a classifier in front of the first noun; CL2 is a classifier in front of the second noun, etc. The dark gray are the zones that are closed. The light gray zones are premodification preferences.

noun may function as a modifier, but it has not lost all its features of nounhood, as it still encodes number and accepts premodification. The ambiguity of the first noun's grammatical status might lead to the irregular premodification discussed in Section 4.2 and found in previous research. In other words, if in the EBNP, particularly the predicative EBNPs, the first noun ascribes an objective or a subjective descriptive modifier property to the second noun, the [N of (a)] chunk would be situated somewhere in the descriptive zones. This might explain why there are no classifiers in front of the first noun that have been selected by the second noun.

This ambiguity is gone in the EM and the BI. In the EM, there is very little modification in front of the first noun, except for subjective descriptive modifiers, and the [N of (a)] chunk functions as a subjective descriptive modifier. In the BI, which essentially functions like an adjective intensifier, the zones in front of the first noun have disappeared apart from the noun-intensifier zones. The reanalyzed [N of (a)] has shifted left in the premodifier zones and premodification predominantly appears in front of the second noun.

In all the constructions, the selector variable did not play a central role in the premodification profiles. Primarily this may be because it could not be unambiguously decided whether the first or the second noun was the selector, and there were too few clear examples of premodifiers selected by the second noun in front of the first noun. A second reason is a problem with the study. Using the selector as a variable of equal weight with the other variables does not make sense. The selector is only an issue when premodifiers appear in front of the first noun, not the second (because the first noun never selects premodifiers in front of the second). Nonetheless, the statistical test factors in this scenario as a viable alternative even though it is not. This would weaken the overall effect of the selector variable and might well explain why it is not a significant feature of the EBNP.

This means that this study can give affirmative answers or provide information in answer to question 1 and question 2, posed at the start of this chapter. Question 3, about the selector, would need a different study.

One issue with the categorization of the premodifiers that became clear in this analysis is that Ghesquière's model of premodifiers does not represent scope relations. This would be important in a number of places when discussing premodification in these constructions, such as in the head-classifier and pseudo-partitive, where one must distinguish the modifier of the reference and referent (although it should also be made clear that the Ghesquière model was not constructed to model *of*-binominals). Furthermore, in the case of the EBNP, example (7.27) is possible only because *hungry-looking* has scope over the whole phrase while *mere* modifies only the first noun. Again, this becomes important in the BI because the [N of a] chunk has scope only over the following modifier and not the noun: this is not distinguished in the Ghesquière model.

(7.27) a **hungry-looking mere** wisp of a fellow

Example (7.27) demonstrates a second problem, namely the categorization of noun intensifiers, in particular for *mere* and *true*. According to the Ghesquière model, *mere*, as a noun intensifier, should appear in the far left of the premodifier zones. However, in this example it is to the right of *hungry-looking*, which is a descriptive modifier. Furthermore, *mere* can have an emotive element, and in other examples even a pragmatic, interpersonal one: *my evil arch enemy was a mere child*. In this example it indicates that the speaker expected an adult, and both these distinctions cannot be accounted for in degree. Later work from both Ghesquière (2017) and Davidse and Ghesquière (2016) (see also Davidse & Breban 2019) address this distinction, and although they show that *mere* has a degree modifier function, it also functions as a focus marker, thus distinct from degree modifiers and descriptive modifiers (or what Davidse & Breban 2019 call Epithets). Focus markers are employed by a speaker to draw a hearer's attention to a certain element of a message (Quirk et al. 1985: 604). They are adverbs and sometimes scalar, like degree modifiers; however, unlike intensifiers, focus markers do not intensify what they modify but activate some sort of scale or set that is related to the element that takes the focus (Traugott 2006: 341).[18] Moreover, scalar focus markers "not only invoke alternatives on a scale but also rank the focus on that scale, usually with other elements of the same type (qualities, events, persons etc.)" (Traugott 2006: 342). Unlike degree modifiers and descriptive modifiers, focus markers have variable scope relations, are no longer compositional, and often require pragmatic

---

[18] There are syntactic differences as well. Unlike intensifiers, which are usually part of the adjective or adverb phrase, focus markers are more flexible (Traugott 2006: 337–8). Furthermore, focus markers do not necessarily need to be placed right next to the element they modify (König 1991: 10; Nevalainen 1991: 39–43). This is shown in the examples below, where *also* can put focus on the verb plus object predicate (i), the verb phrase (ii), or the direct object (iii).

  i. They also <feed the cats>. ('They do not only water the plants.')
  ii. They also <feed> the cats. ('They do not only stroke them.')
  iii. They also feed <the cats>. ('They do not feed only the dogs.')
  (Nevalainen 1991: 42)

information to understand the utterance (Ghesquière 2017; König 1991; Nevalainen 1991). Syntactically speaking, they cannot be used predicatively and do not ascribe a property to the noun phrase head; in the noun phrase, it can have scope over the whole phrase or over an element of the noun phrase (Davidse & Breban 2019: 359–60). In the noun phrase, focus markers typically occur by the linguistic element they have scope over, and if they have scope over the whole noun phrase, appear in the post-determiner position (Davidse & Breban 2019: 360). This requires a more dynamic noun phrase model and scope relations are important.

The second problem is the classification of premodifiers such as *true*, *potential*, or *fake*. *True* and *fake* no longer indicate degree but, instead, indicate how closely the referent matches the property denoted by the noun; *fake* actually negates the property of the noun and *potential* expresses the possibility that the property denoted by the head might apply to the referent. These modifiers cannot be classifiers.[19] A *true Aussi* is not a type of *Aussi*, and *a potential murderer* not a type of murderer, i.e. neither *true* nor *potential* function as classifiers. These words do not determine the referent denoted by the noun head but "comment on the relation between the designation and referent" (Davidse & Breban 2019: 362). Syntactically, these modifiers can be placed close to the determiners and have often been included in the secondary determiner category (Davidse & Breban 2019: 361). They may appear before descriptive modifiers such as *brown* in *fake brown hair* (COCA) or before subjective descriptive modifiers such as *expensive* in *fake expensive brand names* (COCA). However, they may also be placed close to the head, e.g. *last year's bizarre alleged plot* (COCA) (for further discussion see Davidse & Breban 2019: 363–4). These modifiers have scope over the modifiers and the noun that follows (*fake*, for instance, clearly qualifies the application of the properties in question). Davidse and Breban (2019: 362) note that, like classifiers, these modifiers are not gradable (i.e. cannot be intensified) and cannot be used predicatively, and thus cannot be simple modifiers, on par with the other modifiers. They would need to be placed in a separate premodi-

---

[19] Generative theories of modification, which focus more on the relation between modifier and head, do make a distinction between these premodifiers, in that *potential* and *alleged* are non-subsective adjectives, and *fake* and *true* privative adjectives (Kamp & Partee 1995; Morzycki 2016: 24–6, 294; Partee 2010: 275–7).

fier category, and Davidse and Breban (2019: 360–4) call them meta-designatives. As discussed above, this is a case where scope relations play a key role but are not clearly represented in the Ghesquière model. Although these issues are discussed in the context of *of*-binominals, they have repercussions beyond the *of*-binominal research.

PART III

Theoretical Analysis

CHAPTER 8

The EBNP Family: A Construction Grammar Analysis

8.1 Introduction to Construction Grammar

Although the label Construction Grammar may suggest that this is a single theory, it is no more a unified theory than generative or functional paradigms. Indeed Construction Grammar (CxG) is a cover term for a range of models and approaches, including, among others, Sign-Based Construction Grammar (e.g. Boas & Sag 2012; Michaelis 2010, 2012, 2013; Sag 2001, 2012), Radical Construction Grammar (e.g. Croft 2001, 2013), Frame Semantics (e.g. Boas 2003, 2008a, 2008b), and Cognitive Construction Grammar (e.g. Goldberg 1995, 2003, 2006, 2009a, 2009b, 2013, 2019).[1] The cover term sometimes even encompasses Cognitive Grammar (Langacker 1987, 1991; Taylor 2004), a theory with which CxG shares many fundamental assumptions. Cognitive Construction Grammar will be the CxG theory discussed and applied here; however, all the different Construction Grammar approaches share a set of core tenets listed in points (1)–(5) below (Goldberg 2013: 15–16; see further Gisborne & Patten 2011: 94–5). They posit the following:

(1) the conceptualization of grammatical constructions as form–meaning pairings: not only lexical items are learned form and function pairings but also more complex phrasal and syntactic constructions (Goldberg 2013: 15).
(2) the existence of language networks: linguistic knowledge is stored in the form of a network that consists of nodes (aka constructions) that are related by different types of links (Goldberg 2013: 15).

---

[1] These are only the more popular theories; there are also Embodied Construction Grammar (e.g. Bergen & Chang 2005, 2013), and Fluid Construction Grammar (e.g. Steels 2011). For overviews of the different theories, see Boas (2021), Croft and Cruse (2004: 257–90), Goldberg (2013), and Hoffmann and Trousdale (2013).

(3) only surface structure: the theory excludes any underlying transformational or derivational component; any semantic meaning is derived from surface forms (Goldberg 2013: 15).
(4) crosslinguistic variability originating from domain-general cognitive processes: typological differences and crosslinguistic generalizations stem from shared cognitive processes (Goldberg 2013: 15–6; also a basic commitment of cognitive linguistics, see Evans & Green 2006: 40–3).
(5) usage-based knowledge of language: CxG denies the existence of an independent language faculty and claims that linguistic knowledge is acquired through experience with language (Diessel 2015: 296). Hence, "[k]nowledge of language includes both items and generalizations, at varying levels of specificity" (Goldberg 2013: 16; for discussion see Bybee 2010; Divjak 2019; Ellis et al. 2016; Tomasello 2003).[2]

This chapter will introduce the 'construction' (point 1) and the 'construct-i-con' (point 2) in Section 8.2, and the method by which the constructional network emerges via usage patterns (point 5) in Section 8.3, before turning to the analysis in Section 8.4 (points 3 and 4 from the list above are not relevant for this discussion, since point 3 is shared by both FDG and CxG, and point 4 does not play a direct role because this study only looks at English). Looking at the main grammaticalization path (including the N+PP, head-classifier, EBNP, EM, and BI), I argue that it is the notion of the construction network that provides a plausible account for the changes observed in the dataset, in particular the pressure toward formal reanalysis of internal structure that begins in the EBNP and continues in the constructions that follow. To understand these changes, we have to examine these constructions in relation to the larger language network and consider the influence of higher-level constructions such as the simple noun phrase [Det (Mod) N].

8.2 Constructions and Constructional Networks

8.2.1 Constructions

The central linguistic unit in CxG is the construction itself. Constructions are similar to classical Saussurean signs in that they are symbolically linked form and meaning pairings (Diessel 2015: 298; see Figure 8.1). In a construction, no

---

[2] However, this is not necessarily a part of all the CxG programs; Sign-Based Construction Grammar, as a generative-based model, is not usage-based (Diessel 2015: 298).

8.2 Constructions and Constructional Networks

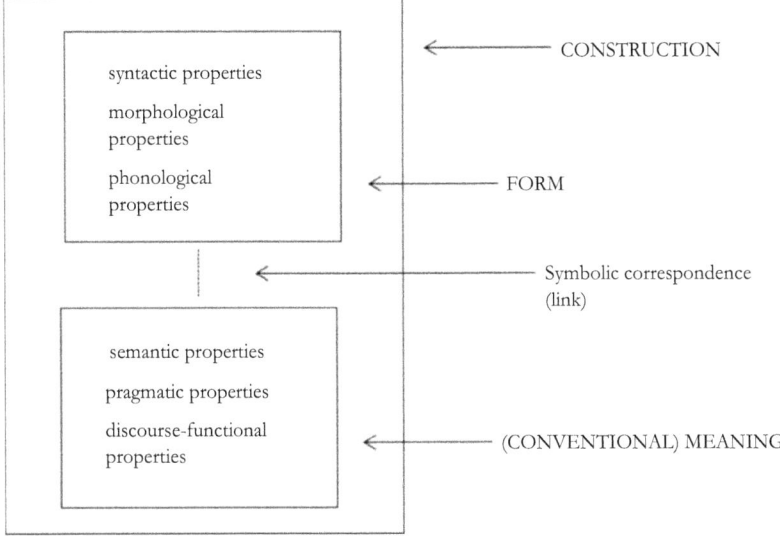

Figure 8.1 The symbolic structure of the construction (Croft & Cruse 2004: 258)

one area of grammar is central or dominant: all levels (syntax, morphology, phonology, semantics, and sometimes pragmatics and discourse) contribute equally to the linguistic unit (Traugott 2008b: 223). Constructions can range from specific and atomic morphological endings to whole, more complex syntactic structures (e.g. the ditransitive construction; see also Goldberg 1995: 141–51). In very broad terms, constructions constitute "a speaker's linguistic knowledge" and are generalizations or patterns formed on the basis of numerous encounters with a certain linguistic form (Hilpert 2014: 9).

In the original definition of a construction in Goldberg (1995: 4), the term *construction* included only unpredictable/noncanonical units of language. In later work, constructions became[3]

> any linguistic pattern . . . as long as some aspect of its form or function is not strictly predictable from its component parts or from other constructions recognized to exist. *In addition, patterns are stored as constructions even if they are fully predictable as long as they occur with sufficient frequency.*
> (Goldberg 2006: 5, my emphasis)

---

[3] In her most recent book, Goldberg (2019: 7) has provided a slightly different definition: "Constructions are emergent clusters of lossy memory traces that are aligned within our high- (hyper!) dimensional conceptual space on the basis of shared form, function, and textual dimensions" (*Lossy* means "not fully specified in all detail" [Goldberg 2019: 6]).

In this new definition, a language element is a construction if it is idiosyncratic and unpredictable, or if it is predictable but very frequent. This definition of construction is based on psychological research which has shown that frequent forms which are compositional may still be stored as a whole, e.g. *cat-s* (see Arnon & Snider 2010; Stemberger & MacWhinney 1988). Therefore, by categorizing these frequent forms as constructions, speakers can store them as separate entries in the construct-i-con (the storage unit for all constructions), where they can develop their own, non-compositional meaning as constructional wholes. This newer definition is the one adopted in this analysis.

Constructions are categorized along three different dimensions: size (either atomic or complex), phonological specificity (substantive, schematic, or in-between), and type of concept (from fully lexical/contentful to fully grammatical/procedural) (see Table 8.1; Croft & Cruse 2004: 255; Traugott & Trousdale 2013: 12–3). Atomic constructions are monomorphic (as in *red*); complex constructions are linguistic forms that consist of more than a word or morpheme (Smirnova & Sommerer 2020: 5–7). The intermediate category consists of forms that are only partly analyzable, as in the case of *bonfire*, where *fire* has semantic-functional value, but *bon* does not (Croft & Cruse 2004: 255). As for the specificity dimension, a substantive construction is fully realized, whereas a schematic construction is an abstraction with empty slots, and an intermediate category (semi-schematic) is partly filled, like the construction V-*ment*, where the slot for the verb (V) remains open (Croft & Cruse 2004: 255).

Table 8.1 *Dimensions of constructions* (Traugott & Trousdale 2013: 13)

	Atomic	Complex	Intermediate
Size	*red, -s*	*pull strings, on top of*	*bonfire*
Specificity	Substantive	Schematic	Intermediate
	dropout, -dom	N, SAI[a]	V-*ment*
Concept	Contentful	Procedural	Intermediate
	red, N	*-s*,[b] SAI	*way*-construction

Note: Traugott and Trousdale (2013) have added the 'concept' dimension to their categorization. Most texts (e.g. Bergs 2008: 270; Croft & Cruse 2004: 255) have only size and specificity.
[a] SAI = subject-auxiliary inversion
[b] s-marker of present tense third person or noun plural (Traugott & Trousdale 2013: 13)

Finally, the concept dimension entails a cline from lexical (contentful) to grammatical (procedural): the lexical/content end of the scale includes linguistic items that can be used referentially, while at the opposing end, we find the grammatical/procedural elements that "signal linguistic relations, perspectives and deictic orientation" (Traugott & Trousdale 2013: 12). In sum, CxG categorizes constructions along a continuum, with schematic abstract constructions at one end and lexical items or lexically filled patterns at the other; therefore, unlike in FDG, there is no strict division between lexemes (lexical constructions) and syntax (syntactic/schematic constructions; see further Goldberg 1995: 7). These various constructions are then organized into networks in a language speaker's mind.

This book primarily looks at complex, schematic, or intermediate (semi-schematic) *of*-binominal constructions. Some of the important forms are shown in (8.1a–b):

(8.1)   a. [[Det] [[N of a]$_{MP}$ [N]]]$_{NP}$
   b. [[Det] [[hell of a]$_{MP}$ [N]]]$_{NP}$

Example (8.1a) depicts the EBNP schema, which is syntactically and semantically idiosyncratic (see Section 8.4.3 for further discussion), and thus is an instance of Goldberg's original definition of a construction (as well as her later one). Example (8.1b) is a semi-schematic EBNP: *hell* fills the first noun position. As was demonstrated in the study of *cake*, *beast*, and *hell* in Chapter 5, the first nouns also impose restrictions on the use and meaning of the *of*-binominals and, therefore, are arguably constructions in their own right.

Another construction that plays an important role in this analysis is the 'simple' NP. This schema is formally and functionally transparent, but, nevertheless, the simple NP would be considered a construction in its own right because it is also extremely frequent and entrenched.[4] The simple NP schema will be represented in the analysis, for simplicity, as [[Det] (mod) [N]]$_{NP}$, but in truth, it is slightly more complex than the representation would lead one to expect; a more detailed representation of the NP schema is presented in Figure 8.2.

Most CxG-oriented models of the NP (Davidse & Breban 2019; Ghesquière 2014) build on the Quirk et al. (1985: 437, 1338–40) zone-based model. Ghesquière (2009, 2014) explicitly links her work to CxG

---

[4] One could also argue that NP's existence cannot be explained by any other construction and must be learned by language users.

Instantiation of a type of entity							
determination			modification				categorization
			degree modification		descriptive modification		
secondary	primary	secondary	noun-intensifier	adjective-intensifier	subjective	objective	classifier	head
				bleached / non-bleached				
all	those			really	pretty	little		garden	flowers
			utter						madness
	those				lovely	long			legs

Figure 8.2 Ghesquière's cognitive-functional NP model (Ghesquière 2014: 24)

8.2 *Constructions and Constructional Networks* 209

and Cognitive Grammar, although her model has also been strongly influenced by Halliday's Systemic Functional Grammar (e.g. 1994: 193). The simple NP schema in this model consists of a head, five premodifier zones, and three determiner zones; the classification of the zones is primarily based on semantic content/function. The zones distinguished by Ghesquière are divided into the determination, modification, and categorization functions. Subsumed under the categorization functions are the head and classifier zones. Under the modification function, Ghesquière distinguishes between subjective and objective descriptive modifiers, as well as adjective intensifiers and noun degree modifiers. Finally, the determination function consists of two secondary determiner slots and one primary determiner slot (see Section 7.3 for a more detailed discussion of this NP model).

The underlying theory is that each zone defines or construes the linguistic unit that fills it; thus, *smart* in *a smart bomb* has a different function from *smart* in *a smart blue bonnet* (see also Feist 2009: 309). In the first example, it is the classifier zone that selects certain semantic information from *smart*, and in the second, this is done by the subjective descriptive zone. It is actually this construction, with premodifier zones, that plays a role in the changes found in the EBNP family.

8.2.2 *The Construction Grammar Network*

Saussure (1959: 114–20) distinguishes between signification, which is inherent in the sign, and the notion of a sign's value, which is the part of a word's semantics that is defined by its relations to other words in a language system. The CxG theory has expanded Saussure's language system to the language network, which includes not only words (signs) but also phrases, clauses, and sentences. In essence, construction grammarians argue that if all linguistic elements, both grammatical and lexical items, are constructions, then it would seem logical that the grammar would be organized similarly to the mental lexicon, i.e. "as a network of related signs or symbols" (Diessel 2015: 302; 2019; see also Hudson's Word Grammar [2007, 2008]). This is CxG's construct-i-con.[5] In the construct-i-con, constructions are the individual nodes and are ordered by links between shared structure, function, and meaning (Diessel 2015: 302; cf. Bybee 2010; Croft 2001; Fried & Östman 2005; Goldberg 1995; Hilpert 2014). Network

---

[5] Kay (1990) first made the link between the mental lexicon and constructions, and Jurafsky (1992) first labeled this inventory of constructions the construct-i-con or constructicon (Bergs 2016: 126).

nodes are positioned in the network along horizontal and vertical dimensions.

The constructional network is hierarchal in that schematic patterns are at the top and fully specified constructions at the bottom. In between are semi-schematic sub-levels (Traugott 2008a, 2016, 2018; Traugott & Trousdale 2013). The different levels are formed on the basis of concrete examples (experiences as utterances in performance): patterns that occur frequently may be generalized and stored as more abstract schemata. For example, *John kicks the dog* and *Peter kisses Mary* share the abstract meaning {A affects B}, and repeated contact with similar constructions triggers the generation of the more abstract transitivity construction [Subj V_{tr} Obj] (Smirnova & Sommerer 2020: 20–1; see also Diessel 2011: 834). Patterns subsequently emerge from several constructions that share functional and formal properties, forming schemata with different degrees of abstractness higher up in the network. Once these constructions have established themselves, then information from the higher nodes flows down to the lower nodes. The lower layers then inherit, to some degree, properties from the higher ones, top-down (Diessel 2015: 303–6; Traugott 2018; see Figure 8.3).

The network consists of different levels of abstraction (Traugott 2008a, 2008b, based on Goldberg 1995, 2003, 2006). The lowest and most concrete level is that of the constructs, the actual language realizations, such as *a lot of* or *a bit of* (Traugott 2006; Traugott & Trousdale 2013: 17). The next level, the micro-construction or substantive level, comprises

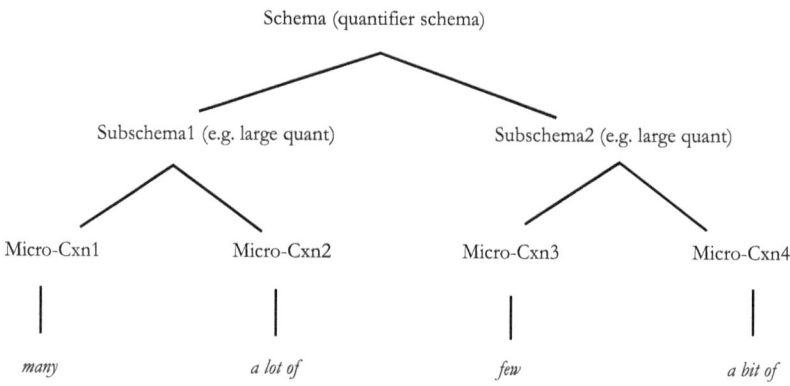

Figure 8.3 Gradient of hierarchic relationships among constructions (Traugott & Trousdale 2013: 17)

abstractions formed from concrete language tokens, rich in semantic and pragmatic content with internal complexity (Goldberg 2006: 5; cf. Traugott 2018). Put in terms of empirical research, if the constructs are the tokens, then the micro-constructions are the types (Norde, De Clerk & Colleman 2014: 240).

The third level or levels consist of meso-constructions (Traugott 2006), or what are now often called subschemata (Traugott & Trousdale 2013: 17),[6] which are sets of constructions that share similar syntactic behavior, such as *many* or *a lot of*. They are generalizations from groups of micro-constructions. Finally, at the top level of the network there are macro-constructions or what are now called schemata: very abstract, schematic form–meaning pairings such as the ditransitive constructions, the NP, or the degree modifier (Traugott 2006, 2018; Traugott & Trousdale 2013: 17). These abstract schemata encompass all subforms that fulfill a given function, meaning that the degree modifier schema would encompass all linguistic elements used as a degree modifier.[7]

The nodes and levels are vertically linked by inheritance links, enabling a downward spread of information; for example, the concept 'car' contains properties of the generic concept 'vehicle', that is, a car, like a vehicle, is a mechanical means of transportation (Trousdale 2013: 500; see also Hudson 2007: 21). For more complex constructions, form and meaning traits are passed down from more schematic constructions, as in (8.1a), to more specified constructions, as in (8.1b), via taxonomic links (Gisborne & Patten 2011; Smirnova & Sommerer 2020: 20). A number of taxonomic inheritance links have been postulated: polysemy, metaphorical, instance, and subpart links (Goldberg 1995: 74–81); the first two are the important ones for this study.

Polysemy and metaphorical links, as their names imply, designate a semantic relationship between two nodes. Polysemy links explain why a single form, such as the ditransitive 'X causes Y to receive Z', might have a range of different extended senses, e.g. 'X enables Y to receive Z' or 'X intends Y to receive Z in the future'. Therefore, in the network, the ditransitive pattern would simply have an 'intended transfer meaning' that is linked to the other senses that inherit a lot

---

[6] Traugott (2018) distinguishes between macro-schemata (previously called macro-constructions), schemata, subschemata, and subgroups (what was previously just called meso-constructions), and then micro-constructions. Smirnova and Sommerer (2020: 20) talk about schemata (at the highest level), multiple layers of subschemata and then fully specified constructions at the bottom.

[7] There is some discussion about whether these highest abstract-level schemata actually exist in the minds of speakers, and linguists have not been able to formalize these forms (for further discussion, see Smirnova and Sommerer 2020: 24).

of their meaning from this more generic form (Goldberg 1995: 75). Metaphorical links, on the other hand, form the connection between a metaphorical sense and an extended sense via a conceptual metaphor (Goldberg 1995: 81; Hilpert 2014: 61). For example, Goldberg (1995: 81) argues that a caused motion construction, exemplified in (8.2a), is linked to a resultative construction by the conceptual metaphor CHANGE IS MOTION, as demonstrated in (8.2b) (Hilpert 2014: 61). The source construction, the caused motion construction, is the source domain, and the same syntactic form is used to indicate a resultative event as in (8.2b). The cognitive link between these constructs which licenses this shared form is a conceptual metaphor (Hilpert 2014: 61). Another example would be the semantic extension of modal auxiliaries from deontic modal meaning to epistemic meaning (Hilpert 2014: 62; see further Sweester 1990).

(8.2)   a. John combed his hair to the side.
        b. Anne tied her hair into a bun.
        (Hilpert 2014: 61)

There are a few different forms of inheritance that have been proposed, but default inheritance is assumed in this representation.[8] Default inheritance assumes that lower-level constructions inherit nonconflicting information from higher-level constructions; conflicting information between nodes can block inheritance. Moreover, default inheritance allows for multi-inheritance, meaning that a construction may form inheritance links with more than one construction (Goldberg 1995: 97).[9] Multiple inheritance is a process that allows constructions to inherit from more than one higher-level construction in the network (Goldberg 1995: 97).[10] This process facilitates language change in that "[n]ew microconstructions often arise at the intersection of existing constructions" (Trousdale 2013: 511) and results in constructions that exhibit properties traceable to more than one construction (Trousdale 2013: 502). For example, in his study Trousdale argues that constructions such as *he gave John a kicking* are hybrids that inherit information from a number of other constructions, more specifically, from V-*ing* constructions

---

[8] There are a number of different types of inheritance being discussed (for an overview, see Barðdal & Gildea 2015).
[9] For further discussion of multiple inheritance and some of its problems, see Sommerer (2020).
[10] Note multiple inheritance is defined differently, and some construction grammarians conceptualize it as an online process in which several constructions are activated for the purpose of creating an actual construct, i.e. an actual utterance (Smirnova & Sommerer 2020: 22 fn 15).

(which provides *kick* its durative or iterative meaning) via a polysemy link, from the composite predicate construction (e.g. *give him a kiss*) via a subpart link, and from the general composite predicate construction via an instance link (Trousdale 2013: 505–6).[11]

Initial research has focused on the vertical links (e.g. Goldberg 2003; Traugott 2008a), and only recently have linguists attempted to incorporate horizontal links, links on a shared level, or horizontal relations between constructions at the same level of abstraction (Diessel 2015: 306–9; 2019: 199–200; Hilpert 2021; Traugott 2016, 2018; Van de Velde 2014).[12] These are found between constructions with similar forms (but different functions) or between different forms but fulfilling the same function or having similar meaning (Diessel 2019: 200; Zehentner 2019; Zehentner & Traugott 2020: 167). The CxG theory has adopted a very loose definition of similarity: "[t]wo (or more) linguistic structures, whatever their degree of schematicity or internal complexity may be perceived to be similar" (Taylor 2004: 52), and similarity can be found in the form and function/meaning (Bergs 2016: 127). This relationship plays a role in the network in that similarity to another construction or lexical expression leads to greater productivity (Bybee 2010: 57–75) and can lead to competition for functions or adaption of functions or characteristics as well (Van de Velde 2014). Some of Goldberg's original network links are used to connect constructions on the same level (horizontal links); polysemy and metaphorical links have been proposed in previous research (for an overview, see Smirnova & Sommerer 2020: 25).[13]

8.3 Grammaticalization in Construction Grammar

A usage-based approach (see point 5 in Section 8.1) assumes that "[g]rammar is a dynamic system of emergent categories and flexible constraints that are always changing under the influence of domain-general cognitive processes

---

[11] The ontological reality of the inheritance links is not always agreed upon. As of yet, inheritance links would appear to primarily have a categorical function, i.e. a linguistic reality, and not necessarily represent neurological links in a speaker's brain. Another suggestion is that there should be less emphasis on the nodes and more on the connections between the nodes (Hilpert 2021; Schmid 2020; cf. Hudson 2017).

[12] This expansion of the network models is due to findings in psycholinguistic research into first language acquisition and research in language change, both of which show that the semantics and morpho-syntax of similar constructions can influence the grammaticalization of a particular construction (Diessel 2015: 307; 2019: 200).

[13] Other potential horizontal relations discussed in the literature but do not play a role in this analysis are syntagmatic and paradigmatic links (see Budts & Petré 2020).

involved in language use" (Diessel 2015: 296), and therefore, the network is not static. The network can change in the following ways:

i. via node creation or node loss (constructionalization and constructional attrition),
ii. via node-internal changes (constructional change), and
iii. via network reconfiguration, the changes of links between constructions, "connectivity changes"

(Sommerer 2018: 148–9; see also Hilpert 2021; Traugott & Trousdale 2013).

Some of the major questions addressed in the diachronic CxG community are the emergence of constructions (constructionalization), changes in constructions (constructional change), and the distinction between grammaticalization and lexicalization (Traugott & Trousdale 2013). Usage-based theories in general and CxG theories in particular are strongly connected to grammaticalization research. Therefore, many concepts or processes discussed in Chapters 5 and 6 have been integrated into the discussion of constructional changes. This link between CxG and grammaticalization has led to a greater awareness of the role of syntactic context (and the language system) in grammatical change (Traugott 2015: 25) and of the interplay between semantic and syntactic changes (Traugott 2015: 58). The predominant benefit in using CxG in grammaticalization theory is that a grammaticalizing linguistic element never undergoes grammaticalization in isolation but in a particular co-text: "the unit to which grammaticalization properly applies are *constructions*, not isolated lexical items" (Himmelmann 2004: 31; emphasis in original).[14]

Noël (2007: 192) makes the distinction between two different types of grammaticalization, which are distinct despite the fact that they can and do occur jointly. One process is the grammaticalization of lexical items in constructions: in the case of the *of*-binominal family here, the progression of first nouns from being used in the N+PP construction to them functioning as intensifiers in the BI. The second is what he calls schematization, but which is also often referred to as constructionalization and defined as "the development through which certain structural patterns acquire their own meanings, so that they add meaning to the lexical elements occurring in them" (Noël 2007: 192). This kind of grammaticalization leads to partially or fully schematic constructions: constructionalization (Noël 2007: 183; see

---

[14] For an overview of grammaticalization and cognitive linguistics, see van der Auwera, van Olmen, and Du Mon (2015).

8.3 Grammaticalization in Construction Grammar

further Gisborne & Patten 2011: 100–2). This process will be discussed in the following analysis.

The theory assumes that constructionalization primarily begins with language use and usually with changes in the semantics before, subsequently, enacting changes in the morpho-syntax and even phonology (Croft 2001: 126–9). Ambiguity in language use on the construct level (i.e. in bridging contexts) leads to changes in higher, more schematic levels. These changes, if frequent enough, are then entrenched and have an effect on the meso-construction level or a higher level of abstraction. This may in turn lead to a change or the development of a new, higher-level schema. This new schema could then lead to coercion and change on lower levels (cf. Gisborne & Pattern 2011: 103; Noël 2007: 184).[15]

A new construction, or a new node in the network, is formed via a change in both form and meaning from an already existing construction (e.g. Traugott & Trousdale 2013: 22; see also Traugott 2018).[16] The change in form includes phonological reduction, obligatorification of a constituent, and host-class expansion; a change in meaning/function entails semantic change, a change from lexical to grammatical, or from grammatical to more grammatical (Hilpert 2021). Brems (2011), for example, argues for a new construction in her network of measure nouns on the basis of a change in semantic prosody and an expansion of collocation patterns; hence, example (8.3a) is a quantifier and example (8.3b) a value quantifier – two different constructions. In the former, the first noun quantifies the second, and in the latter, the first noun functions more as an evaluation of the referent denoted by the second noun (Brems 2011: 174). For evidence of change in form she argues that, in example (8.3b), "[i]n this valuing quantifier use attitudinal subjectification is a work, which leads to new collocational clusterings," and *a load of* can no longer be substituted by *many*, which is still possible in (8.3a) (Brems 2011: 174).

(8.3)   a. I still have *a load of friends* there. (Brems 2011: 172)
        b. What *a load of killjoys*. What's their problem? (Brems 2011: 174)

---

[15] There can also be top-down change in that higher-level constructions link with other constructions via analogy and their idiosyncratic properties are projected onto or coerce lower-level ones (for an overview of both types of change, see van der Auwera et al. 2015: 642).
[16] Particularly in Diachronic CxG circles, this has become rather controversial. For example, Diewald (2015: 119) points out that if the basis of CxG is Saussure's sign, then any distinctive change of form or meaning would, by definition, lead to a new sign; therefore, change in meaning alone (constructional change) would also lead to a new construction.

Two important processes that play a role in this particular study and have also been a topic of discussion in the field is the role of reanalysis and analogy in language change. In order to explain analogy, one has to discuss reanalysis.[17] Reanalysis refers to those instances where a hearer understands a message differently from how the speaker intended (or the speaker intentionally reparses a canonical construction), such as parsing the form and meaning differently from the original intention, e.g. parsing [*Hamburg*] +[*er*] to [*ham* + [*burger*]], which then creates a paradigm for *cheeseburger* and *chicken burger* (Hopper & Traugott 2003: 50). Reanalysis involves a change of a construction's constituency, hierarchical structure, linguistic category, grammatical relations, or boundary types (Traugott 2008b: 225). However, the existence of this mechanism has been called into question by numerous linguists (predominantly discussed in Fischer 2007, 2008, but also in Haspelmath 1998; Kiparsky 2012; De Smet 2009). An alternative that has been suggested is analogy.

Analogy is "[a]ny linguistic change which results from an attempt to make some linguistic forms more similar to other linguistic forms" (Trask 2000: 20). Analogy is a speaker-listener focused process that draws on both ontogenetic and phylogenetic research (Fischer 2007, 2008, 2011). It incorporates processes used by children when they learn language, i.e. intention reading, pattern-finding, entrenchment, and competition (cf. Slobin 1996; Tomasello 2003), and when language is transmitted over generations (cf. Deacon 1997, 2003).[18] For Noël (2007: 183) analogy works in two different areas. Analogy is, first, considered responsible for host-class expansion (Himmelmann 2004: 32), i.e. it results in a construction where the substance is more or less the same, but it adopts broader selection restrictions (also called schematization or expansion) (Noël 2007: 183).[19] The second is in the creation of new substantive constructions in that empty slots in these schematic constructions attract linguistic items, resulting in the grammaticalization of these items (Noël 2007: 183). Noël (2007: 184) exemplifies this with Bisang's (1998) study of verbs marking tense, aspect, and modality (see also Hoffmann 2004; Traugott 2008b), where verbs that occur in certain syntactic positions begin to adopt properties of other verbs that also appear in these positions. Noël (2007: 184) explains that "the schematic construction 'coerces'

---

[17] Also called neoanalysis (Traugott & Trousdale 2013).
[18] For general discussion, see Fischer (2008).
[19] Noël (2007: 183) takes an example from Hopper and Traugott (2003: 66) to illustrate this process, namely *ne ... pas* in French. First, *ne ... pas* only combined with movement verbs and then later could negate all verbs.

a particular interpretation, leading to reanalysis, and a new substantive construction is born."

This book views reanalysis and analogy as two separate but related processes. Reanalysis is essentially the reparsing of the form or meaning of a construction, which results in a new analysis of the same material, whereas analogy is the link to another form already existing in the language system (see also Heine & Narrog 2010: 401).

In sum, CxG sees language change as driven by general cognitive processes of language use that then lead to changes in form and may lead to the creation of a new node/construction in the network. Two cognitive mechanisms that begin this process are analogy and reanalysis, and they are related in that analogy may lead to structural reanalysis. This book takes a conservative stance and posits that a new node is formed only with a change in both meaning/function and form. This new node is positioned in an individual's grammar with vertical links (from substantiated to schematic constructions) and horizontal relations to constructions on the same level of schematicity.

8.4 Modeling the Evaluative *Of*-binominal Family Network

Drawing on evidence from the analysis of the individual constructions in Part I and the empirical studies in Part II, CxG grammar allows us to make predictions about how this family was formed diachronically: more precisely, information from Part I allows us to map out a detailed description of each individual node and demonstrate that these *of*-binominals are indeed constructions in their own right, and the empirical studies in Part II allow us to propose a scenario in which the *of*-binominal constructions developed. This analysis will focus on the main grammaticalization path, discussing the N+PP, head-classifier, EBNP, EM, and BI.

8.4.1 *N+PP*

As was the case with other *of*-binominal families (e.g. Brems 2011; Davidse 2009; Denison 2005; Traugott 2008a, 2008b) and as demonstrated in the case studies in Chapter 5, the grammaticalization process that eventually led to the creation of the evaluative *of*-binominals most likely began with the compositional N+PP construction, where the embedded prepositional phrase ascribes a property to the first noun (*of* functioning similar to *from* or *with*). Figure 8.4 demonstrates an N+PP construction schema where the PP denotes time, such as *the breeze of the morning*. As discussed in Chapter 3

MEANING/FUNCTION

SEMANTICS:

NOUN$_1$	[1] referential
	[2] unrestricted type, e.g. concrete, proper, etc.
NOUN$_2$	[3] referential, denotes a time period
PP	[4] functions as a modifier, anchors or identifies the first noun
	[5] ascribes a temporal property onto the first noun
	[6] preposition *of* means 'from'

FORM

SYNTAX: [$_{NP1}$ [Det$_1$](Mod)[[N$_1$][$_{PP}$[of][$_{NP2}$[[DET$_2$](Mod)[N$_2$]]]$_{TEMP}$]]]

NOUN$_1$	[1] head of whole construction
	[2] head of individual NP$_1$
NOUN$_2$	[3] part of embedded NP in a PP
	[4] heads NP$_2$
	[5] unrestricted type
BOTH Ns	[6] unrestricted modification
	[7] do not have to agree in number
DET$_1$ & DET$_2$	[8] unrestricted, e.g. definite, indefinite, etc.
PP	[9] *of* heads a prepositional phrase
	[10] a separate constituent

MORPHOLOGY: [1] N$_1$ can take singular and plural form
[2] N$_2$ can take singular and plural form
[3] subject-verb agreement with first noun

Figure 8.4 The N+PP temporal construction

(Section 3.2), the first noun is the head of the whole construction, each noun heads its individual noun phrase, and the prepositional phrase modifies the first noun. Both determiner slots are open to all forms of determiners, and the premodification study in Chapter 7 shows that premodification is unrestricted.

At this initial stage, it would make sense to ask whether the N+PP is really a blend or realization of two (or more) separate constructions [[Det$_1$ [N$_1$ [*of*-NP$_2$]]] rather than a single one. Constituency tests (see Section 3.2) indicate that the PP is a separate constituent (unlike the other constructions discussed in this study), and therefore, one could argue that

8.4 Modeling the Evaluative Of-binominal Family Network

it is indeed a noun modified by a separate PP construction. However, in PDE the temporal N+PP construction is unarguably so frequent that it can be considered a construction in its own right, as exemplified by the sub-construction in Figure 8.4. However, a representation with two separate constructions would also fit the present analysis.

Figure 8.5 situates the construction in Figure 8.4 in the larger network. (Note that I have included more detailed nodes than the Traugott & Trousdale [2013] network model; each node includes a short version of both the form and the function of each construction.) The N+PP temporal construction would be on the subschema level and find itself on the same level with other N+PP realizations such as origin or location (*the beast of Prague*),

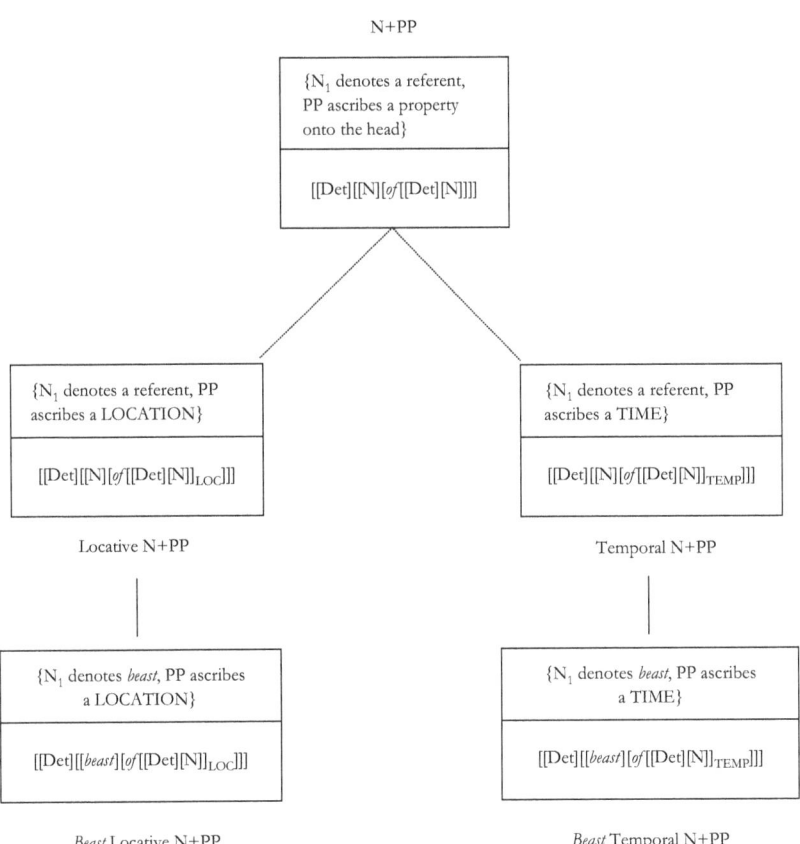

Figure 8.5 The N+PP in the construction network

also depicted in Figure 8.5, and to some degree possession (*the father of the bride*). The different N+PP constructions, e.g. locative and temporal, would constitute different constructional nodes due to their frequency and because the function of the PP puts constraints on the first and second nouns. For example, in the temporal construction, the second noun must be one that can denote or be construed as denoting time. These different realizations of the *of*-binominal construction are joined by the more schematic 'mother node', the very frequent N+*of*-PP construction on a higher level; in this more schematic construction, the PP simply ascribes a property to the head. Only on a lower microconstruction level, do we find constructions where the first noun position is filled, e.g. *a beast of* NP. These are the basic forms that the more idiosyncratic constructions develop from. In particular, this higher-level schema, I argue, drives the changes that result in the other constructions.

8.4.2 Head-Classifier

The diachronic studies in Chapter 5 show that the head-classifier appears after the prototypical examples of N+PP (*cake* is an exception). This means that at some point, on the construct level, the PP in the N+PP was reconceptualized, metaphorically extended, as denoting the first noun's class: *the breeze of the morning* became *a breeze of morning* or *a morning breeze* (so in theory one can have *a morning breeze* in the night because it is a type of breeze; see Section 3.3 for further discussion). The analogy between the origin, location, property, or time ascribed by the PP as classifying the noun head led to formal reanalysis. In the head-classifier, the PP is no longer a separate constituent and *of* has become a linking device and no longer means *from* or *with*.[20] The change in the function of the second noun would then result in it no longer being referential but instead denoting a category: the nouns are co-referential. The second noun is realized as a bare plural, bare abstract, or mass noun, so the second determiner position is empty: *a beast of the field* becomes *a beast of field*. Figure 8.6 models the schematic head-classifier construction. These formal and semantic changes differentiate the head-classifier from the N+PP and warrant a separate node for the head-classifier in the network.

Figure 8.7 situates the head-classifier in the larger network level (for simplicity, this discussion will focus on location and temporal constructions; however, in theory any N+PP construction could be used in the head-classifier: *a dress of your cloth* could become *a dress of cloth*). The N+PP

---

[20] For the discussion of this change in many *of*-binominals, see Tyler and Evans (2003: 209).

8.4 Modeling the Evaluative Of-binominal Family Network

MEANING/FUNCTION

SEMANTICS:

NOUN$_1$		[1] semantic head, denotes overall referent
		[2] unrestricted, e.g. concrete, proper, etc.
NOUN$_2$		[3] nonreferential
		[4] denotes a category of N$_1$
		[5] mass noun, bare abstract noun or bare plural count noun
BOTH Ns		[6] co-referential
PP		[7] qualifies or classifies N$_2$
		[8] *of* functions as a linking device

FORM

SYNTAX: [$_{NP1}$ [Det$_1$](Mod)[[N$_1$][of]$_{LE}$ [$_{NP2}$(Mod)[N$_2$]]]]

NOUN$_1$	[1] syntactic head of whole construction
	[2] unrestricted, e.g. concrete, proper, etc.
	[3] open premodification
	[4] modifiers in front of N$_1$ modifies N$_1$ or the referent
NOUN$_2$	[5] no longer heads NP$_2$
	[6] premodification restricted
Both Ns	[7] do not have to agree in number
Det$_1$ & Det$_2$	[8] Det$_1$ unrestricted
	[9] no Det$_2$
PP	[10] no longer a separate constituent
	[11] *of* functions as a linking device

MORPHOLOGY: [1] N$_1$ is marked for the plurality of the referent.
[2] Det$_1$ agrees in number with N$_1$
[3] subject-verb agreement with first noun

Figure 8.6 The head-classifier construction

construction and the head-classifier are joined by a metaphorical link (M) on the micro-construction level. The change from N+PP location to head-classifier is a classic metaphorical shift from concrete source domain to abstract target domain: the actual conceptual metaphor used depends on the first noun. In the case of *breeze* in Figure 8.7, the metaphor would be a breeze linked to a season, e.g. *a breeze of spring*. This link would have to be on the lower micro-construction level, because not all first nouns used in the temporal or locative N+PP constructions are reconceptualized as head-classifiers,

8 The EBNP Family: A Construction Grammar Analysis

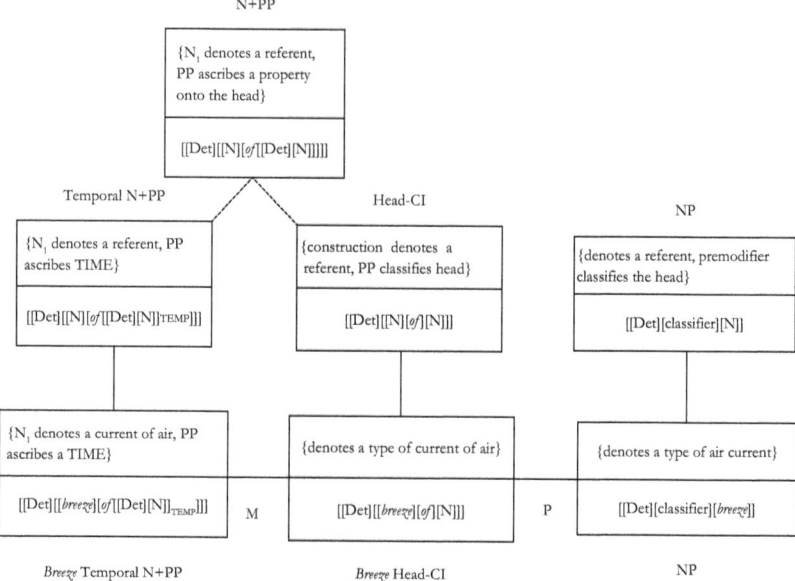

Figure 8.7 The N+PP and head-classifier in construction network

i.e. not all first nouns can be classified by a locative or temporal property. This link is not systematic but facilitated by the first noun. The head-classifier is entrenched enough to warrant a separate, open head-classifier schema on a higher level, which in turn has a taxonomic link to the schematic N+PP mother node.

Not only is the head-classifier construction formally similar to the N+PP, but it shares functions with classifier premodifiers: *a book of poetry* can also be *a poetry book* (see Gunkel & Zifonun 2009; see Section 7.3.1 for discussion of this category). The PP in the head-classifier construction and the classifier premodifier in the simple noun phrase function very much alike, and in some cases, as shown above, the two constructions are interchangeable. This shared function indicates that the classifier premodifier and the head-classifier construction are connected via a polysemy link (P) in the construct-i-con; the two forms are in some cases syntactic alternates.[21] The primary semantic difference between the two constructions is that the head-classifier disambiguates the

---

[21] *Breeze* in the NP has been represented as a separate node in this representation in order to illustrate the argument. Naturally, the question arises as to whether it would warrant a separate node in the network or whether constructs such as *a sea breeze* are actually just formed in online production via links between a *breeze* node and the simple NP node, and not an individual node itself.

8.4 Modeling the Evaluative Of-binominal Family Network

premodifier reading. In the premodifier position, the modifier can function as both a classifier and a descriptive modifier, as in the case of *wooden* in example (8.4).

(8.4)   a. a toy wooden boat
          b. a wooden toy boat

In (8.4a) *wooden* denotes the type of boat, most likely a rowboat or a small boat usually made of wood, but, in theory, it could be made of plastic. In (8.4b), the toy is made of wood, but the boat could be a large trawler, usually made of steel or iron. In many cases, such as *wooden*, the premodifier is ambiguous, whereas the head-classifier can denote only a classifier relationship. Some reasons for the speaker to choose one construction over the other include end-weight considerations, head noun semantics, or genre. Therefore, despite the fact that the two forms are in competition with each other, they manage to coexist (see Zehentner 2019; Zehentner & Traugott 2020 for a similar scenario with the benefactive ditransitive).

Based on the information presented in this book, it is hard to judge the systematicity of these alternations, i.e. if these two higher-level schemata are actually linked in the minds of speakers. Interchangeability between both forms appears to be dependent on the first noun and the construction: for example, we have *breeze* in the N+PP temporal construction for *a breeze of spring* and this allows for the classifier alternative, *spring breeze*. *An ocean breeze* is fine, but *a breeze of ocean*, however, would be read as a pseudo-partitive rather than a head-classifier. Particularly the more entrenched head-classifiers, such as *a bird of prey*, do not appear to have the premodifier alternative at all: **a prey bird*. Thus, it is most likely that the two forms are connected only on the micro-construction level, between the partially filled schemata, since the first noun enables or restricts the alternation.

Noël (2007: 184) points out that "[c]onstructions of a higher level of abstraction can play a role as an analogical force behind grammaticalization, enhancing a substantive construction's expansion or triggering the establishment of a new substantive construction." This connection between the head-classifier and the classifier premodifier in the simple noun phrase might have created a relationship between the head-classifier and the very schematic and very frequent simple noun phrase (see Figure 8.7). This connection could then be the driving force behind the changes that follow, namely a pressure to reduce the complex N+PP to a simple NP as has been observed in this study and in other English *of*-binominal studies, e.g. *sorta*, *kinda*, or pseudo-partitives

(Brems 2011; Davidse 2009; Keizer 2007a; Traugott 2008a, 2008b). In other words, the hypothesis is that by sharing the functions with elements in the simple noun phrase, in this case the classifier premodifier, certain *of*-binominals create a network link to the more schematic noun phrase construction. This sets the two forms, the *of*-binominal and the simple noun phrase, in competition with each other. The competition created by activation of both constructions in the minds of the speakers then motivates an analogy with the simple NP and the subsequent reanalysis of the internal structure of the *of*-binominal that follows.

8.4.3 Evaluative Binominal Noun Phrase

Both formally and functionally, the EBNP is different from all other *of*-binominal constructions in English, hence justifying a node of its own (see Section 4.2). Semantically, the EBNP functions completely differently from the head-classifier: the first noun ascribes a property to the second, which denotes the referent and is the clear semantic head. The change in the semantic functions of the nouns means that the selection of the first noun is restricted, while almost any first noun can be used in the head-classifier construction. On the other hand, the second noun slot has almost no restrictions. Formally, in the EBNP, the second noun is the most likely syntactic head, unlike the first noun head in the head-classifier. Furthermore, there are restrictions on both first and second determiners, whereas the head-classifier allows unrestricted determiners in the Det_1 position. Finally, the EBNP exhibits idiosyncratic premodification patterns (see Figure 8.8).

As discussed in Section 4.2, the origin of the EBNP construction is unclear. Previous research has claimed that the EBNP has entered English via French or Latin, but this claim has yet to be substantiated. A second scenario would be that the present EBNP construction might have developed from another English *of*-binominal construction, separately from the French version (although the dissemination of EBNPs in European languages would make this the less likely scenario). Either way, the CxG network allows for grammaticalization paths or developing networks to create links to already existing constructions. Traugott (2018a) points out that networks are not static structures but materialize, change, and can be completely reorganized (see also Colleman 2011; Van de Velde 2014). This would also provide evidence in support of the Constructional Convergence Hypothesis, which proposes that historically unrelated constructions can

8.4 Modeling the Evaluative Of-binominal Family Network

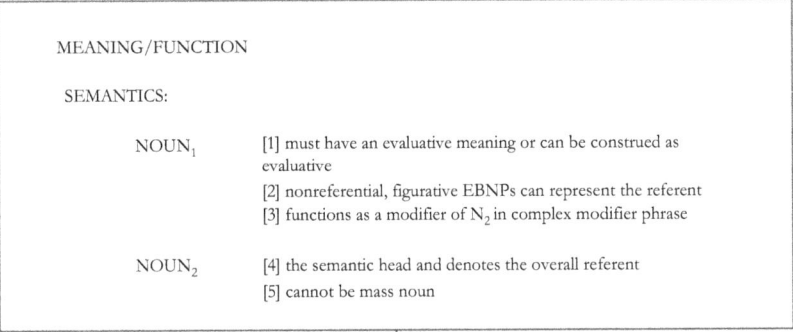
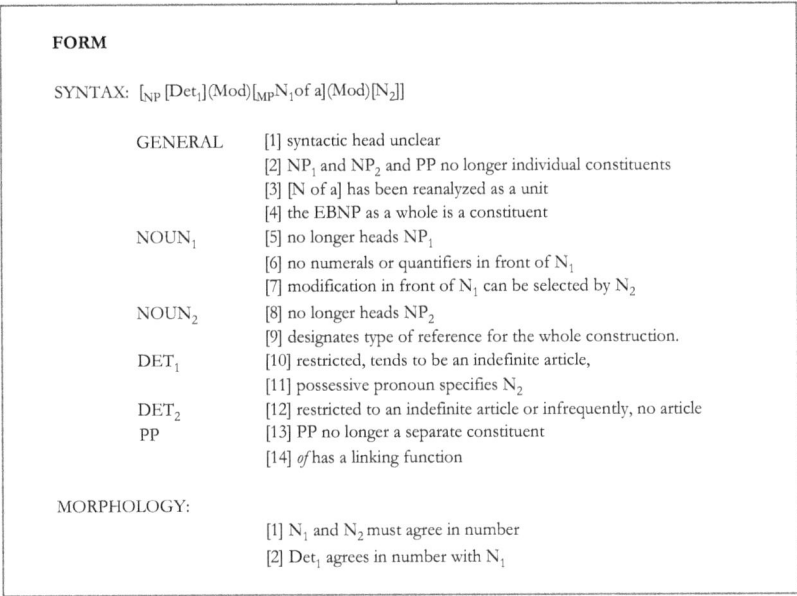

Figure 8.8 The EBNP construction

eventually take a position in a formally and functionally related network (Torrent 2015). Therefore, it is possible that the EBNP construction already existed in English, having entered via French or Latin, and this construction was adopted into this *of*-binominal family.

Although some first nouns may come to be used in the EBNP via the pseudo-partitive, the most frequent progression is from the head-classifier to the EBNP (see Section 6.4). Although the actual reanalysis would happen on the construct level, frequency of use with particular first nouns would result in nodes formed on the micro-construction level; in the network the EBNP and head-classifier constructions are connected via metaphorical extension (M). This transition can be seen most clearly in the diachronic study with *beast* (see Section 5.4): in the head-classifier, *beast* denotes an animal, and in the EBNP, *beast* is used to ascribe animal-like features (manner or size) to first humans and then objects (see Figure 8.9).

The EBNP construction is established and salient enough to have a higher-level schema. Despite the internal reanalysis found in the EBNP, this schema would then have a taxonomic link to the more schematic N+PP mother node, as was the case with the previous constructions. Although the functions of many of the internal elements in the EBNP, such as *of* and the second determiner, are idiosyncratic, formally the preposition *of* is not optional, and the second determiner still marks number. The inheritance link between the EBNP and the N+PP would explain the reappearance of the indefinite article in the second determiner position in the EBNP. This slot remains unfilled in the head-classifier

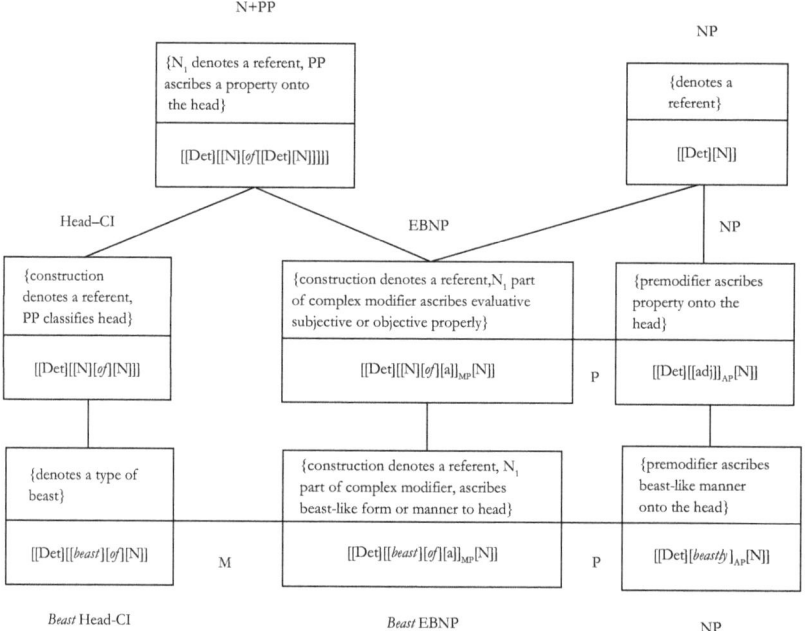

Figure 8.9 The Head-classifier and EBNP in the construction network

8.4 Modeling the Evaluative Of-binominal Family Network

because of functional restrictions on the second. However, the EBNP is defined by its indefinite article in the second determiner position (see Section 4.2).

The EBNP also has a link to the simple noun phrase, in that it shares functional properties with descriptive premodifiers: the first noun ascribes a subjective or objective evaluative property to the second noun. As was the case with the head-classifier, some first nouns license both an EBNP form and a premodifier form with very little difference in meaning, e.g. *a hell of a hotel* and *a hellish hotel* or *a beast of a boy* and *a beastly boy*. An alternative is that the first nouns can take the *-like* suffix and can be used as a premodifier to mean something similar to the EBNP, e.g. compare *her round moon of a face* (COCA) to *her moon-like face* (COCA). Nonetheless, this is not true for all first nouns used in the EBNP, e.g. *a breeze of a girl* is fine, but $^?$*a breeze-like girl* is noncanonical if not ungrammatical. This greater systematicity would lead to the conclusion that there is a polysemy link (P) between the EBNP schema and the simple noun phrase at the subschema level. A subschema link would then motivate the reconceptualization of the first nouns as denoting attributes and as a part of a noncanonical [N of a] modifier phrase. This is the first step in the *of*-binominal reducing to a simple NP (see Figure 8.9).[22]

The first noun's change in function initiates the subsequent debonding and reanalysis of the [N of (a)]. This connection to the simple noun phrase and *of*-binominal has an effect on the semantic development of these constructions: the EBNP grammaticalizes further, coalescing into the simple NP, and semantically, progressing along a similar path to that of premodifiers: from objective to subjective descriptive modification to intensification.

8.4.4 Evaluative Modifier

The EM construction modeled in Figure 8.10 is very similar to the EBNP construction, but there are both critical meaning and form differences. The semantics of the first noun has bleached to speaker evaluation of the referent denoted by N_2: it can no longer ascribe physical attributes. There are a number of morpho-syntactic differences, such as the first

---

[22] As was true with the head-classifier, one can argue that *beastly* as a premodifier does not warrant a separate node in the network. However, syntactic position does indeed restrict the meaning of the modifier: *beastly* can have a range of meanings in the premodifier position (see OED entry for 'beastly'), but only mean animal-like, e.g. *Let's not be Beastly to the Germans* (COCA) or an intensifier, e.g. *the Gazoo was beastly hot* (COCA), in other positions.

228   8 The EBNP Family: A Construction Grammar Analysis

```
┌─────────────────────────────────────────────────────────────────────────────┐
│  MEANING/FUNCTION                                                            │
│                                                                              │
│     SEMANTICS:                                                               │
│              [1] N₂ is the semantic head and denotes the ovrerall referent  │
│              [2] N₁ is nonreferential, must have a subjective evaluative reading │
└─────────────────────────────────────────────────────────────────────────────┘
┌─────────────────────────────────────────────────────────────────────────────┐
│   FORM                                                                       │
│                                                                              │
│        SYNTAX:       [_NP [Det₁](Mod)[_MP N₁ of (a)](Mod)[N₂]]              │
│        GENERAL       [1] Np₁ and Np₂ and PP are no longer individual constituents │
│                      [2] [N of (a)] has been reanalyzed as a unit           │
│                      [3] [N of (a)] increased scope                          │
│        NOUN₁         [4] a part of [N of (a)], functions as evaluative modifier, modifying N₂ │
│                      [5] N₁ no longer heads NP₁                              │
│                      [6] modification in front of N₁ can be selected by/have scope over N₂ │
│        NOUN₂         [7] syntactic head                                      │
│                      [8] no longer heads NP₂                                 │
│                      [9] designates type of reference for the whole construction. │
│        DET₁          [10] restricted: an indefinite article, or emphatic some or one │
│                      [11] possessive pronoun specifies N₂                    │
│        DET₂          [12] indefinite article or no article, no longer marks number for N₂ │
│        PP            [13] of no longer has a function                        │
│                                                                              │
│     MORPHOLOGY:                                                              │
│                      [1] N₁ and N₂ no longer must agree in number           │
│                      [2] N₁ is always in singular                            │
│                                                                              │
│     ORTHOGRAPHY:     [1] orthographic reduction in the most frequent forms: helluva, hella, whaleuva │
└─────────────────────────────────────────────────────────────────────────────┘
```

Figure 8.10 The EM construction

noun must be singular, the second determiner no longer marks number, and the second and first nouns do not have to agree in number, although they usually do (see Section 4.3 for more discussion). Formally, the internal reanalysis culminates with the orthographic reduction of the most frequent forms to *hella, helluva,* and *whaleuva*.

In many cases, there is a clear metaphorical extension from the EBNP to the EM on the micro-construction level, as shown in Figure 8.11. For example, in the case of *whale,* the large size meaning in the EBNP (*a whale of a ship*) bleaches in the EM to a simple positive evaluation of the referent (*a whale of a movie*) along the lines of the metaphors GOOD IS BIG (see discussion in Section 6.5.1).

The formal and functional changes in the EM construction weaken the link between the EM and the schematic *of*-binominal mother node (hence the dotted taxonomic link in Figure 8.11). The existence of a polysemy link between the particularly filled EM construction to premodification in the

8.4 Modeling the Evaluative Of-binominal Family Network

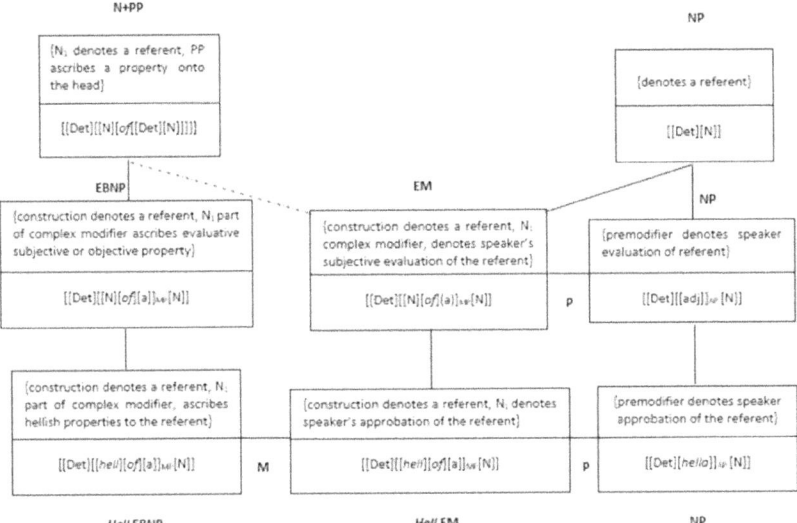

Figure 8.11 The EBNP and the EM in the construction network

Note: In an expanded version of this network, *hella*, *helluva*, and *whaleuva* would be represented by separate lexical nodes in the network; for simplicity and readability, I have just included *hella* in the NP.

simple NP on the micro-construction level depends on the first noun. *Beastly* can be used as an evaluative premodifier in examples such as *beastly configurations* (COCA), and the OED also lists *hellish* as having an EM-like meaning in phrases such as *a hellish speed*, starting to appear in the mid-eighteenth century, around the time when the first EM examples appear. This link resulted in the creation of *hella*, which is clearly an EM in the following examples: *You mess with them even once, believe me, you'd better be* **one hella witch** *to keep me from strangling you.* (COCA) (see Figure 8.11). However, most other first nouns in the EM do not have an evaluative premodifier alternative, e.g. *honey* or *dog*.

Although many EMs are not linked to the simple NP on the micro-construction level, there is semantic overlap between EMs and other evaluative premodifiers like *wonderful*, and the EM shares more formal features with the simple NP than with the *of*-binominal. Therefore, the EM must share a horizontal link to evaluative modifiers in the noun phrase, but on the subschema level, rather than the micro-construction (see Figure 8.11). The presence of this polysemy link to the simple NP is further supported by the findings in the premodifier study in Chapter 7.

This study shows that in the EM, the [N of (a)] unit positions itself in the subjective modifier zone in front of intensifiers and after descriptive and classifier premodifiers. Descriptive modifiers were not found in front of the first noun, and the use of classifiers is restricted. This means that although the preposition *of* and second determiner remain in the EM, the construction has formally been reanalyzed as a simple NP.

8.4.5 Binominal Intensifier

In the BI, the [N of (a)] chunk has been integrated into the adjective phrase and functions as an intensifier of the following adjective, as shown in Figure 8.12. This function differentiates it from both the EBNP and EM constructions. In the BI, the second determiner slot has lost all functionality (neither marking number nor definiteness), and the first determiner has

---

MEANING/FUNCTION

SEMANTICS:

[1] N_1 part of a [N of (a)] which functions as an intensifier, modifying the following adj.

[2] N_2 is semantic head, denotes the whole construction's denotation

[3] N_1 is nonreferential

FORM

SYNTAX: [$_{NP}$ [Det$_1$] [$_{MP}$ [$_{INT}$N$_1$of (a)][Adj]][N$_2$]]

NOUN$_1$	[1] part of a [N of (a)]
	[2] [N$_1$ of (Det) Adj] separate constituent in AP
	[3] restricted modification
NOUN$_2$	[4] N$_2$ is syntactic head
	[5] modified descriptive modifiers and classifiers
DET$_1$	[6] restricted, indefinite article, or emphatic *some* or *one*
DET$_2$	[7] an indefinite article or no article, no longer marks number with N$_2$
	[8] in some forms of can be left out
PP	[9] *of* no longer has a function

MORPHOLOGY:

[1] N_1 and N_2 no longer must agree in number

[2] N_1 is always in singular

[3] N_2 takes plural marking

ORTHOGRAPHY:

[1] orthographic reduction in the most frequent forms: *helluva, hella, whaleuva*

Figure 8.12 The BI construction

8.4 Modeling the Evaluative Of-binominal Family Network

scope over the whole construction, as was true for the EM. However, unlike the EM, premodification appearing in front of the first noun is severely restricted; it allows for *whole* as in *a whole hell of a lot of time*, but no others (see Section 7.6.6 for discussion). Further evidence that BI is indeed a separate construction from the EBNP and EM is that the [N of (a)] chunk in some cases has become an autonomous constituent used predicatively, as demonstrated in examples like *Young believes they "did Britain a hell of good by coming here"* (NOW). As was the case with the EM, the most frequent forms are orthographically reduced to *helluva*, *hella*, and *whaleuva*, and the most frequent of these are autonomous nodes in the network.

The EM and BI are connected on the micro-construction level via shared first nouns in partially schematic constructions, as modeled in Figure 8.13. These two constructions also share very similar internal structure, but in the case of the BI, [N of (a)] has shifted into the AdjP. Given that in the BI the [N of (a)] chunk is syntactically autonomous in some cases, this would indicate that the BI is connected to the simple adjective phrase, not the whole NP. Only on a more abstract schematic level would the AP link with the NP node. As was the case with the EM constructions, first nouns in the BI do not usually

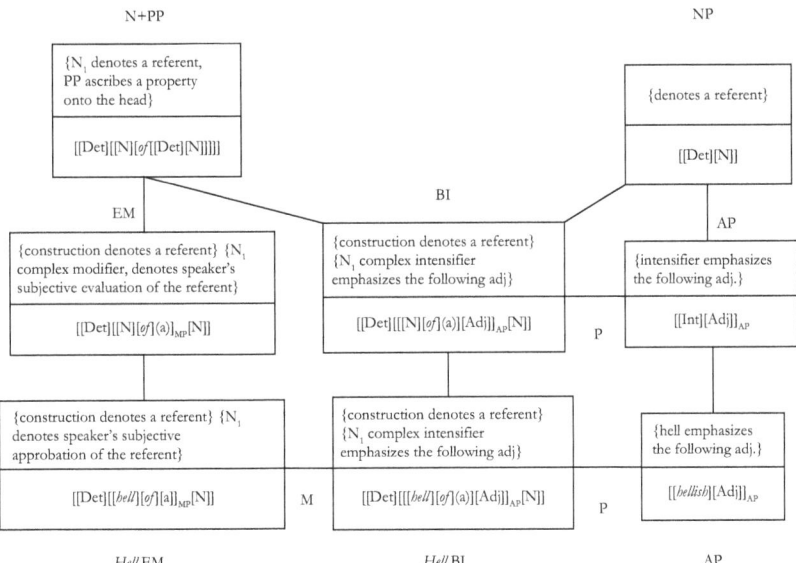

Figure 8.13 The EM and BI in the construction network

have a premodifier alternative: *a whale of a good time* but not **a whale/whalish good time*. The two exceptions are *beastly* and *hell*. *Beastly* appears to be a relatively frequent intensifier found in examples like it was *a beastly aggressive player* (COCA). *Hellish* has functioned as an intensifier since the seventeenth century: *A mouth O hellish wide* (OED). More recently, *hell* has been construed as an intensifier in its own right, as demonstrated in examples such as *there are some hell tough ladies in those books* (COCA). However, this form is most likely not frequent enough yet to have created a separate node but is a product of online, multiple inheritance links.

The link to the schematic *of*-binominal has weakened (dotted line in Figure 8.13): the chunk [N of (a)] functions as an intensifier in an adjective phrase, the first noun is always singular, and the second determiner may be dropped. Furthermore, the results from the premodification study in Section 7.6.6 show that the [N of (a)] part of the BI has inserted itself in the intensifier end of the premodification zones and has become a separate constituent.

8.5 Conclusion

In this chapter, a multiple inheritance account models the ways in which other linguistic elements in the language might have triggered, driven, or influenced the grammaticalization path shown here. I propose that in the N+PP, the function of the construction is to allow the speaker to denote a referent and specify the referent by providing locative, temporal, or further information about this referent. Analogical extension led to a change in the function of the prepositional phrase and reanalysis of the internal structure in the head-classifier. This results in polysemy links between the head-classifier and the classifier premodifier in the noun phrase because the head-classifier with certain first nouns share semantic functions with the same noun functioning as a classifier premodifier. These variations create a link between the two partially filled constructions on the micro-construction level and, thereby, a link to the simple NP. This study proposes that this connection created tension between the simple NP and the N+PP mother nodes, and the resulting competition facilitated the change of head and the internal reanalysis of the *of*-binominal in the constructions that followed. This would explain why the evaluative *of*-binominals (EBNP, EM, and BI) then follow the prototypical grammaticalization path observed in prototypical premodifiers shifting from objective descriptive to subjective descriptive modifiers and finally intensifiers. Furthermore, this construction network model demonstrates how changes in the lower levels in the network, i.e. in the head-classifier, results in connections between higher-level, more schematic nodes. Like Zehentner and Traugott's (2020) study of the benefactive ditransitive, this chapter also shows the importance of horizontal links in driving the constructionalization of higher-level schemata. This study shows that the resulting competition between the *of*-binominals and the premodifiers did not always result in the loss of one construction, but in this case, two constructions with shared functions coexisting. The different schematic layers in the network also allow us to explain why some of the *of*-binominals have premodifier variations, e.g. *a beastly boy* and *a beast of a boy*, while others do not. Furthermore, it can explain why first nouns used in the EM and BI have premodifier functions and yet do not offer this variation, e.g. *a whale of a good time* but not **a whale good time*.

Unlike Zehentner and Traugott's (2020) study, I represented the connection between the *of*-binominals and the simple noun phrase as a polysemy link. They explained the creation of the benefactive ditransitive using allostructions. Allostructions are constructions that share functions or meaning but vary in form. They are linked horizontally on the same level and also connected by a higher schema, the constructeme, which encodes those elements shared by both allostructions (Capelle 2006). Zehentner and Traugott adopt a looser definition in that allostructional links are "the relations between formally different but *semantically overlapping* constructions" (2020: 172; my emphasis); syntactic alternatives "*may* vertically connect to a constructeme" (2020: 174; my emphasis). In their definition, allostructional links do not have to be exact synonyms and do not have to share a more schematic, higher-level constructeme. Positing allostructions might provide a viable explanation here as well and would need to be explored with a more focused quantitative study. Even without allostructions, the representations in this chapter become relatively complex and have the potential of being even more complex.

Ultimately this chapter shows that CxG provides the tools to create a model that explains the changes that first nouns undergo when they progress along this grammaticalization path. More importantly, despite the data collection issues inherent in a study of the EBNP, CxG allows us to predict how this path may have been created. However, some features that the CxG account cannot explain are why the intensifier zones for the second nouns are lost in the head-classifier, or why, in the EBNP, the descriptive premodification shifts from being placed in front of the second noun to placement in front of the first one. It can map but does not explain why the internal changes happened in the order shown in the data. This can be explained by the second language model discussed here, namely, Functional Discourse Grammar.

CHAPTER 9

The EBNP Family: A Functional Discourse Grammar Analysis

9.1 Introduction to Functional Discourse Grammar

This chapter examines the evidence from Parts I and II of this monograph from a Functional Discourse Grammar (FDG) perspective. Looking at this phenomenon from an FDG perspective raises a number of theory-relevant questions, such as how a more formal linguistic theory would model the internal changes found in these constructions, whether FDG can explain the development of the EBNP, EM, and BI, and whether it can account for the changes in the premodification patterns. This chapter also addresses some more general questions, such as the potential role of constructions in this theory. Many formal models, e.g. Sign-Based Head-Driven Phrase Structure Grammar (Boas & Sag 2012; Sag 2001, 2012; Michaelis 2010, 2012, 2013) and Role and Reference Grammar (van Valin 2005; van Valin & LaPolla 1997), have adopted variations of the theoretical concept of construction (as defined in Chapter 8) into their models. In this study, the EBNP would be a strong candidate for being a construction, and this project asks if the FDG model can explain the noncanonical behavior of the EBNP construction without having to posit the existence of constructions.

The rest of Section 9.1 will introduce the FDG model (Section 9.1.1), the primitives in the grammar (Section 9.1.2), give an example of an FDG analysis of the noun phrase (Section 9.1.3), and finally, FDG's classification criteria (Section 9.1.4). The analysis is presented in Section 9.2. Section 9.3 discusses FDG's modeling of the diachronic development of these *of*-binominals before concluding in Section 9.4.

9.1.1 General Overview

FDG developed as the successor of Dik's Functional Grammar (FG) (1997a, 1997b) and "seeks to reconcile the patent fact that languages are structured complexes with the equally patent fact that they are adapted to function as instruments of communication between human beings" (Hengeveld & Mackenzie 2008: ix; cf. Dik 1997a: 3). It is a functional, typologically based model of language characterized by a form-oriented "function-to-form," top-down approach to grammar (Hengeveld & Mackenzie 2008: 1–3, 25–41). The theory is form-oriented in that it focuses on and accounts for linguistic facts, and therefore, only takes into account linguistic phenomena that are actually encoded in the grammar of a language: in other words, it only accounts for pragmatic and semantic phenomena that are systematically encoded in the grammar. It is function-to-form in that an underlying premise is that function, either directly or indirectly, influences form, and it is top-down because each analysis begins with a speaker's intention and ends with articulation (for more details, see Hengeveld & Mackenzie 2008: 25–42). These final two premises are clearly reflected in the model's architecture (see Figure 9.1),[1] which begins with a speaker's communicative intention on the prelinguistic level in the Conceptual Component.[2] This mental representation feeds into the Grammatical Component and triggers the operation of formulation, which translates these conceptual representations into pragmatic representations at the Interpersonal Level and semantic representations at the Representational Level.

Formulation draws on frames to structure representations at the Interpersonal Level and the Representational Level, and lexemes and operators provide the lexical and grammatical information, respectively. Lexemes either carry pragmatic meaning or designate entities (Genee et al. 2016: 885; see also García Velasco & Hengeveld 2002); operators symbolize "the grammatical distinctions required in the language under analysis" (Hengeveld & Mackenzie 2008: 2). At the two levels of analysis resulting from formulation, a range of modifiers can be found, providing further lexical information, and being lexical, these modifiers can themselves be modified. Operators, on the other hand, specify an abstract property of the entity and cannot be modified (Keizer 2007b: 48–9).

The configurations from these two levels are then encoded on the Morphosyntactic Level, using the templates, grammatical morphemes, and operators available in the language in question. Next, information from all three levels feeds into the phonological encoding, resulting in a representation at the Phonological Level. Finally, the information at this level feeds into the final operation of articulation and the Output

---

[1] The model's structure is based on Levelt's (1989) psycholinguistic model.
[2] Words that are used as technical terms in the FDG theory are capitalized in the text.

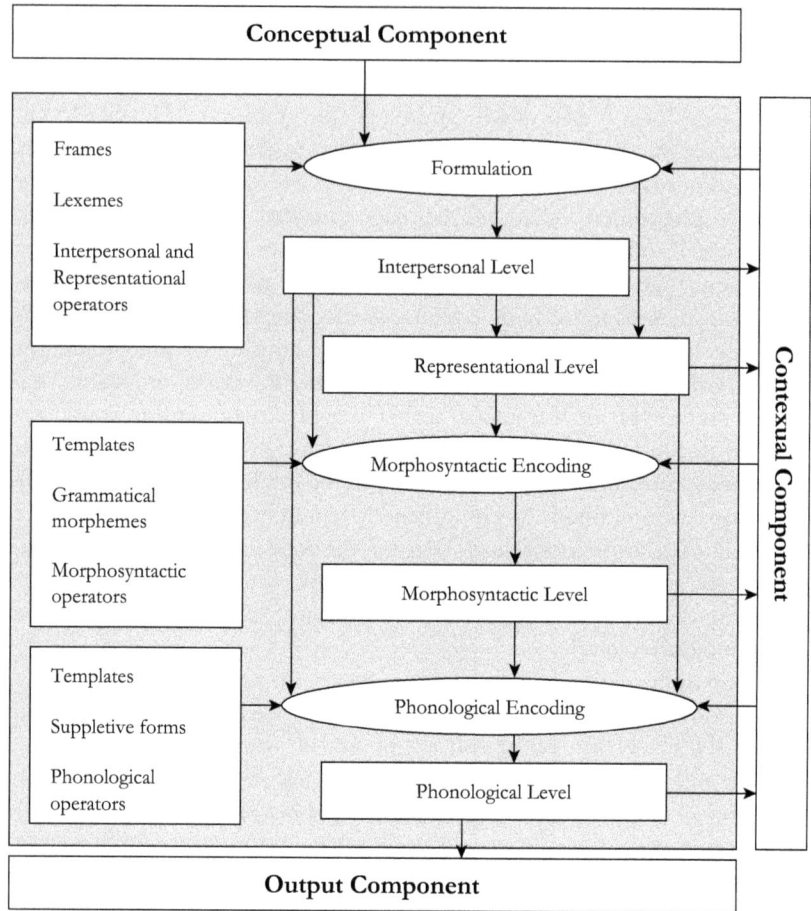

Figure 9.1 General layout of FDG (Hengeveld & Mackenzie 2008: 13)

Component (Hengeveld & Mackenzie 2008: 12–13). Information from the Contextual Component (i.e. relevant aspects of the context) feeds into both of the formulation levels as well as into both operations of encoding (see Figure 9.1).

In its underlying organization "FDG takes the functional approach to language to its logical extreme: pragmatics governs semantics, pragmatics and semantics govern morphosyntax, and pragmatics, semantics, and morphosyntax govern phonology" (Hengeveld & Mackenzie 2008: 13). The FDG theory distinguishes between lexical and grammatical elements,

9.1 Introduction to Functional Discourse Grammar

and all language-specific, long-term linguistic knowledge is stored in the Fund (Genee et al. 2016: 881).

Further information about the various primitives is provided in the next section, which is followed by a discussion of the NP in FDG, and the FDG approach to categorization.

9.1.2 Primitives: Units of the FDG Grammatical Component

In the FDG model, the grammar consists of primitives, which form the building blocks of linguistic utterances, as well as of the operations (formulating and encoding) which "combine these primitives in order to produce the various levels of representation" (Hengeveld & Mackenzie 2008: 19; see Figure 9.1). On the formulation levels (Interpersonal and Representational), these primitives take the form of frames, operators, and lexemes, and on the encoding level (i.e. the Morphosyntactic and Phonological Levels), of words, morphemes, feet, syllables, and templates (see Table 9.1). All these elements are stored in the Fund, the storehouse of long-term linguistic knowledge (Genee et al. 2016: 880–1).[3] The Fund is divided into three parts: the grammatical elements reside in the grammaticon, the templates and frames in the frameset (or structicon), and the lexical items in the lexicon (Genee et al. 2016: 881, 885–7). Therefore, although FDG acknowledges that the distinction between lexical and grammatical is fuzzy, the model still distinguishes between grammatical and lexical categories and stores them separately (see Hengeveld & Mackenzie 2008: 9; Keizer 2015: 13).

Table 9.1 *The primitives in the Fund at the different levels*

FORMULATION LEVELS	ENCODING LEVELS
INTERPERSONAL & REPRESENTATIONAL LEVELS	MORPHOSYNTACTIC & PHONOLOGICAL LEVELS
Frames Lexemes Operators	Templates Grammatical morphemes Operators Suppletive forms

---

[3] The term Fund was introduced in Functional Grammar, FDG's predecessor (see Dik 1978, 1980, 1989, 1997a, 1997b).

The frameset (structicon) consists of frames and templates. Frames "are language-specific pragmatic and semantic configurations allowed by the grammar of the language" (Hengeveld & Mackenzie 2016: 1141) and "are constructed according to language-independent general schema" (Genee et al. 2016: 882). There are frames on both of the formulation levels: interpersonal frames define "the expressive or communicative nature of Discourse Acts, the encoded configurations of information structure, and the rhetorical functions of Discourse Acts" (Hengeveld & Mackenzie 2008: 19), whereas representational frames define "quantitative and qualitative valency, the combinations of semantic categories allowed, and the possible modification structures" (Hengeveld & Mackenzie 2008: 19). The last two features, defining the semantic categories and delineating the modification structures, are important for this study.

During the operation of morpho-syntactic encoding, use is made of templates, which include language-specific realizations of Linguistic Expressions, Clauses, Phrases and Words (Genee et al. 2016: 884; Hengeveld & Mackenzie 2008: 20). Templates are the syntactic realization (in terms of clause, phrase, and word structure) of information from the pragmatic and the semantic levels. It is only with the selection of the Noun Phrase template at the Morphosyntactic Level that, technically, we talk about the noun phrase in FDG.

Operators appear at all the levels, and they distinguish grammatical relations, such as emphasis, degree of commitment, definiteness, number, etc. (see Hengeveld & Mackenzie 2008). Lexemes are selected at the formulation levels: at the Interpersonal Level they include non-descriptive elements such as interjections, proper names, illocutionary adverbs, performative verbs, etc. (Hengeveld & Mackenzie 2008: 19), and at the Representational Level, they closely resemble what would prototypically be considered lexical items, i.e. elements used to designate Properties (e.g. *furious, red*), Individuals (e.g. *woman, cat*), Propositional Contents (e.g. *hope, love*), etc. (Genee et al. 2016: 885). Words and Morphemes, on the other hand, are introduced during morpho-syntactic encoding.

One of the reasons for distinguishing between lexemes and words is that there does not have to be a one-to-one relationship between them (although that is normally the case). Thus, an adjectival lexeme (heading a Property, functioning as a modifier, e.g. *quick*) may correspond to an adverb at the Morphosyntactic Level: in that case the mismatch is between the prototypical function of an adjective (designating Properties of Individuals) and its current function (designating the manner in which an action is performed); the encoding on the Morphosyntactic Level involves a derivational process (Genee et al. 2016: 890).[4] The second reason is that the distinction between lexemes and words is also used to account for the appearance of dummy elements, which only appear in encoding to satisfy syntactic concerns. Thus, the dummy *it* appears in examples such as *it's raining* to fulfill the need for a subject in English (Keizer 2015: 232–3; cf. Hengeveld & Mackenzie 2008: 347–50), or in the case of this study, *of* links two nouns although it no longer has semantic content as in *a beast of a game*.[5] This morpho-syntactic Word does not, however, correspond to a lexeme at the Interpersonal or Representational Level; *of* in many cases is not even represented on the Interpersonal and Representational Levels but appears as a linking element between two nouns that do not have a compound frame.

Lexemes are usually prototypically associated with certain positions within frames (Keizer 2016: 1009); thus, the distinction between the lexicon and frameset provides the flexibility to capture the distinction between the noncanonical variation from more iconic uses within a language (Genee et al. 2016: 894–5). In other words, FDG provides a systematic explanation for nondefault uses of lexemes in frames that would account for noncanonical formulations and would yet still explain their more canonical features, such as *a jewel of a city*, where the noun *jewel* is placed in a modifier frame and coerced.[6]

A final important point concerning the interaction of primitives at different levels is that, unlike in CxG, there is no symbolic link between form and meaning. Thus, as explained by Hengeveld and Mackenzie (2016: 1146):

---

[4] Some very frequent forms (e.g. conventionalized derivations like *writer*) can, for instance, be both stored in the lexicon and productively derived in the grammar, i.e. these elements may be produced or retrieved via a "dual access route" (Hay 2002).

[5] For more details about the reasoning behind this distinction, see Hengeveld and Mackenzie (2008: 400–1), and for a discussion specifically of English, see Keizer (2015: 232–5).

[6] Coercion is defined as "the adaptation of a lexical item to an unexpected syntactic environment" (Genee et al. 2016: 894). Drawing on the classic CxG example of resultative constructions shown in (ia) and (ib), Genee et al. (2016: 894–5) explain that in FDG, this type of formation would also be a case of coercion, with intransitive verbs like *smile* or *laugh* being coerced into a transitive construction. This allows the model to account for the canonical aspects of the resultative construction, such as the premodification in (ib), as well as for the noncanonical features, such as the use of a verb normally appearing in an intransitive frame in combination with a direct object.

(i) a. She smiled herself an upgrade. (Goldberg 2006: 6–7)
    b. We laughed our *boring* conversation to an *unfortunate* end.
    (modified example from Goldberg 2006: 6–7)

there is no one-to-one relation between semantic and morpho-syntactic organization, as there necessarily is in Construction Grammar. Since the frameset indicates the range of possible configurations available for the operation of formulation, the frames capture semantic information in terms of categories and functions they contain and are not directly connected to the encoding levels at which form is established.

Thus, all language production, both regular and creative, proceeds in a top-down manner, starting with changes in conceptualization and speaker intention, triggering changes in the internal organization at the formation levels; these changes, in turn, may lead to nontransparent relations between elements at the various levels, ultimately resulting in novel forms of expression. In Section 9.2, we will see how this approach can account for the changes taking place in the development of the various constructions within the EBNP family. In the following section, an FDG analysis is demonstrated for a simple noun phrase, before continuing to the more complex *of*-binominal noun phrases and premodification in the noun phrase.

9.1.3   The Noun Phrase in FDG

Example (9.1) is a (somewhat simplified) representation of the phrase *a ferocious beast* in FDG. In this theory, the Noun Phrase is a technical term that only appears at the Morphosyntactic Level (ML; (9.1d)), where Np stands for a Noun Phrase, i.e. a phrase with a Nominal Word (Nw) as its head. The Np prototypically relates to a Reference Act (R) at the Interpersonal Level (IL; example (9.1b)), an Individual (x) at the Representational Level (RL; (9.1 c)), and a Phonological Phrase (PP) at the Phonological Level (PL; (9.1e)).

(9.1)   a. a ferocious beast
   b. IL: (-id R_1: [(T_1) (T_2)] (R_1))
   c. RL: (1 x_1: (f_1: beast (f_1)) (x_1): (f_2: ferocious (f_2)) (x_1))
   d. ML: (Np_1: [(Gw_1: a (Gw_1)) (Ap_1: (Aw_1: ferocious (Aw_1)) (Ap_1)) (Nw_1: beast (Nw_1))] (Np_1))
   e. PL: (PP_1: [(pw_1: / ə / (pw_1)) (pw_2: / fə'rəʊʃəs / (pw_2)) (pw_3: / 'biːst / (pw_3))] (PP_1))

The IL is made up of linguistic units that represent those aspects of Speaker and Addressee interaction that are encoded in a language. At this level, the Communicated Content of the message consists of two Subacts, a Subact of Reference or Referential Subact (R) and a Subact of Ascription (T).

Subacts of Ascription "reflect the speaker's attempt to evoke a property or relation" (Keizer & Van Staden 2009: 817).[7] They function either as independent parts of the Communicated Content (in which case they tend to be expressed as verbs), or as part of a Subact of Reference, in which case they tend to be expressed as nouns and adjectives ascribing Properties to the referent evoked by the Referential Subact in question (see Hengeveld & Mackenzie 2008: 107–24). In example (9.1), there is a single entity R_I whose head consists of two Subacts of Ascription (T_I) and (T_2), one evoking the property 'beast' and the other the property 'ferocious'. Operators at the layer of the Referential Subact usually mark referent identifiability, e.g. in (9.1b) '-id' indicates that the speaker does not think the addressee will be familiar with the entity evoked.

At the next level of formulation, the Representational Level, the information from the Interpersonal Level is provided semantic content. Semantics here is used in the sense of Halliday's (1985) 'ideation' and is restricted to the meanings of the linguistic items, divorced from their communicative use, which is already captured on the Interpersonal Level (Hengeveld & Mackenzie 2008: 128–9). The units at this level represent entities in a nonlinguistic world, but only those that are linguistically relevant. The four basic semantic categories on this level, all of which can have a nominal head, are an Individual (x) (e.g. *chair*), a Property (f) (e.g. *color*), State-of-affairs (e) (e.g. *meeting*), and Propositional Content (p) (e.g. *idea*) (Hengeveld & Mackenzie 2008: 131–2). In the case of (9.1), the Referential Subact (R_I) on the IL coincides with the Individual (x_I) on the RL. The Individual designated by (x_I) is ascribed the Property 'beast' (f_I) and is further modified by the Property 'ferocious' (f_2). The operator '1' indicates that this is a single entity.

On the Morphosyntactic Level, the information from the previous two levels is encoded using a set of language-specific morpho-syntactic primitives (Hengeveld & Mackenzie 2008: 282–7). These primitives include templates that encode the ordering patterns at the clause, phrase, and word layers. Example (9.1d) is based on the prototypical Noun Phrase template,

---

[7] The evoked property need not always be ascribed to an entity (Keizer & Van Staden 2009: 817). An example would be the so-called weather verbs in English (Keizer & Van Staden 2009: 817; see also Keizer 2015: 85). In this example the property 'rain' is not assigned to any referent:

(i) It is raining.
    IL: $(C_I: [(T_I)] (C_I))$

which includes a determiner slot, an adjective slot (filled by an Adjectival Phrase), and a noun slot (heading the Np). Operators at this level take the form of 'placeholders' ('sg' for singular; see Section 9.2.3 for more details), triggering the use of the appropriate form of bound morphemes or suppletive forms at the Phonological Level.

All the input from the previous three layers feed into the Phonological Level, and this level is, therefore, entirely dependent on information from these upper levels for its operations (Hengeveld & Mackenzie 2008: 422). To structure this content, it has three different sets of primitives: (i) prosodic patterns for the information from each layer of analysis, (ii) forms expressing grammatical information such as irregular verb forms (on the basis of grammatical information triggered by operators at a higher level), and (iii) tertiary operators (e.g. rising or falling intonation). An example of a noun phrase Phonological Level analysis can be seen in (9.1d).

Premodifiers in FDG can be analyzed either as modifiers or as operators at the Interpersonal and Representational Levels. As mentioned above Referential Subacts evoke entities and usually consist of at least one Subact of Ascription, which evoke a property to be ascribed to the entity evoked by the Referential Subact (Hengeveld & Mackenzie 2008: 107–24). Operators of the Ascriptive Subact that are realized as premodifiers are grammaticalized forms of approximation such as *sort-of* in (9.2). Modification at this level is strictly interpersonal, i.e. expressing the speaker's attitude toward the referent or the property ascribed. One example would be *really* in (9.3), which signals the emphatic commitment on the part of the speaker ascription of the Property 'nice', whereas the adjective *proper* expresses the speaker's evaluation of the referent's conformity to the Property *fool*, in this case indicating exactness (see Hengeveld & Keizer 2011: 1969). The Referential Subact at the Interpersonal Level can also be modified; however, *poor* in (9.5) does not ascribe a property to an entity but expresses the speaker's sympathy for the referent (Hengeveld & Mackenzie 2008: 121). Owing to their subjective, speaker-oriented nature, these adjectives are represented at the Interpersonal Level.

(9.2)   a. sort-of blue
        b. (approx T_1)
        (Hengeveld & Mackenzie 2008: 112)

(9.3)   a. a really nice example
        b. (-id R_1: [(T_1) ((T_2): really (T_2))]) (R_1))
        (simplied version of Hengeveld & Mackenzie 2008: 111)

(9.4) a. A proper fool
b. (-id R_I: ((T_1): proper (T_1)) (R_I))

(9.5) a. Why do they have to be out there pestering *a poor innocent dinosaur*?
b. (-id R_I: [(T_1) (T_2)]: poor (R_I))
(Keizer 2015: 220)

Other modifiers, such as *ferocious*, appear on the Representational Level. At this level descriptive modifiers would be a Property that modifies an Individual, as in example (9.6) (a repetition of example (9.1) discussed above). In (9.6), the Individual designated by (x_1) is ascribed the Property 'beast' (f_1) and is further modified by the Property 'ferocious' (f_2). As to the subjective/objective distinction found in previous studies (see Adamson 2000; Alexiadou, Haegeman & Stavrou 2007: 313; Hetzron 1978; Seiler 1978; Trueswell 2009), FDG only stipulates that if there is more than one descriptive modifier, the more objective modifiers tend to be closer to the head and the subjective ones further away (Hengeveld & Mackenzie 2008: 241–2), as demonstrated in example (9.7). In the underlying representation, *old* is considered the more objective modifier and thus appears closer to the head than the more subjective *beautiful*.

(9.6) a. a ferocious beast
b. RL: (1 x_1: (f_1: beast (f_1)) (x_1): (f_2: ferocious (f_2)) (x_1))

(9.7) a. the beautiful old man
b. RL: (1 x_1: (f_1: man (f_1)) (x_1): (f_2: old (f_2)) (x_1): (f_3: beautiful (f_3)) (x_1))

Ghesquière's distinction between classifiers and descriptive modifiers can be captured in the FDG framework, where both would appear on the Representational Level (for more discussion see Portero Muñoz 2013). However, classifiers, as distinct from descriptive modifiers in (9.6) and (9.7), are represented in FDG as a Property modifying another Property, as in example (9.8), where the Property 'student' is restricted by the Property 'medical', and these two properties together describe the Individual (Hengeveld & Mackenzie 2008: 230). Example (9.9) represents the descriptive modifier frame, where the Property (f_2) modifies (has scope over) the reference (f_1). Thus, descriptive modifiers and classifiers occur in two separate frames (Portero Muñoz 2013: 130–2).

(9.8) a. a medical student
b. (1 x_1: (f_1: student (**f_1**): (f_2: medical (f_2)) (f_1)) (x_1))

(9.9) a. a clever student
b. (x_1: (f_1: student (f_1)) (**x_1**): (f_2: clever (f_2)) (x_1))

Degree modifiers in FDG fulfill a variety of roles and can be more or less subjective (speaker-oriented), meaning that in the FDG framework they can be rendered as operators or modifiers of the Ascriptive Subact or Referential Subact on the Interpersonal Level or as an operator of a Property on the Representational Level (Van de Velde 2007: 216; see García Velasco 2013 for an overview). For example, a degree modifier such as *very* functions as an operator on the Representational Level (García Velasco 2013: 87–9; example (9.10)), and the more subjective -*ly* degree adverbs such as *dreadfully* appear on the Interpersonal Level (García Velasco 2013: 93–4; example (9.11)). Examples (9.10) and (9.11) would be what Ghesquière designates as bleached (9.10) and unbleached (9.11) adjective-intensifiers, respectively.

(9.10) very tall
  RL: (**intens** f_1: tall (f_1))
  ML: (Ap_1: (**Gw_1: very (Gw_1)**) (Aw_1: tall (Aw_1)) (Ap_1))
  (García Velasco 2013: 89)

(9.11) dreadfully sorry
  IL: (T_1: [ ] (T_1): dreadfully (T_1))
  RL: (f_1: sorry (f_1))
  (García Velasco 2013: 94)

The important distinctions made by FDG are that there are speaker-oriented intensifiers and subjective modifiers at the Interpersonal Level and intensifiers, subjective and objective modifiers, and classifiers at the Representational Level. Whereas Ghesquière only distinguishes between subjective and objective descriptive modifiers, FDG adds a further distinction, between interpersonal subjective modifiers and representational subjective modifiers. Classifiers are captured by means of scope relations, modification of the Individual or the Property seen in examples (9.8) and (9.9). FDG posits a subjective-objective ordering of adjectives on the Representational Level as well as the ordering distinction between modifiers that appear on the Interpersonal Level and those on the Representational Level (discussed in more detail in Section 9.2.3). Finally, as is the case with descriptive modifiers, degree modifiers are either modifiers/operators at the Interpersonal and the Representational Levels.

FDG categorizes premodification primarily by its function; however, as has already been demonstrated in Chapter 7, accounting for the linear order of premodification is an important aspect of premodification categorization. Syntactic order will be discussed in more detail in

Section 9.2.3. A few final theoretical issues will be discussed in Section 9.1.4 before turning to the FDG analysis of the EBNP family.

9.1.4 FDG Categorization

Three central theoretical principles in FDG apply to the categorization issues in this particular study: the first concerns the criteria that need to be fulfilled in order to distinguish a new category, the second is the distinction made between lexical and grammatical items, and the third is the notion of transparency. For general categorization criteria, FDG is a functional model and therefore, by definition, it takes a function-to-form approach. Nonetheless, it is at the same time expressly a form-oriented theory (Hengeveld & Mackenzie 2008: 38–9). This means that FDG accounts only for those pragmatic, semantic, conceptual, and contextual phenomena that are expressed in the morpho-syntax of an utterance (Hengeveld & Mackenzie 2008: 40); this is referred to as the Principle of Formal Encoding (Keizer 2015: 14–15). In other words, semantic/pragmatic changes are only accounted for by the model if those changes are systematically encoded in the language (Hengeveld & Mackenzie 2008: 194; Keizer 2015: 133). Other pragmatic and semantic changes will still be regarded as important for the interpretation of an expression but are not represented at the Interpersonal and Representational Levels. In the case of lexical items, this means that any changes in their semantics and pragmatics are regarded only as cases of polysemy or lexical extension, and not as new lexical elements.

The second important distinction that FDG makes is between lexical and grammatical items, i.e. between those elements that function as lexemes (functioning as heads or modifiers) and those that are grammatical elements (functioning as operators) (for more discussion of this distinction in the functional paradigm, see Boye & Harder 2012).[8] Using the changes found in the stages of grammaticalization as the classification criteria to judge if a linguistic item is either lexical or grammatical, Keizer (2007b)

---

[8] With a wish to move away from inadequate definitions based on phonological, morphosyntactic, or semantic features, Boye and Harder (2012: 3–6) redefine grammatical status and thereby propose an alternative view of grammaticalization. They maintain the grammatical and lexical distinction (which conforms with FDG but not CxG), and approaching the question from a usage-/discourse-based perspective, they define grammatical items as those "that by linguistic convention are ancillary and as such discursively secondary in relation to other expressions." As such, grammaticalization "consists in the diachronic change that lead to such expressions" (Boye & Harder 2012: 2). This would then make lexical items those that have primary discourse prominence (Boye & Harder 2012: 2).

proposes the following criteria to distinguish between lexemes, secondary lexemes, lexical operators, and operators (Keizer 2007b: 44):[9]

No ascriptive function
Mutually exclusive
Fixed position
Not modifiable
No predicate formation
Closed class
Increased frequency
Little or no semantic content
Phonetically reduced
Syntactic paradigm
No focus/emphasis
Fusion

These criteria allow for the representation of the stage-like process of grammaticalization, leading to a distinction between primary and secondary grammatical and lexical items. Lexemes and operators have been discussed in detail in Section 9.1.2, and therefore, the discussion here will focus on secondary lexical items and operators. Secondary lexemes are defined as an intermediary position between lexeme and operator and are realized as linguistic forms such as idioms and lexicalized phrases like *sort-of* in examples, such as *a sort of holiday*, meaning 'something like a holiday' (Keizer 2007b: 45–7). In these forms, *sort* in *sort-of* no longer evokes an entity, is semantically bleached, no longer takes the plural form or a NP complement, and the whole phrase can be phonologically reduced to *sorta*. *Of* no longer has a relational function. However, *sort-of* can co-occur with other modifiers, and it does not have a fixed position in the clause. It can take the focus function, is optional, and does not fuse with other linguistic elements (Keizer 2007b: 45–6). Therefore, it is more grammatical than a prototypical lexical item, but it is not an operator; hence, it can be categorized as a secondary lexeme (note this is a different use of *sort-of* from the approximate function of *sort-of* exemplified in example (9.2)).

Lexical operators can be defined in terms of their function in that they are nondescriptive and function more like grammatical operators (Keizer 2007b: 50; see García Velasco 2013, Olbertz 2016); in terms of their formal

---

[9] In a recent publication, Hengeveld (2017) adopts this lexeme, lexical operator, and operator dichotomy. He also reduces the classifying criteria to two elements: modification and focalization (for focalization discussion, see Harder & Boye 2011 and also Boye & Harder 2012).

behavior, however, they have more in common with lexical items. A classic example is the demonstrative *that*. In an example such as *that man*, the demonstrative exhibits grammatical properties in that it does not modify or restrict the head, cannot be modified, is part of a closed class, has a relatively fixed position, and does not have a predicate formation. However, *that* does retain some lexical features in that it can be focalized, cannot be fused with other linguistic elements, or phonetically reduced, and is not completely void of semantic information (Keizer 2007b: 44; see also Hengeveld 2017). *That* fulfills half of the criteria above and is, therefore, considered to be neither a lexeme nor an operator, but a lexical operator.

The final important concept is transparency. Based on principles of iconicity, domain integrity, and function stability, transparency is "the extent to which there is in a language a one-to-one correspondence between units of meaning and units of form" (Hengeveld & Mackenzie 2008: 291).[10] The prototypical example presented in (9.12) (a repetition of example (9.1)) demonstrates a high degree of transparency between the different levels of analysis, resulting in default relations between the units at the different levels (a Referential Subact at the Interpersonal Level coincides with an Individual at the Representational Level and is encoded as an NP on the Morphosyntactic Level and a PP at the Phonological Level). However, due to processes of lexicalization and grammaticalization, this is not always the case, and particularly not the case of the EBNP and related constructions. The changing relationships between elements at the different levels will play a role in the development of the various non-prototypical *of*-binominals discussed in Part I.

(9.12)   a ferocious beast
    IL: (-id R_I: [(T_1) (T_2)] (R_I))
    RL: (1 x_I: (f_I: beast (f_I)) (x_I): (f_2: ferocious (f_2)) (x_I))
    ML: (Np_I: [(Gw_I: a (Gw_I)) (Ap_I: (Aw_I: ferocious (Aw_I)) (Ap_I)) (Nw_I: beast (Nw_I))] (Np_I))
    PL: (PP_I: [(pw_I: /ə/ (pw_I)) (pw_2: /fəˈrəʊʃəs/ (pw_2)) (pw_3: /ˈbiːst/ (pw_3))] (PP_I))

---

[10] It should be noted that Hengeveld and Mackenzie (2008), in their typological model, use a broader definition of transparency than Keizer (2015) in her application of the model in English. For Hengeveld and Mackenzie, transparency would entail any one-to-one relation between any of the four levels of analysis. For Keizer (2015: 178–81), transparency is a one-to-one correspondence between certain variables on the different levels, i.e. Referent (R) coincides with an Individual (x) and is encoded by a Noun Phrase (Np), and an Ascriptive Subact (T) corresponds to a Property (f) and is encoded as a Nominal Word (Nw), etc. Keizer's definition is adopted here.

248   9 The EBNP Family: An FDG Analysis

9.2 A Functional Discourse Grammar Account of the EBNP Family

This section has two primary aims. First, it examines the evidence from Part I and Part II of this study from a FDG perspective and provides an FDG account of the development of these constructions. As was the case in Chapter 8 on Construction Grammar, it focuses on the main constructions in the path: N+PP, head-classifier, EBNP, EM, and BI. Second, it addresses the question of whether constructions (as defined by CxG) can or should be integrated into the FDG model. The first question is addressed in Sections 9.2.1, 9.2.3, and 9.2.4. The role of constructions in FDG is discussed in 9.2.2.

9.2.1 The EBNP Family

9.2.1.1 The Prototypical N+PP Construction

Example (9.13) below represents what could be regarded as a prototypical example of the *of*-binominal: the first noun is the head, both nouns can take the singular and plural form and do not have to agree in number, both nouns head a referential NP, and both determiners indicate the identifiability and number of their respective referents. (The Phonological Level has been omitted as it does not play a role until the last stages of the analysis.)

(9.13)   In early times the Esquimaux killed *the whale of the North* with harpoons ... (COHA)
   IL: (+id R_1: [(T_1) (+id R_2: (T_2) (R_2))] (R_1))
   RL: ($1x_1$: (f_1: whale (f_1)): (l_1: (f_2: [(f_3: of$_{Adp}$ (f_3)) ($1l_2$: (f_4: North (f_4)) (l_2))$_{Refl}$] (f_2)) (l_1)) (x_1))
   ML: (Np$_1$: [(Gw$_1$: the (Gw$_1$)) (Nw$_1$: whale (Nw$_1$)) (Adpp$_1$: [(Adpw$_1$: of (Adpw$_1$)) (Np$_2$: (Gw$_2$: the (Gw$_2$)) (Nw$_2$: North (Nw$_2$)) (Np$_2$))] (Adpp$_1$))] (Np$_1$))

In the Conceptual Component (not represented here), the speaker has singled out a particular entity (*the whale*) for reference and has related it to a particular geographical location (*the North*). During the operation of formulation, the speaker's intention is then structured at the Interpersonal Level as two separate Referents, (R_1) and (R_2), the second specifying the first. Both Referential Subacts are marked as identifiable (+id) and each is headed by an Ascriptive Subact evoking a property, represented by the variables (T_1) and (T_2). At the Representational Level, the semantic representation comprises an Individual (x_1), and a location (l_1) with the semantic function of Reference (Ref) (a general function indicating argument status, in this case in relation to the adposition *of*). The first Individual (x_1), headed by the Property 'whale', represents the referent of the expression as a whole; the location (l_2) corresponds to the lexeme 'North'. The preposition *of* is a lexical item indicating origin or source.

With a high degree of transparency between the Interpersonal and Representational Levels, with Referents at the Interpersonal Level correlating with Individuals at the Representational Level and with the preposition *of* designating a semantic property, there is a relatively straightforward relation between the interpersonal and representational units and the units at the Morphosyntactic Level. There, the two Referential Subacts (R_1) and (R_2), corresponding to (x_1) and (l_2) at the Representational Level, are realized as a Noun Phrase (Np_1) and an Adpositional Phrase ($Adpp_1$), with the embedded location (l_2) corresponding to another Noun Phrase (Np_2). The lexical Properties (f_2) and (f_4), functioning as the heads of (x_1) and (l_2), are realized as Nominal Words (Nw_1 and Nw_2) heading the two Noun Phrases, with the (Nw_1) *whale* functioning as the head of the overall expression. At the Morphosyntactic Level, the nominal head is followed by an Adpositional Phrase ($Adpp_1$), consisting of the Adposition Word *of* and the second Noun Phrase *the North*. The relative transparency between the different levels, the fact that two Referents correlate to two Individuals, which are both encoded as Noun Phrases, would then predict relatively prototypical premodification on both the Interpersonal and the Representational Levels, which was indeed shown in the premodifier study. This is the basic frame and template that the other constructions subsequently adapt.

9.2.1.2 The Head-Classifier Construction

An FDG analysis of a head-classifier can be found in example (9.14). From this analysis, it is clear that the changes in the Conceptual Component, i.e. the changes in the speaker's intention, trigger two key changes at the formulation levels, subsequently leading to changes at the Morphosyntactic Level. First, because the second Noun Phrase is no longer referential (see Section 3.3), the second Referential Subact is lost at the Interpersonal Level; instead, it is analyzed as a property by means of an Ascriptive Subact (T_2). This Ascriptive Subact, however, still corresponds to an Individual (or a class of Individuals) at the Representational Level, accounting for the fact that it can accept premodification such as *angry* and *public* (see example (9.15)), can still be realized in the plural form (as demonstrated by *rocks* in (9.14)), and does not have to agree in number with the first noun. At the Representational Level, the Property (f_2) functions as the head of the construction, while the Individual (x_2) functions as a modifier. *Of* no longer has semantic content but functions as a grammatical linking device (a dummy element), and thus does not appear at the Representational Level.[11]

(9.14) I returned to Pryor Mountain, which rises like *a huge whale of rocks* from the Bighorn River Basin ... (COHA)
IL: (-id R_I: [(T_I) (T_2)] (R_I))
RL: ($1x_I$: (f_I: (f_2: whale (f_2)): (m x_2: (f_3: rock (f_3)) (x_2)) (f_2)) (f_I)) (x_I))
ML: (Np_I: [(Gw_I: a (Gw_I)) (Nw_I: whale (Nw_I)) (Gw_2: of (Gw_2)) (Np_2: (Nw_2: rock.pl (Nw_2)) (Np_2)] (Np_I))

(9.15) devoured by *the great land whale of **angry public** opinion* ... (modified COHA example)

These changes thus create a mismatch between the Interpersonal and Representational Levels, as an Ascriptive Subact (T_2) at the Interpersonal Level (usually realized by a Property at the Representational Level) now corresponds to an Individual (x_2).[12] This mismatch affects the morphosyntactic form of the expression: because the identifiability operator applies only to Referential Subacts and not to Ascriptive Subacts, and because the Ascriptive Subact corresponds to an unbounded entity at the Representational Level, the second Ascriptive Subact, corresponding to and Individual (x_2), appears as a bare noun at the Morphosyntactic Level.

In the head-classifier, the preposition *of* no longer has semantic content; however, it still appears as a linking element. The reason is that, since in combinations of nouns such as *beast* and *prey* there is no frame available to express this particular configuration of nouns, the speaker is forced to choose the closest morpho-syntactic template, that of the prototypical N+PP construction, adapting it where necessary. However, this is only true in some cases. As was discussed in Section 3.3, there is often a functional overlap between the head-classifier construction and constructions with a premodifier (as shown in (9.16a) and (9.16b)). One possible explanation for the coexistence of these two templates is that the premodifiers, like

---

[11] This analysis is representative of the whole head-classifier category. However, more recent work (Keizer & Ten Wolde forthcoming) shows that the head-classifier category is more heterogenous than expected. Therefore, the underlying representation for an intrinsic head-classifier (which example (9.14) would be) is slightly different from the one presented here, but this difference would not change the underlying argument.

[12] This phenomenon is not unique to the head-classifier but is also discussed in relation to the copular constructions (for a discussion of the English copular construction, see Keizer 2015: 139–40).

wooden, allow for ambiguity, i.e. whether, in (9.16a), *wooden* functions as a classifier (the table in question belongs to the group of 'wooden tables') or as a modifier (the speaker ascribes the property of 'woodenness' onto the table) is unclear. In (9.16b), on the other hand, we clearly have a head-classifier (see Quirk et al. 1985: 1330–1, 1243–4). In other words, the head-classifier has the advantage of unambiguously coding the classifying function of the modifier. The N-of-N templates have the additional advantage of allowing for categorization diversity that would be less acceptable in pre-modification, as demonstrated in (9.17a–b) and (9.18a–c).

(9.16)   a. a wooden table
           b. a table of wood

(9.17)   a. If the fragrance of my living does not call the soul to suck *the honey of eternal bliss* then? (COHA)
           b. *the eternal bliss honey

(9.18)   a. the laws of the universe are prescribed *the bitch of necessity the bitch of chance* and the DNA overlord (COCA)
           b. *the necessity bitch
           c. *the chance bitch

This mismatch between the Interpersonal and the Representational Levels has an effect on the premodification patterns. Because the second noun is no longer realized as a Referential Subact on the IL, it can no longer be modified by modifiers or operators of the Referential Subact, as demonstrated in (9.19). As shown in this example, *proper* (a modifier at the Interpersonal Level; see Section 9.1.3.2) can be used to modify the whole construction (9.19a) and can also modify *burden* (9.19b), but not when *burden* is used in the head-classifier construction (9.19c). This analysis would then explain the loss of the noun-intensifier zones in the head-classifier (see Section 7.6.2) and predict the acceptability of (9.20), where *very* and *slimy* are operators and modifiers at the Representational Level.

(9.19)   a. A **proper** beast of burden
           b. A **proper** burden
           c. ?A beast of **proper** burden
           (Ten Wolde 2019)

(9.20)   a. A hell of fish
           b. A hell of **very slimy** fish

One reason for the head-classifier modification to favor the first premodifier zones over the second would be that the category includes a range of first nouns that are more idiomatic than others: *a whale of stone* or *a book of comics* are less idiomatic than *a beast of burden*. The more idiomatic examples, such as *a beast of burden*, would be less likely to have premodification in front of the second noun, e.g. **a beast of heavy burden*.

The loss of the second Referential Subact at the Interpersonal Level distinguishes the head-classifier from the N+PP construction and is shared by all the constructions that follow. As this construction grammaticalizes further, the repercussions of this change permeate into the lower levels.

9.2.1.3 The EBNP Construction

An FDG analysis of the EBNP would look something like example (9.21), where the speaker is either comparing the *wolf* to the *whale* or ascribing whale-like properties to the wolf (presumably size):

(9.21) I slammed that' er hunk o' lead into the pack leader – *a whale of a wolf*.
(COHA)
IL: (-id R_1: [(T_1) (T_2)] (R_1))
RL: ($1x_1$: (f_1: wolf (f_1)) (x_1): (f_2: whale (f_2)) (x_1))
ML: (Np_1: [(Gw_1: a (Gw_1)) (Nw_1: whale (Nw_1)) (Gw_2: of (Gw_2)) (Np_2: (Gw_3: a (Gw_3)) (Nw_2: wolf (Nw_2)) (Np_2))] (Np_1))

Although the Interpersonal Level is similar to that of the head-classifier, with only one Referential Subact (R_1) which consists of two Ascriptive Subacts (T_1) and (T_2), in the EBNP the first noun no longer has referential value, and the second noun designates the referent. At the Representational Level, (R_1) is realized as a single Individual (x_1), headed by the Property *wolf* (f_1), and ascribed the Property *whale* (f_2). The first noun no longer designates an Individual; instead, it has become a dependent of the second noun (which is now the head), as shown by the fact that it must agree in number with the second noun. In this construction, transparency has been reestablished between the Interpersonal and the Representational Levels with a Referential Subact (R_1) aligning with an Individual (x_1), and the Ascriptive Subacts (T_1) and (T_2) corresponding with the Properties (f_1) and (f_2), very similarly to the prototypical noun phrase example in (9.1) above.

The EBNP template, however, creates a mismatch between formulation levels and the Morphosyntactic Level, as *whale*, filling a modifier slot at the Representational Level, is realized as a noun at the Morphosyntactic Level. Subsequent confusion concerning the status of the first noun can be seen in the fact that premodifiers positioned before the first noun can actually be

9.2 An FDG Account of the EBNP Family

selected by both the first noun and the second (see Section 4.2). Finally, since Ascriptive Subacts are not coded for identifiability, the second determiner in the EBNP no longer expresses this feature (and therefore no longer contrasts with the definite article). Number in both determiners is triggered by the number of the overall Individual, since the two nouns have to agree in number. However, since the second noun is the head, it is this noun which selects the first determiner, as seen in examples such as (9.22a–b), where *your* specifies *brother* not *jerk*. Since the two nouns clearly do not form a compound (and as discussed above, not all nouns can be coerced into a modifier slot), the preposition *of* is still present at the Morphosyntactic Level. Since the second determiner must be indefinite, both the indefinite article and the preposition can be regarded as fixed elements in a new construction, added at the Morphosyntactic Level (where the article is represented as a placeholder, with its final form dependent on the number of the overall phrase).

(9.22) a. your jerk of a brother
       b. your brother is a jerk

In the cases of lexemes, such as *beast*, that have an adjectival as well as a nominal form, the outcome of the operation of formulation can trigger two different morpho-syntactic forms: *a beastly child* or *a beast of a child* (see Figure 9.2). Although there is semantic overlap between the two encodings, at least in the case of *beast*, the EBNP retains a distinction in meaning: where *beastly* refers only to behavior, *beast* in the EBNP can be an evaluative comment on both behavior and size.[13] A possible explanation for the retention of the two options is that although the simple premodifier template is more prototypical and frequent, the EBNP offers the speaker a range of linguistic advantages. First, it sanctions the use of nouns as modifiers that lack adjectival

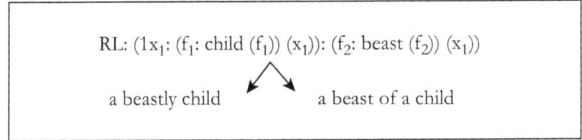

RL: $(1x_1: (f_1: \text{child} (f_1)) (x_1)): (f_2: \text{beast} (f_2)) (x_1))$

a beastly child   a beast of a child

Figure 9.2 Two possible frames triggered by the template at the Representational Level

---

[13] This semantic distinction between the two forms is not always so clearly defined. With *hell*, there is no clear difference between *a hellish hotel* or *a hell of a hotel*.

forms, such as *whale* in (9.21) (*a whalish wolf would be awkward), and second, it allows for creative premodification, e.g. *a 17th-century wedding cake of a building* (COCA).

The information on the Representational Level can, therefore, trigger two possible templates. In either case, however, the choice of template creates a mismatch between the Representational and Morphosyntactic Levels: either the nominal modifier at RL is adapted and takes the form of an adjective (e.g. *beastly*), or, in the EBNP template, the nominal modifier is expressed as an Np, but in an unconventional position, triggering the element *of* as a linking element. In the latter case, the mismatch between the semantic function and syntactic encoding of the first noun may explain the shift of premodification into the first noun premodification zones. The first noun in the EBNP semantically functions either as an objective or as subjective descriptive modifier (depending on the noun and the context, e.g. *a beast of a car* for a large car or *a beast of a child* for a child that acts in a beastly manner), and therefore, there might be some ambiguity about the placement of subjective and objective modifiers, even those selected by the second noun.

In conclusion, by using the distinction between the different levels of analysis in FDG, and the interfaces between them, we can capture the noncanonical function and features of the EBNP, such as premodification in front of the first noun and first determiner use. However, the appearance of the second determiner in the encoding on the Morphosyntactic Level and its function is not adequately explained in this analysis. This would then raise the question of whether this unique formulation and its link to a specific, noncanonical template would require positing the existence of constructions. This question will be addressed in Section 9.2.2.

9.2.1.4 *The Evaluative Modifier Construction*

With the EM, the modifier phrase as a whole coalesces and becomes more subjective; the first noun no longer conveys semantic content but the speaker's subjective evaluation of the head, and the linguistic unit's meaning is context dependent (see discussion in Section 4.3). In modeling this construction, two central issues need to be addressed: whether it is a modifier or an operator and at which level it appears (Interpersonal Level or Representational Level).

The first noun's loss of semantic content raises the question to what extent can the first noun in the EM still be considered lexical. Returning to Keizer's (2007b) cline (see Section 9.1.4), the first noun in the EM demonstrates the following grammatical criteria:

No ascriptive function (can no longer evoke an entity)
Little semantic content
Increased frequency of use (when compared to the EBNP)
Decategorialized (the first noun has lost nominal properties, e.g. no plural form)
Fixed position
No predicate formation

The first noun can still be modified; however, the premodification is less frequent than in the case of the EBNP and predominantly consists of degree modifiers (see Section 7.6.5). The first noun still exhibits some lexical features, in that it has not joined a closed class or a syntactic paradigm. It can be assigned focus function; it cannot be fused to other lexical items. It can be orthographically reduced, but this is only found with some first nouns (predominantly *hell*, *whale*, and infrequently *beast*). If lexemes are "restrictors [that] restrict the denotation of an expression by describing a property of the entity/set of entities designated (and as such function as predicates)" and "operators specify more abstract, non-descriptive properties of the entity/set of entities in question" (Keizer 2007b: 48), then the EM cannot be considered a prototypical lexeme or a prototypical operator and is, therefore, best analyzed as a secondary lexical element, with varying degrees of grammaticalization. The most frequent and entrenched forms, primarily *hell*, are more operator-like (i.e. semantically bleached and do not take modification) than others such as *beast*, which still retains some semantic variation depending on the context (e.g. *a beast of a golf course*, example (4.33), could mean *difficult* or *amazing*). These more lexical forms can still be modified although this modification is greatly restricted, e.g. *his little honey of a mule* (the descriptive modifier *little* more likely functions as an intensifier than as an objective descriptive modifier, ascribing a size property).

As to the question of level, Van de Velde (2009: 216–17) and García Velasco (2013) point out that degree modifiers like *very* or *astonishing* could be represented either as an operator of a Property at the Representational Level or as a modifier of an Ascriptive Subact at the Interpersonal Level. Van de Velde argues that since they do not encode some representation of reality but rather the speaker's subjective stance, they should appear at the discourse-pragmatic level.[14] Although EMs are not degree modifiers, they

---

[14] Note that García Velasco (2013) actually argues for dual distinction between degree words such as *dreadfully* and *very*: degree modifiers such as *dreadfully* function as modifiers on the Interpersonal Level and *very* as an operator on the Representational Level. Since his findings will be discussed in

are not prototypical modifiers either. Like degree modifiers, they do not encode some representation of reality but are the speaker's subjective evaluation of the head; thus, they can be placed on the Interpersonal Level.

The first noun of the EM would be a secondary lexical element with a reinforcing function of an Ascriptive Subact, whose interpretation is determined by context. The appropriate morpho-syntactic template would then be triggered by the modifier and Ascriptive Subact together. Example (9.23) represents a possible FDG analysis of the EM:

(9.23)   And apparently the weather outside is perfect for pandas. Take a look at this guy having *a whale of a time* in the winter weather in his pen at the Yun (inaudible) Zoo in China the other day, his buddy romping around in the snow nearby, too. (COHA)

IL: (-id R$_1$:   [(T$_1$)   (T$_2$: [...] (T$_2$): whale (T$_2$))] (R$_1$))

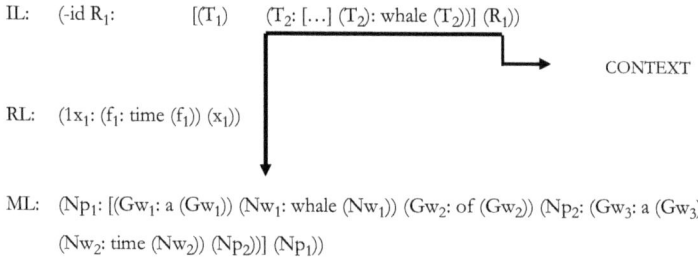

CONTEXT

RL: (1x$_1$: (f$_1$: time (f$_1$)) (x$_1$))

ML: (Np$_1$: [(Gw$_1$: a (Gw$_1$)) (Nw$_1$: whale (Nw$_1$)) (Gw$_2$: of (Gw$_2$)) (Np$_2$: (Gw$_3$: a (Gw$_3$)) (Nw$_2$: time (Nw$_2$)) (Np$_2$)] (Np$_1$))

In example (9.23), neither the original meaning of the lexeme *whale* (a large, marine mammal used in the N+PP and the head-classifier), nor the bleached meaning, simply large (found in the EBNP), are present anymore; the speaker is essentially reinforcing an evaluation, usually positive, of a referent.[15] This EM meaning of *whale* may well be a metaphorical extension along the lines of 'big is good'. The Interpersonal Level representation of the EM is similar to that of the EBNP except that *whale* now acts as a modifier of an unspecified property T$_2$. With the loss of its semantic content, however, *whale* no longer appears at the Representational Level but is immediately triggered at the Morphosyntactic Level, where it appears only in singular form. The property (T$_2$) that the modifier reinforces is defined by

---

more detail in the next section and does not contradict the analysis here, the discussion is saved for Section 9.2.1.6.

[15] This step is not surprising when considering the grammaticalization of *great* from denoting physical size to subjective modifier indicating prominence, importance, and significance (OED).

9.2 An FDG Account of the EBNP Family

context; the loss of the semantic content of the first noun thus leads to possible ambiguity in the semantic interpretation (see Section 4.3).

As is also the case with the head-classifier and some cases of the EBNP, the speaker in (9.23) has two means at her disposal to express her enthusiasm about the *time*: she could either use an EM (as in 9.23) or have used a subjective modifier construction, e.g. *a great time*. The combination of units on the Interpersonal and Representational Levels in (9.23) triggers the EM template on the Morphosyntactic Level.

The changes at the two formulation levels have led to further alterations at the Morphosyntactic and Phonological Levels. First, the change on the Interpersonal Level has an effect on the premodification distribution patterns of the construction in that the premodification primarily appears in front of the second noun, and the speaker-oriented evaluative modifier appears in the left of the premodifier zones (for a discussion on syntactic placement, see Section 9.2.3). Since it does not have semantic content and does not appear on the Representational Level, it cannot take Representational Level modification. This would explain the lack of descriptive modifiers and classifiers modifying the first noun found in the empirical study in Chapter 7. Furthermore, although the N-of-N template is still being used, both the preposition *of* and the second determiner have lost their meaning and function, and this allows for phonological reduction. Crucially, as demonstrated in (9.24), [N_1 of (a)] can, in some very frequent cases, become orthographically reduced to a single lexical item.

(9.24) Tom Hirst, who has done *a whaleuva job* of organizing everything, hopes those of you within a couple hours drive will plan to join us for the day. (Creesy 1986)

IL: (-id R_1: [(T_1) (T_2: [...] (T_2): whaleuva (T_2))] (R_1))

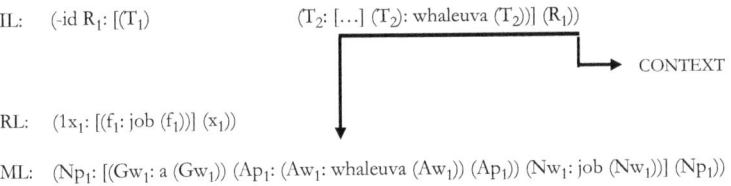

CONTEXT

RL: ($1x_1$: [(f_1: job (f_1))] (x_1))

ML: (Np_1: [(Gw_1: a (Gw_1)) (Ap_1: (Aw_1: whaleuva (Aw_1)) (Ap_1)) (Nw_1: job (Nw_1))] (Np_1))

At this stage, with the orthographic reduction, the mismatch between the formulation stages and the Morphosyntactic Level in the EBNP has been resolved, and transparency has been reestablished through reduction.

Unlike the EBNP, this *of*-binominal can be adequately explained using the tools provided by the English grammar and the model. Furthermore, what becomes clearer in the FDG analysis than in the CxG grammar analysis (where each syntagm is simply a new construction) is that the EM in the reduced form is no longer an *of*-binominal, but an [N of (a)] chunk in a simple NP template.

9.2.1.5 The Binominal Intensifier

In the BI, the degree function in the EM is forefronted, the contextual link is lost, and the first noun functions as an intensifier. Degree modifiers fulfill a variety of different roles and can be more or less subjective, meaning that, in the FDG framework, they can be rendered as operators or modifiers of the Ascriptive Subact on the Interpersonal Level or as operators of a Property on the Representation Level (García Velasco 2013; Van de Velde 2007: 216). Therefore, the BI function, as was the case with the EM above, raises two different issues. The first issue is which level, Interpersonal or Representational, would this linguistic unit be realized on (as discussed in Section 9.1.3.2, a degree modifier such as *very* functions as an operator on the Representational Level [García Velasco 2013: 87–9], and the more subjective *-ly* degree adverbs such as *dreadfully* are modifiers on the Interpersonal Level [García Velasco 2013: 93–4]). The second question is whether, in this construction, the first noun functions as an operator or a modifier.

With reference to the first question, it is clear that most degree adverbs no longer encode some representation of reality; moreover, numerous studies have shown that when descriptive premodifiers grammaticalize from descriptive adjectives to degree adverbs they tend to lose semantic content and become more subjective (e.g. Adamson 2000; Paradis 2001). This is also the case with the BI: this construction conveys a subjective (and in the case of *whale* or *hell* emphatic) comment from the speaker on the message's content and, therefore, conveys pragmatic and not semantic information. Thus, the degree modifier should appear on the Interpersonal Level.

As was the case with the EM above, the BI is actually a simple noun phrase consisting of an [N of (a)] unit and no longer an *of*-binominal.[16] Therefore, the second issue concerns the question of whether the first noun

---

[16] Unlike in the EM, the BI can function as an autonomous constituent, as seen in examples such as *this donut is hell of good*. This would then raise the question of whether the BI is actually the whole NP with the [N of (a)] chunk or the chunk itself. This is briefly discussed in the conclusion.

functions as an operator or a modifier of an Ascriptive Subact on the Interpersonal Level.[17] Returning to the criteria proposed by Keizer (2007b), the BI use gives positive values for the following grammatical criteria:

> No ascriptive function (can no longer evoke an entity)
> Little or no semantic content
> Mutually exclusive
> High frequency of use
> Decategorialized ('hell' has lost all nominal properties)
> Not modifiable
> Fixed position
> Phonetically reduced
> Fusing with other elements

When it comes to the loss of semantic content, although only a few first nouns from the original group have reached this final stage, i.e. *hell, whale, devil*, it would appear that these first nouns can be predominantly used interchangeably: *a hell of a long day, a whale of a long day,* or *a devil of a long day*. Each might denote different shades of the same meaning or exhibit subtle semantic nuances (this might be because all these first nouns continue to function as productive lexical items in English and evoke different concepts), but the use of one first noun instead of the other does not seem to change the overall message, i.e. 'it was a very long day'. Therefore, in this construction, the first noun is construed to have little or no semantic content.

Nonetheless, the noun that fills this unit still exhibits some lexical features. It has not joined a closed class. It can take focus and emphasis, and the phrase is optional. Therefore, it would appear that this linguistic unit may be regarded as a grammatical item, albeit not as prototypical as other operators (such as those expressing identifiability), hence, a lexical operator.[18] Thus in the transition between the EM and the BI, the first noun has transitioned from lexical to grammatical.

Examples (9.25) and (9.26) then demonstrate how FDG might model the BI's underlying structure. On the Interpersonal Level, the BI is represented as lexically realized in an operator position, acting as a reinforcer of an Ascriptive Subact (T_2). Because *whale* no longer has semantic content, it does not appear on the Representational Level and is

---

[17] The fact that [N of (a)] is a constituent is argued in Section 4.4 and will not be discussed further here.
[18] This analysis would also conform to Hengeveld's (2017) definition of lexical operator, i.e. it takes focus but cannot be modified.

only realized on the Morphosyntactic Level. As is often the case with these *of*-binominals, the prominent exception being the N+PP, this combination of Interpersonal Level and Representational Level features triggers two potential templates. The speaker can select a regular adjective-intensifier such as *extremely* (e.g. *an extremely ambitious goal*) or the N-of-N template (e.g. *a hell of an ambitious goal*). However, as with the EM, triggering the N-of-N template creates a mismatch between the information from formulation and the templates used for encoding. Similarly to the EM, transparency here is reestablished with the reduced form in (9.26). In this final example, the lexical operator with a reinforcer function at the Interpersonal Level is realized by a Grammatical Word on the Morphosyntactic Level.

(9.25) World peace? That's *a whale of an ambitious goal* for a minnow-sized fish market in Seattle. (COCA)
IL: (-id R$_1$: [(T$_1$) (**whale** T$_2$)] (R$_1$))
RL: (ıx$_1$: (f$_1$: goal (f$_1$)) (x$_1$): (f$_2$: ambitious (f$_2$)) (x$_1$))
ML: (Np$_1$: [(Gw$_1$: a (Gw$_1$)) **(Nw$_1$: whale (Nw$_1$)) (Gw$_2$: of (Gw$_2$))** **(Np$_2$: (Gw$_3$: a (Gw$_3$))** (Ap$_1$: (Aw$_1$: ambitious (Aw$_1$)) (Ap$_1$)) (Nw$_2$: goal (Nw$_2$)) (Np$_2$))] (Np$_1$))

(9.26) Let's drink to a ***helluva*** wonderful country (COHA)
IL: (-id R$_1$: [(T$_1$) (**helluva** T$_2$)] (R$_1$))
RL: (ıx$_1$: (f$_1$: country (f$_1$)) (x$_1$): (f$_2$: wonderful (f$_2$)) (x$_1$))
ML: (Np$_1$: [(Gw$_1$: a (Gw$_1$)) (Ap$_1$: **(Gw$_2$: helluva (Gw$_2$))** (Aw$_1$: wonderful (Aw$_1$)) (Ap$_1$)) (Nw$_1$: country (Nw$_1$))] (Np$_1$))

Primarily, the N-of-N template offers novelty, something particularly sought after with intensifiers. As mentioned above, although one intrinsically feels that the use of the different first nouns does add a semantic nuance of difference, in general they are so bleached that they can be used interchangeably; this is supported by the fact that these forms are often found in similar constructions, as seen in (9.27a–c).[19] As linguists have pointed out (e.g. Bolinger 1972; Lorenz 2002), with an increase in frequency, a new intensifier soon loses its 'shock effect' or its 'uniqueness' (this is particularly the case here, since these first nouns are often expletives or taboo words).

(9.27) a. a hell of a good time
b. a whale of a good time
c. a beast of a good time

---

[19] However, through frequent use with certain forms, they probably form individual collocation patterns.

9.2 An FDG Account of the EBNP Family

This analysis would also explain the empirical findings found in the premodification study in Chapter 7. As a lexical operator, or a grammatical item, it can no longer be modified. Since it is being used as a lexical operator on the Interpersonal Level, it would be placed at the left of the noun phrase. This would explain why modification only modifies the head (the second noun), i.e. *girl* in example (9.28), and not *hell*; this is why example (9.29a) would be considered grammatical, with *beautiful* modifying *country*, but questionable with *beautiful* before *helluva* in (9.29b).

(9.28)   Yes, that was surely Doina. Bracing. The same as twenty years ago. Sarcastic, and feisty, and sincere, always helpful, and funny and conscientious. And what else? Yes, *one hell of a sweet girl*.
IL: (-id R$_1$: [(T$_1$) (**hell** T$_2$)] (R$_1$))
RL: (1x$_1$: (f$_1$: girl (f$_1$)) (x$_1$): (f$_2$: sweet (f$_2$)) (x$_1$))
ML: (Np$_1$: [(Gw$_1$: a (Gw$_1$)) (**Nw$_1$: hell (Nw$_1$)**) (**Gw$_2$: of (Gw$_2$)**) (**Np$_2$: (Gw$_3$: a (Gw$_3$))** (Ap$_1$: (Aw$_1$: sweet (Aw$_1$)) (Ap$_1$)) (Nw$_2$: girl (Nw$_2$)) (Np$_2$))] (Np$_1$))

(9.29)   a. It must be *one helluva **beautiful** country*.
         b. ?It must be *one **beautiful** helluva country*.

In the BI, the first noun is a lexical operator on the Interpersonal Level and functions as a reinforcer of an Ascriptive Subact (T). The linguistic unit's lack of semantic content means that it does not appear on the Representational Level. On the Morphosyntactic Level, it is encoded as a [N of (a)] chunk. With the orthographic reduction to *helluva* or *hella* and *beasta*, transparency is reestablished on all three levels. As in the case of the EM, the BI can be explained using the tools provided by the FDG model.

9.2.2 Constructions in FDG

Of all five constructions discussed above, only the EBNP poses features that are difficult for the FDG model to capture, and thus the question remains as to whether the FDG model would need to resort to positing the epistemological (if not ontological) existence of constructions to explain the encoding of the EBNP. In the following sections, I will argue that at least on the basis of the analyses proposed in this book, they are not needed. Instead, a different kind of primitive must be introduced, namely the Combination of Partially Instantiated Frames (and Templates) or ComPIFs (Keizer 2016), to explain some of the encoding issues raised by the EBNP.

9.2.2.1 Combinations of Partially Instantiated Frames

The ComPIF is a new kind of primitive that has recently been added to the Fund. Situated between the frameset and the lexicon, these ComPIFs are meant to account for the large variation in the morpho-syntactic realization of idioms. Essentially, this is meant to provide an explanation of why certain idioms, such as *spill the beans* in (9.30a), allow for modification in (9.30b), quantification in (9.30c), and passivization in (9.30d), while other idioms, such as *kick the bucket* in (9.31a), do not, as demonstrated in (9.31b–c) (Keizer 2016: 985–6).

(9.30)   a. Edith spilled the beans.
             b. Benecio Del Torro just spilled the official beans.
             c. The informative trailer has already spilled most of the beans.
             d. The beans were spilled by Edith. (Keizer 2016: 985–86)

(9.31)   a. Matthew kicked the bucket.
             b. *The bucket was kicked by Matthew.
             c. *?Mathew kicked the empty bucket/ several buckets. (Keizer 2016: 986)

By distinguishing between different types of idioms, Keizer (2016) tries to find an explanation for both the regularity and the irregularity in their morpho-syntactic behavior. She concludes that in order to account for the partly idiosyncratic and partly compositional nature of idioms, without surrendering the lexical-grammatical distinction (as CxG has done), FDG needs partially filled frames and templates. These are frames and templates which include an invariable element, i.e. an element that is partly "sealed off" and stored as part of the frame or template, while the rest of the frame or template are filled in accordance with the normal rules of the grammar (Keizer 2016: 1009, 1012). A ComPIF is demonstrated in example (9.32), which shows the underlying interpersonal, representational, and morpho-syntactic structure for *to hit the ceiling*. At the Interpersonal Level, the whole idiom is realized as a single Ascriptive Subact (T_1); *ceiling* does not evoke an individual Referent, as it does not evoke an individual entity. At the Representational Level, *hit the ceiling* forms a single, complex predicate (f_2), within which *ceiling* is realized as a separate Individual (x) undergoing the action designated by the verb; this Individual accepts certain kinds of modification. The operator position for number is fixed as singular (1), reflecting the fact that number is invariable, and no other operators are allowed (underlined). In addition, the fact that *hit* and *ceiling* form one complex predication accounts for the fact that syntactic processes like passivization and nominalization are blocked (*the ceiling was hit*; *the hitting of the ceiling*) (Keizer 2016: 1004–5).

9.2 *An FDG Account of the EBNP Family* 263

(9.32) **Lexicon**: Meaning: 'become very angry'
  IL: $(\pi\ T_I)_\Phi$
  RL: $(\pi\ f_1: [(f_2: hit_V\ (f_2))\ (\underline{\iota x_1}: ceiling/roof_N\ (x_1))_U]\ (f_1))$
  ML: $(Vp_1: (Vw_1: hit\ (Vw_1))\ (Vp_1))\ (Np_2: [(Gw_1: \underline{the}\ (Gw_1))\ (Nw_2:$
     $ceiling/roof\ (Nw_2))]\ (Np_2))$
(Keizer 2016: 1010)

Despite certain similarities, a ComPIF is not the same as a construction. Keizer (2016: 1011) explicitly states that

> unlike Construction Grammar, FDG does not regard every (partly) unpredictable and/or frequently used linguistic element or pattern as a ComPIF: the notion of a ComPIF is restricted to multi-word expressions which, in terms of transparency and productivity are situated between traditional lexemes and fully productive (abstract) frames.

Whereas most CxG theories categorize all linguistic elements as constructions (or at least all linguistic elements with enough frequency and irregularity) and posit a scalar relation between lexical constructions and more schematic (or more procedural) constructions, in FDG a clear distinction is still retained. The ComPIF would be an alternative to the CxG construction.

9.2.2.2 ComPIFs or Constructions in the EBNP Family
The EBNP would be, of all the *of*-binominals discussed above, the potential candidate for a construction: the morpho-syntactic behavior (i.e. the noncanonical linguistic behavior of the second determiner) is not predictable from productive mechanisms. This would be a case where the interpersonal and representational information, as well as existing language-specific templates, cannot completely account for the production of this particular expression. Thus, in the EBNP the relation between frames and templates is not straightforward. It, therefore, seems justified to analyze the EBNP as a more schematic form of a ComPIF, as demonstrated in (9.33).

(9.33) RL: $(\mathbf{1x_1}: (f_1: wolf\ (f_1))\ (x_1): (f_2: whale\ (f_2))\ (x_1))$
   ML: $(Np_1: [(Gw_1: a\ (Gw_1))\ (Nw_1: whale\ (Nw_1))\ (\mathbf{Gw_2}: \underline{\mathbf{of}}\ (\mathbf{Gw_2}))$
    $(\mathbf{Np_2}: (\mathbf{Gw_3}: \underline{\mathbf{a}}\ (Gw_3))\ (Nw_2: wolf\ (Nw_2))\ (Np_2))]\ (Np_1))$

As a ComPIF, the determiner position encoding number in front of the second noun is sealed off, with the form of the indefinite article being triggered by the number of the overall Individual (in bold on Representational Level in (9.33)). This second determiner, furthermore, no longer marks identifiability of the overall referent; this is done by the first determiner. If *of* is also a fixed element in this template, then this would explain the irregular premodification patterns. Since the first noun functions as a modifier and [of a] are fixed elements in the template, then other premodifiers selected by the second noun could appear in front of either the first noun or the second. Since there appears to be a general practice that the more objective a premodifier is, the closer to the head it is placed, and if in examples such as *a bitchy iceberg of a woman* both the premodifier *bitchy* and the first noun *iceberg* function as subjective modifiers of the second noun (the head), then this would predict that when there are premodifiers selected by the second noun in front of the first noun, these would predominantly be subjective descriptive modifiers. In cases such as these, where the first noun functions as a subjective descriptive modifier, it would be less likely to find objective descriptive modifiers or classifiers in this slot, e.g. ?*a young iceberg of a woman*. However, the first noun might also ascribe an evaluative but more objective property to the Individual denoted by the second noun, as in *a huge, black-bearded bull of a man*, where *bull* denotes the size and/or shape of the man in question. In these cases, it would make sense to find more objective descriptive modifiers, selected by the second noun, in front of the first noun (however, this would need to be investigated in more detail).

This analysis would also explain why the first determiner is selected by the second noun, e.g. why **an idiot of a Rebecca* is dispreferred. Therefore, the ComPIF is an adequate tool to explain the irregularity of the EBNP and has the benefit of being able to explain the regular features of the EBNP, as well as the irregular, without having to resort to postulating constructions (in the CxG sense). Furthermore, the introduction of constructions would force FDG as a model to sacrifice the motivated link between meaning and form, while the ComPIF does not.

9.2.3 Placement in FDG

One cannot talk about premodification without discussing the linear ordering of the modifying elements. CxG-based models of the noun phrase posit zones to explain ordering; FDG has a unique placement apparatus which is applied here to demonstrate how FDG would deal with the irregular forms and premodification patterns in the three evaluative *of*-binominals.

9.2.3.1 Syntactic Ordering in Functional Discourse Analysis

In FDG, the ordering of elements in a phrase proceeds in a top-down and inward manner with Interpersonal Level elements being placed first and

9.2 *An FDG Account of the EBNP Family* 265

Representational Level elements second, with elements from outer layers being placed before elements on inner layers, and with all the non-core units (first IL and then RL) placed before core units (Hengeveld & Mackenzie 2008: 377; Keizer 2015: 219–24). In addition, for a language like English, functions are placed before operators and modifiers. The stages are listed in (9.34):

(9.34) a. Placement of elements triggered by *interpersonal non-core units*, i.e. the functions, operators, and modifiers of the Referential or Ascriptive Subact in question.
   b. Placement of elements triggered by *representation non-core units*, i.e. the functions, operators, and modifiers of the Individual, followed by those of the Property.
   c. Placements of elements triggered by *core units*, i.e. the predicate and its arguments, starting with the predicate.
   d. Placement of *dummy elements*.
   (Keizer 2015: 219)

The core units are those units that contain the essential information at each level, which in the phrase layer includes the predicate and its arguments. Non-core units consist of the remaining units, which for the phrase layer would include functions, operators, and modifiers, first of the Individual and then the Property (Keizer 2015: 184–5, 219). For the placement of elements, at both clausal and phrasal level, there are three absolute positions: the Phrase-initial position (P^I), the Phrase-medial position (P^M), and the Phrase-final position (P^F); once filled, these open up relative positions (P^{I+1}, P^{F-1}, etc.) (Hengeveld & Mackenzie 2008: 379; Keizer 2015: 219–20).

The example in (9.35) and (9.36) illustrates how the interpersonal and representational analysis of the phrase *a poor innocent dinosaur* (a repetition of example (9.1)), together with the ordering principles specified above leads to the syntactic structure in (9.36). Starting at the Interpersonal Level with the non-core elements, first the operator (-id) and then the modifier of the Referent, *poor*, are placed, in P^I and P^{I+1} positions. Moving to the Representational Level, the singularity marker (1) is placed in P^M, where it functions as a placeholder for the head. Then the modifier *innocent*, as the last non-core element, is placed in P^{I+2}. Finally, the only core element, the head of the Individual *dinosaur*, joins the singularity marker in P^M.

(9.35) Why do they have to be out there pestering *a poor innocent dinosaur*?
   (Keizer 2015: 220)
   IL: (-id R_I: [(T_I) (T_2)] (R_I): poor (R_I))
   RL: ($1x_I$: (f_I: dinosaur (f_I)) (x_I): (f_2: innocent (f_2)) (x_I))
   ML: (Np_I: [(Gw_I: a (Gw_I)) (Ap_I: (Aw_I: poor (Aw_I)) (Ap_I)) (Ap_2: (Aw_2: innocent (Aw_2)) (Ap_2)) (Nw_I: dinosaur (Nw_I))] (Np_I))

(9.36) a poor innocent (dinosaur)

P^I P^{I+1} P^{I+2} P^M

π^Rindef Σ^Rpoor σ^xinnocent dinosaur π^xsg

1   2   4   5–3

The next section will discuss FDG's ability to deal with the noncanonical premodification patterns of the EBNP and the other constructions.

9.2.3.2 Linear Placement of Modifiers in Functional Discourse Analysis

Example (9.37) is a good demonstration of the creativity in premodification placement allowed in the EBNP. *Hungry-looking* is clearly selected by *fellow* and would be a descriptive modifier, while *mere* modifies *wisp*. In the FDG circles, no one has really discussed how a ComPIF would affect word order, and I present here a possible scenario that accounts for the flexibility of premodification placement in (9.37). The speaker selects the EBNP ComPIF frame to structure her message. *Of* is a fixed element in the template as is the second determiner slot (filled by the indefinite article or a zero article); together they fill one phrasal position, hence the brackets. Starting at the Interpersonal Level, the indefinite article is placed in P^I in the compositional part of the ComPIF. *Mere*, as an operator on the Interpersonal Level is placed in P^M. On the Representational Level, the singularity marker, as an operator, is set as a placeholder in P^F, where it will trigger the appropriate form of the head noun; this operator also triggers the singular form of the first determiner (an indefinite article). Then the modifiers *hungry-looking* and *wisp*, as the last non-core entities, are placed in P^{I+1} and P^{M+1}, respectively. Next, the core element *fellow* is placed in the open P^F slot. Finally, the fixed elements, functioning as dummy elements, are placed in P^{M+2}, whereby the form of the article that is part of the dummy is determined by the number of the overall expression.

(9.37) A hungry-looking mere wisp of a fellow
  IL: (-id R$_1$: [(T$_1$) (T$_2$) (T$_3$: mere (T$_3$))] (R$_1$))
  RL: (1x$_1$: (f$_1$: fellow (f$_1$)) (x$_1$): (f$_2$: hungry-looking (f$_2$)) (x$_1$): (f$_3$: wisp (f$_3$)) (x$_1$))
  ML:

P^I P^{I+1} P^M P^{M+1} P^{M+2} P^F

π^Rindef σ^fhungry-looking Σ^Tmere σ^f**wisp** [of a] fellow π^xsg

1   4   2   5   7   6–3

The placement of elements in the EM is more straightforward and demonstrated with example (9.38). On the Interpersonal Level, first the indefinite article is placed in P^I and then the secondary lexical element in

P^{I+1}. [N of a] has now been reanalyzed as a chunk and thus is encoded as a single construction. On the Representational Level, the singularity marker operator is placed first in P^M, followed by the Property modifier *football* in P^{I+2} and the head *player* in P^M. As a unit at the Interpersonal Level, [N of a] is placed relatively early in the process, and therefore toward the left end of the premodifiers; nevertheless, it can take Interpersonal Level modification, e.g. *an utter beast of a cartridge*.

(9.38) A hell of a football player
 IL: (-id R_1: [(T_1) (T_2) (T_3: [...] (T_3): hell (T_3))] (R_1))
 RL: ($1x_1$: (f_1: player (f_1): (f_2: football (f_2)) (f_1)) (x_1))
 ML:

P^I P^{I+1} P^{I+2} P^M

π^Rindef π^Thell-of-a $^{\sigma f}$football   player $^{\pi x}$sg

  1   2   4   5–3

Finally, the process in the BI is very similar to the EM, as demonstrated in (9.39). With [hell of a] functioning as a lexical operator on the Interpersonal Level, it would be placed second in the P^{I+1} position on the Morphosyntactic Level. As an operator it would not receive premodification, and as a lexical operator on the Interpersonal Level it would require placement immediately after the determiner, thus disallowing modification before [hell of a].

(9.39) A hell of a sweet girl
 IL: (-id R_1: [(T_1) (T_2) (**hell** T_3)] (R_1))
 RL: ($1x_1$: (f_1: girl (f_1)) (x_1): (f_2: sweet (f_2)) (x_1))
 ML:

P^I P^{I+1} P^{I+2} P^M

π^Rindef π^Thell-of-a $^{\sigma f}$sweet   girl $^{\pi x}$sg

  1   2   4   5–3

The placement criteria provided by the model is flexible enough to account for noncanonical syntax found in these three *of*-binominals. However, more research needs to be done to account for the role of ComPIF templates in syntactic placement.

9.2.4 Conclusions

The analysis of the synchronic information above already provides an outline for a proposed diachronic development discussed in the following section. This analysis demonstrates, in the case of the head-classifier, how a speaker's intention and contextual ambiguity can trigger a particular structure at the Interpersonal Level, which may lead to a mismatch between the Interpersonal and Representational Levels. It shows that changes on the Interpersonal Level, in particular the loss of the second Referent, destabilized the system and resulted in changes on the Representational, Morphosyntactic and finally Phonological Levels. Finally, these changes lead to the creation of a new type of modifier and lexical operator on the Interpersonal Level and reestablishing transparency between the levels.

The next section discusses the scenario that FDG would propose as to how these different constructions link together and how they may have historically developed.

9.3 A Diachronic Functional Discourse Grammar Explanation

9.3.1 Grammaticalization in FDG

FDG was created for and has predominantly been used as a typologically based theory of language structure, and only a few more recent studies have applied the framework to diachronic questions (e.g. Giomi 2020; Honselaar & Olbertz 2016; Olbertz 2016; Pérez Quintero 2013; Van de Velde 2009; some papers in Hengeveld et al. 2017).[20] However, as a grammatical model, FDG, with its different levels and layers, can model the diachronic changes and their processes, such as grammaticalization, pragmaticalization, lexicalization, or constructionalization (in the sense of the creation of a new frame or template).

The FDG model would predict that language change begins in the pragmatics and semantics of a linguistic expression, and these changes may lead to changes in formal behavior (Heine 1997b; Heine & Kuteva 2002; Hengeveld et al. 2017); thus, language change begins with changes in the meanings and works its way down to the form, i.e. morpho-syntax and phonology (Boye & Harder 2012; Heine 2002, 2003; Heine & Kuteva 2002; Keizer 2007b). Heine (2003: 579; for an overview see Heine & Narrog 2010: 410) takes Lehmann's parameters, links them to a functional theory of change, and argues for four basic mechanisms of

---

[20] Nonetheless, Hengeveld et al. (2017) point out that the strength of a typological approach to grammaticalization is that only through examining the grammaticalization of features in a range of different languages can an analysis capture general processes of change (see also Bisang 2011).

9.3 A Diachronic FDG Explanation

grammaticalization, each of which affect one aspect of grammar (pragmatics, semantics, morpho-syntax, and phonology):

(1) Extension
(2) Desemanticization
(3) Decategorialization
(4) Erosion

The process begins with extension, which is "the rise of new grammatical meanings when linguistic expressions are extended to new contexts (context-induced reinterpretation)" (Heine & Narrog 2010: 410). Extension involves three different components: sociolinguistic, text-pragmatic, and semantic (Heine & Narrog 2010: 411). In the sociolinguistic component, grammaticalization starts with a speaker's innovation that is then adopted by an entire speech community. The text-pragmatic component of grammaticalization involves the extension of a linguistic element from regular context to new context or contexts and then its spread to more general paradigms of contexts. Finally, the last component is closely linked to the text-pragmatic component and entails that the linguistic element develops a new meaning, either evoked or developed in this new context (Heine & Narrog 2010: 411); only the last form of extension is important for this study. The change in pragmatics then leads to a change in semantics (i.e. desemanticization, semantic reduction, or bleaching), which results in a loss in meaning or content (Heine & Narrog 2010: 412).

Next, these changes may have an effect on the morpho-syntactic form, leading to decategorialization. Decategorialization, also found in Lehmann's parameters (2002: 110) and Hopper's principles (1991: 22–33), denotes the loss of features which are typically associated with a particular lexical category; decategorialization in nouns results in the loss of the distinctions of number and gender and results in an inability to take anaphoric reference, to combine with determiners, and to take modifiers (Heine & Narrog 2010: 412–13; see Chapter 5). The final stage of grammaticalization is erosion or phonetic reduction; this is often linked to high frequency of use and may include morphological or phonetic erosion (Heine & Narrog 2010: 413). Like the FDG theory, Heine would theorize that change begins at the formation levels and then progresses down to the encoding ones. These stages are found in the analysis below and can be clearly modeled in FDG's underlying representation.

9.3.2 *The FDG Diachronic Analysis*

The qualitive diachronic case studies support the claim that the initial stages of grammaticalization began with the formation of the head-classifier. The FDG analysis shows that taking the prototypical and primarily transparent N+PP as the starting point, a reconceptualization of the relationship between the two nouns in the mind of the speaker (part of the Conceptual Component) allots the PP a classifying function. This leads to a change in the pragmatics of the construction (Heine's first stage of grammaticalization: semantic extension). This reconceptualization led to the second noun no longer denoting a referent, and at the Interpersonal Level, the second Referential Subact is lost. However, at the Representational Level the second noun still designates an Individual, which then creates a mismatch between the two levels and changes in the morpho-syntactic encoding: the second noun is nonreferential, and identifiability and number of the whole *of*-binominal is realized by the first determiner. The preposition *of* no longer has semantic meaning.

With the transition to the head-classifier, the internal structure of the template changes as the relationship between the two nouns is reconceptualized. The changed status of the second noun led to a different frame on the Interpersonal Level, and the mismatch between the Representational and Interpersonal levels led to restrictions on the Morphosyntactic Level. However, although the mismatch results in restrictions in the encoding, the frames and templates used are those already available in the English language.

Harder and Boye (2011; see also Boye & Harder 2012) would argue that the loss of the second referent in the head-classifier and the preposition's loss of semantic value resulted in the preposition's bleached form encoding some sort of linking relationship between the two nouns. This change allows the speaker/hearer to interpret what this relationship might be and, in turn, sets the two nouns in direct competition with each other for head status and discourse prominence. Thus, grammaticalization arises out of this competition between two linguistic elements. In this particular grammaticalization path, the first noun 'loses'. This can be seen in the constructions that follow.

In the EBNP, the Interpersonal Level is similar to that of the head-classifier. The second noun is the head at the Representational Level, and the first noun has bleached and was reconceptualized as ascribing an evaluative property to the second noun (Heine's second stage of grammaticalization: desemanticization). The first noun must agree in number with

9.3 A Diachronic FDG Explanation

the second noun. This also results in a mismatch between the Representational and Morphosyntactic Level because a linguistic element usually encoded by a noun (often without an alternative adjectival form) fills a property slot in a frame. The first determiner is selected by N_2, and the use of this frame as well as the function–form mismatch explains the preference for premodification in front of the first noun, even when selected by the second. The idiosyncratic features of the syntagm can be explained by positing that the template is a ComPIF, with a fixed [of det$_2$] position. The FDG account would be able to explain, a posteriori, the reappearance of the second determiner by assuming some sort of cognitive link with the N+PP; however, the model would not predict it.

The transition between the head-classifier to EBNP entails not only a loss or redistribution of semantics properties but also decategorialization (Heine's third stage of grammaticalization). Although the loss of a referent in the head-classifier might have started this process (since an NP prototypically evokes a referent), it is only in these constructions that the first nouns begin to lose their properties of nounhood.

It is only in the EM, where [N of (a)] has become a separate chunk, that the first noun changes from a lexeme to an element with the [N of (a)] functioning as a secondary lexical element, an intermediary stage between a lexical item and a grammatical element (see Hengeveld 2017; Keizer 2007b). Thus, the process of decategorialization from noun to modifier finishes in the EM, where the first noun can appear only in singular form and premodification is restricted. In the EM, [N of (a)] bleaches to the extent that it shifts from functioning as a property at the Representational Level to an unspecified extreme modifier at the Interpersonal Level. In this stage, there is evidence of orthographic reduction in some of the more frequent forms (Heine's fourth stage of grammaticalization: erosion).

Finally, with the BI the [N of (a)] becomes a lexical operator, a grammatical element, modifying an Ascriptive Subact on the Interpersonal Level. The corpora provide orthographic evidence of the reduction of [N of (a)] to a single lexical item (i.e. erosion), and in the case of *hella*, this form is very productive. This final step then reestablishes transparency between all levels.

The direction of the process itself, i.e. the pressure to reduce the complex NP to a simple NP, might be explained by a very loose interpretation of Dik's Principle of Formal Adjustment, which states that "derived, secondary constructions of type X are under pressure to adjust their formal expression to the prototypical expression model of non-derived, primary constructions of type X" (1997b: 20, 158). Dik (1997b: 157–64) uses this principle to explain why embedded constructions such as *John denied the charges* may also take the form of *John's denial of the charges*. This might be a case where the *of*-binominal is then under pressure to form a simple NP.

In sum, the whole process, from the N+PP to the BI, would be a classic example of grammaticalization. The process begins with a lexeme functioning as the head of a noun phrase and denoting a referent. This lexeme changes to secondary lexical element and then finally becomes a lexical operator. At the same time there is a shift from encoding semantic information to encoding pragmatic information. This analysis shows that FDG can model the interplay between form and meaning in the grammaticalization process, and can also make testable predictions and provide restrictions for the paths a lexeme can take. As Giomi (2017: 46) argues:

> [b]y mapping directional universals explicitly onto the structure of the four levels, the FDG approach gains a decisive advantage over most functionally oriented theories of grammaticalization: that of showing how language change is not only compatible with general cognitive principles, but directly reflects the same underlying grammatical hierarchy as is observable synchronically across the languages of the world. In this way, it provides precise grammar-internal constraints on possible and impossible patterns of grammaticalization.

The analysis also demonstrates how a change at the Interpersonal Level and the loss of transparency leads to changes on the lower levels and finally ends with reestablishing transparency in the phonetically reduced BIs, e.g. *hella*.

9.4 Conclusion

The FDG theory provides a plausible, testable explanation for the patterns found in the empirical analysis. In the head-classifier, the irregular premodification patterns essentially stem from the loss of the second Referential Subact on the Interpersonal Level and the subsequent mismatch between the Interpersonal and Representational Levels. In the EBNP, the change of function in the first noun is reflected in the restricted premodification in front of the first and second noun. However, in the EBNP, transparency between the Interpersonal and Representational Levels is reestablished, but instead there is a mismatch between the Representational Level and the encoding on the Morphosyntactic Level,

9.4 Conclusion

again resulting in a change in the premodification patterns. In the EM, this mismatch between the Representational and Morphosyntactic Levels is then resolved with the first noun becoming an extreme modifier only realized on the Interpersonal Level. In the BI, the first noun functions as a lexical operator at the Interpersonal Level and, therefore, cannot be modified. Despite its irregular syntactic form, its function allows [N of (a)] to integrate into the premodifier patterns in front of the second noun as an adjective-intensifier.

The use of the ComPIF adequately explains the changes found in the EBNP without having to resort to making the whole phrase a construction (in the CxG sense). The ComPIF provides the tool to explain the irregular features of the template, while still being able to explain the regular elements. Therefore, in the context of this book, there is no need for the model to adopt constructions as symbolically linked form and meaning pairings. Furthermore, the motivated link between frames and templates and a clear delineation between lexicon and frameset allows the model to distinguish between noncanonical and more iconic features.

The historical analysis in the FDG frameworks shows that we are looking at the reduction of the internal components of the N-of-N template to a simple NP template, with a reanalyzed chunk [N of (a)], functioning first as a modifier and then as a lexical operator. Thus, the EM and BI is not the whole N-of-N construction (as would be proposed in CxG theory), but this [N of (a)] element. Therefore, although we are structurally looking at an *of*-binominal, to call this linguistic structure an *of*-binominal is a misnomer.

This analysis, furthermore, demonstrates the interplay between external and internal factors in language change. In this case, an external factor, i.e. speaker intention, changed the message, which then led to a series of mismatches within the language system as language-internal pressures, such as transparency, facilitated further changes. In terms of internal factors, FDG not only distinguishes between modifiers of pragmatic and semantic information but also captures the interplay between the changing roles of the nouns in the different *of*-binominals, and the effect these changes have on the different constructions' premodification patterns. Finally, FDG can provide a plausible explanation for why, in the EBNP, modifiers in front of the first noun can be selected by the second noun. Although this variable did not ultimately turn out to be a significant feature in the premodifier study in Chapter 7, it is still a phenomenon that requires clarification.

In sum, this analysis shows that FDG can capture the distinctions and changes between the different *of*-binominals. Furthermore, it provides, based on mechanisms already in the grammar and grammar-internal constraints, an explanation for the idiosyncrasies of these *of*-binominal constructions without having to resort to the adoption of constructions as arbitrary form–meaning pairings. What is clear is that FDG as a model cannot capture the role of the language network in motivating these changes and, therefore, has little to add about the role of the language network in the grammaticalization change (see Boye & Harder 2012). This is one of the strengths of the CxG model, as was discussed in Chapter 8.

PART IV

Discussion

CHAPTER 10

Discussion and Conclusions

10.1 Classification Discussion

This monograph has examined the EBNP *of*-binominal, asking questions such as what explanations linguistic theories can provide for both its irregularity and its persistence despite these irregularities. In addition, the study has addressed the question of the way in which the EBNP is related to other *of*-binominals that share a similar form.

One of the most challenging parts of a study of *of*-binominals is the fact that the different constructions are structurally so similar, but the relation between the two nouns so different that sometimes it is impossible to say what exactly the speaker might have meant. For this reason, this book began with a comprehensive discussion of the criteria used in previous studies to delineate and distinguish between *of*-binominal constructions. These criteria were then applied to the corpus data. Based on a large sample of nouns used in the first noun position in the EBNP, this study differentiated between different types of *of*-binominals that appear to be historically related: the prototypical N+PP, the head-classifiers, the pseudo-partitives, the EBNPs, the EMs, and the BIs. The EM then acts as a bridge between the EBNP and the intensifier *of*-binominal (the BI), a category which some researchers hypothesized would exclude evaluative first nouns. The existence of the EM and BI *of*-binominals, furthermore, supports Aarts' (1998) analysis of the EBNP, namely the internal structure of the EBNP has been reanalyzed to form a modifier phrase.

The premodification analysis shows that beginning in the head-classifier, and particularly in the EBNP, the EM, and the BI, there has been a loss and conflation of the premodifier zones in front of the nouns, thus providing evidence for an analogical link to the simple NP template. The diachronic study of first nouns that have progressed along this path more recently has shown that the grammaticalization path most likely diverges at the head-classifier, with either the pseudo-partitive developing before the EBNP, or with both uses beginning at about the same time. Only in the case of *snake* is there evidence that the EBNP use might have developed from the pseudo-partitive. Only with *cake* do we find pseudo-partitives before head-classifiers. In general, the diachronic evidence supports the grammaticalization path suggested by the synchronic analysis. In sum, this book suggests that the historical developments of this family did not just randomly take place but followed a specific pattern and adhered to inherent language-internal rules: when the relation between the two nouns changed, the morpho-syntactic patterns changed to adapt to this. Jackendoff (2002: 180) claims that "the range of meanings associated with N-of-NP constructions is too great for the meaning to be attributed to the construction itself. Rather, all the semantic relations come from the head verb or noun, and the construction is merely a form to be filled." This study has shown that this solution is too simplistic. The change in the relationship between the two nouns has led to systematic changes of the morpho-syntactic form/FDG template; this has been clearly shown by the premodifier study and the irregularity in the EBNP.

Jackendoff, however, is not completely incorrect. This project raises a question about the extent to which the grammaticalization path proposed here can tell the whole story. Once the different *N-of-N* constructions exist, it is more likely the semantics of the first noun that constrains or incites this noun to be used in certain constructions, rather than more general pragmatic and semantic features of the *of*-binominal templates. This means that although this study has presented this grammaticalization path as one unbroken 'branch' in the *of*-binominal forest (with a slight detour to the pseudo-partitive), I cannot eliminate the possibility that some first nouns enter the path in later stage constructions. For example, *Watergate* can be creatively used in the EBNP in examples such as *the "Cosmic Watergate" of a UFO coverup* (blog).[1] *Watergate* might be used in N+PP, *the Watergate of this generation*, but is less felicitous in the head-classifier, ?*a Watergate of secrecy*. It is exactly this flexibility of the *of*-binominal constructions that allows for first noun metastasis from one construction to the next. Ultimately, this study has shown that the N-of-N network is extremely intricate, subtle, and 'incestuous'.

The second contribution that this book has made is the juxtaposition of a CxG analysis of the data and an FDG one. It has asked how each theory

---

[1] Robert Sheaffer. Comments on the History Channel show "UFOs on the Record" [blog post], August 30, 2011, *Bad UFOs: Skepticism, UFOs, and the Universe* (http://badufos.blogspot.co.at/2011/08/).

accounts and delineates between the categories proposed in Part I, and how each theory would explain the historical development of these constructions described in Part II. Both models have provided interesting, albeit different, insights.

10.2 Comparing the Two Models

Compared to the theoretical 'distance' between generative theories and cognitive-functional theories, the differences between the CxG and FDG (as two theories in the functional-cognitive paradigm) are relatively few and small. FDG and CxG are both theories situated in the cognitive-functional space (Butler & Gonzálvez-García 2005, 2014; Gonzálvez-García & Butler 2006), meaning that their conceptualizations of language share some ontological and epistemological principles. Both theories perceive language as a tool used in social interaction and, hence, assume that pragmatics and semantics predominantly shape linguistic form and that language changes through use. Both theories view language as being grounded in cognitive processes, meaning that psycholinguistic evidence is used to support arguments or motivate changes in their theory, or, at the least, neither theory would make claims contradicting robust findings from psycholinguistic research. Both theories are usage-based in that, where possible, they use real-world data. Unlike generative-based theories, both posit that language only has a surface level; there is no deep or underlying structure (the underlying representations in FDG are epistemological tools for linguistic analysis and do not have ontological or psychological reality), and there is no movement. Furthermore, both theories acknowledge that the lexical–grammatical divide is gradient, although they deal with this gradience differently in the specific models: CxG does away with the lexical–grammatical dichotomy, while FDG still retains a divide between the two in the model (but not in conceptualization).

Both theories have very similar classification methods. In the FDG theory, only those semantic and pragmatic changes which systematically affect the morpho-syntactic structure result in new categories. This distinction is currently being discussed in CxG circles. Some construction grammarians would agree with this FDG distinction, whereas others have argued that a change in meaning is enough to posit a new type of construction (Traugott & Trousdale 2013; cf. Diewald 2015). Nonetheless, both theories can describe the functional and formal changes that have led from the prototypical (original) N-of-N construction (N+PP) to the other *of*-binominals discussed in this book. In addition, both theories capture the syntactic change in which what was originally a complex NP (consisting of a noun modified by a prepositional phrase) is reduced in form to a simple NP and allow for the subsequent repercussions of this formal change on the premodification patterns of the individual *of*-binominals.

One of the fundamental differences between these two approaches is the information that they seek to model. FDG is a model that "seeks to describe the knowledge that underlies a language user's potential to communicate in his/her language in an explicit and highly formalized way" (Hengeveld & Mackenzie 2008: 26), and its purpose is "to describe and, as far as possible, explain the formal properties (syntactic, morphological, and phonological) of Discourse Acts from a functionalist perspective" (Hengeveld & Mackenzie 2008: 31). This means that this approach provides grammar-internal explanations for phenomena. It offers defined primitives and combinatorial constraints that are the basis of the analysis and constrain possible outcomes. When there are changes, the model initially looks for explanations for these changes in the grammar, because the model was conceptualized to represent and explain the conventional and systematic part of the language system.

In the context of this project, this means that FDG allows us to capture the distinction between the five central *of*-binominal categories discussed using the linguistic (English-language specific) tools that already exist in the model. It provides the tools to demonstrate how changes on the pragmatic and semantic levels can explain the noncanonical behavior on the morpho-syntactic and phonological levels. It, furthermore, captures the first noun's shift from being the complex NP's head in the N+PP and head-classifier to [N1 of a]'s reanalysis as a chunk and shift from the Representational Level in the EBNP to functioning as a secondary lexical element at the Interpersonal Level.

The FDG theory posits a top-down approach in which change (or difference) in meaning should trigger a change (or difference) in form for this change to be accounted for in the analysis. Thus, this analysis ascribes a motivated link between meaning and form; the elements of the meaning (pragmatic and semantic levels) influence the final form. This results in very different explanations of the diachronic changes. The existence of motivated links allows FDG to show how the changing functions of the nouns in the *of*-binominals constructions have an effect on these constructions' premodification patterns, and thereby, explain noncanonical patterns, e.g. the loss of referential status of the second noun in the head-classifier. Using the variables and tools provided by the language model, FDG can represent the different *of*-binominal constructions and model the differences between them. This model then predicts the changes found in the premodification patterns and can model the different stages of the grammaticalization process. Furthermore, the model showed that in the last two stages of this path, the EM and BI are no longer an *of*-binominal, but an [N of (a)] chunk that is used in a simple NP template. This analysis demonstrates how FDG can account for system-internal and external factors that contribute to the grammaticalization of these *of*-binominals. However, the FDG account lacks a network view of these phenomena. A network perspective can more fully account for the reappearance of the second determiner in the EBNP but also hypothesize what drove the internal reanalysis.[2]

On the basis of the analysis of this family of constructions, I have argued that FDG does not need to introduce constructions into the primitives already provided by the model; the linguistic tools provided by the model offer a plausible explanation of the phenomena. The ComPIF offered a frame that could adequately explain the restricted determiner selection in front of the second noun in the EBNP without having to posit whole constructions. The set features on the ComPIF allow us to capture the irregular features of the EBNP, while the *of*-binominal frame accounts for regular features as well.

Work done in CxG has focused a lot more on the cognitive processes. CxG takes a cognitive approach in that it "represents a mentalistic approach to language that aims to describe speakers' knowledge of language" (Hilpert 2018). Its goal is "to develop a framework for the analysis of linguistic structure that is grounded in general cognitive processes" (Diessel 2015: 296). This means that changes are linked to frequency, entrenchment, schematicity, and networks.

The most interesting aspect of the CxG contribution to this study is that it offers a network view of the changes in constructions and links linguistic phenomena to more entrenched patterns in the language system. This means that it can capture the co-evolution of constructions in the language system. This point is clearly demonstrated in the polysemy link between similar functions of the PP in the head-classifier and the classifier premodifiers; this link then motivated structural changes in the *of*-binominal. This network analysis suggests that it is not just semantic and pragmatic factors

---

[2] A network approach is also compatible with FDG, since the frames/templates of the original constructions are still available and may be assumed to be activated when the new constructions are produced (certainly before they have become completely established). However, this has not been explicitly proposed by FDG linguists.

driving the changes (e.g. Hopper & Traugott 2003: 75–6), but that form also must have played a role in the changes that took place (what might be considered grammar-internal pressures in FDG). In particular, the CxG analysis posits a link to the simple NP schema, and that would account for the internal changes that took place in the EBNP, EM, and BI. Furthermore, the persistence of the inheritance link to the N-of-N construction would offer a plausible explanation for the reappearance of the indefinite determiner in the EBNP, as an element required to distinguish the EBNP from the head-classifier (and the pseudo-partitive although it was not discussed in the analysis).

One issue that has arisen in this analysis is the exact nature of the link between, for example, the head-classifier and the classifier modifier. Can there be an underspecified classifier function, a constructeme, that has two separate realizations, e.g. as a head-classifier or as a premodifier (see Zehentner & Traugott 2020 for more discussion)? Are these realizations actually allostructions of a higher underspecified function, or are they all separate nodes in the network, linked paradigmatically through a shared function but with taxonomic links to different higher constructions? For example, in a similar study, Norde, De Clerk and Colleman (2014: 242) propose the macro-construction degree modifier. However, the degree modifier function can, as has been shown here, be expressed in a range of forms; hence, FDG's positing no one-to-one link between form and function. A related issue is that construction grammarians talk about verbs, adverbs, and the noun phrase, but their ontological status in the network is not completely clear. Are they considered more entrenched schematic forms? It would appear logical that a more entrenched form like the simple NP is then more likely to attract a new construction than another type.[3]

The second fundamental difference between the two theories that played a role in this analysis is the link between meaning and form already briefly mentioned above. CxG claims this link is arbitrary, while FDG would claim it is (in most cases) motivated. This distinction limits CxG to some extent to that of a descriptive model, in that function no longer influences form, and constructions are classified with dictionary-like entries. This also means that CxG is unable to distinguish between the canonical and noncanonical elements: they are all constructions. In the context of this book, this means that CxG categorizes each of the

---

[3] Taylor (2004: 57–8) in his Cognitive Grammar network model talks about constructions that are more motivated, i.e. ones that have more links to other constructions in the network, and those that are less so. Traugott (2016: 105) claims that this is one of the functions her specific micro-construction map should fulfill.

of-binominals discussed here as different constructions but then fails, particularly in the case of the evaluative constructions, to see that [N of a] is an irregular form that has integrated into a canonical NP form. In the case of premodification patterns, in particular, noncanonical premodification patterns, CxG provides a tool to systematically capture patterns in the data but would not require an explanation of the changes found. This means it provides convenient categories for a larger empirical study; however, it fails to offer an explanation as to why the head-classifier lost its degree modifier zones or why the EBNP premodifier zones developed so idiosyncratically.

This problem lies in the limitations of a zone-based approach and in the nature of the CxG approach itself. Researchers addressing the use of constructions in Role and Reference Grammar and the Lexical Construction Model have noted constructional models' inability to explain constraints, meaning constraints in terms of lexical choice to fill constructions (Butler 2009; Ruiz de Mendoza Ibáñez & Mairal Usón 2006), but in the case of this particular study, it is also an inability to explain constraints on the premodification selection of the constructions that have developed. Nuyts (2011) points out that rules or language norms create a third dimension to language, a meta-linguistic level that purely form–meaning pairings miss. Instead, CxG models language as a Wittgensteinian undertaking, where old constructions breed new constructions through similarities and frequency of form and function. The language model fails to separate changes licensed by the language system itself from those that are not.

The real strength of the CxG approach is the fact that it is a network model; this was particularly important when looking at the diachronic development of a linguistic item and when looking for a language-internal explanation for changes, i.e. competition between two forms, as was the case with this grammaticalization path. In the Construction Grammar chapter, I have argued that a formal representation of this change has to model not only the changes in meaning but those in form. Only then can CxG explain the internal changes that have taken place in the grammaticalization of these constructions.

The FDG framework and other more formal models have language parameters that have been tested and which put constraints on what is possible in a language. The framework has less to say about mechanisms of change, but it can incorporate psycholinguistic findings and, in principle, also allows for links between different frames (functional links) and templates (formal links), thus integrating the network model. Therefore, although this analysis did not find any reason in which to integrate the

CxG construction into the FDG model, the network analysis would be compatible with an FDG analysis, although the repercussions would have to be explored in more detail in future work. In this way, these two models do not appear to be mutually exclusive, and a possible integration of these two approaches, i.e. integrating the network analysis into an FDG analysis might be fruitful for future research.

10.3 Future Research

The preposition *of* has proven an interesting subject of research for linguists for over sixty years. Its allure stems from both its allusive character and its 'incestuous' behavior: lack of semantics allows this preposition to denote a range of relationships between two nouns. Despite extensive work in the past, a number of issues still remain.

In the context of this book, a few issues that have not been adequately addressed (despite dedicating over a hundred pages to classification) is whether the EM and BI really are *of*-binominals at all? At what point do the EMs and BIs stop being *of*-binominal NPs and are simply NPs? Is *of*-binominal a formal criteria or a functional one? Other questions about this *of*-binominal family that are still open to discussion are, first, the role of the *of*-appositional construction, e.g. *the city of Chicago* (see Keizer 2007a: 73–82). It appears in the data with some of the first nouns and may be a transition stage between the head-classifier and the EBNP. In general, this construction has been underresearched and would need to be explored in more detail so that any findings would be important. Second, the focus of this project was on the EBNP and the evaluative constructions that followed. However, the head-classifier in English has not been discussed in detail. Some open questions that remain are, for example, whether there are more than the two head-classifier types listed in this project? What is the exact relation between the premodifier and *of*-binominal classifier forms and is this alternation systematic? Finally, a large-scale diachronic study, pulling in the *of*-apposition and possibly even the partitive construction (*a piece of the cake*), needs to be conducted in order to answer the questions of how these constructions entered or developed in English and their relation to other *of*-binominal families. A study of this kind would also need to take into account French influence.

On the theoretical level, this study touches on how FDG accounts for syntactic placement, in particular noncanonical syntactic placement. This part of the model has, as yet, been underresearched and a larger, more comprehensive study is needed to expand on these rules. A conservative Construction Grammar analysis has been presented in this book, but the network theory is currently in the process of being developed and elaborated on. A more focused quantitative study of the *of*-binominal family has the potential to offer evidence for allostructions and constructemes.

References

Aarts, B. (1998). English binominal noun phrases. *Transactions of the Philological Society*, 96, 117–58.

Abney, S. P. (1987). The English noun phrase in its sentential aspect. Ph.D. dissertation, Massachusetts Institute of Technology, Cambridge, MA.

Abraham, W. (1998). Ein Schatz von einem Kind: Zur Pradikatsyntax binominaler Nominalkonstituenten. *Deutsche Sprache*, 26, 337–47.

Adamson, S. (2000). A lovely little example: Word order options and category shift in the premodifying string. In O. Fischer, A. Rosenbach, and D. Stein, eds., *Pathways of Change: Grammaticalization in English*. Amsterdam: John Benjamins, pp. 39–66.

Aijmer, K. (2002). *English Discourse Particles: Evidence from a Corpus*. Amsterdam: John Benjamins.

Akmajian, A. and Lehrer, A. (1976). NP-like quantifiers and the problem of determining the head of an NP. *Linguistic Analysis*, 2(4), 395–413.

Alexiadou, A., Haegeman, L., and Stavrou, M. (2007). *Noun Phrase in the Generative Perspective*. Berlin/Boston: Mouton de Gruyter.

Anttila, R. [1972] (1989). *Historical and Comparative Linguistics*, 2nd rev. ed. Amsterdam: John Benjamins.

Arnon, I. and Snider, N. (2010). More than words: Frequency effects for multi-word phrases. *Journal of Memory and Language*, 62(1), 67–82.

Athanasiadou, A. (2007). On the subjectivity of intensifiers. *Language Sciences*, 29, 554–65.

Austin, F. O. (1980). A crescent-shaped jewel of an island: Appositive nouns in phrases separated by of. *English Studies*, 61, 357–66.

Bache, C. (2000). *Essentials of Mastering English: A Concise Grammar*. Berlin/New York: Mouton de Gruyter.

Baker, N. (2014). *Occultus Liber*. Bloomington, IN: AuthorHouse.

Barðdal, J. and Gildea, S. (2015). Diachronic Construction Grammar: Epistemological context, basic assumptions and historical implications. In J. Barðdal, E. Smirnova, L. Sommerer, and Spike Gildea, eds., *Diachronic Construction Grammar*. Amsterdam: John Benjamins, pp. 1–50.

Bauer, L. (1998). When is a sequence of two nouns a compound in English? *English Language and Linguistics*, 2(1), 65–86.

Bauer, L. (2004). Adjectives, compounds and words. *Nordic Journal of English Studies*, 3(1), 7–22.
Bell, M. J. and Plag, I. (2012). Informativeness is a determinant of compound stress in English. *Journal of Linguistics*, 48(3), 485–520.
Bell, M. J. and Plag, I. (2013). Informativity and analogy in English compound stress. *Word Structure*, 6(2), 129–55.
Bennett, W. A. (1976). One type of expressive noun phrase in French. *Nottingham Linguistic Circular*, 5(2), 20–1.
Bennis, H., Corver, N., and den Dikken, M. (1998). Predication in nominal phrases. *The Journal of Comparative Germanic Linguistics*, 1, 85–117.
Bergen, B. K. and Chang, N. (2005). Embodied construction grammar in simulation-based language understanding. In J. O. Östman and M. Fried, eds., *Construction Grammar(s): Cognitive and Cross-Language Dimensions*. Amsterdam: John Benjamins, pp. 147–90.
Bergen, B. K. & Chang, N. (2013). Embodied Construction Grammar. In T. Hoffmann and G. Trousdale, eds., *The Oxford Handbook of Construction Grammar*. Oxford: Oxford University Press, pp. 168–90.
Bergs, A. (2008). Can we take Construction Grammar beyond sneezing napkins off tables? In K. Stierstorfer, ed., *Anglistentag 2007 in Münster: Proceedings*. Trier: Wissenschaft Verlag Trier, pp. 269–76.
Bergs, A. (2016). Response to Traugott. *Constructions and Frames*, 8(1), 126–30.
Bisang, W. (1998). Grammaticalization and language contact: Constructions and positions. In A. Giacalone Ramat and P. Hopper, eds., *The Limits of Grammaticalization*. Amsterdam: John Benjamins, pp. 13–58.
Bisang, W. (2011). Grammaticalization and linguistic theory. In H. Narrog and B. Heine, eds., *The Oxford Handbook of Grammaticalization*. Oxford: Oxford University Press, pp. 105–17.
Bloomfield, L. (1933). *Language*. New York: Henry Hold & Co.
Boas, H. C. (2003). *A Constructional Approach to Resultatives*. Stanford, CA: Center for the Study of Language and Information.
Boas, H. C. (2008a). Determining the structure of lexical entries and grammatical constructions in Construction Grammar. *Annual Review of Cognitive Linguistics*, 6, 113–44.
Boas, H. C. (2008b). Towards a frame-constructional approach to verb classification. *Revista Canaria de Estudios Ingleses*, 57, 17–48.
Boas, Hans, C. (2021) Construction Grammar and Frame Semantics. In X. Wen and J. R. Taylor, eds., *Routledge Handbook of Cognitive Linguistics*. New York/London: Routledge, pp. 43–77.
Boas, H. C. & Sag, I. A., eds. (2012). *Sign-Based Construction Grammar*. Stanford, CA: Center for the Study of Language and Information.
Bolinger, D. (1967). Adjectives in English: Attribution and predication. *Lingua*, 18, 1–34.
Bolinger, D. (1972). *Degree Words*. The Hague: Mouton.
Börjars, K., Vincent, N., and Walken, G. (2015). On constructing a theory of grammatical change. *Transactions of the Philological Society*, 113(3), 363–82.

Bouchard, D. (2002). *Adjectives, Number and Interfaces: Why Languages Vary*. Amsterdam/Boston/London: Elsevier.

Boye, K. and Harder, P. (2012). A usage-based theory of grammatical status and grammaticalization. *Language*, 88(1), 1–44.

Breban, T. (2010). *English Adjectives of Comparison: Lexical and Grammaticalized Uses*. Berlin/Boston: Mouton de Gruyter.

Breban, T. and Davidse, K. (2016). A functional-cognitive analysis of the order of adjectival modifiers in the English NP. Paper presented at Deutsche Gesellschaft für Sprachwissenschaft (DGfS) Conference, Konstanz, February 24–26, 2016.

Brems, L. (2003). Measure noun constructions: An instance of semantically-driven grammaticalization. *International Journal of Corpus Linguistics*, 8(2), 283–312.

Brems, L. (2004). Measure noun constructions: Degrees of delexicalization and grammaticalization. In K. Aijmer and B. Altenberg, eds., *Advances in Corpus Linguistics: Papers from the 23rd International Conference on English Language Research on Computerized Corpora (ICAME 23)*. Amsterdam: Rodopi, pp. 249–65.

Brems, L. (2007). The grammaticalization of small size nouns: Reconsidering frequency and analogy. *Journal of English Linguistics*, 35, 293–324.

Brems, L. (2010). Size noun constructions as collocationally constrained constructions: Lexical and grammaticalized uses. *English Language and Linguistics*, 14(1), 83–109.

Brems, L. (2011). *Layering of Size and Type Noun Constructions in English*. Berlin/Boston: Mouton de Gruyter.

Brems, L. (2012). The establishment of quantifier constructions for size nouns: A diachronic case study of heap(s) and lot(s). *Journal of Historical Pragmatics*, 13 (2), 202–31.

Brems, L. and Davidse, K. (2010). The grammaticalisation of nominal type noun constructions with *kind/sort of*: Chronology and paths of change. *English Studies*, 91, 180–202.

Brinton, L. J. & Traugott, E. C. (2005). *Lexicalization and Language Change*. Cambridge: Cambridge University Press.

Brugman, C. (1981). The story of 'over.' MA thesis, University of California, Berkeley.

Brugman, C. and Lakoff, G. (1988). Cognitive topology and lexical networks. In S. L. Small, G. W. Cottrell, and M. K. Tanenhaus, eds., *Lexical Ambiguity Resolution: Perspectives from Psycholinguistics, Neuropsychology, and Artificial Intelligence*. San Mateo: Morgan Kaufmann, pp. 477–508.

Bucholtz, M., Bermudez, N., Fung, V., Edwards, L., and Vargas, R. (2007). Hella nor cal or totally so cal? The perceptual dialectology of California. *Journal of English Linguistics*, 35, 325–52.

Budts, S. and Petré, P. (2020) Putting connections centre stage in diachronic Construction Grammar. In L. Sommerer and E. Smirnova, eds., *Nodes and Networks in Diachronic Construction Grammar*. Amsterdam: John Benjamins, pp. 318–51.

Butler, C. S. (2008). Interpersonal meaning in the noun phrase. In J. Rijkhoff and D. García Velasco, eds., *The Noun Phrase in Functional Discourse Grammar*. Berlin/Boston: Mouton de Gruyter, pp. 221–62.

Butler, C. S. (2009). The lexical constructional model: Genesis, strengths and challenges. In C. S. Butler and J. Martín Arista, eds., *Deconstructing Constructions*. Amsterdam: John Benjamins, pp. 117–52.

Butler, C. S. and Gonzálvez-García, F. (2005). Situation FDG in functional-cognitive space: An initial study. In L. J. Mackenzie and M. Gómez-González, eds., *Studies in Functional Discourse Grammar*. Bern: Peter Lang, pp. 109–58.

Butler, C. S. and Gonzálvez-García, F. (2014). *Exploring Functional-Cognitive Space*. Amsterdam: John Benjamins.

Bybee, J. L. (2010). *Language, Usage, and Cognition*. Cambridge: Cambridge University Press.

Cali Abokor, A. (1987). *The Camel in Somali Oral Traditions*. Trans. Axmed Arten Xange. Motala: Motala Grafiska.

Capelle, B. (2006). Particle placement and the case for "allostructions." *Constructions Special*, 1, 1–26.

Cave, D. (2007). *Four Trails to Valor: From Ancient Footprints to Modern Battlefields, a Journey of Four Peoples*. Santa Fe, NM: Sunstone Press.

Chesterman, A. (1991). *On Definiteness: A Study with Special Reference to English and Finish*. Cambridge: Cambridge University Press.

Cinque, G. (1994). On the evidence for partial N movement in the Romance DP. In G. Cinque, J. Koster, J.-Y. Pollock, L. Rizzi, and R. Zanuttini, eds., *Paths Towards a Universal Grammar*. Georgetown: Georgetown University, pp.85–110.

Cinque, G. (2010). *The Syntax of Adjectives: A Comparative Study*. Cambridge, MA: MIT Press.

Cinque, G. (2014). The semantic classification of adjectives: A view from syntax. *Studies in Chinese Linguistics*, 35(1), 1–30.

Colleman, T. (2011). Ditransitive verbs and the ditransitive construction: A diachronic perspective. *Zeitschrift für Anglistik und Amerikanistik*, 59(4), 387–410.

Corver, N. (1998). Predicative movement in pseudo partitive constructions. In A. Alexiadou and C. Wilder, eds., *Possessors, Predicates and Movement in the Determiner Phrase*. Amsterdam: John Benjamins, pp. 215–58.

Creesy, C. (ed.) (1986). *Princeton Alumni Weekly*. Princeton: Princeton University Press, September 30.

Croft, W. (2001). *Radical Construction Grammar: Syntactic Theory in Typological Perspective*. Oxford: Oxford University Press.

Croft, W. (2013). Radical Construction Grammar. In T. Hoffmann and G. Trousdale, eds., *The Oxford Handbook of Construction Grammar*. Oxford: Oxford University Press, pp. 211–32.

Croft, W. and Cruse, D. A. (2004). *Cognitive Linguistics*. Cambridge: Cambridge University Press.

Curme, G. O. (1914). The development of the analytic genitive in Germanic, Part II. *Modern Philology*, 11(3), 289–313.
Curme, G. O. (1931). *A Grammar of the English Language*, Vol. III: *Syntax*. Boston, MA: Heath and Co.
Davidse, K. (2009). *Complete* and *sort of*: From identifying to intensifying? *Transactions of the Philological Society*, 107(3), 262–92.
Davidse, K. and Breban, T. (2019). A cognitive-functional approach to the order of adjectives in the English noun phrase. *Linguistics*, 57(2), 327–71.
Davidse, K., Brems, L., and De Smedt, L. (2008). Type noun uses in the English NP: A case of right to left layering. *International Journal of Corpus Linguistics*, 13 (2), 139–68.
Davidse, K. and Ghesquière, L. (2016). Content-purport, content-substance and structure: Focusing *mere* and *me rely*. *Acta Linguistica Hafniensia*, 48(1), 85–109.
Davies, M. (2010–). *Corpus of News on the Web* (NOW). http://corpus.byu.edu/now/.
Davies, M. (2018). *iWeb Corpus: 14 Billion Words, 1990–2015*. http://corpus.byu.edu/iweb.
De Clerck, B. and Colleman, T. (2013). From noun to intensifier: *Massa* and *massa*'s in Flemish varieties of Dutch. *Language Sciences*, 36, 147–60.
De Smet, H. (2009). Analyzing reanalysis. *Lingua*, 119, 1728–55.
Deacon, T. W. (1997). *The Symbolic Species: The Co-Evolution of Language and the Brain*. New York: Norton.
Deacon, T. W. (2003). Universal grammar and semiotic constraints. In M. H. Christiansen and S. Kirby, eds., *Language Evolution*. Oxford: Oxford University Press, pp. 111–39.
Den Dikken, M. (1998). Predicate inversion in the DP. In A. Alexiadou and C. Wilder, eds., *Possessors, Predicates and Movement in the Determiner Phrase*. Amsterdam: John Benjamins, pp. 215–58.
Den Dikken, M. (2006). *Relators and Linkers: The Syntax of Predication, Predicate Inversion and Copulas*. Cambridge, MA: MIT Press.
Denison, D. (2002). History of the *sort of* construction family. Paper presented at the Second International Conference on Construction Grammar, Helsinki. 7 September 2002.
Denison, D. (2005). The grammaticalisations of *sort of*, *kind of*, and *type of* in English. Paper presented at New Reflections on Grammaticalization 3, University of Santiago de Compostela, July 17–20, 2005.
Denison, D. (2011). The construction of SKT. Second Vigo-Newcastle-Santiago-Leuven International Workshop on the Structure of the Noun Phrase in English (NP2), Newcastle upon Tyne, September 15–16, 2011.
Dewell, R. B. (1994). Over again: Image-schema transformations in semantic analysis. *Cognitive Linguistics*, 5(4), 351–80.
Diessel, H. (2011). Review of *Language, Usage and Cognition* by Joan Bybee. *Language*, 87(4), 830–44.

Diessel, H. (2015). Usage-Based Construction Grammar. In E. Dąbrowska and D. Divjak, eds., *The Cognitive Linguistic Handbook*. Berlin: Walter de Gruyter, pp. 296–321.
Diessel, H. (2019). *The Grammar Network: How Linguistic Structure Is Shaped by Language Use*. Cambridge: Cambridge University Press.
Diewald, G. (1999). *Die Modalverben im Deutschen: Grammatikalisierung und Polyfunktionalität*. Tübingen: Niemeyer.
Diewald, G. (2011). Grammaticalization and pragmaticalization. In B. Heine and H. Narrog, eds., *Oxford Handbook of Grammaticalization*. Oxford: Oxford University Press, pp. 450–61.
Diewald, G. (2015). Review of Traugott, Elizabeth Closs; Trousdale, Graeme. 2013. *Constructionalization and Constructional Changes*. Oxford: Oxford University Press. *Beiträge zur Geschichte der deutschen Sprache und Literatur*, 137, 108–21.
Dik, S. C. (1978). *Functional Grammar*. Amsterdam: North-Holland Linguistic Series.
Dik, S. C. (1980). *Studies in Functional Grammar*. London: Academic Press.
Dik, S. C. (1989). *The Theory of Functional Grammar*. Dordrecht: Foris Publications.
Dik, S. C. (1997a). *The Theory of Functional Grammar, Part I: The Structure of the Clause*, 2nd ed., ed. K. Hengeveld. Berlin: Mouton de Gruyter.
Dik, S. C. (1997b). *The Theory of Functional Grammar, Part II: Complex and Derived Constructions*, ed. K. Hengeveld. Berlin: Mouton de Gruyter.
Divjak, D. (2019). *Frequency in Language: Memory, Attention and Learning*. Cambridge: Cambridge University Press.
Dixon, R. M. W. (1982). *Where Have All the Adjectives Gone?* Berlin: Mouton de Gruyter.
Dixon, R. M. W. (2010). *Basic Linguistic Theory*, Vol. II. Oxford: Oxford University Press.
Dobrovie-Sorin, C. and Beyssade, C. (2012). *Redefining Indefinites*. Heidelberg: Springer.
Doetjes, J. and Rooryck, J. (2003). Generalizing over quantitative and qualitative constructions. In M. Coene and Y. D'hulst, eds., *From NP to DP: The Syntax and Semantics of Noun Phrases*, Vol. I. Amsterdam: John Benjamins, 277–96.
Ellis, N. C., Römer, U., and O'Donnell, M. B. (2016). *Usage-Based Approaches to Language Acquisition and Processing: Cognitive and Corpus Investigations of Construction Grammar*. Malden, MA: Wiley-Blackwell.
Evans, V. and Green, M. C. (2006). *Cognitive Linguistics: An Introduction*. Edinburgh: Edinburgh University Press.
Evans, N. and Wilkins, D. (1998). *The Knowing Ear: An Australian Test of Universal Claims about the Semantic Structure of Sensory Verbs and Their Extension into the Domain of Cognition*. Cologne: Institut für Sprachwissenschaft.
Everaert, M. (1992). Nogmaals: "Een schat van een kind." In H. Bennis and J. W. de Vries, eds., *De binnenbouw van het Nederlands: Een bundel artikelen voor Piet Paardekooper*. Dordrecht: Foris, pp. 45–54.

Feist, J. (2009). Premodifier order in English nominal phrases: A semantic account. *Cognitive Linguistics*, 20(2), 301–40.
Feist, J. (2012). *Premodifiers in English: Their Structure and Significance*. Cambridge: Cambridge University Press.
Ferris, C. (1993). *The Meaning of Syntax: A Study in the Adjectives of English*. London: Longman.
Fischer, O. (2000). Grammaticalisation: Unidirectional, non-reversable? The case of *to* before the infinitive in English. In O. Fischer, A. Rosenbach, and D. Stein, eds., *Pathways of Change: Grammaticalization in English* [Studies in Language Companion Series 53]. Amsterdam/Philadelphia: John Benjamins, pp. 149–69.
Fischer, O. (2007). *Morphosyntactic Change: Functional and Formal Perspectives*. Oxford: Oxford University Press.
Fischer, O. (2008). On analogy as the motivation for grammaticalization. *Studies in Language*, 32(2), 336–82.
Fischer, O. (2011). Grammaticalization as analogically driven change? In H. Narrog and B. Heine, eds., *The Oxford Handbook of Grammaticalization*. Oxford: Oxford University Press, pp. 105–17.
Foolen, A. (2004). Expressive binominal NPs in Germanic and Romance languages. In G. Radden and K. U. Panther, eds., *Studies in Linguistic Motivation*. Berlin: Mouton de Gruyter, pp. 75–100.
Fried, M. (2010). Grammaticalization and lexicalization effects in participial morphology: A Construction Grammar approach to language change. In A. Van Linden, K. Davidse, and J.-C. Verstraete, eds., *Grammaticalization and Grammar*. Amsterdam: John Benjamins, pp.191–224.
Fried, M. and Östman, J. O. (2005). Construction Grammar and spoken language: The case of pragmatic particles. *Journal of Pragmatics*, 37(11), 1752–78.
Gallagher, L. (2009). S*nowboarding: Learning to Ride from All-Mountain to Park and Pipe*. Seattle, WA: The Mountaineers Books.
García Velasco, D. (2013). Degree words in English: A Functional Discourse Grammar account. *Revista Canaria de Estudios Ingleses*, 67, 79–96.
García Velasco, D. and Hengeveld, K. (2002). Do we need predicate frames? In R. Mairal and Q. Pérez, eds., *New Perspectives on Argument Structure*. Berlin/Boston: Mouton de Gruyter, pp. 95–123.
Genee, I., Keizer, E., and García Velasco, D. (2016). The lexicon in Functional Discourse Grammar. *Linguistics*, 54(5), 887–906.
Ghesquière, L. (2009). From determining to emphasizing meanings: The adjectives of specificity. *Folia Linguistica*, 43(2), 311–43.
Ghesquière, L. (2014). *The Directionality of (Inter)Subjectification in the English Noun Phrase*. Berlin/Boston: Mouton de Gruyter.
Ghesquiere, L. (2017). Intensification and focusing: The case of "pure(ly)" and "mere(ly)." In M. Napoli and M. Ravetto, eds., *Exploring Intensification: Synchronic, Diachronic and Cross-linguistic Perspectives*. Amsterdam: John Benjamins, pp. 33–53.

Ghesquière, L. and Davidse, K. (2011). The development of intensification scales in noun-intensifying usages of adjectives: Sources, paths and mechanisms of change. *English Language and Linguistics*, 15(2), 251–77.
Giacalone Ramat, A. (1998). Testing the boundaries of grammaticalization. In A. Giacalone Ramat and P. Hopper, eds., *The Limits of Grammaticalization*. Amsterdam: John Benjamins, pp. 107–27.
Giegerich, H. J. (2004). Compound or phrase? English noun-plus-noun constructions and the stress criterion. *English Language and Linguistics*, 8, 1–24.
Giegerich, H. J. (2005). Associative adjectives in English and the lexicon–syntax interface. *Journal of Linguistics*, 41(3), 571–91.
Giegerich, H. J. (2009). The English compound stress myth. *Word Structure*, 2 (1), 1–17.
Giomi, R. (2017). The interaction of components in a Functional Discourse Grammar account of grammaticalization. In K. Hengeveld, H. Narrog, and H. Olbertz, eds., *The Grammaticalization of Tense, Aspect, Modality and Evidentiality: A Functional Perspective*. Berlin/Boston: De Gruyter Mouton, pp. 39–74.
Giomi, R. (2020). Shifting structures, contexts and meanings: A Functional Discourse Grammar account of grammaticalization. Ph.D. dissertation, University of Lisbon.
Gisborne, N. and Patten, A. (2011). Grammaticalization and Construction Grammar. In H. Narrog and B. Heine, eds., *The Oxford Handbook of Grammaticalization*. Oxford: Oxford University Press, pp. 92–104.
Givón, T. (1984). *Syntax*, Vol. I. Amsterdam: John Benjamins.
Givón, T. (1993). *English Grammar: A Function-Based Introduction*, Vol. I. Amsterdam: John Benjamins.
Goldberg, A. E. (1995). *Constructions: A Construction Grammar Approach to Argument Structure*. Chicago: University of Chicago Press.
Goldberg, A. E. (2003). Constructions: A new theoretical approach to language. *Trends in Cognitive Sciences*, 7(5), 210–24.
Goldberg, A. E. (2006). *Constructions at Work: The Nature of Generalization in Language*. Oxford: Oxford University Press.
Goldberg, A. E. (2009a). The nature of generalization in language. *Cognitive Linguistics*, 20(1), 93–127.
Goldberg, A. E. (2009b). Constructions at work. *Cognitive Linguistics*, 20(1), 201–24.
Goldberg, A. E. (2013). Constructionist approaches. In T. Hoffmann and G. Trousdale, eds., *The Oxford Handbook of Construction Grammar*. Oxford: Oxford University Press, pp. 15–31.
Goldberg, A. E. (2019). *Explain Me This: Creativity, Competition, and the Partial Productivity of Constructions*. Princeton, NJ: Princeton University Press.
Gonzálvez-García, F. and Butler, C. S. (2006). Mapping functional-cognitive space. *Annual Review of Cognitive Linguistics*, 4, 39–96.

Grady, J., Oakley, T. and Coulson, S. (1999). Blending and metaphor. In G. J. Steen and R. W. Gibbs, eds., *Metaphor in Cognitive Linguistics: Selected Papers from the Fifth International Cognitive Linguistics Conference, Amsterdam, 1997*. Amsterdam: John Benjamins, pp. 101–24.

Grestenberger, L. (2013). Number marking in German measure phrases and the structure of pseudo-partitives. *The Journal of Comparative Germanic Linguistics*, 18(2), 93–138.

Gries, S. (2009). *Statistics for Linguistics with R: A Practical Introduction*. Berlin/Boston: Mouton de Gruyter.

Guisti, G. (1991). The categorical status of quantified nominals. *Linguistische Berichte*, 136, 439–52.

Guisti, G. (1997). The categorial status of determiners. In L. Haegeman (ed.), *The New Comparative Syntax*. London: Longman, pp. 95–124.

Gunkel, L. and Zifonun, G. (2009). Classifying modifiers in common names. *Word Structure*, 2(2), 205–18.

Haas, F. (2007). The development of English *each other*: Grammaticalization, lexicalization, or both? *English Language and Linguistics*, 1(1), 31–50.

Halliday, M. A. K. (1985). *An Introduction to Functional Grammar*. London: Edward Arnold.

Halliday, M. A. K. (1994). *An Introduction to Functional Grammar*, 2nd ed. London: Edward Arnold.

Halliday, M. A. K. and Matthiessen, C. (2014). *An Introduction to Functional Grammar*, 4th ed. London: Routledge.

Harder, P. and Boye, K. (2011). Grammaticalization and functional linguistics. In H. Narrog and B. Heine, eds., *The Oxford Handbook of Grammaticalization*. Oxford: Oxford University Press, pp. 56–68.

Haspelmath, M. (1998). Does grammaticalization need reanalysis? *Studies in Language*, 22, 315–51.

Hay, J. (2002). From speech perception to morphology: Affix ordering revisited. *Language*, 78(3), 527–55.

Heine, B. (1997b). Grammaticalization theory and its relevance to African linguistics. In R. K. Herbert, ed., *African Linguistics at the Crossroads: Papers from Kwaluseni*. Cologne: Köppe, pp. 1–15.

Heine, B. (2002). On the role of context in grammaticalization. In I. Wischer and G. Diewald, eds., *New Reflections on Grammaticalization*. Amsterdam: John Benjamins, pp. 83–101.

Heine, B. (2003). Grammaticalization. In R. D. Janda and B. D. Joseph, eds., *The Handbook of Historical Linguistics*. Oxford: Blackwell, pp. 573–601.

Heine, B. and Kuteva, T. (2002). On the evolution of grammatical forms. In A. Wray, ed., *The Transition to Language*. Oxford: Oxford University Press, pp. 376–97.

Heine, B. and Narrog, H. (2010). Grammaticalization and linguistic analysis. In B. Heine and H. Narrog, eds., *The Oxford Handbook of Linguistic Analysis*. Oxford: Oxford University Press, pp. 401–23.

Hengeveld, K. (2017). A hierarchical approach to grammaticalization. In K. Hengeveld, H. Narrog, and H. Olbertz, eds., *The Grammaticalization of Tense, Aspect, Modality, and Evidentiality: A Functional Perspective*. Berlin: De Gruyter Mouton, pp. 13–38.

Hengeveld, K. and Mackenzie, J. L. (2008). *Functional Discourse Grammar: A Typologically-Based Theory of Language Structure*. Oxford: Oxford University.

Hengeveld, K. and Mackenzie, J. L. (2016). Reflections on the lexicon in Functional Discourse Grammar. *Linguistics*, 54(5), 1135–61.

Hengeveld, K., Narrog, H., and Olbertz, H. (2017). A functional perspective on the grammaticalization of tense, aspect, modality, and evidentiality. In K. Hengeveld, H. Narrog, and H. Olbertz, eds., *The Grammaticalization of Tense, Aspect, Modality, and Evidentiality: A Functional Perspective*. Berlin: De Gruyter Mouton, pp. 1–12.

Hetzron, R. (1978). On the relative order of adjectives. In H. Seiler, ed., *Language Universals: Papers from the Conference Held at Gummersbach/Cologne, Germany, October 3–8, 1976*. Tübingen: Gunter Narr, pp. 165–84.

Hilpert, M. (2013). *Constructional Change in English: Developments in Allomorphy, Word Formation and Syntax*. Cambridge: Cambridge University Press.

Hilpert, M. (2014). *Construction Grammar and Its Application to English*. Edinburgh: Edinburgh University.

Hilpert, M. (2018). Three open questions in Diachronic Construction Grammar. In P. Andersson & E. Coussé, eds., *Grammaticalization Meets Construction Grammar*. Amsterdam: John Benjamins, pp. 21–39.

Hilpert, M. (2021). Lecture 3: Three open questions in Diachronic Construction Grammar. In *Ten Lectures on Diachronic Construction Grammar*. Leiden: Brill.

Himmelmann, N. P. (2004). Lexicalization and grammaticalization: Opposite or orthogonal? In W. Bisang, N. P. Himmelmann, and B. Wiemer, eds., *What Makes Grammaticalization? A Look from Its Fringes and Its Components*. Berlin/Boston: Mouton de Gruyter, pp. 21–42.

Hoffmann, T. (2004). Are low-frequency complex prepositions grammaticalized? On the limits of corpus data – and the importance of intuition. In H. Lindquist and C. Mair, eds., *Corpus Approaches to Grammaticalization in English*. Amsterdam: John Benjamins, pp. 171–210.

Hoffmann, T. and Trousdale, G. (2013). Construction Grammar introduction. In T. Hoffmann and G. Trousdale, eds., *The Oxford Handbook of Construction Grammar*. Oxford: Oxford University Press, pp. 1–14.

Honselaar, W. and Olbertz, H. (2016). The use of *moeten* without an infinitive: A case of degrammaticalization?. In A. Bannink and W. Honselaar, eds., *From Variation to Iconicity: Festschrift for Olga Fischer on the Occasion of Her 65th Birthday*. Amsterdam: Uitgeverij Pegasus, pp. 185–201.

Hopper, P. (1991). On some principles of grammaticalization. In E. C. Traugott and B. Heine, eds., *Approaches to Grammaticalization*. Amsterdam: John Benjamins, pp. 17–35.

Hopper, P. and Traugott, E. C. [1993] (2003). *Grammaticalization*, 2nd ed. Cambridge: Cambridge University Press.

Hudson, R. A. (1984). *Word Grammar*. Oxford: Blackwell.
Hudson, R. A. (2007). *Language Networks: The New Word Grammar*. Oxford: Oxford University.
Hudson, R. A. (2008). Word grammar and Construction Grammar. In G. Trousdale and N. Gisborne, eds., *Constructional Approaches to English Grammar*. Berlin/Boston: Mouton de Gruyter, pp. 257–302.
Hudson, R. A. (2017). Pied-piping in cognition. *Journal of Linguistics*. Online ed. www.cambridge.org/core/journals/journal-of-linguistics/article/piedpiping-in-cognition-1/FAFC2CCF34F7DE3B4C2B797498C6096D (June 19, 2017).
Iannuzzi, J. N. (2008). *Condemned*. Xlibris.
Jackendoff, R. (1977). *X-syntax: A Study of Phrase Structure*. Cambridge, MA: MIT Press.
Jackendoff, R. (1991). Parts and boundaries. *Cognition*, 41, 9–45.
Jackendoff, R. (1997). *The Architecture of the Language Faculty*. Cambridge, MA: MIT Press.
Jackendoff, R. (2002). *Foundations of Language: Brain, Meaning, Grammar, Evolution*. Oxford: Oxford University Press.
Jensen, B. and Chalkley, T. (2021). *A History Lover's Guide to Baltimore*. Charleston, SC: The History Press.
Jespersen, O. (1924). *The Philosophy of Grammar*. London: Allen and Unwin.
Jurafsky, D. (1992). An on-line computation model of human sentence interpretation: A theory of the representation and the use of linguistic knowledge. Ph.D. dissertation, University of California, Berkeley.
Kamp, H. and Partee, B. (1995). Prototype Theory and compositionality. *Cognition*, 57(2), 212–191.
Kay, P. (1990). Even. *Linguistics and Philosophy*, 13(1), 59–111.
Kayne, R. S. (1994). *The Antisymmetry of Syntax*. Cambridge, MA: MIT Press.
Keizer, E. (2004). Postnominal PP complements and modifiers: A cognitive distinction. *English Language and Linguistics*, 8(2), 323–50.
Keizer, E. (2005). What to do with those fools of a crew? In H. Broekhuis, N. Corver, R. Huybregts, U. Kleinhenz, and J. Koster, eds., *Organizing Grammar: Linguistic Studies in Honor of Henk van Riemskijk*. Berlin/Boston: Mouton de Gruyter, pp. 300–9.
Keizer, E. (2007a). *The English Noun Phrase: The Nature of Linguistic Categorization*. Cambridge: Cambridge University Press.
Keizer, E. (2007b). The lexical-grammatical dichotomy in Functional Discourse Grammar. *ALFA: Revista de Linguística*, 51(2), 35–56.
Keizer, E. (2011). English preforms: An alternative account. *English Language and Linguistics*, 15(2), 303–34.
Keizer, E. (2015). *A Functional Discourse Grammar for English*. Oxford: Oxford University Press.
Keizer, E. (2016). Idiomatic expressions in Functional Discourse Grammar. *Linguistics*, 54(5), 981–1016.
Keizer, E. (2017). English partitives in Functional Discourse Grammar: Types and constraints. *Glossa: A Journal of General Linguistics*, 2(1), 1–40.

Keizer, E. (2020). Noun phrases. In B. Aarts, J. Bowie, and G. Popova, eds., *The Oxford Handbook of English Grammar*. Oxford: Oxford University Press, pp. 335–57.

Keizer, E. and ten Wolde, E. (forthcoming). Of birds of prey and men of honour: head-classifier constructions in English. In L. Gardelle, E. Mignot, and J. Neveux, eds., *Nouns and the Morphosyntax/Semantics Interface*. Palgrave Macmillan.

Keizer, E. and Van Staden, M. (2009). Introduction. *Linguistics*, 47(4), 799–824.

Kendall, B. J. et al. (1880). *A Treatise on the Horse and His Diseases*. Claremont, NH: Claremont Manufacturing Co.

Kennedy, C. and McNally, L. (2005). Scale structure and the semantic typology of gradable predicates. *Language*, 81, 345–81.

Kim, J. B. and Sells, P. (2015). English binominal NPs: A construction-based perspective. *Journal of Linguistics*, 51, 41–73.

Kiparsky, P. (2012). Grammaticalization as optimization. In D. Jonas and J. Whitman, eds., *Grammatical Change: Origins, Nature, Outcomes*. Oxford: Oxford University Press, pp. 15–52.

Knopp, L. (2012). *What the River Carries: Encounters with the Mississippi, Missouri, and Platte*. Columbia/London: University of Missouri Press.

König, E. (1991). *The Meaning of Focus Particles: A Comparative Perspective*. London: Routledge.

Kreitzer, A. (1997). Multiple levels of schematization: A study in the conceptualization of space. *Cognitive Linguistics*, 8(4), 291–325.

Kruisinga, E. (1932). *A Handbook of Present-Day English Part II: English Accidence and Syntax 2*, 5th ed. Groningen: Noordhoff.

Laenzlinger, C. (2005). French adjective ordering: Perspectives on DP-internal movement types. *Lingua*, 115, 645–89.

Lakoff, G. (1987). *Women, Fire and Dangerous Things: What Categories Reveal about the Mind*. Chicago: Chicago University Press.

Langacker, R. W. (1987). *Foundations of Cognitive Grammar*, Vol. I: *Theoretical prerequisites*. Stanford, CA: Stanford University Press.

Langacker, R. W. (1990). Subjectification. *Cognitive Linguistics*, 1, 5–38.

Langacker, R. W. (1991). *Foundations of Cognitive Grammar*, Vol. II: *Descriptive Application*. Stanford, CA: Stanford University Press.

Langacker, R. W. (1999). *Grammar and Conceptualization*. Berlin/Boston: Mouton de Gruyter.

Langacker, R. W. (2002). *Concept, Imagine, and Symbol: The Cognitive Basis of Grammar*, 2nd ed. Berlin/Boston: Mouton de Gruyter.

Langacker, R. W. (2010). A lot of quantifiers. In S. Rice and J. Newman, eds., *Empirical and Experimental Methods in Cognitive/Functional Research*. Stanford, CA: Center for the Study of Language and Information.

Larson, R. K. (1999). Semantics of adjectival modification. Lectures presented at the Dutch National Graduate School (LOT), Amsterdam. http://semlab5.sbs.sunysb.edu/~rlarson/LOT(99)/Contents.htmld/index.html (June 19, 2017).

Lehmann, C. [1982] (2002). *Thoughts on Grammaticalization*. 2nd ed. Erfurt: Seminar für Sprachwissenschaft der Universität.
Lehmann, C. (2020). Univerbation. *Folia Linguistica Historica*, 41, 205–52.
Lehrer, A. (1986). English classifier constructions. *Lingua*, 68(2–3), 109–48.
Levelt, W. J. M. (1989). *Speaking*. Cambridge, MA: MIT Press.
Leys, O. (1997). 'Ein Engel von (einer) Frau'. Emtionalität als konstruktionale Bedeutung. *Leuvense Bijdragen*, 86, 27–52.
Lieberman, M. and Sproat, R. (1992). The stress and structure of modified noun phrases in English. In I. A. Sag and A. Szabolcsi, eds., *Lexical Matters*. Stanford, CA: Center for the Study of Language and Information, pp. 131–82.
Lightfoot, D. (2011). Grammaticalization and pragmaticalization. In H. Narrog and B. Heine, eds., *The Oxford Handbook of Grammaticalization*. Oxford: Oxford University Press, pp. 438–49.
Löbel, E. (1989). Q as a functional category. In C. Schmidt, E. Löbe,l and C. Bhatt, eds., *Syntactic Phrase Structure Phenomena in Noun Phrases and Sentences*. Amsterdam: John Benjamins, pp. 133–58.
Löbel, E. (2001). Classifiers and semi-lexicality: Functional and semantic selection. In N. Corver and H. Riemsdijk, eds., *Semi-lexical Categories: The Function of Content Words and the Content of Function Words*. Berlin/Boston: Mouton de Gruyter, pp. 221–71.
Lorenz, G. (2002). Really worthwhile or not really significant? A corpus-based approach to the delexicalization and grammaticalization of intensifiers in modern English. In I. Wischer and G. Diewald, eds., *New Reflections on Grammaticalization*. Amsterdam: John Benjamins, pp. 143–61.
Lundskær-Nielsen, T. (1993). *Prepositions in Old and Middle English: A Study of Prepositional Syntax and the Semantics of* At, In *and* On *in some Old and Middle English Texts*. Odense: Odense University Press.
Lyons, J. (1977). *Semantics*, Vol. II. Cambridge: Cambridge University Press.
Maiorana, S. and Pitoniak, S. (2005). Slices of Orange: Great Games and Performers in Syracuse University Sports History. Syracuse, NY: Syracuse University Press.
Margerie, H. (2011). Grammaticalising constructions: To death as a peripheral degree modifier. *Folia Linguistica Historica*, 45(32), 115–47.
Masini, F. (2016). Binominal constructions in Italian of the N1-di-N2 type: Towards a typology of Light Noun Constructions. *Language Sciences*, 53, 99–113.
Matthews, P. H. (2014). *The Positions of Adjectives in English*. Oxford: Oxford University Press.
McCawley, J. D. (1987). A case of syntactic mimicry. In R. Dirven and V. Fried, eds., *Functionalism in Linguistics*. Amsterdam: John Benjamins, 459–70.
McCawley, J. D. (1988). *The Syntactic Phenomena of English*. 2 vols. Chicago: Chicago University Press.
McGregor, W. B. (1997). *Semiotic Grammar*. Oxford: Clarendon Press.

Michaelis, L. A. (2010). Sign-based Construction Grammar. In B. Heine and H. Narrog, eds., *The Oxford Handbook of Linguistic Analysis*. Oxford: Oxford University Press, pp. 139–58.

Michaelis, L. A. (2012). Making the case for Construction Grammar. In H. C. Boas and I. Sag, eds., *Sign-Based Construction Grammar*. Stanford, CA: Center for the Study of Language and Information, pp. 31–67.

Michaelis, L. A. (2013). Sign-based construction grammar. In T. Hoffmann and G. Trousdale, eds., *The Oxford Handbook of Construction Grammar*. Oxford: Oxford University Press, pp. 133–52.

Mortley, R. (1973). The theme of silence in Clement of Alexandria. *Journal of Theological Studies*, 24(1), 197–202.

Morzycki, M. (2016). *Modification*. Cambridge: Cambridge University Press.

Mustanoja, T. F. (2016). *A Middle English Syntax: Parts of Speech*. Amsterdam: John Benjamins.

Napoli, D. J. (1989). *Predication Theory: A Case Study for Indexing Theory*. Cambridge: Cambridge University.

Nevalainen, T. (1991). *But, Only, Just: Focusing Adverbial Change in Modern English 1500–1900*. Helsinki: Société Néophilologique.

Noël, D. (2007). Diachronic construction grammar and grammaticalization theory. *Functions of Language*, 14(2), 177–202.

Norde, M. (2009). *Degrammaticalization*. Oxford: Oxford University Press.

Norde, M., De Clerck, B. and Colleman, T. (2014). The emergence of non-canonical degree modifiers. In R. Boogaart, T. Colleman, and G. Rutten, eds., *Extending the Scope of Construction Grammar*. Berlin/Boston: Walter de Gruyter, pp. 207–50.

Nuyts, J. (2011). Pattern versus process concepts of grammar and mind: A cognitive-functional perspective. In M. Brdar, S. Th. Gries, and M. Fuchs, eds., *Cognitive Linguistics: Convergence and Expansion*. Amsterdam: John Benjamins, pp. 47–66.

Olbertz, H. (2016). Lexical auxiliaries in Spanish: How and why? *Linguistics*, 54(5), 947–79.

Olsen, S. (2000). Compounding and stress in English: A closer look at the boundary between morphology and syntax. *Linguistische Berichte*, 181, 55–69.

Paardekooper, P. C. (1956). Een schat van een kind. *De Nieuwe Taalgids*, 49, 93–9.

Paradis, C. (1997). *Degree Modifiers of Adjectives in Spoken British English*. Lund: Lund University Press.

Paradis, C. (2000). Reinforcing adjectives: A cognitive semantic perspective on grammaticalization. In R. Bermúdez, D. Denison, R. Hogg, and C. McCully, eds., *Generative Theory and Corpus Studies*, Berlin: Mouton de Gruyter, pp. 233–58.

Paradis, C. (2001). Adjectives and boundedness. *Cognitive Linguistics*, 12(1), 47–65.

Paradis, C. (2008). Configurations, construals and change: Expressions of DEGREE. *English Language and Linguistics*, 12(2), 317–43.

Partee, B. H. (2010). Privative adjectives: subsective plus coercion. In R. Bäuerle, U. Reyle, and T. E. Zimmermann, eds., *Presuppositions and Discourse: Essays Offered to Hans Kamp*. Cambridge, MA: Emerald Group, pp. 273–85.

Partington, A. (1993). Corpus evidence of language change: The case of the intensifier. In M. Baker, F. Tognini-Bonelli, and E. Tognini-Bonelli, eds., *Text and Technology: In Honour of John Sinclair*. Amsterdam: John Benjamins, pp. 177–92.

Payne, J. and Huddleston, R. (2002). Noun and noun phrases. In R. Huddleston and G. K. Pullum, eds., *The Cambridge Grammar of the English Language*. Cambridge: Cambridge University Press, pp. 323–524.

Payne, J., Pullum, G. K., Scholz, B. C., and Berlage, E. (2013). Anaphoric one and its implications. *Language*, 89(4), 794–829.

Pérez Quintero, M. J. (2013). Grammaticalization vs lexicalization: The Functional Discourse Grammar view. *Estudios Inglese*, 67, 97–122.

Pins, R. (2018). *How to Kill an Elephant: Eighteen Months to Save the Planet*. Bloomington, IN: AuthorHouse.

Plag, I. (2006). The variability of compound stress in English: Structural, semantic, and analogical factors. *English Language and Linguistics*, 10(1), 143–72.

Plag, I. (2010). Compound stress assignment by analogy: The constituent family bias. *Zeitschrift für Sprachwissenschaft*, 29(2), 243–82.

Plag, I., Kunter, G., and Lappe, S. (2007). Testing hypotheses about compound stress assignment in English: A corpus-based investigation. *Corpus Linguistics and Linguistic Theory*, 3(2), 199–232.

Plag, I., Kunter, G., Lappe, S., and Braun, M. (2008). The roles of semantics, argument structure, and lexicalization in compound stress assignment in English. *Language*, 84(4), 760–94.

Portero Muñoz, C. (2013). Adjective-Noun sequences at the crossroads between morphology and syntax: An FDG perspective. *Revista Canaria de Estudios Ingleses*, 67, 123–40.

Pustejovsky, J. (1995) *The Generative Lexicon*. Cambridge, MA: MIT Press.

Quirk, R., Greenbaum, S., Leech, G., and Svartvik, J. (1985). *A Comprehensive Grammar of the English Language*. London: Longman.

Radden, G. and Dirven, R. (2007). *Cognitive English Grammar*. Amsterdam: John Benjamins.

Radford, A. (1988). *Transformational Grammar: A First Course*. Cambridge: Cambridge University Press.

Ralli, A. and Stavrou, M. (1998). Morphology–syntax interface: A–N compounds vs A–N constructs in Modern Greek. In G. Booij and J. Van Marle, eds., *Yearbook of Morphology 1997*. Amsterdam: Springer, pp. 243–64.

Rijkhoff, J. (2002). *The Noun Phrase*. Oxford: Oxford University Press.

Rosenbach, A. (2002). *Genitive Variation in English: Conceptual Factors in Synchronic and Diachronic Studies*. Berlin: Mouton de Gruyter.

Rosenbach, A. (2014). English genitive Variation: The state of the art. *Genitive Variation in English*, 18(2), 215–62.

Ross, J. R. (1967). Constraints on variables in syntax. Ph.D. dissertation, Massachusetts Institute of Technology, Cambridge, MA.

Rothstein, S. (2011). Counting, measuring and the semantics of classifiers. *The Baltic International Yearbook of Cognition, Logic and Communication*, 6, 1–42.

Ruiz De Mendoza Ibáñez, F. J. and Mairal Usón, R. (2006). Levels of semantic representation: Where lexicon and grammar meet. *Interlingüística*, 17, 26–47.

Sag, I. A. (2001). Dimensions of natural language locality. Unpublished paper presented at the Eight Annual Conference on Head-Driven Phrase Structure Grammar, Norges Teknisk-Naturvitenskapelige Universitet, Trondheim, Norway.

Sag, I. A. (2012). Sign-based construction grammar: An informal synopsis. In H. C. Boas and I. Sag, eds., *Sign-Based Construction Grammar*. Stanford, CA: Center for the Study of Language and Information, pp. 69–202.

Saussure, Ferdinand de. 1959. *Course in General Linguistics*. London: McGraw-Hill.

Schlücker, B. and Plag, I. (2011). Compound or phrase? Analogy in naming. *Lingua: International Review of General Linguistics*, 121(9), 1539–51.

Schmid, H. (2020). *The Dynamics of the Linguistic System: Usage, Conventionalization and Entrenchment*. Oxford: Oxford University Press.

Schneider, C. J. (2011). Culture, rap music, "bitch," and the development of the censorship frame. *American Behavioral Scientist*, 55(1), 36–56.

Scontras, G., Degen, J., and Goodman, N. D. (2017). Subjectivity predicts adjective ordering preferences. *Open Mind*, 1(1), 53–66.

Scott, G. J. (1998). Stacked adjectival modification and the structure of nominal phrases. *SOAS Working Papers in Linguistics and Phonetics*, 8, 59–89.

Scott, G. J. (2002). Stacked adjectival modification and the structure of nominal phrases. In G. Cinque, ed., *Functional Structure in DP and IP*. Oxford: Oxford University Press, pp. 91–120.

Seiler, H. (1978). Determination: A functional dimension for interlanguage comparison. In H. Seiler, ed., *Language Universals: Papers from the Conference Held at Gummersbach/ Cologne, German, October 3–8, 1976*. Tübingen: Gunter Narr, pp. 301–28.

Selkirk, E. (1977). Some remarks on noun phrase structure. In P. W. Culicover, T. Wasow, and A. Akmajian, eds., *Formal Syntax*. New York: Academic Press, pp. 285–316.

Slobin, D. (1996). From "thought and language" to "thinking for speaking." In J. J. Gumpertz and S. Levinson, eds., *Rethinking Linguistic Relativity*. Cambridge: Cambridge University Press, pp. 70–96.

Smirnova, E. and Sommerer, L. (2020). Introduction: The nature of the noted and the network – Open questions in Diachronic Construction Grammar. In L. Sommerer and E. Smirnova, eds., *Nodes and Networks in Diachronic Construction Grammar*. Amsterdam: John Benjamins, pp. 1–44.

Sommerer, L. (2018). Article Emergence in Old English: A constructionalist approach. Berlin/Boston: Mouton de Gruyter.

Sommerer, L. (2020). Why we avoid the "Multiple Inheritance" issue in usage-based Cognitive Construction Grammar. *Belgian Journal of Linguistics*, 34, 320–31.

Sproat, R. and Shih, C. (1988). Prenominal adjective ordering in English and Mandarin. In J. Belvins and J. Carter, eds., *Proceedings of NELS 18*. Amherst, MA: Graduate Linguistics Student Association, University of Massachusetts, pp. 465–89.

Sproat, R. and Shih, C. (1991). The cross-linguistic distribution of adjective ordering restrictions. In C. Georgopoulos and R. Ishihara, eds., *Interdisciplinary Approaches to Language*. Dordrecht: Kluwer Academic Publishers, pp. 565–93.

Steels, L. (2011). Introducing Fluid Construction Grammar. In L. Steels, ed., *Design Patterns in Fluid Construction Grammar*. Amsterdam: John Benjamins, pp. 3–30.

Stemberger, J. R. and MacWhinney, B. (1988). Are inflected forms stored in the lexicon? In M. Hammond and M. Noonan, eds., *Theoretical Morphology*. New York: Academic Press, pp. 101–16.

Stirling, L. and Huddleston, R. (2002). Deixis and anaphora. In R. Huddleston and G. K. Pullum, eds., *The Cambridge Grammar of the English Language*. Cambridge: Cambridge University Press, pp. 1449–564.

Sweester, E. (1990). *From Etymology to Pragmatics: Metaphorical and Cultural Aspects of Semantic Structure*. Cambridge: Cambridge University Press.

Tayler, A. and Evans, V. (2003). *The Semantics of English Prepositions: Spatial Scenes, Embodied Meaning, and Cognition*. Cambridge: Cambridge University Press.

Taylor, J. R. (2004). The ecology of constructions. In G. Radden and K.–U. Panther, eds., *Studies in Linguistic Motivation*. Berlin/Boston: Mouton de Gruyter, pp. 49–73.

Ten Wolde, E. (2019). Linear vs. hierarchical: Two accounts of premodification in the *of*-binominal noun phrase. *Linguistics*, 57(2), 283–326.

Ten Wolde, E. and Keizer, E. (2016). Structure and substance in Functional Discourse Grammar: The case of the binominal noun phrase. *Acta Linguistica Hafniensia*, 48(1), 134–57.

Tomasello, M. (2003). *Constructing a Language: A Usage-Based Theory of Language Acquisition*. Cambridge, MA: Harvard University Press.

Torrent, T. T. (2015). On the relation between inheritance and change: The constructional convergence and the Construction Network Reconfiguration Hypotheses. In J. Barðdal, E. Smirnova, L. Sommerer, and S. Gildea, eds., *Diachronic Construction Grammar*. Amsterdam: John Benjamins, pp. 173–212.

Trask, R. L. (2000). *The Dictionary of Historical and Comparative Linguistics*. Edinburgh: Edinburgh University Press.

Traugott, E. C. (1982). From propositional to textual and expressive meanings: Some semantic-pragmatic aspects of grammaticalization. In W. P. Lehmann and Y. Malkiel, eds., *Perspectives on Historical Linguistics*. Amsterdam: John Benjamins, pp. 245–71.

Traugott, E. C. (1995). Subjectification in grammaticalisation. In S. M. Wright and D. Stein, eds., *Subjectivity and Subjectivisation: Linguistic Perspectives*. Cambridge: Cambridge University Press, pp. 31–54.
Traugott, E. C. (2003). Constructions in grammaticalization. In B. Joseph and R. Janda, eds., *The Handbook of Historical Linguistics*. Malden, MA: Blackwell, pp. 624–47.
Traugott, E. C. (2006). The semantic development of scalar focus modifier. In A. Kemenade and L. Bettelou, eds., *The Handbook of the History of English*. Oxford: Blackwell, pp. 335–59.
Traugott, E. C. (2007). The concepts of constructional mismatch and type-shifting from the perspective of grammaticalization. *Cognitive Linguistics*, 18(4), 523–57.
Traugott, E. C. (2008a). The grammaticalization of *NP of NP* patterns. In A. Bergs and G. Diewald, eds., *Constructions and Language Change*. Berlin/Boston: Mouton de Gruyter, pp. 23–45.
Traugott, E. C. (2008b). Grammaticalization, constructions and the incremental development of language: Suggestions from the development of degree modifiers in English. In R. Eckardt, G. Jäger, and T. Veenstra, eds., *Variation, Selection, Development: Probing the Evolutionary Model of Language Change*. Berlin/Boston: Mouton de Gruyter, pp. 219–50.
Traugott, E. C. (2011). Grammaticalization and mechanisms of change. In H. Narrog and B. Heine, eds., *The Oxford Handbook of Grammaticalization*. Oxford: Oxford University Press, pp. 19–30.
Traugott, E. C. (2015). Toward a coherent account of grammatical constructionalization. In J. Barðdal, E. Smirnova, L. Sommerer, and S. Gildea, eds., *Diachronic Construction Grammar*. Amsterdam: John Benjamins, pp. 109–40.
Traugott, E. C. (2016). Do semantic modal maps have a role in a constructionalization approach to modals? *Constructions and Frames*, 8(1), 98–125.
Traugott, E. C. (2018). Modeling language change with constructional networks. In S. Pons Bordería and O. Loureda Lamas, eds., *New Insights into the Grammaticalization of Discourse Markers*. Leiden: Brill, pp. 17–50.
Traugott, E. C. and Dasher, R. B. (2002). *Regularity in Semantic Change*. Cambridge: Cambridge University Press.
Traugott, E. C. and Trousdale, G. (2013). *Constructionalization and Constructional Changes*. Oxford: Oxford University Press.
Trousdale, G. (2012). Grammaticalization, constructions, and the grammaticalization of constructions. In K. Davidse, T. Breban, L. Brems, and T. Mortelmans, eds., *Grammaticalization and Language Change: New Reflections*. Amsterdam: John Benjamins, pp. 167–94.
Trousdale, G. (2013). Multiple inheritance and constructional change. *Studies of Language*, 37(3), 491–514.
Trueswell, R. (2009). Attributive adjectives and nominal templates. *Linguistic Inquiry*, 40, 525–33.

Van Caspel, P. P. J. (1970). Een schat van een (niet meer zo jong) kind. *De Nieuwe Taalgids*, 63, 280–87.
Van de Velde, F. (2007). Interpersonal modification in the English noun phrase. *Functions of Language*, 14, 203–30.
Van de Velde, F. (2009). The emergence of modification patterns in the Dutch noun phrase. *Linguistics*, 47(4), 1021–49.
Van de Velde, F. (2014). Degeneracy: The maintenance of constructional networks. In R. Boogaart, T. Colleman, and G. Rutten, eds., *Extending the Scope of Construction Grammar*. Berlin: De Gruyter, pp. 141–80.
Van der Auwera, J. (2002). More thoughts on degrammaticalization. In I. Wischer and G. Diewald, eds., *New Reflections on Grammaticalization*. Amsterdam: John Benjamins, pp. 19–29.
Van der Auwera, J., Van Olmen, D., and Du Mon, D. (2015). Grammaticalization. In E. Dabrowska and D. Divjak, eds., *Handbook of Cognitive Linguistics*. Berlin/Boston: De Gruyter Mouton, pp. 634–50.
Van Goethem, K. and De Smet, H. (2014). How nouns turn into adjectives: The emergence of new adjectives in French, English and Dutch through debonding processes. *Languages in Contrast*, 14(2), 189–214.
Van Riemsdijk, Henk. 1998. Categorial feature magnetism: The edocentricity and distribution of projections. *Journal of Comparative Germanic Linguistics*, 2, 1–48.
Van Valin Jr., R. (2005). *Exploring the Syntax–Semantics Interface*. Cambridge: Cambridge University Press.
Van Valin Jr., R. and LaPolla, R. J. (1997). *Syntax: Structure, Meaning and Function*. Cambridge: Cambridge University Press.
Vendler, Z. (1967). *Linguistics in Philosophy*. Ithaca, NY: Cornell University Press.
Villalba, X. and Bartra-Kaufmann, A. (2010). Predicate focus fronting in the Spanish determiner phrase. *Lingua*, 120(4), 819–49.
Von Eye, A. (2002). *Configural Frequency Analysis: Methods, Models and Applications*. Mahwah, NJ: Erlbaum.
Vos, R. (1999). A grammar of partitive constructions. Ph.D. dissertation, Tilburg University.
Vuillaume, M., Marillier, J. F., and Behr, I. (1993). Dieser Schuft von einem Hausmeister. Überlegungen zu den morphosyntaktischen und semantischen Eigenschaften von Strukturen nach dem Muster "N-von-N." In M. Vuillaullle, J. F. Marillier, and I. Behr, eds., *Studien zur Syntax und Semantik der Nominalgruppe*. Tübingen: Gunter Narr, pp. 167–84.
Zehentner, E. (2019). *Competition in Language Change: The Rise of the English Dative Alternation*. Berlin/Boston: De Gruyter Mouton.
Zehentner, E. and Traugott, E.C. (2020). Constructional networks and the development of benefactive ditransitives in English. In L. Sommerer and E. Smirnova, eds., *Nodes and Networks in Diachronic Construction Grammar*. Amsterdam: John Benjamins, pp. 167–212.
Zwicky, A. (1985). Heads. *Journal of Linguistics*, 21, 1–29.

Corpora

Biber, D. and Finegan, E. (2004–5) A Representative Corpus of Historical English Registers (ARCHER 2). CQPweb Main Page (lancs.ac.uk)

Davies, M. (2008–). The Corpus of Contemporary American English: 450 Million Words, 1990–2015 (COCA). Available online at http://corpus.byu.edu/coca/.

Davies, M. (2010–). Corpus of News on the Web (NOW). Available online at http://corpus.byu.edu/now/. Davies, M. (2010–). The Corpus of Historical American English: 400 Million Words, 1810–2009. Available online at http://corpus.byu.edu/coha/.

Davies, M. (2017). *Early English Books Online* (EEBO). Part of the SAMUELS project. Available online at http://corpus.byu.edu/eebo/.

Davies, M. (2018). iWeb Corpus: 14 Billion Words, 1990–2015. Available online at http://corpus.byu.edu/iweb.

Kroch, A. and Taylor A. (2000). Penn–Helsinki Parsed Corpus of Middle English (PPCME2). Department of Linguistics, University of Pennsylvania. CD-ROM, 2nd ed. (www.ling.upenn.edu/hist-corpora/).

Kroch, A., Santorini B., and Delfs L. (2004). Penn-Helsinki Parsed Corpus of Early Modern English (PPCEME). Department of Linguistics, University of Pennsylvania. CD-ROM, 1st ed. (www.ling.upenn.edu/hist-corpora/).

OED Online. Oxford University Press, June 2015. Web. Accessed April–May 2017.

Index

adjective intensifiers, 172
allostructions, 233, 282
analogy, 95, 167, 216–17
anaphora, 12–13, 14, 15, 31, 48, 49, 67, 87, 121, 167, 269
apposition *of*-binominal, 24, 118, 142, 145, 284
Archer Corpus, the, 97
associative adjectives, 83

beast, 24, 40, 41–3, 64–5, 75–6, 82, 96, 103–6, 110–13, 151
beasta, 96, 105
binominal intensifiers (BIs), 4, 5, 22, 84–93, 119
  beast as first noun, 105
  bitch as first noun, 151
  Construction Grammar, 230–2
  diachronic development, 153–5, 156
  Functional Discourse Grammar, 258–61, 267
  hell as first noun, 109–10
  premodification, 89, 192
  whale as first noun, 149
bitch, 145, 149–55, 156, 189
bleaching, 21, 40, 84, 93, 98, 172, 244, 246, 255, 269, 270
boundedness, 52–3
breeze, 130–3, 143, 156
bridging context, 109, 122–3, 127, 128, 130, 133, 135, 137, 138, 143, 155, 215

cake, 36, 51, 59, 64–5, 96, 99–102, 110–12, 278
classifiers, 4, 35, 41, 42, 59, 149, 162, 164–5, 173, 194, 196, 198, 209
  BIs, in, 89, 192
  classifiers and head-classifiers, 222–4, 232
  classifiers vs compounds, 165–8
  classifiers vs descriptive modifiers, 170–2
  Construction Grammar, 281–2
  EBNPs, in, 189
  EMs, in, 79, 189–92
  Functional Discourse Grammar, 243, 244
  head-classifiers, in, 38–9, 182

N+PPs, in, 180
pseudo-partitives, in, 55, 185
collocation, 16–17, 83, 108, 121–2, 153, 215
combination of partially instantiated frames, 262–4, 266, 267, 271
compounds, 164, 165–8, 173
Conceptual Component, 235
constituency tests, 10
  coordination, 14
  postposing, 14
  preposing, 14
construct-i-con. *See* construction network
construction network, 203, 204, 209–17, 232–3, 281–2
  evaluative *of*-binominal family network, 217–32
constructionalization, 268
constructions, 204–7
  classification, 206–7
  noun phrase, 207–9
Contextual Component, 236
conventionalization, 122
co-referential, 15, 220
Corpus of Contemporary American English, the, 21, 120, 124, 173
Corpus of Historical American English, the, 21, 97, 120, 124

debonding, 98, 112, 227
decategorialization, 56, 112, 269, 271
definiteness, 45, 71, 73, 80, 81, 230, 238
degree modifiers, 19, 75, 91–2, 95, 112, 162, 172–3, 197
  adjective degree modifiers, 173
  BIs, in, 192
  EBNPs, in, 189
  EMs, in, 191
  Functional Discourse Grammar, 244, 255–6
  head-classifiers, in, 182–4
  N+PPs, in, 182
  noun degree modifiers, 173
  pseudo-partitives, in, 185

306

Index

delexicalization, 16, 85, 123, 157
descriptive modifiers, 159, 160, 162, 168–70, 175, 194, 197
   BIs, in, 89, 192
   descriptive modifiers vs classifiers, 170–2
   EBNPs, in, 70, 187, 189
   EMs, in, 83, 191
   Functional Discourse Grammar, 243, 244
   head-classifiers, in, 39
   N+PPs, in, 182
   objective descriptive modifiers, 168, 173
   pseudo-partitives, in, 54–5, 185
   subjective descriptive modifiers, 159, 169, 173
   subjective vs objective descriptive modifiers, 169–70
desemanticization, 269, 270

Early English Books Online, Corpus of, 96
emphasizers, 172
encoding, 237, 238
erosion, 269, 271
evaluative binominal noun phrases (EBNPs), 2–3, 63–74
   beast as first noun, 104–5
   bitch as first noun, 151–3
   breeze as first noun, 133
   cake as first noun, 101–2
   Construction Grammar, 224–7
   diachronic development, 92, 95, 112, 118–20, 153–5, 156
   Functional Discourse Grammar, 252–4, 261, 263–4, 266, 277–8
   hell as first noun, 5, 107–8
   husk as first noun, 137–8
   nub as first noun, 127, 128–30
   premodification, 70, 187–9
   snake as first noun, 142
   whale as first noun, 146–8
evaluative modifiers (EMs), 4, 5, 22, 74–84
   beast as first noun, 105
   bitch as first noun, 151–3
   cake as first noun, 102
   Construction Grammar, 230
   diachronic development, 95, 119, 153–6
   Functional Discourse Grammar, 254–8, 266–7, 271
   hell as first noun, 108, 109
   premodification, 78, 189–92
   whale as first noun, 148
extension, 102, 121, 153, 212, 232, 269, 270
extreme adjectives, 75, 85

focus, 246
focus markers, 197–8

formulation, 235
frames, 235, 237, 238
   interpersonal frames, 238
   representational frames, 238
Fund, 237
fusion, 97, 113

Generative Grammar, 44, 46, 160
Ghesquière, 161, 173, 196–9, 207–9
Grammatical Component, 235
grammaticalization, 16, 18, 63, 80, 81, 83, 84, 89, 91, 92, 93–5, 96, 97–9, 111, 113, 117–23, 149, 214
   Construction Grammar, 213–17, 223, 224, 232–3, 283
   Functional Discourse Grammar, 245–7, 255, 268–72, 280–1

head-classifiers, 2, 4, 34–43
   beast as first noun, 103–4
   breeze as first noun, 130
   cake as first noun, 100
   Construction Grammar, 220–4, 282
   diachronic development, 284
   Functional Discourse Grammar, 249–52, 270
   hell as first noun, 106–7
   husk as first noun, 135
   intrinsic head-classifiers, 41, 100, 103, 107, 125, 130, 135, 146
   nub as first noun, 125
   premodification, 38–9, 182–5
   snake as first noun, 140
   taxonomic head-classifiers, 60, 103, 117, 130, 140
   whale as first noun, 146
headedness, 10, 44
   binominal intensifiers (BIs), 86–7
   discourse-pragmatic tests, 12–13
   evaluative binominal noun phrases, 65–8
   evaluative modifier binominals, 76–7
   head-classifiers, 35–7
   morpho-syntactic tests, 11–12
   N+PPs, 29–30
   pseudo-partitives, 46–50
   semantic tests, 10–11
hell, 3–5, 25, 63, 74–5, 82, 92–3, 96, 106–10, 112
   Functional Discourse Grammar, 255
   hella, 58, 96, 108, 110, 113, 229
      Construction Grammar, 229
      Functional Discourse Grammar, 261
   helluva, 96, 108, 109–10, 113, 227
      Functional Discourse Grammar, 261
   intensifier, as, 232
Hierarchical Configural Frequency Analysis, 175
horizontal links, 213, 233

host-class expansion, 121, 122, 215, 216
husk, 133–8, 143, 145

Individuals, 238, 241, 265
inheritance, 212
  default inheritance, 212
  multiple inheritance, 212, 232
inheritance link, 211, 212, 213, 226, 232, 282
instance links, 213
intensifiers. *See* degree modifiers
Interpersonal Level, 235, 240–1, 244, 247, 252, 266
  diachronic change, 270–2
  operators, 238
  placement, 264–5, 266
  premodification, 242, 244
interpersonal modifiers, 169, 242, 244, 251

lexemes, 235, 237, 238, 246
  lexemes and words, 238–9
lexical operators, 246, 247, 259, 261, 267
lexicalization, 96, 97–8, 111, 113, 214, 247, 268
locative *of*-binominal, 4, 30, 103, 117, 130, 220, 221, 232

macro-constructions, 211, 282
meso-constructions, 211
metaphorical extension, 52, 86, 100, 102, 106, 130, 135, 145, 213, 226, 228
metaphorical links, 211, 212, 220–2
micro-constructions, 210–11, 212, 220–1, 223, 226, 231
mismatch, 238, 250, 251, 252, 254, 257, 260
modifiability, 246, 255
modifiers, 265
  Functional Discourse Grammar, 235
Morphosyntactic Level, 235, 238–9, 241–2
  operators, 242
  syntactic placement, 264–7

N+PPs, 4, 28–34
  beast as first noun, 103
  breeze as first noun, 130
  cake as head, 100
  Construction Grammar, 217–20
  diachronic development, 112
  Functional Discourse Grammar, 249, 270, 271
  hell as first noun, 106–7
  husk as first noun, 135
  nub as first noun, 125
  premodification, 32, 177, 180–2
  snake as first noun, 140
  whale as first noun, 146
nodes, 203, 209–10, 211–12, 214, 215, 217, 219, 220, 226, 282

mother nodes, 220, 222, 226, 228, 232
noun intensifiers, 172–3, 197
nub, 125–30, 143

objective descriptive modifiers. *See* descriptive modifiers
of-genitive, 1, 4
one
  emphatic, 72, 77, 79, 82, 90
  proform, as a, 12–13, 15, 30, 36, 48, 53, 67, 87, 167, 168, 173
operators, 235, 237, 238, 241, 242, 246, 255, 265, 267
Output Component, 236
Oxford English Dictionary, 96

paradigmatic links, 282
Penn-Helsinki Corpus, 21, 96
phonetic reduction, 247, 269, 272
Phonological Level, 235, 242
polysemy links, 211, 213, 222, 227, 228, 229, 232, 233, 281
pragmaticalization, 268
premodification, 16
  diagnostic tool, as, 18–19
  Functional Discourse Grammar, 242–4
primitives, 237–40, 241, 242, 262, 280
Properties, 238, 241, 265
pseudo-partitives, 2, 4, 43–60
  beast as first noun, 104
  breeze as first noun, 131
  cake as first noun, 100–1
  container nouns, 44, 45, 50, 54
  diachronic development, 60–2, 113, 118, 124–45, 155–6
  hell as first noun, 107
  husk as first noun, 137
  measure nouns, 9, 16, 28, 44, 45, 49, 54, 62, 63, 99, 123, 215
  nub as first noun, 127
  part nouns, 45, 54, 101
  premodification, 53–6, 185
  quantifier nouns, 4, 19, 45, 50, 52, 53, 54, 84
  snake as first noun, 140

quantification, 19, 45, 47, 54, 56, 85

reanalysis, 44, 73, 81, 82, 92, 112, 118, 119, 153, 155, 156, 216–17, 220, 224, 225–6, 227, 228
reinforcers, 172
Representational Level, 235, 241
  diachronic change, 270–2
  operators, 238
  placement, 264–5, 266, 267
  premodification, 243, 244
representational modifiers, 243, 244

Index

secondary lexemes, 246, 255, 256, 266
semantic reduction, 269
s-genitive, 1
snake, 138–43, 155, 156, 278
some emphatic, 72, 77, 79, 82, 90
sort/kind/type constructions, 18–19, 45, 63, 84, 92, 246
stacking, 165
Subacts of Ascription, 241, 242, 244, 249, 250
  modification, 242, 258
Subacts of Reference, 241, 244, 247, 249
  modification, 242
subjectification, 98–9, 102, 112, 215
subjective descriptive modifiers. *See* descriptive modifiers
subpart links, 213
subschema level, 229

taxonomic links, 222, 226, 228, 282
templates, 235, 238, 241
temporal *of*-binominal, 4, 30, 34, 117, 130, 219–20, 221, 223, 232
transparency, 245, 246, 247, 249, 252, 257, 261

univerbation, 96, 97, 113
usage-based approach, 204, 213, 214, 279

value adjective, 83, 93
vertical links, 213, 217

whale, 65, 82, 86, 145–9, 153–5, 156, 191
  Construction Grammar, 228
  whaleuva, 58, 96, 113, 229

zone-based premodification, 160–4, 207–9, 283

For EU product safety concerns, contact us at Calle de José Abascal, 56–1°, 28003 Madrid, Spain or eugpsr@cambridge.org.

www.ingramcontent.com/pod-product-compliance
Ingram Content Group UK Ltd.
Pitfield, Milton Keynes, MK11 3LW, UK
UKHW022125060326
468743UK00020B/3523